MW00625488

TOVE
JANSSON

TOVE
JANSSON

LIFE, ART, WORDS

Boel Westin

TRANSLATED BY
SILVESTER MAZZARELLA

University of Minnesota Press
Minneapolis

Copyright 2007, 2014 by Boel Westin

First published in Swedish as *Tove Jansson: Ord, bild, liv* by Albert Bonniers Förlag, Sweden. English translation copyright 2014 Sort Of Books / Silvester Mazzarella.

First University of Minnesota Press edition, 2024

All rights reserved. No part of this publication may be reproduced, stored in a retrieval system, or transmitted, in any form or by any means, electronic, mechanical, photocopying, recording, or otherwise, without the prior written permission of the publisher.

Published by the University of Minnesota Press
111 Third Avenue South, Suite 290
Minneapolis, MN 55401-2520
http://www.upress.umn.edu

ISBN 978-1-5179-1729-6 (hc)
ISBN 978-1-5179-1730-2 (pb)

A Cataloging-in-Publication record for this book is available from the Library of Congress.

Printed in Canada on acid-free paper

The University of Minnesota is an equal-opportunity educator and employer.

30 29 28 27 26 25 24   10 9 8 7 6 5 4 3 2 1

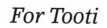

For Tooti

Contents

CHAPTER 1

I'm Busy

The birth of a very unusual and talented Moomintroll

The Exploits of Moominpapa

'Maybe we'll have a great artist in Tove one day. A really great one!': a young soldier writes from the front to the woman he loves during a fierce civil war. This is Finland in the late winter of 1918. The sculptor Viktor Jansson from Helsinki and the illustrator Signe Hammarsten from Stockholm had been married for a little more than four years when he enlisted on the White (anti-Bolshevist) side in the Finnish civil war, which broke out that January and lasted till May. For young Viktor, barely thirty years old, there was no choice. He was a sculptor who loved his country so much he was prepared to die for it, and for the independence of Finland and a freedom he believed to be his own and everyone else's right.

He begged Signe not to grieve for him. There could be no life without this conflict. 'My darling Signe. Now your husband is going out to do battle. God be with us and our arms. I may never see you again,' wrote Viktor on 14th February, hours before going into battle for the first time. His letters are beautiful and touching, full of the terrible realities of war, but they also tell of the glorious moments when a longed-for letter arrives, of moments with a cigarette in the spring sunlight, and of the joy (his own word) of fighting for his country and for what he believes in more than

Signe and Viktor are married on Ängsmarn on 17th August 1913 by Fredrik Hammarsten. Next to Signe are her sister Elsa and brother Einar.

anything else: his family. These letters, often written in pencil on thin paper, shine with love and longing for Signe and their daughter: 'our little darling'. Their daughter is barely three-and-a-half-years old. She was baptised Tove Marika Jansson.

Art and family were holy for Viktor Jansson, and Signe and his children would carry this inheritance forward into the world beyond the war. Little Tove represented hope, something to believe in, something to long for and dream about. Gender was irrelevant to Viktor as a father. He never spoke of woman or man, or boy or girl, not even of sculptor or illustrator. He talked of becoming an *artist*, nothing more. 'How I love our little girl and long to see you both,' he wrote to Signe during a brief respite on Easter Day.

Like all loving fathers he wanted the best for his child. And art held the key to life. Viktor was delighted with the sketches by Tove of 'old men' that Signe sent with her letter, and he wished he could have seen how his daughter 'stared at the paintings' when she was taken to the National Museum. She was his firstborn and would carry his profession of artist into the future.

Viktor Jansson's dream became reality. Tove became an artist whose pictures and writings would carry the name Jansson far beyond the borders of Finland and Europe.

A Really Great One

Tove Jansson was conceived in Paris, city of art and artists, in the autumn of 1913. When on 9th August the following year she was born in Helsinki, Viktor immediately sent a telegram to his wife's parents at Västra Trädgårdsgatan 17 in Stockholm: '*une fille, Signe bien portant[e]*' ('a girl, Signe doing well'). Tove came into the world on a Sunday, and next day Signe began 'The Book of Our Sunday Child'. In it she drew her daughter for the first

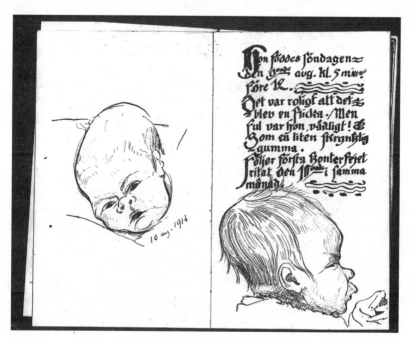

Signe's first drawings of her daughter, 10th August 1914.

'You can see how her eyes shine,' Signe wrote to Viktor.

time and wrote on the same page in beautiful script: 'She was born on Sunday 9th August at five minutes to twelve. It's nice she was a girl. But she was so ugly, awful! Like a little wrinkled old woman. The first sketch, made on the tenth of the same month.'

Tove was depicted into life and from the start drawn by her mother and sculpted by her father. Soon the eye of the camera was in action too, and photographs of Tove as baby and toddler fill several photo albums. 'This is typical of Tove when she's especially happy. Look how her eyes are shining,' wrote Signe on the back of a photograph she sent Viktor from Stockholm. There are many pictures from her visits to her mother's parents: Tove in the bath, eating a banana, going out in her pram, playing in Kungsträdgården park, sleeping among the prams, and these snapshots form a narrative of little Tove's life. She was born at the beginning of the First World War; times were troubled during the new family's first years, and they were involved in those troubles. During the Finnish civil war (January to May 1918), mother and daughter lived with Signe's parents.

There are photos from the spring of 1915, and some from autumn 1917 and spring 1918. For Viktor the little snapshots and Signe's letters were all he had to alleviate his longing for his daughter. When some years later he sculpted her head, it was as an Egyptian princess, solemn and as if inaccessible in white marble (1920). The face has geometrically clean features and the hair is as smooth and straight as a pageboy's. It is as if her father is creating his daughter anew and infusing the white stone for ever with his longing for her. He is researching her, discovering her secrets. There is a portrait mask of Tove's face from the same period. Later the teenage Tove would pose as a model for many of Viktor's sculptures of young women, ethereal figures with names like 'Spring' and 'Convolvulus'. Her father's love found a language in art. 'To Tove from Dad', he wrote in white on a photograph of his sculpture 'Spring'.

The instinct to make pictures was in Tove Marika Jansson's blood. 'Studio' was synonymous with 'home' and she could draw almost before she could walk. One of Signe's early sketches of her daughter shows her absorbed in drawing, only 18 months old. She is sitting on a little cushion in front of a low table and a sheet of paper. The pencil is firmly held in her right hand while her left hand holds the paper down, and she is concentrating totally on her work. This was the beginning.

Tove's Busy

Tove Jansson was active as an artist and writer for more than seventy years. When she published her first illustrations in a couple of newspapers in 1928 she was only fourteen, followed a year later by a seven-part comic strip in the children's paper *Lunkentus*. She published her first cartoon at 15, first exhibited in the spring of 1933 and saw her first illustrated book printed the same year. She exhibited at the Konstnärsgillet (Artists' Guild) in Helsinki (1937) and later joined a group called 'The Five Young People' who came together to exhibit in a gallery in 1940. She had to wait several years to exhibit on her own – it was a time of war and crisis – but in autumn 1943 the artist Tove Jansson was able to announce her first private show at the Konstsalongen (Art Salon) in Helsinki.

By now she had also started writing stories and publishing them in various periodicals. Two years later, in autumn 1945, her first Moomin work, *The Moomins and the Great Flood*, reached the bookshops, being published in both Helsinki and Stockholm. It excited no response to speak of – I have found just one review – but after the next two Moomin books, *Comet in Moominland* (1946) and particularly *The Hobgoblin's Hat* (1948 – known in English as *Finn Family Moomintroll*), Tove Jansson began to be known as a writer in Finland and Sweden.

She had already been recognised for some time as a cartoonist and illustrator, and her second one-woman show as a painter had attracted attention. Painting was her passion, but it was the Moomin stories that brought her to the notice of the public at large. She became a megastar in the 1950s, when her Moomin strip series took off in England.

Her books came out like pearls in that busy decade, three in seven years, while Moomin dramatisations were performed throughout the Nordic countries and the Jansson Moomin philosophy was discussed in

Tove drawing, sketch by Ham.

universities and on the arts pages of newspapers. Reviewers saw the books more as general literature than children's stories. In fact, Tove had a double artistic identity. For a long time she presented herself as painter and writer in that order, and throughout all the successes and overwhelming diffusion of the Moomin world she held fast to her painting, even if this was restricted to particular periods. It became more difficult with time to combine painting and Moomins and she was afflicted by a painful tension between demands, expectations and her own longing. Behind the trolls and the paintings lay a continual struggle between pleasure and duty, desire and responsibility.

This conflict stayed with her for life. Inclination was for her what mattered most, a concept she returned to again and again in her notes: 'Duty and pleasure are a long story for me, permanently relevant, and I've gradually reached an unusual and altogether personal conclusion. The only honest thing is pleasure – desire, joy – and nothing I've forced myself to do has ever given pleasure to the people round me,' she wrote in April 1955, in the middle of one of the first major outbreaks of Moomin fever. For Tove nothing could be more terrifying than the disappearance of pleasure.

'I'm busy' is a constant expression in the young Tove's diaries, which she began to write when she was twelve, and busy-ness set a heavy stamp on her path through artistic life. To be busy is to do something, to be active, to find an idea and work with it. Words like 'create' and 'inspiration' were taboo in Viktor and Signe's studio home at Lotsgatan 4B in Helsinki; rather one discussed work and pleasure. The illustrated diaries Tove kept as a child and adolescent are full of activities of various kinds: she writes, draws, paints, sews, does craftwork, produces newspapers, builds fleets, huts and small houses. In the summer of 1929 she wandered round Pellinge archipelago wearing a pair of fur trousers she had sewn for herself during the winter, and she described them in detail:

> At the back and in patches in front I have cats' fur and at the sides long-haired white goatskin from Anna's [home help] collar. The legs are a little tight by mistake at the top and very broad lower down, and they are made of grey goatskin with curly white hair inside and long tassels at the front. On the left leg there's a little bit of black rabbit skin. Of course everyone who lives in Pellinge was flabbergasted at the sight of them.

She loved her fur trousers and sketched herself wearing them many times in her diary. They clothed her legs throughout the summer and this get-up (never mind how hot it must have been) clearly made an impact. People really noticed the fifteen-year-old Tove Jansson. That was the intention.

Her life from start to finish consisted of work – plus a great deal of love – and her capacity for work was unbelievable. As an artist in training she worked away for dear life to keep herself from one job to the next: '... work, work. It has been noticed that I produce work in oils, Indian ink, charcoal, etc, this has become a real register of work,' wrote Tove at twenty-one in October 1935. Between the first drawings she presented to the public in 1928 and her last book, the story collection *Messages* seventy years later in 1998, came still-lifes, landscapes, portraits, cartoons, illustrations and abstract paintings, novels and picture books, short stories, illustrated strips, plays and opera librettos, poems and songs, murals, altarpieces and stage sets, paintings on glass, book covers and drawings for cards, posters, advertisements and much else. Like her immense productivity

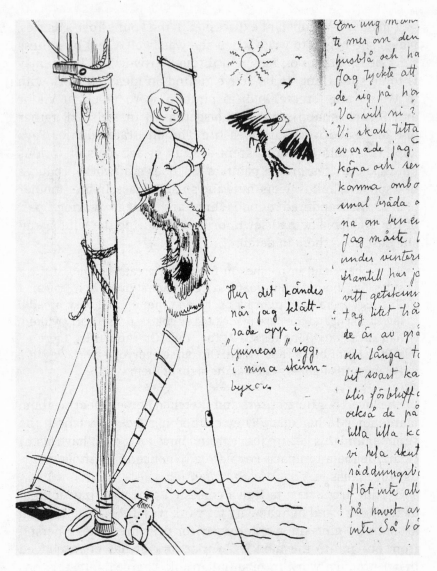

Tove in her fur trousers. Diary entry, summer 1929.

her repertoire continued to develop much longer than might have been expected. The satirical political paper, *Garm*, to which she contributed for some fifteen years, alone published more than 600 of her pictures.

From her first drawings to her last book Tove Jansson was a universal genius with a greater than average need to express herself. She was driven by her craving to use words and her determination to set pictures moving – a perpetual hunger for a new aesthetic. It was vital to her to understand the significance of each artistic act in relation to herself. 'I'm a real artistic snob, Eva,' she wrote to her friend Eva Konikoff just after the end of the war in 1945. They were discussing the justification of art: 'Art for art's sake. You write, "Dali only works for himself." Who else could he work for? When you've got work to do you don't worry about others! You try to express yourself, your own perceptions, make a synthesis, explain, set free. Every still-life, every landscape, every canvas is a self-portrait!!'

She was never to lose track of these thoughts, and pondered them anew when she came to write her late novels after the Moomin books. But every artist who depicts herself also depicts the times she lives in.

Cennini

One of Tove's household gods was the Florentine painter Cennino Cennini, famous for his *Il Libro dell'Arte o Trattato della Pittura* (The Book of Art or Treatise on Painting), a handbook on Renaissance painting which advises on the various kinds of brushes, colours and other things needed for tempera and frescoes; it was written, while the author was in prison, to bring comfort to all artists. Tove's notes (to the Swedish edition of 1948) are detailed, respectful and charming, and she also wrote short pieces on the importance of Cennini for the artist and artistic work. Mostly she wrote for herself, but she spared a thought for others too. Cennini had been locked up in the delle Stenche prison in Florence because he could not pay his debts:

> He seems never to have been released. But as he waited there, Cennino Cennini wrote a book on the art of painting. He wanted to help young painters with their work. He calculated that thirteen years should be devoted to basic studies, before the moment when, after much invocation and prayer, one might start upon one's first panel. He not only warns, but makes cheerful promises too: 'In the name of the whole Trinity, put some flowers on your lawns, and a few small birds. I will tell you all you need to know about how to colour a river, with or without fish... But the main

thing is to follow your own ideas in all you do and let yourself be guided by your own feelings. All art requires proficiency, but you must also take joy in your work.

All art requires proficiency, but joy as well. Tove Jansson, all her life, worked with herself as artist, writer and human being.

'Work and Love' was one of her favourite mottoes, in her early years clearly expressed in the mass of symbolic illustrations on one of her first *'ex libris'* bookplates (1947). Here we find work and sex, love and passion, fidelity and temptation, and not least Leo, her personal star sign. She crammed an enormous amount into a space of 9cm by 6cm, as she later noted with a touch of self-criticism:

> A lion, a rose, a thistle, a woman, a number of stars, a Moomintroll, two anchors, two pillars with capitals and grapevines, a palette, a sea at night, a sun, various grasses and fruit and undefined vegetation, a burning heart, several confused ornaments and a pathetic device in Latin, which furthermore would seem to be grammatically incorrect.

(Tove had made the motto read *'Labora et Amare'* but it should perhaps have read *'Labora et Ama'*, work and love [in the imperative mood of the verb]). This view was typical of her later *ex libris* of the early 1960s, when she was exalting the principle

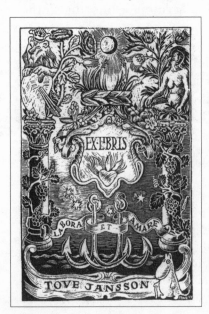

Bookplate with lion, flowers, stars, Moomintroll and Latin inscription, 1947.

22

Three Tove Jansson bookplate designs from the 1960s.

of simplicity and thinking about writing books beyond the world of the Moomins. By this time she preferred a monogram (though she alluded to her very first *ex libris* with a stylised picture of a tree). Put together, these three simpler bookplates form three self-portraits: the young Tove Jansson as a growing tree, Tove Jansson in a tumultuous time of painting and Moomins, and Tove Jansson in a time of words and clear writing, symbolised by simple stylised lettering.

'You must be aware of the time needed for learning,' wrote Tove in her notes on Cennini, and she followed this maxim all her life. She was herself her own most important teacher and never felt at home in the world of formal instruction. Whether painting or writing, everything she did was founded on rigorous self-study. In the preliminary work for her books she was capable of documenting such things as the variability of winds and the flight of birds (as in the manuscript of *Moominpappa at Sea*), or of giving instructions about technical matters to do with printing and possible colour combinations (as in the draft of the picture book, *The Book About Moomin, Mymble and Little My*). Her successive workbooks are filled with reflections and thoughts, facts and information about characters, and notes on changes, publication and translation.

It's the same with the pictures. A little sketchbook from the 1930s, which I found stuck in her bookshelves, describes in expert terms the principles of 'Golden Leather and Leather-colouring', talks of glass-painting on parchment and gives

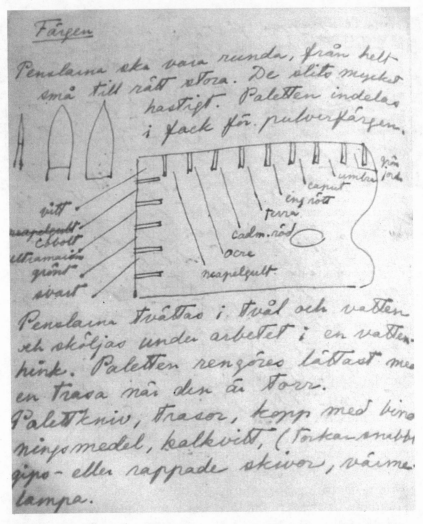

Notes on fresco painting, 1947.

notes on insulating substances, cloth, oil tempera and other things. A notepad dated 1943 and headed 'Material' discusses in lyrical phrases the care of new palettes – 'oil both sides with hot linseed oil' – considers the use of colours and describes the technique of painting *al fresco*. These notes relate very closely to the two murals Tove painted in the basement of Helsinki Town Hall in 1947. The process is described exhaustively in words and pictures: preparing the wall, making the sketches, sand, box, tools, colours, and further on in the same pad there is a description of the *al secco* mural that she worked on the following year (1948).

Like Cennini Tove Jansson wrote a book on painting, but she wrote it for herself alone.

Self-Portraits

The first picture Tove exhibited was a drawn self-portrait, contributed in spring 1933 to an exhibition entitled 'Helsinki Humorists'; the paintings in her last exhibition of new work in 1975 included one too. She wrote no autobiography – she left that to Moominpappa. The nearest thing was her collection of stories of childhood, *Sculptor's Daughter* (1968). But she spent her whole life writing a book about herself in pictures and words. Together, her many self-portraits, from those sketched in her diaries up to her last large-scale paintings, create a narrative of the self known as Tove Jansson and form a visual autobiography. It presents her, launches her, masks her and documents her. She constructed her self through self-portraits, transforming it as she passed through a variety of poses: the busy girl, the highly strung embryo artist, the solemn young painter, the artistic aesthete.

A portrait from the 1940s, 'The Lynx Boa', shows her in a sober suit with a fur boa slung across her shoulders, wildly beautiful in a boldly dramatic combination. She presents herself as both animal and human. Her hair is combed back, her gaze evades the viewer, her bronzed face has sharply slanting eyes. 'I'm like a cat in my yellow fur, with cold slanting eyes and freshly smoothed hair in a knot. And a whole firework display of flowers,' she wrote of this picture in a letter. She was not yet thirty. There was still a long way to go to the frank, self-searching study she was to present at the age of 61 in 1975. (See coloured plates 7, 15 and 32).

Tove writes herself into her stories, sometimes unmasked, free and open, sometimes hidden behind a variety of names and disguises. Everything from the free-thinking Thingummy in *Finn Family Moomintroll* (1948), the reflective Whomper in *Moominvalley in November* (1970), the sculptor's child in *Sculptor's Daughter*, the listener in the short story collection, *The*

Listener (1971), the drawer of comic strips in *The Doll's House* (1978) and the writer of children's books, Anna Amelin, in *The True Deceiver* (1982), to the word-hunting Jonas in *The Stony Field* (1984) and the short story writer, Mari, of the narratives in *Fair Play* (1989).

Her last book, *Messages*, simply deals with either a Tove or a Jansson. Traces of Tove Jansson herself run backwards and forwards through the words and pictures, constantly creating new patterns. 'Effective children's books are full of symbols, identifications and obsessions,'she wrote in an essay, a statement that holds good for her own work in general. 'I am the theme of my book,' Montaigne once wrote. The same can be said of Tove Jansson. She is the theme of her own work and she is constantly changing. When after years of war deprivation her friend Eva Konikoff sent her money and a new coat from the USA, Tove immediately bought a blue autumn hat and drew herself wearing it in her next letter to Eva.

During the 1930s and 1940s, the period when she was training herself and developing her identity as a painter, she made a large number of self-portraits, at least fifteen. She drew herself in charcoal and painted herself in oils. She linked herself to tradition, painting herself in Renaissance style against a background of her own paintings, including herself as a signature in her frescoes and portraying herself within the circle of her family. In her striking painting 'The Family' (1942), which she was working on at the height of the war, she emphasised her presence as an artist in the fashion of the fifteenth-century Italian painters she so much admired, and placed herself in the middle. In her crowded frescoes on the walls of Helsinki Town Hall, Tove the artist sits in the midst of the throng (together with a Moomin), and is transformed into a part of a work of art, in the same way that Renaissance painters painted themselves into their frescoes. Thus she presented herself in her various roles. It was a way for the young artist to consolidate her identity as a painter, to nail herself fast to tradition and establish a relationship for herself with the great male masters.

'Self-portrait with Fur Cap' (1941) is an excellent example. It is a salute to the Great Master himself, Rembrandt, and to one of his most famous self-portraits, from 1640. Rembrandt is

*Self-portrait,
charcoal, 1930s.*

wearing his characteristic fur headgear, Tove a fur cap in Davy
Crockett style. She also has on a fur gilet – the fur trousers of
her childhood were the beginning of a lifelong love affair with
fur. The subject faces the viewer, turned slightly to one side in
the same way as the master does, with the right arm and hand
held forward. Rembrandt's hand rests on a balustrade, Tove's
on her knee. Her pose, the body, the perspective, everything
breathes Rembrandt, and just as his portrait was a tribute to
Titian, so is Tove's a tribute to him. The fact that she painted
herself into the great visual history of the self-portrait is
evidence of the demands she was making on herself. This is
the portrait of a woman who challenged tradition and men,
and faced the world with a confident gaze. An entirely different
impression from the one given in her notes and letters, in
which painting is the object of constant reflection and her
self-belief shoots up and down like a rollercoaster. (See colour
plates 7, 8 and 9.)

Her back straight, she fixes her eye gravely on the viewer to reveal herself. She is sitting in front of one of her own paintings, a landscape from Brittany from the late-1930s. This completes her link with the Renaissance. She has created space behind her figure and opened the landscape behind herself. She reveals herself as painter and artist, but without using palette and brush to advertise her identity. We have to interpret her identity from her interplay with tradition. In her many self-portraits she represented herself in various roles and poses, expressing herself as a painting Tove in a constant state of change. For a long time she signed herself 'Tove' but later changed to 'Jansson'. As a writer she always worked under her whole name, Tove Jansson.

Biography

Tove Jansson is one of those writers and artists who excite strong feelings. She possessed an unusual combination of integrity and openness, an ability to make the other person feel especially chosen at the same time as keeping her secrets to herself. Her books and pictures made of her someone whom people wanted to come close to. Many readers feel a strong emotional relation-ship to the Moomin world; the enormous correspondence she had from readers is proof of this, and a good number of these letter writers were not happy to acknowledge the existence of other visitors to Moominvalley than themselves. An obstinate relationship with the self and individualism is an important feature in the magnetism of the Moomin stories.

Tove Jansson has been depicted as a gracile child of nature, an easily surprised painter on an island in the Gulf of Finland who was transformed in a twinkling into a writing Moominmamma, an artist who became a writer without further ambitions. She has been described as an ingenuous Moomin with no real awareness of banks, money, negotiations or business. Nothing could have been further from the truth. Such ideas are superficial romanticisations (needs to create a mythology) that have very little connection with the deeply aware artist who had worked hard ever since the age of fifteen, who had been writing stories for publication since her early teens and who herself looked after all negotiations to do with trolls and pictures till well into the 1950s. She was already pondering Moomin marketing possibilities in her letters in around 1950, despite having published only two of the books.

The best known and most frequently quoted of the few things she wrote about her own profession is her shrewd essay from 1961, 'The Deceitful Writer of Children's Books'. In it she discusses the motive force of writing and presents a portrait of herself that is as far from an innocent Moomin or a cosy Moominmamma as it is possible to get. Hidden behind her books is a self-centred author who writes children's books as a way of coping with childishness in herself, certainly not to please children. A dangerous writer. A childishness unsuitable for the grown-up world, a writer looking for something that existed in the past, something she wants to create again. In the words of the deceitful author, she wants to describe and experience 'something lost or unattainable'. The search for this is connected to the arcane secrecy of the Moomin books. It gives form to a certain longing that exists in all of us. It can relate to our attempts to break away from roles or expectations, and to our dreams of becoming someone else or disappearing into some other existence.

Escapism, which has raised so many questions and socially committed misgivings about the Moomin books, is a part of our narrative about ourselves. But the truly deceitful writer is not content just to tell us a story about a family of Moomins in a valley. She writes relentlessly on, crushes the dreams, empties the valley and sends the family and herself away towards new realities and awakenings of various kinds. In the same way she steers her writing and her painting towards new forms of expression. After the Moomin books – there were eventually to be nine in all – the many Moomin comic strips and the three picture books, Tove wrote novels and collections of stories between 1971 and 1998, and for a time in the 1960s went in for abstract painting. By then the years of being a humble student of painting were over and she was working towards new ideas.

My aim in this biography of Tove Jansson as writer and artist is to come close to her through her words, pictures and life. The figure of Moominpappa writing his memoirs was inspired by one of Tove's favourite Italian artists, Benvenuto Cellini, the

Tove in her Ulrikasborgsgatan studio, 1940s.

famous sixteenth-century sculptor whose autobiographical *Vita* is one of the great classics of the genre. Cellini's view was that anyone who has done well here in the world (and reached the age of forty) may go ahead freely and write his autobiography. Tove (after 1954) amply satisfied these conditions. Her life is a tale in itself, full of painting and Moomins, writing and searching, work and love. She is the most widely translated writer to come out of Finland, read all over the world, and her

Moomins, for better or worse, are a part of Finland. But behind the trolls and the pictures lies a constant struggle between pleasure and duty, inclination and responsibility. Tove Jansson searched for new forms of artistic expression all her life, from her first drawings to her last book. 'Give me a picture, a longing to express something. It doesn't need to be much, but it must be *something*, a little pleasure, a little need,' she wrote in a note in 1960. She never consciously sat down herself to write the story of her life, but there are many lesser texts and presentations. All parts of the story of Tove Jansson. At the beginning of the 1990s she wrote a short account of her life in relation to words and pictures. It hasn't been published, but I have the manuscript and will return to it at the end of this book.

It is the nature of biography to pick a path through work and life, and move backwards and forwards between various types of material – in Tove Jansson's case between words and pictures. This involves an often multiple process of keeping notebooks with richly abundant sources. I have wanted to give an articulate and dynamic picture of the Tove who can be found in her work – everything we think of when we hear the name Tove Jansson: Moomins, stories and huge numbers of pictures.

As the first researcher, I have had free access to the whole of the private archive Tove Jansson built up over the years, from the early stories, drawings and diaries of her childhood to material relating to her late writings at the end of the 1990s. It fills hundreds of bulging files and folders, not to mention piles of loose material in boxes and on shelves, masses of notes, manuscripts of stories and talks, lists, drafts, sketches, drawings, plans for projects of various kinds, photographs, diary notes, cuttings, articles, every kind of letter and correspondence, programmes, catalogues, and so on. And it provides a picture of the writer and artist who built up this large memorial to herself and her work. It is personal and at the same time strictly documented.

Tove Jansson was a systematic person who spared herself no more than she spared those round her. She was capable of generosity to journalists and researchers – for example, by sending a neatly handwritten little analysis, or a cutting or photocopy of some document – but she liked to keep the reins firmly in her own hands. She was precise about what she gave researchers, and often made notes of what she had given to whom so as not to cause confusion. That in the course of time she skilfully came to direct accounts of her own life and work speaks for itself. It was part of the strategy she used to manage and come to terms with her own great fame. For instance, she kept all the letters readers sent her, normally about two thousand a year.

This archive became an essential part of the activity that grew up around her work, particularly the Moomin stories. She made many workbooks in which she documented facts and miscellaneous information, such as the answers to 'recurring' questions. How Moomintroll came into existence was and remained the commonest of these. The material about her writings is the richest, but there is also a great deal on her art work. I have been through this archive in many directions since I started my work on this book, both with Tove Jansson and without her. Thus I have been able to benefit from two perspectives on the material, and have been through it and reworked my ideas many times.

Tove was a great letter writer, not least of private letters. Letters to and from those who were closest to her, her parents, friends and lovers, have been very important for my book. I have had free access to these. One of the biggest and most important series of correspondence is that between Tove and Tuulikki Pietilä; another between Tove and Eva Konikoff, a friend who emigrated to the USA in 1941. Tove's correspondence with Eva lasted twenty-five years and contains more than a hundred letters from Tove. 'I've lost the urge to write letters after too many years of Moomin business, a daily and overwhelming correspondence with people I don't know and don't like,' she wrote to Eva on Christmas Eve 1961. But a little margin was left free, for 'privacy and free will'. Another, who with time became a close friend, was Maya Vanni (at one time married to Tove's mentor and lover for several years in the 1930s, the painter Sam Vanni), a correspondence that became prolific with time.

There are a good many other important series of letters in the various Tove Jansson archives, the chief one of which is preserved in her old studio in Helsinki. Over the years she also made two major donations, one of manuscripts and readers' letters to Åbo Akademi and one of more than a thousand illustrations to Tampere Museum of Art.

Tove Jansson had the same studio in Helsinki for nearly sixty years, and the mounds of papers, letters and notes simply grew and grew. Fortunately the ceiling of her tower studio is six metres high. For me this unique archive has proved spellbinding, and my work on her words, pictures and life became like exploring a bottomless treasure chest. But the time came in the end to close the lid.

Viktor and Signe in the studio in Montparnasse.

CHAPTER 2

Family

Mamma sat down on the rail of the bridge and said:
And now finally I want to hear a little more about our
forefathers.

Moominland Midwinter

Signe and Viktor met in Paris in 1910 at the Académie de la
Grande Chaumière. This was at the time a contemporary school
(it had been founded in 1904) for painting and sculpture in
Montparnasse, and it was here that Tove also started, many
years later, when she came to Paris to study art. Thus, she was
to follow a family tradition but she did not spend long there – by
then it had become too conservative.

After their marriage in 1913 the Hammarsten-Janssons
returned to Paris – it was after all their city – on a combined
honeymoon and scholarship trip. They planned to live and
work there for a considerable time and settled down in a studio
on the Rue du Moulin de Beurre, a grassy *impasse* near the Rue
de la Gaîté, west of the Cimetière Montparnasse. They were
happy in Paris. Signe drew and sketched, and Viktor worked
on his sculpture 'Woman', which was sent to Finland, where
it won first prize in a national art competition in 1914. The
quarter is long gone now (the last traces of it vanished when
the old Gare Montparnasse was pulled down at the end of the
1960s), but when Tove and her father were in Paris together in
the spring of 1938, artists were still living in the low garage-

35

like buildings. Back in 1913, the newly married couple pose in a photograph full of atmosphere, Viktor on one side and Signe on the other, in the doorway leading out to the little lane. Studio doors were often kept open to the street. The photo was taken from inside the studio. The sculptor is in his white overall. His sculptor's turntable is in the foreground, with a small sculpture of a sitting girl on top. The man on one side, the woman on the other, and between them the work of art. He is looking at her and she is turning her head a little towards the camera; it is as if a perfect line connects them. The beginning of a shared life of work and love.

Signe Hammarsten

Tove's mother, Signe Hammarsten – always known as Ham by her children – was a clergyman's daughter from Stockholm. She was born in 1882 at Hannäs in the Kalmar district in south-east Sweden, the second child in a brood that eventually grew to six – there was an elder sister and after her came four brothers. Signe was in her early teens when the family moved to Stockholm, where her father had been appointed to a position in Solna. The Census of 1900 describes her as a 'home daughter' – at that time they were living in the centre of Stockholm at Drottninggatan 68 – but two years later she began her higher education at HKS, the College of Industrial Art, a department of the Stockholm School of Technology where she had already completed several courses.

Signe had gained excellent reports and dreamed of becoming a sculptor, but such a career would have been very difficult for a young woman at the turn of the century. The family's limited finances were needed to provide for her brothers, and she had already qualified as a teacher of drawing. But she had continued to worry away at sculpture on several courses: plaster-casting, figure-modelling and wood-carving; and a photograph from her student days shows her radiantly proud after the casting of her 'Borghese Swordsman'. Beside her is Jerker Bergman, a fellow artist. Ham never secured admission to the female section of the Academy of Art, but she had trained herself in a field she had marked off for herself.

Signe's father, Fredrik Hammarsten, was from the province of Östergötland, and after various posts as assistant pastor, curate and pastor in the provinces of Småland, Östergötland and Stockholm, in 1908 he became pastor of the Jacob parish in Stockholm. He had already been appointed a court preacher in 1898. He has been described as a humble, simple, unpretentious man whose published collections of sermons marked him out as one of the most widely read writers of edifying texts of the time. But above all, writes his biographer, he had no equal in Stockholm as a preacher on the subject of God's grace, and filled his church with devout listeners for decades. For him, his texts were no mere formal introductions to his sermons but the foundation of what he wanted to say; and it was claimed emphatically for him that he preferred people to listen to him preach than have them read his words later. His manner of speaking was described as simple and unaffected, and phrased with captivating beauty. In other words he was a storyteller, and there were several of these in the Hammarsten family.

Fredrik was the youngest brother of Wilma Lindhé, one of those women writers of the 1880s who emphasised the conflict between home and profession; one of her best-known short stories carries the significant title 'Imprisoned and Free'. In her memoir *From Times Gone By* (1917), she traced the history of the family as far back as the end of the eighteenth century. Its first known member was the village shoemaker of the parish of Rönö in Östergötland. More widely known Hammarstens came with time, not only Wilma Lindhé herself but several scientists; her brother Olof Hammarsten became internationally famous for research in biochemistry. Long after Wilma's death in 1922 the family acquired a star in the form of her great-niece Tove, even if she was not a Hammarsten on her father's side. Fredrik had set his sights on a career in natural history, but as was the case later for his daughter, he was forced to tailor his ambitions to fit the family finances. To save money he decided to read Theology, which required a shorter period of study. Fredrik was eight years younger than his sister Wilma and she had little to say about him in her book. But she did remember that he had been known as the 'Golden Nugget', and to judge from her descriptions of family life he must have had a very pleasant childhood, even though the family suffered from economic problems.

In 1879 Fredrik Hammarsten married Elin Emanuelsson, daughter of a well-known revivalist dean. In her early years Elin had been known as the 'pastor's wild lassie' but little more is known about her. As the times demanded, she accepted her roles as pastor's wife and mother. But she did pass the free spirit of her youth on to Signe, who became pastor's wild lassie for the next generation. Signe loved riding horses without a woman's saddle, was a crack shot, and is said to have appeared on one famous occasion as a circus rider with the King and Queen of Sweden in the audience. Photographs of her at this time emphasise physical activities. She trekked in the mountains, paddled canoes in the archipelago, went sailing and rowing, climbed hills and skied, altogether an adventurous young woman with a spring in her step, free from the restrictive indoor ideals the period upheld for women. She could not have been further from a 'home daughter' in the literal sense. Her photo albums present her as horsewoman, adventurer and traveller to Paris. She was a young woman anxious to educate herself, practise a profession and create her own prospects.

Active outdoor life was physically fashionable at the time, and Signe's involvement in the budding Swedish Girl Guide movement was part of the preparation of a new generation of girls for a new freedom – the freedom of getting out of the home, circulating freely and experiencing nature without restrictive clothing; literally of taking the air. As a teacher at the Wallinska School in Stockholm she started a troop of Girl Guides together with the two fellow teachers who were her best friends, Emmy Grén-Broberg and Esther Laurell; many of their pupils supported their initiative. Girls should get out of doors like boys – that was the slogan of the day. The Guides organised excursions, cycle trips, flag exercises and rowing. A photograph shows the pioneers around their camp fire, wearing divided skirts, shirts and big hats, a very different sort of clothing from the long dresses they had to wear in town. Scouting was the equivalent of freedom.

This was before the official foundation of the Swedish Girl Guide movement, and its story as written later records their contribution under the heading 'Preludes'. The trio were known as Shem, Ham and Japhet (after Noah's three sons in the Book of Genesis: Esther was Shem, Signe, of course, Ham, and Emmy

Japhet), and they were unquestionably among the New Women of the day. Fresh winds were blowing for emancipation and the movement for women's suffrage was on the march. An international congress in favour of votes for women was held in Stockholm in 1911 with Selma Lagerlöf (the first woman to win a Nobel Prize for Literature in 1909) as principal speaker. The Girl Guide movement was founded in the same year. Later Signe also enrolled as a suffragette. Esther went from school to university, while Emmy became a key figure in the new Guide movement and later one of its historians. But for Signe the fresh-air life of the Guides was not enough; she wanted to see Europe, study art and go to Paris, London and Dresden. It was during her second trip to Paris that she met Viktor.

When Signe fell pregnant with Tove the family moved from Paris to Helsinki. The young art student and teacher Signe, who had wanted to be a sculptor, was thus transformed into the illustrator, wife and mother Ham. With time she became a well-known draughtswoman, caricaturist and designer of postage stamps, and can step forward as a modern career woman, as she did when interviewed for the periodical *Astra* ('The Newspaper of the Swedish-speaking Women of Finland')

The Girl Guide pioneers. From the left: Shem (Esther Laurell), Ham (with the oars) and Japhet (Emmy Grén-Broberg).

The priest's wild lass.

in 1922 on the subject of 'A Married Woman's Work Outside the Home'. The cover picture shows Ham and Tove, cheek to cheek. At first she had little time for art, she tells us in the article, but as Tove got bigger her 'longing for art' was aroused and an environment without art became unthinkable – despite the fact that by now 'a little boy had been added to the family'; Tove's brother, Per Olov, was born in 1920. It took a good deal of hard work at the drawing table to support the family and there was never room for any independent general longing for art. Ham became a virtuoso caricaturist, known for better or worse as the 'little cobra', but her field was limited. The minimal entry on her in the *Swedish Biographical Lexicon* expresses the accepted attitude to women of the time; they are always defined in relation to other people: 'a sister of Olof, Einar and Harald Hammarsten, the illustrator Signe Hammarsten-Jansson (born 1882), active in Helsinki, is through her marriage to the sculptor Viktor Bernhard Jansson mother of the Finnish-Swedish artist and writer Tove Jansson'.

Sister, wife and mother are the epithets used to present a woman who makes a living by drawing. In a summary of her life written by herself she says not a word about art, mentioning only work and love. She imitated the style of Edgar Lee Masters as part of her cover design for a 1927 edition of *Spoon River Anthology*:

I was   a clergyman's daughter
        suffragette
        teacher
        Guide leader
        interested in
        care of the sick
        books and drawing
        in religion an idealist

I was   loved
        an artist
        moved to his country
        survived four wars
        worked hard for
        the meatballs of life
        gave birth to three wonderful
        fantastic children
        so really
        the whole thing wasn't so
        crazy.

Ham

Viktor Jansson

The artist Ham loved – Viktor Jansson – was born in 1886 and came from a family of industrialists, civil servants and teachers; it was a petit bourgeois family, concluded Ari Latvi in his presentation of Viktor Jansson at the opening of an exhibition in his memory in 1988. Viktor's father, Julius Viktor Jansson, had worked in the Stockmann department store in Helsinki, eventually starting his own haberdashery business. He and Viktor's mother, Johanna Karlsson, had four children but only Viktor and his brother Julius Edvard (known as Jullan) survived;

Viktor's twin sister died at the age of five months. He himself was only six when his father died, so the family was soon reduced to just Johanna, Viktor and Jullan. Their resources were limited but Johanna Jansson, who had been educated at a girls' high school and gone on to business college, took over the running of the business, kept the little family going and managed to give her boys an education. When despite all her efforts the business collapsed in 1911, Viktor was already in Paris on a scholarship.

Ever since his early years Viktor Jansson had been known as 'Faffan' and, as with 'Ham', this became a name their children used. It was said to go back to a time when he was woken from his daydreams by a cry from the teacher in a gym lesson to the effect that he shouldn't just stand there like a 'fafa' (short for *'farfar'*, 'grandfather'); this was later changed to 'Faffan'. But Viktor was far from being a daydreamer. From his earliest years as an artist he cultivated an adversarial and rebellious attitude, and took a stand against traditional art-school teaching. Later, with his colleagues Marcus Collin, Tyko Sallinen and Uuno Alanko, he founded a free art academy (1915) that offered instruction according to foreign models in painting and sculpture, but it only lasted a year. Tove followed in his footsteps some twenty years later, when a group of students left the Drawing Class of the Academy of Art to work on free forms in a shared studio. Viktor was a family rebel; no relative had previously chosen to be an artist.

This choice of a life outside the traditions of his family was something he shared with Ham. Each broke free of their background to devote themselves to pictorial art. Viktor enrolled in the Drawing Class of the Academy of Art (1903), became a pupil of the sculptor Robert Stigell (who became a father figure to him) and worked and studied for long periods in Paris. A couple of erotic groups called 'Passion' and 'Nightfall' (exhibited in Finland in 1911) caused a commotion, referred to by art historians as a 'scandalous breakthrough'.

Faffan was a hard-working professional, but he also knew how to cut loose and have fun. This could go on for days and the description of the art of 'partying' in *Sculptor's Daughter* on the whole gives an accurate picture of the phenomenon. There is a fine atmospheric description in Tove's diary. She was twenty-one years old and painting with the artist Sam Vanni; it was a night in January 1936 and she had come home to the family studio home in Lallukka:

> When I unlocked the door I could hear laughter and the clinking of glasses. Marcus Collin's yellow dog came running with the doormat in its mouth. Tobacco smoke had formed a billowing quilt under the studio ceiling. The musician Hirn got up from the bottle-filled table and came swaying towards me. His large, lumpy face strained and searching. With a magnificent gesture he offered me a seat. Marcus was sitting as usual in a corner, chuckling to himself; Tunström was walking about and looking at Dad's sculptures.

> Dad was playing a *haidare* [a kind of accordion] with a radiant and distant look. I lit a cigarette and crept silently onto the sofa. Mum had gone to bed and the night looked set to be long.

One of the core participants was the artist Tyko Sallinen, whom Viktor Jansson had met in Paris in about 1910, when there had been long 'drinking sessions on the café terraces', and these

Party at Lotsgatan. Diary, 1929.

wild ways continued back home in Helsinki. Others in the circle included Marcus Collin (already mentioned) and Jalmari Ruokokoski, but closest to Faffan was the painter Alwar Cawén. They were born in the same year (1886) and had been in the Art Class together. They had lived in the same accommodation in Paris, sharing life and art and making portraits of each other. Cawan (Cawén's nickname) was a regular guest in the Hammarsten-Jansson home. Tove drew a picture of him when she was six years old. When he died in 1935 it was a severe blow, and on 3rd March she wrote in her diary: 'Cawan has died of a heart attack. Dad is desperately sad. We are all tremendously sorry.'

Viktor Jansson was a key figure in the local art world and a committed member of artists' organisations. His life became to a large extent a story of competitions, prizes won and lost, triumphs and disappointments. It was a cut-throat world and like the other sculptors of his generation in Finland he worked in the shadow of Wäinö Aaltonen. When he won second prize in 1929 in a competition for a memorial to the writer Zachris Topelius, it sent the whole family 'wild with joy' and a party was planned. 'We've got apples and pears and jam and chocolate at home', an elated Tove reported to her diary: 'We're having a party today, with Finne, Felix, Malmberg and a Swede.' (The sculptors Gunnar Finne and Felix Nylund; the Swede was presumably the artist Arnold Strindberg.) When a later competition, in Vaasa in 1935, went badly, an upset Tove wrote: 'The competition for the monument is over. Outcry among the artists. [Yrjö] Liipola 1st prize! Finne 2nd. The Prize Committee bumbled about till 6 in the morning then issued a reduced and miserable judgement. Dad's proposal bought for 5000. But he was better than all the others, and I'm proud he did complete the design anyway!'

The next day she added triumphantly that the papers gave her dad a 'handsome revenge'. Monuments were vital for Viktor and his fellow sculptors – there were many to be erected after the war – and competing for them was a chance to make money. But he preferred to fill his home with female figures and small sculptures of children and cherubs in various forms. This has been described as a decorative streak in Viktor Jansson's sculpture, but it was more a question of a total trend

After plaster-casting: Faffan and Ham.

towards a softer style. In these small carvings, hard material and forms were transformed into a rugged kind of openness, an appeal to the viewer to see beneath the sculptured surface. This particularly applies to the sculptures Ham and Tove modelled for.

Signe and Viktor were both strong-willed artists, but conditions for man and woman were entirely different. Even before their marriage, Signe had had to lay aside her more radical artistic plans. But she chose to marry a sculptor. The course she had taken in plaster-casting was not wasted and in the studio working together was their practice from the first. The camera caught the couple in a moment of after-work exhilaration during their happy year in Paris, both covered with plaster, particularly

Viktor. Signe has a big, delighted smile. At Ängsmarn they worked on a female head with Ham's features. Little by little, Ham began signing her husband's work and she was capable of improving his efforts if necessary; for instance, remaking a hand which had gone wrong.

The coming together of Ham and Faffan became a union of two countries, two family cultures and two lives. They worked and loved and had a daughter, later two sons. They were happy. But they also lived in times of war and revolution, and during the First World War they were separated for a time. Viktor was lonely in their home in Lotsgatan Street while Signe was in Stockholm with Tove. Many photographs were taken to send home to Viktor in the spring of 1915. But the most painful period was the Finnish civil war, which permanently changed the life-loving artist Signe had fallen in love with, the stylish plaster-caster who had smiled at the camera with a glint in his eye. The Viktor who returned from the front was reserved and gloomy, a quite different man who hardly ever laughed. He was only 32 years old but his experiences and the horrors of war left an enduring mark on family life. 'This is no ordinary war,' he told Ham in his letter of 6th March 1918, but 'something much worse. Here no quarter is received or given.' All he could do was look forward to the future: 'We'll be so merry and happy after this war. A new world will open for us and we'll meet happy days head on,' he continued on 7th April. German troops had begun landing in Finland and that very day 2,500 men arrived at Loviisa; they went north and took Lahti, the crossing point of two railways.

Viktor's letters are living history, the tales of a soldier, full of feeling, impressions and longing. An epic strain in them links father to daughter, an exciting impulse to express himself in writing. He wanted to 'talk with' Signe; that is the expression he uses again and again (and this is how Tove will write later, too). He uses words to try to come near the woman he loves. When (very briefly) he describes things he has been doing himself, such as running across an open field under heavy fire to fetch ammunition, his words are clear and sharp with life. There were many storytellers in the Hammarsten family, an inheritance cultivated by Signe, who passed it on to her daughter. But Viktor's writing is just as close to the storyteller in Tove. Moominpappa the writer is there.

Mother's Dynamic Brothers

The family inheritance of foremothers and forefathers was in Signe's case a throng of brothers and sisters and, in the course of time, many children. The Hammarsten country house at Ängsmarn, Blidö, was iconised early as a model for the Moomin house. The opening of *Sculptor's Daughter* has become a classic of Tove's narrative style:

> Grandfather was a clergyman and used to preach to the king. Once, before his children and his children's children and his children's children's children covered the face of the earth, Grandfather came to a long field which was surrounded by forests and hills so that it looked like paradise. At one end it opened out into a bay for his descendants to bathe in.

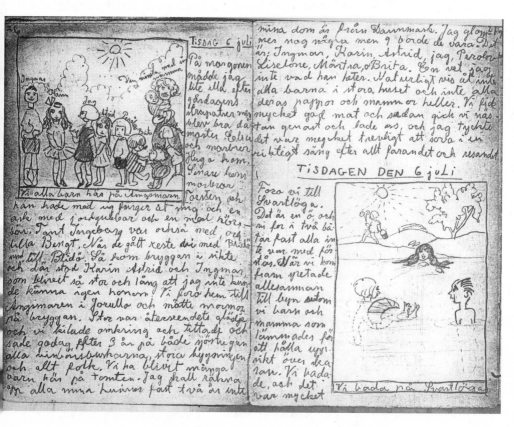

'All of us children here on Ängsmarn'. Tove's diary, summer 1926.

His grandchild Tove writes about this paradise-like valley in her very first diary in 1926. By then Grandfather was dead, but Grandmother stood on the landing stage at Ängsmarn to welcome the Hammarsten-Jansson family for years to come. All round swarmed parents, cousins and children of various sizes: 'There've been lots of us children here in the grounds,' wrote Tove (soon to be twelve) in the summer of 1926, and went on to draw the crowd over the caption: 'All of us children here at Ängsmarn'. In the 1920s the family would sometimes go to Stockholm in summer, call on relatives and spend a few days shopping at the NK department store and visiting Skansen and Gröna Lund open-air museum and amusement park and the theatre and cinema. Then everyone would go on to Blidö, where Tove often stayed with her little brothers while their parents returned to the city to work. The summer 1926 holiday on Blidö fills many pages of the diary with bathing excursions, berry-picking expeditions and games. Tove had bought a Native American outfit at NK and appeared many times as big chief 'Ironheart', while her cousin Karin was 'Black Hand' and Per Olov 'Hawkeye'. (Her younger brother Lasse was born in autumn the same year.) The endangered palefaces included Tove's maternal uncles, Einar and Olov.

Tove with her wild Uncle Harald, 1930s.

Signe's brothers and sisters were very important. As a student in Stockholm in the early 1930s, Tove boarded in the home of Einar Hammarsten, one of the family's many scientists, and during her first trip abroad stayed with his sister Elsa, who was married to a priest in Germany. Elsa was the mother of Cousin Karin, to whom Tove was very close. The Hammarsten brothers – Torsten, Olov, Einar and Harald – all specialised in scientific or technological subjects: a mining engineer, a biologist, a chemist and a mathematician. They were eccentric and stubborn, each in their own way individualists, like Signe. They built houses, went sailing and skiing, preferably in storms and blizzards, and enjoyed rock climbing and more or less risky experiments of various kinds. Torsten Hammarsten loved explosions and making people jump, and once filled a grindstone with gunpowder, placed it inside a porcelain tiled stove and lit the fuse, whereupon it flew out of the window and landed in their neighbour's greenhouse (as told by Tove in her story 'My Beloved Maternal Uncles'.)

There was an undeniable aura of adventure and excitement about her mother's brothers, particularly Torsten, Harald and Einar, and their explosive tendencies made a deep impression on their niece. Their rare visits to the Finnish archipelago, where the Jansson family rented holiday accommodation, were special events. When her 'wild and redhaired Uncle Harald with his big yacht, *Thalatta*, and three guests with him' was due for a three-day visit, Tove became sick with anticipation. The Hammarstens were storytellers – Torsten especially – and on Blidö they organised ghost-story competitions. Once, Torsten spoke in such a hair-raising manner about his own and others' experiences that it merited a special note in Tove's diary. Earlier she had herself entertained the children with 'stories of ghosts and trolls', while her apparently horror-struck listeners preserved a 'deathly silence'. This delight in telling tall stories was a family characteristic, as a note in her diary makes clear. It is 'a family failing I can't help', she wrote on 24th March 1932. She had used up her 'stock of smuggler stories' at a studio party and was 'troubled' afterwards by 'pangs of conscience' for her 'horrible' exaggerations.

Einar, who became Professor of Chemistry and Pharmacy at the renouned Karolinska Institute, always made a pugnacious and contentious impression, according to his colleague Ulf

Swimming at Blidö with several versions of Tove. Diary, 1930.

Lagerkvist, who came to know him in the years after the war. Every Easter, equipped with a number of sodium plugs from his laboratory, he would organise a great firework display on Blidö. He would make holes in the plugs and thread them onto a wire that was then wound into a 'light ball' and thrown into the sea. As Lagerkvist put it: 'According to him this was extremely satisfying. The sodium reacted on the water with extreme violence and on the magnificent scale on which Einar conducted the experiment; the result must have resembled a small atomic bomb.' He was a nightmare for conformist research directors and university administrators, Lagerkvist continues, but he had the ability to build a creative milieu around himself and his fellow workers and students: 'an unparalleled fisher of men, and everyone drawn into his magic circle was marked and formed by the experience'. This magic circle also impressed the young Tove, who loved her Uncle Einar deeply. In a letter home from the Hammarsten apartment at Norr Mälarstrand 26, she tells Ham excitedly about Einar's latest adventures on Blidö in April 1933. Together with Anna Lisa and little Ulla (his wife and child) he rashly ventured out onto thin ice, fell through, miraculously pulled himself out and then fell in again three times on his way back to the shore. 'What d'you think of that?' she asked Ham, adding: 'Now Uncle Einar's chuckling happily over the fact that *even Harald* thinks he's reckless.'

Faffan's family doesn't make the same vivid impression in Tove's diaries as the energetic Hammarstens, but it's fair to say that there was no obvious context in which they could express themselves. Visits to Jansson relatives were less frequent, mostly mentioned only in passing in the diaries. But as a mature writer in *Sculptor's Daughter* Tove introduces us to her father's mother, an enterprising woman who owns a button shop, and who when bankruptcy threatens hides boxes of buttons under her skirts just as she once hid weapons during the Finnish 'war of independence'.

Hammarsten and Jansson

'A tour of Signe and Faffan's home' is the name Ham gave her 1922 album of photographs of the flat in Lotsgatan in the Skatudden district of Helsinki. The tour begins in the hall, then takes us into the living room, where there are a few small pieces of sculpture, including a head of Ham. On one wall are oval portraits of Fredrik and Elin Hammarsten, and other walls are hung with pieces of textile and various pictures. The entrance to the studio is screened off by a curtain and Signe's drawing table stands in one corner. We see into the studio, catch a glimpse of the sculptor's stand and are allowed to look into the bedroom.

Samma rum från annat håll.

'A look-in at Signe and Faffan's'. The studio at Lotsgatan 4B, with Ham's writing desk in the right-hand corner.

There is a photograph of the children, Tove and Per Olov, together in a basketwork chair, which seems entirely undamaged despite its similarity to the one the sculptor in *Sculptor's Daughter* attacks with his bayonet when the party is at its height. The general effect is of light colours, in pure fin-de-siècle style with a personal touch, but not strikingly bohemian. Yet this was how the outside world must have seen this family of artists. For Erik Tawastsjerna, who lived on the same staircase, they represented *'la vie de bohème'*.

Home and studio were one, with no clear distinction between work and family life; this was the milieu that Tove and her two brothers grew up in. Art and pictures dominated, but there were also plenty of books. Ham illustrated novels, volumes of poetry, textbooks, everything under the sun, and with her own and Faffan's personal books, these volumes formed a motley library. The bookshelves stretched from floor to ceiling.

An article entitled 'Inside One of the Most Amusing Studio Homes in the World' appeared in the daily newspaper *Hufvudstadsbladet* in 1927, when Tove was thirteen years old. The reporter was Ester Åkesson, whom Tove would later work for as a young illustrator. Åkesson compares the flat to 'a box with endless secret compartments'; no sooner do you think you have seen it all than you come on yet another secret drawer and make new discoveries. An example was the shelf that served as a bunk for Tove herself. When the family needed more space (Lars had been born in 1926), they started literally climbing the walls. Tove, told to get down from her shelf and come and say hello to the journalist, is described as a 'long-legged girl in her very early teens', already at that tender age the publisher of an illustrated magazine called *Kakta knopp* ('Cactus bud'), which she describes in her diaries. But, the reporter writes, this fact is kept secret by her parents, who do not want to have undue influence on their 'wonder child'. *Kakta knopp* was a typical Tove project. Her diary tells us how 'busy' she was with this paper during the autumn of 1927, printing it in multiple copies. The number grew rapidly, from ten for the first issue to twenty-three for the third.

Many newspaper articles of this kind were written about the family; Faffan often did most of the talking but Ham and her work always featured as well. Yet there was little room for Ham. Åkesson noticed that her writing table stood at one end of the room, while the rest of the studio was dominated by her husband's work. Signe Hammarsten did not have a workroom of her own until the family moved into the brand-new artists' home, Lallukka, between Hesperiagatan and Apollogatan. A 1933 article in *Astra* emphasised the close relationship of home and art in the Hammarsten-Jansson household, as far as domestic comfort was concerned:

> Plaster, dust and wet clay often get onto the old curly-grained furniture in Faffan Jansson's studio, but it is none the less pleasant for that. Here housewife, children and guests relax from stress and work. The artist himself sits for a moment in court-preacher Hammarsten's shiny writing chair to sip the coffee which is diligently served to him and gather his strength for new efforts. It is rare to see an artist's home in which the work of colleagues is so richly represented. Swedish and Finnish art rub shoulders here.

Tove and Per Olov, 1922. From the family album.

The key figure in this description is clearly the sculptor, defined as the artist, while Signe is 'the housewife', contrasting with their daughter Tove, who has a 'workroom'. Tove, 19 years old, had just graduated from Stockholm Technical School.

Lallukka had been made possible by a generous donation. Its purpose was to provide a peaceful environment in which creative artists could afford to work. Rents were generally understood to be 'phenomenally' low. Faffan and Ham were among the first to move in; other residents included the artist couple Marcus Collin and Eva Törnwall-Collin, and the painters Ellen Thesleff and Ester Helenius. It was a sort of functionalist collective with a general dining room on the ground floor, though each apartment also had its own kitchen or cooking alcove. The large windows of the Jansson studio overlooked Hesperiagatan, and the studio itself was described in the article as enormous and containing sculptures of various sizes made from different materials. One whole wall was lined with pieces of sculpture arranged on shelves, wrote *Allas Krönika* in 1933:

> On the opposite wall a *soupente* has been built, a great platform almost like a separate room, with under it an open fireplace, sofa, table and chairs. The other rooms in the flat are next to the studio. This is where Mrs Signe Hammarsten has her room, the place where some of her brilliantly stylish vignettes and illustrations are created. She also shows us with justifiable pride a collection of pictures that the daughter of the house, the young Tove Jansson, has sent home from her recent years as a student at the Technical School in Stockholm. The pictures of this promising young artist show both imagination and style. In a back room the family's two young sons live like princes, as they themselves insist. Tove, shortly to come home, wrote from Stockholm: 'I'm very pleased about my "platform", but can't it also be extended as far as the window and the light there?'

It was of course only to be expected that the home would be dominated by Faffan's sculpture, but the places where Ham worked were fixed points, for both the 'promising artist' and her brothers. 'I best remember her sitting bent over her writing table with a strong magnifying glass before her eyes, working late into the night on the minute details of her postage stamp sketches,' recalls Per Olov Jansson in a memoir.

In 1924 Ham had begun a part-time job in the art department of the Bank of Finland, where she worked on designs for postage stamps, bonds, watermarks and banknotes – 'earning jobs', as Tove was often to describe the work she herself came to do on illustrations, caricatures and book covers. Work and family grew side by side for Ham, Faffan and the children, but in different ways. The three Hammarsten-Jansson children saw their parents constantly at work on sculpture and illustration and, at one time or another, they too all came to work in the world of the visual arts. Tove became a painter and draughtswoman, Per Olov a photographer, and Lasse, by degrees and, among many

The studio at Lotsgatan. Diary entry, 1929.

other things, a Moomin artist; in his early years he had devoted himself for a time to sculpture.

They were a genuine family of artists and this was how the public saw them in the 1930s. When Tove published her first short story in 1934 she was introduced in the newspaper *Helsingfors-Journalen* as a young member of 'the well-known artist family', so she had now also become a literary debutante. When Ham, Faffan and Tove took part in the first exhibition at Lallukka in 1941 (Tove called it 'the inmates' first exhibition'), the art critic Signe Tandefelt commented sarcastically: 'The Jansson family are displaying their wares. What else would you expect?' Tove was very indignant. 'That Tandefelt woman has dismissed us,' she commented. 'I'm sure it's simply that old age is beginning to rot her brain. Being an artist has little to do with family connections!'

The cultural world of Swedish-speaking families in Finland is indeed rich with luxuriant family trees, and there are families of artists and writers where the mere name (Enckell, Parland and many others) is enough to indicate some form of cultural activity. Various explanations have been put forward for this phenomenon: the position of a linguistic minority, a fear of isolation and exclusion that makes their need for self-expression particularly strong, and what has been termed the aesthetic of the narrow room. But Tove's family never fitted this pattern. For Faffan, and for Ham (who came from Sweden anyway), it was a love of art that had struck the spark and neither came from an artistic family. The Hammarsten-Jansson family was an artistic enclave of its own. Its members supported each other, worked together and criticised each other's work. Gradually a form of family criticism developed. Tove has told how Faffan would emerge from the studio and say, 'Now you can come and look.' There was a pecking order: Ham first, then Tove. That tradition was to live on, if in new forms.

All three children worked with words. Soon Tove's two brothers followed her into print. In 1941 Lars, only fifteen, published an adventure story, *The Treasure of Tortuga*, which was well received. Ham designed its cover and also those of several later books he wrote: *The Ruler* (1945) and *I Am My Own Disquiet* (1950). In the year of Tove's Moomin debut, Per Olov brought out a collection of stories, *A Young Man Walks Alone*. The illustrations and cover design were signed by Ham, who was also responsible for the cover for his novel, *Book with Happy Ending* (1946). This artistic co-operation between sister and brothers went further and they had projects in common all their lives. In the 1940s Lars and Tove collaborated on stories in verse for the magazine *Garm*, and later on the Moomin comic strips. In her journals of the 1940s Tove described how Per Olov photographed rooms and pictures in her studio, and the portraits he took of her as a writer were used in a great number of introductions, surveys and reference works. The photographic picture book, *The Scoundrel in the Moomin House* (1980), is a later example of their sibling co-operation. Family unity was close, both in work and everyday life.

Like Tove's *Sculptor's Daughter*, the brothers' books of the 1940s were rooted in their home and family. In *Book with Happy Ending*, Per Olov described a son's return home after the war. His father is a sculptor and the description of him in his studio with an 'eternal' cigarette in the corner of his mouth and a 'modelling tool in his hand' has clear traces of Faffan. The setting is similar to that described much later by Tove in *Sculptor's Daughter*, but her brother's contemporary novel about a war-hardened young soldier has a different purpose: it contains an outspoken critique of the family and of the power of a father who will accept no theories of art but his own. The Hammarsten-Jansson childhood world of adventure books and games (with lots of Tarzan) and of enjoyable storms and voyages of discovery, one of Tove's hallmarks as a writer, is also found in her brothers' work. An extreme example is Lasse's novel *...And Yet Day Dawns* (1946). But the family portraits could be rearranged and appear differently in different contexts and moods. For all three children, writing became a rebellion against the domination of pictures, a road away from the sculptor's and illustrator's studio in the direction of words and stories.

When Tove described her childhood and adolescence and the family she grew up in, it was in terms of fellowship and freedom, responsibility, family loyalty and harmony. It was a childhood full of games, excursions and shared time, particularly during their summers in Pellinge archipelago. 'My father was a melancholy man,' she once wrote in a letter, 'but when a storm threatened he became a different person, cheerful, entertaining and ready to join his children in dangerous adventures.' Storms, high water, bad weather – everything that was dangerous and could be evaded or fought off – in Tove's words, had a positive effect: 'these (fairly) minor catastrophes proved that in the end everything was really all right, and that we were together'. Storms signified excitement and rescue – the two were always linked – and a guarantee of companionship within the family. Traces survived of the civil war warrior, the man who constantly worried about his little family and how he could protect them.

The family in the new artists' home, Lallukka. From left Tove, Per Olov, Ham, Lasse, the critic Sigrid Schauman, and Faffan.

Minor catastrophes became a way for him to take the family into his protection (like Moominpappa in the books), while at the same time they made everyday life exciting. 'The water is rising! The landing stage is floating away!' exclaimed Tove in her diary in the summer of 1928, happily drawing a dramatic picture.

But there were storms within the walls of the studio too. Ham had left her home country for love and emigrated to an entirely unfamiliar land and culture. Even though many people in Finland understood Swedish, she never learned Finnish properly and was linguistically isolated. And she had been forced to set aside her earlier interests and work hard to support her family. This sapped her strength and her love, as did the change in Faffan's temperament after the war. There were periods when money was short and Ham's job at the Bank of Finland was the family's only regular source of income. As a sculptor, Faffan had no choice but to depend almost entirely on prizes, grants and commissions, which made for a highly unreliable income.

For this reason Tove very early came to feel a sense of responsibility for helping to support the family, and at fourteen was already speaking of her longing to 'help Mamma' with drawings. During her time at the Technical School in Stockholm she was torn between a longing to complete her education on the one hand, and on the other a strong wish to help her mother, who was weighed down by the burden of her responsibility for supporting the family. The pressure on Tove was sometimes very severe, and the conflicting demands of Uncle Einar (who was financing her college studies) and of Ham became a litany of despair in her diary. 'Am I to let Mamma slave alone,' she wrote, aged sixteen in spring 1931, 'when Uncle Einar thinks I can help her?' Ham's letters tell of exhaustion and overwork. 'I must go home and help if I can,' Tove decides, then in the next sentence writes of her hope of being able to continue her studies. Viktor seems not to have been involved in these discussions. Ham's plan to attend Tove's graduation ceremony in May 1931 had to be cancelled because of the state of the family finances, 'so dreadful that such a small sum of money must stop you coming to me here,' Tove writes. She herself had won an award and wanted to send Ham 100 Swedish kronor: 'We could have such a good time in all simplicity.'

Tove was not forced to make a choice between study and work in the spring of 1931, but the worries expressed in her diary and letters have little in common with the untroubled childhood and adolescence she was so often to describe in later years. 'I have to become an artist for the sake of the family,' she wrote during her first year in Stockholm. It was a vow she never forgot. Responsibility to work and family came first. That was where love was to be found. And so it was for Tove: work and love came before everything else.

CHAPTER 3

The Embryo Artist

We were eight boys and Eva Cederström and me.

'Graduation Day' from Messages

'I think you understand me better than anyone else,' wrote the sixteen-year-old Tove to Ham in January 1931. It was her second term at the Technical School and she was homesick for her family. The relationship between Ham and Tove was a close and warm one. Tove had been an only child for six years before the birth of her brother Per Olov in 1920. The photographs tell a story of love. 'Look what beautiful hands,' wrote Ham of Tove, aged one, making a lifesize drawing of them: 'one flat, with outstretched fingers, one with a clenched fist'. Hands are the tools of people who draw and paint.

Ham's sketch of Little Tove drawing at the age of eighteen months is another statement of the relationship between mother and daughter. With a mother who was always drawing, it was natural for her daughter to take after her and do the same. They mirrored each other through their pens. 'Mamma draws me and I draw Mamma,' wrote Tove in June 1931. She drew the family and herself in her diaries and on her sketch block from an early age. Her drawings show her mother reading a book (when Tove was four), their family friend Cawan, the family when Per Olov was born, and Faffan and Tove on a stair.

The diaries were created by a child who could draw and would grow into an 'embryo artist' and gradually be transformed into a young painter. It was obvious from the first that Tove would work with pictures, but words were there from the beginning too. Viktor could write and Tove later bore witness many times to Ham's suggestive way of telling stories, most beautifully in *Sculptor's Daughter,* in which storytelling becomes magic: 'We turn off the lights in the studio and she says: "Once upon a time".' And there were words inside Tove herself too. Her school compositions in Swedish won high marks, and she loved telling stories and wrote a whole series of miniature books before moving on to bigger projects like her novel 'Matilda and Art', and the story about the flying hero, Yachin, in 'Invisible Powers', part I and part II. 'It would be best to give her imagination free rein,' said her drawing teacher Agnes Kihlman much later. It was a wild imagination and must be allowed to develop in peace.' Tove's diaries and stories are powerful evidence of this wild imagination. She wrote about and drew all manner of things and worked away at various means of expression.

The Tove Publishing Co!!!

As an adult writer of children's books Tove would talk about the importance of the happy ending and the principle of pulling everything together on the last page, but for the child storyteller other methods applied. The story of Prick the dog, written by Tove when she was seven, deals with illness and death; Prick rapidly departs this life (1921). She wrote, drew and assembled the pages of her manuscript to make a little book, and named the edition after herself, writing 'Prick!' and 'The Tove Publishing Co!!!' on the first page. Fourteen small books containing short narratives, fairy tales and verses, neatly dated between 1921 and 1925 and numbered like a series, have been preserved. All give the name of the author as 'Tove Marika Jansson'. The last page of one of the first books, 'Sir Blue the Knight', carries a list of forthcoming titles in the series *Tove's Books for Children* and many of these were actually completed. The Christmas calendar *Among Goblins and Trolls*, illustrated by the much-admired John Bauer, was an important model.

Tove's series included traditional fairy tales with titles like 'Princess Glittergirl' (which has certain comic touches) and

Cover for 'Death', 1925.

'Sir Blue', but central to her storytelling were ghost and horror stories and verses on angels, death, hell and paradise. Such titles as 'Death', 'Assault' and 'A Dreadful Night' are firm evidence of the young storyteller's favourite reading. As a teenager she carried a basket full of 'ghost and troll stories', and when she visited relatives in Stockholm it was not easy to avoid horror-thirsty cousins of all sizes: 'Tove, tell us a horrible story' was the cry at Whitsun 1932. Even the adult Tove Jansson often talked happily about 'horror stories'.

The devil appears in many of her childhood tales, and in 'Travelling Round the Earth' he is a menacing figure pursuing the chief editors, an angel and a girl. There are also biblical elements here and there too. The young Tove based her stories on tradition and the miscellaneous literature that Ham illustrated; stories, chatty columns, poems and textbooks, all left their mark. In 'The Wizard' a magician loses his cloak and a young woman makes convenient use of it to send a persistent admirer to heaven.

Tove watched Ham working at her table every day and, as is the way with children, she wanted to do the same. But there is something more than wanting to play mother in these little books, a longing to tell stories that makes them more interesting than mere children's games. This desire to make books was realised in projects that were planned and carried through from idea to execution, including the co-ordination of text and pictures on the page. When Tove was not quite fourteen she had her first story accepted for publication, a series of pictures with accompanying verses for the weekly *Allas Krönika*. The intermediary was the editor, Ester Åkesson. The author was presented as a 'young woman' named 'Totto'. The text was a poem of homage to the President with the title 'Hey, Hurrah for Mannerheim' (after his triumphal progress through Helsinki in 1928).

In the same year Tove contributed fairy-tale illustrations to *Julen* (the Christmas publication of the Finland-Swedish Office-workers' Association), and a year later her first cartoon appeared in *Garm* (1929). She had sent in two pictures, the texts written together with Ham. From the very first Tove recorded her publications in her diary: 'In the magazine Julen there are 10 drawings for 2 fairy tales and I did the drawings,' she noted proudly in December 1928. But her greatest achievement was her contribution to the children's paper *Lunkentus* (also edited by Ester Åkesson), a story in pictures in no fewer than seven parts about two caterpillars called 'The Adventures of Prickina and Fabian' (see colour plate 2). It was in the gyrations of the caterpillars that the signature 'Tove' was born. Earlier she had written T.J. or, as in her first published work, 'Totto' – a pet name within the family.

This was the beginning of her professional life as an illustrator. It all started when she deputised for Ham, whose mother Elin Hammarsten had fallen seriously ill and was near death. Ham had to leave suddenly for Stockholm and her work for the children's paper passed to her daughter. Trembling with fear and excitement, Tove noted in her diary:

> Mamma could not do the cover and end-page for Lunkentus so I got the job of doing them. The front page shows St George and the Dragon in red and blue, the back page 'The Adventures of Prickina and Fabian' in green and black (caterpillars). I'm so afraid they won't like them. So much depends on it, whether I'll get another commission, if this goes well.

At the same time Tove worked away at her fur trousers, adding uneasily: '(Surely it can't be wrong to sew fur trousers even though one's dearly loved grandmother is ill?)' A few days later her grandmother died and everything changed: 'so strange and

Sketch above the signature 'Totto' in Allas Krönika, 1928: 'Hi, hurrah for Mannerheim.'

sad. Pappa and I talked of things we would never have talked about otherwise.'

Lunkentus needed an illustration for the front cover and a story in pictures with words under each picture for the back. Tove finished the whole thing off with speech bubbles and her first comic strip was done. The formula for the story was the world in microcosm. The leading actors are a pair of caterpillars in love, and their aim is simply to save their own skins, seen realistically from a caterpillar's point of view. 'Prickina and Fabian' was created with fresh humour and a feeling for comic touches all the way to its happy ending: 'How happy their idyll when Fabian's wife/ said mildly one day, O my darling now/ I've brought seven little caterpillar kids into the world for you.' But the editor thought the story too long-winded and one of Tove's teachers couldn't accept her inaccurate zoological fantasising. 'I dragged out the strip endlessly,' she said in an interview in 1944, 'and rapidly changed the caterpillars to butterflies. Because I'd made my caterpillars have caterpillar babies and my zoology teacher was upset by this error. That's not how it works, he said.'

This strip was Tove's first major work to reach print and a lot depended on it. She had seen an early chance to help support the family, and her concern for the family and for Ham is touching. Work is like love; a way of helping people to be together. 'I long for the time when I'll be able to help Mamma with drawings. Mamma does so much work on her own,' Tove wrote just before her fourteenth birthday. Work brought with it professional pride. The printing of that first cover was not of a good enough standard. When the paper came out in April 1929 she wrote crossly in her diary: 'They've ruined it by making it all red. What a sad disappointment. I'm cross with Mrs Åkesson.' It was an important first experience. The adult Tove would always take care to send precise instructions about her pictures to editors, publishers and printers.

The Storyteller

Work on Tove's magazine *Kakta knopp*, mentioned in Ester Åkesson's article on the Hammarsten-Jansson family, is described in detail in Tove's diary. This was the first of three issues of the magazine, and Tove as sole entrepreneur was responsible for the whole production from A to Z. She wrote, drew, duplicated, boiled glue and eventually sold copies at school. *Kakta knopp* ('Cactus Paper', three issues in autumn 1927) was followed by *Julkorven* (Christmas Sausage) a year later. Tove noted: 'I have published a newspaper: "Julkorven". It was very successful and everyone in the class bought it' (December 1928). The following spring found her back in action with a new paper, *Sexan* (The Sixth), which was devoted to her own class. But not all her classmates co-operated. Tove wrote: 'I gave out "Sexan" at school. Everyone except Kalle, Frese and Francke bought it.' Unfortunately she did not reveal why this trio resisted. She published no more newspapers during her school days, but later at art college she would be involved with student publications.

School was difficult, but it had its lighter moments. In her first diary Tove herself promised that the book would concentrate on 'happy summers – not school', and the summer months to

Geography lesson in the Broberg school. Tove is on the left in the second row from the bottom.

which 'conditions' (extra school work after failing exams) had to apply were a torment. But she got by with room to spare. She worked hard at Finnish during the summer of 1929. Her drawing talent was known to her classmates and she was happy to show what she could do. When they challenged her to draw a portrait of one of the teachers and his new red-haired girlfriend on the blackboard she couldn't refuse, especially since her most dangerous rival, Hertta (who couldn't draw anything but horses, noted Tove caustically), would otherwise get the job. 'Competition is severe between Hertta and me, so I did the drawing.' But on the whole, school was a straitjacket to the young 'busy bee'. She would fill the long walk from Lotsgatan in Skatudden to the Broberg School ('Broban') at Högsbergsgatan 23 with stories, and sometimes one of her friends would join her to listen to them. By the time she left school she already had several long stories behind her, neatly written out in black oilcloth-covered exercise books of various sizes.

I'm a Writer

After her little books, Tove plunged into the world of the story-teller. She spent a lot of time on 'Matilda and Art' and worked hard on 'Invisible Forces'. She began the latter in spring 1928 and wrote it in two parts: Part I contains thirteen chapters on 118 handwritten pages, and Part II five chapters on 64 pages. She drew inspiration from Jules Verne, Conan Doyle and Edgar Rice Burroughs (*Tarzan*) and her cast of characters includes a scientist, a beautiful daughter and a villain with 'piercing black eyes'. The hero's name is Yachin, an early Superman whose ability to fly has been granted to him by 'invisible forces'. With this story Tove assumed the role of author. She read the chapters aloud in private to Per Olov and presented herself in her diary at her author's desk. 'I'm rewriting the whole of "Invisible Forces" in a big new book, and I'm changing nearly everything in it,' she wrote in September 1928, adding a picture, 'Me Writing Yachin', which shows her tearing her hair and writing so vigorously that the ink splatters. But she drew no pictures for the story, and the stories she wrote at this early stage of her writing career often aren't illustrated. She was exploring words and finding out what they could do.

The young Tove was very ambitious. She wanted to tell stories and write, publish and be read, earn her own living and help support the family. In the year of her fourteenth birthday these projects set each other in motion. She had to become a professional. Picture-books were an important part of this process and she had several in progress. 'The Princess Who Shingled Herself' was written in verse and illustrated in three colours. It was written during two intensive weeks in February 1928. Her purpose is crystal clear: 'In February I began working on "The Princess Who Shingled Herself". By the 19th it was almost completely finished. I hope it will get published.' It was sent to Oscar Furuhjelm at the Bildkonst (Art Picture) publishing company but was 'sent back', a disappointment noted in the diary.

They thought it was too 'artistic', she wrote angrily. But there could be no question of giving up and she started a new book, 'Sara and Pelle and the Octopuses of the Water-Sprite', about a brother and sister who enter the Watersprite's 'underwater world'. This world is full of octopuses and the children get to look after the littlest ones. When they return home, the baby fish end up in Mother's casseroles and become the family dinner.

Tove cycled to the Tilgmann Printing Press with her new book. 'I had to wait a long time, but in the end Furki (Furuhjelm) came and he gave me some hope. Maybe - - - ??? Today I'll go there again and then I'll know for sure. If they turn this one down I'll start a new book.' But this time they took the bait and she celebrated in her diary: 'It worked! Oh I'm so happy! Now I've taken the first step in my career as an artist.' It was May 1928. Tove Jansson was on the way to becoming an illustrator. Her royalty was to be 300 Finnish marks and the book would probably be printed on the first of August, she wrote ecstatically a month later: 'Think what fun, a book by me getting published!' But publication was delayed for a couple of months and then set aside. The book finally came out five years later in 1933 under the pseudonym 'Vera Haij' – a friend at the Technical School in Stockholm, named a couple of times in Tove's letters of the time. The book ('Sara and Pelle') is mentioned in her notes, but there's no longer any trace of the excitement of her school days; rather the opposite, the book seems almost to disgust her. Such childish adventures are nothing to a young painter en route to the Parnassus of art education in Finland, the Ateneum in Helsinki. Perhaps this was why she didn't want to see her own name on the cover.

During the first years of her studies at Stockholm Technical School Tove worked intensively on several picture books and as always recorded the progress of her work in her diary. 'I have begun a more modern version of 'The Princess Who Shingled Her Hair', she wrote, adding 'pretty decent'. She hoped to get it 'printed and a little money for it'. Work went quickly during September 1930: 'All the drawings are done, 10 in all plus front and back covers, but the text still needs work', she wrote on 15th September. Two days later she noted: 'The Princess Who Shingled Her Hair is finished.'

She was working at the same time on another picture book,

Tove's picture-books from the 1930s. On the left a page from the unpublished Pelle Who Won't Go to School; *on the right the cover of* Sara and Pelle and the Octopuses of the Water-Sprite *(1933).*

'Pelle Who Won't Go to School'. It *must* be published, 'I've made up my mind about that', she wrote just before New Year 1930. She had already tried to get this paraphrase of an old children's jingle about a boy who wouldn't go to school published the year before by Söderströms Publishers in Helsinki. On 15th November 1929 she wrote in her diary:

> After school I walked to Söderströms and Mr Lüchow. That is to say, I searched for the publishers in the twilight, and when I finally found them, I was completely done in. Mr Lüchow roared 'sit down' and leafed to and fro through 'Pelle Who Won't Go to School' and then said, 'Come again on Monday'.

It was to be the fate of the Pelle book to have to call on several publishers. The Finnish-language firm of Otava declined and Bonniers in Sweden weren't interested either. The return of the manuscript is dated immediately after the book was submitted, in January 1931. It was all recorded in Tove's diary: 'On Thursday I handed in the book at Bonniers. No response yet. It'll come back – of course.' Her pessimism was justified a couple of days later. 'The book's back again. Oh well, it wasn't very good.'

But it was an important book for Tove herself; she regarded it as her first book for children. 'One wants to start at the top,' she wrote many years, and a couple of Moomin books later, to her friend Eva Konikoff in 1948, in a discussion on the requirements of youthful artistic endeavour: 'It is a natural part of the rash decision-making of a very young person.' That's how I myself wanted to start,' she went on. 'That's how it was for me when Bonniers rejected my first children's book.'

The young Tove Jansson worked hard to make her plans come true. Naturally not all she wrote and drew is memorable, and often the story her diaries tell carries more sting – there is an unaffected openness and boldness about it. The most arresting thing about these early diaries full of picture books and literary attempts is the diarist's strong will and powerful need for self-expression: this explains her persistent pursuit of publishers and editors. Some of her commissions were mediated through Ham as illustrator, but many were initiated by Tove herself. Her writing had to grow. When she was writing her first short stories in her twenties she noted in her diary: 'Mamma says: Write a book.'

A Free Young Lady

In May 1930 Tove finished her school days and walked out of the Broberg School for the last time. Freedom beckoned and the future was her own: 'Now I'm a free young lady, because school has shut its jaws behind me for ever. And now I shall begin to live.' That autumn she entered Stockholm Technical School, section B for 'female pupils'. It was 23rd September 1930 and the schoolgirl had turned into the art student Tove Jansson, with special reference to the drawing of advertisements and general design. Another school, but this time involving construction drawing, freehand drawing, painting, text-writing, the art of perspective, figure-drawing and planned professional industrial drawing. She had not been required to give prior evidence of ability. Signe Hammarsten-Jansson's name had been enough to guarantee her 'quality'.

Tove's much-loved Uncle Einar was to play a big part in her training at 'Teknis', as the Technical School was popularly known. A wonderful offer from him had cast a glow over her last term at the Broberg School: 'I shall be able to live with him and his wife and co. in Stockholm and try for the Academy. I'm incredibly happy, but anxious too because I really don't know how to do anything at all,' wrote Tove in April 1930.

It was with huge expectation that she started at Teknis. She sailed for Stockholm in the ferry *Oihonna* and was installed with Uncle Einar and his family at Norr Mälarstrand 26, after a short stay in Äppelviken with Uncle Olov and his family. She wrote a detailed description of her first day at college in her diary. It involved clover-leaf figures in various forms, in connection with practice in the stylisation of natural models. In figure drawing '8.30–10.20' the fixed point was a plaster model. The whole thing is described in the conversational style that was to become typical of the diaries of her Teknis period. It was a way of creating distance, of keeping oneself under control, that also left room for the contrast between free imagination – what the young Tove called 'creative joy' – and the regulated school instruction she was never able to reconcile herself to:

> A plaster clover leaf was set before one – some were lucky enough to get the chance to draw a convoluted lily stalk, also made of plaster. This was Teknis. Trembling fingers grasped their pens and a great many crooked clover leaves saw the light of day. However, if I was not aware of any real joy of creation, it was perhaps partly because the clover leaf I had so painfully assembled found no favour with my own critical eye.

According to the teacher (said to be a nice little woman), Tove's clover leaves were too small and she had to start again:

> So I started to draw on a large scale, while the woman at the desk behind burst out indignantly: 'But how can you make such strokes!? It really cuts me to the heart.' I understood her only too well – how dismal it must be for her heart to be to be faced by such a mass of clover leaves when just one was enough to fill my own heart with gloom? We also drew clover leaves freehand. When it was over I walked home. It wasn't like it had been in the morning. Now I could no longer see the tunnel under the railway bridge as a gorge full of ghosts, or Karduansmakaregatan Street as a dangerous ravine and the square in front of the town hall as a dismal forest. My thoughts were prosaic, and their only embellishment was clover leaves.

The first thorn had pierced her wild imagination; there would be many more during her time at Teknis.

Her three years at college in Stockholm came to have great importance for Tove. She was sixteen when she started and would be 19 when she finished in 1933. It was a time of decision, of new experiences and development. She became ever more secure in the saddle and made many friends, surrounded by a steady set of 'embryo artists', richly described in her diaries in connection with various activities: college work, excursions and parties. She won prizes and scholarships, drew and painted, wrote student shows and worked on her stories. She posed confidently, palette in hand in a painter's overall, for college photographs. And she worked hard. On one particular day during that first autumn of 1930, 'I began with an acrostic on the letters ABC and in the evening started on a leather folder for mamma. I bought a jazzophone and sang through it but Uncle Einar didn't like it.' The next day she was given the job of 'setting up a simple group' of paintings and got it done. The teacher, 'Miss Bolin', said it was 'good' and contained 'airy colours'. In the evening she finished the leather folder, after which she spent a 'pleasant evening in' around the long family table. She quite often made music and one of her best-loved possessions was her balalaika (she liked drawing herself with it), even if Uncle Einar and Aunt Anna Lisa didn't enjoy her playing as much as Tove herself did.

Anxiety about Ham and her responsibility for the family was never far away. Mostly for herself and the family, she prepared a description of her first term at the Technical School in the form of a picture book entitled 'Homecoming'. It is like an illustrated narrative film of her life in Stockholm, a mixture of homesickness, fear and independence. She pondered her professional role and the identity that seemed to have been chosen for her from the start: 'Certainly, my God, I'm grateful to have my profession (phew!) in a little box; it's absolutely the only thing I do have. What would become of me otherwise? Nothing,' she wrote in September 1930. It was all settled, but there was a 'phew' in the picture too. Writing was firmly fixed inside the young Tove and the day she started at Teknis a future in pictures became a reality. When she wrote to Ham about gratitude and talent she already had her first term behind her, and there was more in what she wrote of responsibility than of pleasure and joy: 'Isn't it something one should be grateful for and try to be worthy of, this ability to draw, I had it from the beginning, just have to develop it myself?'

During that first year the conflict between possibly going on to 'higher' education at the College of Industrial Art (HKS), and the need to go home to Helsinki and work as an artist for money, became acute. Tove was anxious to shoulder her share of the responsibility of supporting the family, which would have enabled a longed-for work partnership with her beloved Ham, but deepest of all inside her was a longing to go on studying. In January 1931 she told her mother: 'I don't know whether I'll go on to "higher" – or what – I only know one thing for sure – I want to be able to sit opposite you and help you to draw.' But in her diary she struck a different note. After all, a year at Teknis was no more than basic training and the wonderful idea of trying to go on to the College of Industrial Art had suddenly vanished from the picture. The fact that Ham actually hoped that her daughter would not aspire to higher education shows how sharp the conflict was. By 17th April 1931 she was in despair: 'Mamma hopes I won't go on. And of course I want to go home and help Mamma. But I also want to go on to higher. But three years – can I let darling Mamma slave away on her own for three years, when uncle Einar believes I would be able to help her with the drawing. What shall I do?'

Tove's strong feeling of responsibility was now firmly established. What she wanted was to paint, to stay in Stockholm and apply for entry to the College of Industrial Art, but Ham and the family needed her. She had already shown what she was capable of with her drawings, and now the problem had become serious. If she could go on to 'higher' in autumn 1931, that would solve the problem, and she would never have to face the dutiful daughter's only alternative: to go home.

Students usually applied for entry to the College of Industrial Art (HKS) after a year or two of preliminary training. Ham had studied to be a teacher of drawing, but Tove had specialised in 'drawing for printed material', a training for illustrators and designers of advertisements, which included such subjects as higher art-industrial professional drawing, script and heraldry, figure drawing, decorative painting and book design. A great deal of her student work from this period survives: bound books, exercises in heraldry, designs for book covers and various exercises involving script. She drew advertisements and worked in all kinds of printed material, but her constant dream was to paint. She was also awarded the highest marks in decorative painting at the end of her studies in spring 1933: a little 'a'. The advertisements she drew were modern, though she was no admirer of the Functionalist trends of the 1930s. She was capable of producing a fashionably modern scene such as a rectangular courtyard with brownish yellow, greyish pink and other more or less indeterminate colours, all illuminated by a single street lamp, and of dismissing the whole with the words 'Really modern, my God!' She could draw book covers and geometrical compositions, but what she longed to do was to draw pictures of wet sand and people collecting shells, and of skies in natural colours. By this time she was in her last term at Teknis, spring 1933. During her student years the distinction between painting and printed work grew ever greater for her. She wrote: 'There must always be a ramshackle lamp in any composition that aims to be up-to-date, nor can you leave out the decrepit fir-tree, the consumptive girl drinking through a straw or the man or woman made of wire – UGH! Yet even I from time to time produce such desperate specimens of city life!'

But she was more contemporary in her artistic views than she liked to show, and worked with colour and form in a new way. She filled pages of her diary with 'modern' portrayals of herself and relaxed with pictures of 'Ellen's sketching Monday' (Ellen was an alter ego in the diary) or a 'modern' representation of her first swim.

She worked on her diary entries in a more literary manner, and her student days in Stockholm fill more than two notebooks. She drew and painted as if possessed, but was far from abandoning her projects as a writer. One of her diaries takes the form of a picaresque novel made up of letters addressed to 'Fabian, knight of the sad figure', and dated 1931. *Don Quixote* was the obvious pattern for this study of fellowship and artistic life, written during Tove's second year at Teknis. It is a strongly self-reflective tale, in which the diarist struggles with three narrators, 'Fernanda', 'Dulcinea' and 'Ellen', and paints self-portraits as if on a conveyor belt. The writer soon reveals she won't be using 'her usual Tove, but rather other and more well sounding names'. One of these names relates to action, one to thought and one to poetry – but all three characters are energetic illustrators. The plan is set out as

EPISODES
FROM FERNANDA'S DAILY LIFE.
   THOUGHTS
EMANATING FROM DULCINEA'S BRAIN.
   POEMS
WRITTEN BY ELLEN.
   EVENTS.
   EVENINGS.
   DAYS.
   NIGHTS.

WITH ILLUSTRATIONS BY THE THREE NAMED LADIES.
TAKING PART: FABIAN.
   SEEDPOD.
   KA.
   HIPPIGAIGAI.
   THE PESSIMIST   THE LAST TWO TAKE TURNS WITH THE PEN
   THE OPTIMIST

The description of contents is extremely detailed, with narrative subtitles in archaic Roman script for the nine letters and an interspersed play in five acts, but after sixty pages the whole thing goes over to a calm diary style with elements of summer poesy and a concluding comment from the author. The principal parts are taken by a group of companions known as 'The Embryo House', and their exploits and offences: 'Nalle' (Brita Edquist), 'Hammarberg' (Elis Hammarberg) and 'Johanna' (Johannesson). An obscure nightclub also features, and two companions who belong to an outer circle, called 'Nilsson' and 'Fryholm'. The scene is often an attic alcove six floors up at Norr Mälarstrand 26.

The letters to Fabian reveal an appetite for expression that nearly ties itself in knots, an exhilaration that knows no limits. Colour illustrations lavishly set on whole pages portray the three narrators in various stressful situations. Everything is written in the parodic style characteristic of many of Tove's writings from this period. The first letter introduces the principal actors:

Dear Fabian,

You, my faithful knight, my companion on lonely expeditions, you who never tire of hearing of troubles and sorrows and never criticise or disapprove although you often have good reason to do so, you who have never before been entrusted with anything amusing, let me present a few embryo artists to you. I am not sure whether you have any interest in art. I have never heard you talk of what you occupy yourself with, or of what interests you, and I've never really believed that you concern yourself with anything at all beyond listening to my own effusions. It was for this purpose that you were created.

Fabian is the diary, the principal listener and the receiver of the writer's 'effusions', but after a couple of terms Tove returns to her usual diary style. The exploits of the Embryo House laid a

Self-portrait.
From diary, 1931.

definite emphasis on nightlife, but now the notes move more and more in the direction of work.

Colour was important to the young Tove in Stockholm, as it will continue to be over the years during her career as a painter. In her diaries and notes, she discusses again and again the importance of colour, its nuances and the 'power spectrum'. 'I want to see real colours on the painter's palette,' she writes during her last term at Teknis (1933), talking lyrically about glorious orange, pale green and carmine. When she was noticed by the senior lecturer in painting, Oscar Brandtberg, it was precisely in relation to colour that he advised greater restraint. His comments aroused new feelings in her, a mixture of euphoria, pride and fear, and huge expectation. The legendary Brandtberg was known not only as a man of few words but also for his respect for the artistic individuality of his students. His words of praise made a strong impression on Tove and played an important part in encouraging the concentration on painting she developed during her time at Teknis. When Tove described her brief interview with Brandtberg, and her own reactions to it, she dramatised as always – making herself little and the teacher big – but her serious attitude to painting was no subject for jokes. She described their meeting on 10th May 1932 in her diary:

> Today I was busy with a tempera painting I was very deeply involved with. Buzzing like a bee, naturally – terrified of possible dismissive criticism, blushing up to my ears and spraying bucketfuls of sweat for a distance of three metres all round, I was sploshing away at breakneck speed, bright red and in a state of nerves – in fact, just as I always *am* when something interests me. Brantberg arrived. He stood behind me and just looked. I shrank into myself, licked my brush out of sheer absentmindedness and nerves and got a throatful of formalin. 'My girl,' said Brantberg. 'You're putting on too much colour.' Pause. Then he said, 'Apply for the Academy. Worth your while,' and vanished. Now I'm so proud it almost feels unpleasant.

The value of this laconic judgement could not be clearer: the teacher's words contrast with the silence of the student painter. But Tove never applied for entry to the Academy of Art and Uncle Einar's wonderful idea never became a reality. She completed her final year at the Technical School and went back to her family,

The embryo artist, the teacher and colour. From diary, 1932.

who had now settled into their new studio home at Lallukka. During her last spring in Stockholm she wrote seriously to Ham about solidarity, independence and responsibility, everything that related to the concept of love. She told them she loved them all and sent a big hug to Pappa and the boys. It was May 1933 and it looked as if Ham's trip to Stockholm, which they had both been looking forward to, would come to nothing. But Tove was happy to be coming home:

> I am a part of you, more than the boys are – it makes no difference *how* I am, your sadness is mine – how can I care a damn for the whole of Sweden when you aren't here? I'm coming home, soon. I'm coming home, exactly as I was when I came here, just that I've managed to do a little work, make a few friends and spend a little time with my relatives and sorting myself out. It may be that I'll be better able to understand you now, and to help you and understand how lucky I am to have you.

An exhibition of comic art entitled 'Humour and Satire', to which Ham contributed several pictures, was shown in Stockholm during the spring and Tove went to see it twice. Her comments are full of family loyalty. She reported that the illustrator Adolf Hallman had nearly a whole room to himself: 'beautiful, but Mother should have sent in more contributions. I saw a great deal that was more straight illustration than comic pictures; the Ham group could have filled a whole wall with mixed acts – at least that's my opinion.'The Stockholm exhibition had a successor in Helsinki the same spring and in it Tove made her first appearance as an exhibitor, with a drawn self-portrait. Press cuttings arrived from Helsinki, where Ham and Hjalmar Hagelstam were two of the driving forces behind the exhibition, and Tove commented in a letter: 'Amusing that Salon Strindberg was in such a hurry to set up an exhibition of this sort. I've been sent cuttings that mention Mamma and Hageli. [...] It amuses me a good deal to think that my self-portrait's in it.'

The *Svenska Pressen* critic Sigrid Schauman related this portrait to a feeling for decorative art and 'freshly understood interpretation of character'. Tove had acquired not only her decorative sense at Teknis, but even more her fresh interpretation of character. Her diaries are full of similar self-analysis.

The Painter at the Ateneum

When Tove started in the Drawing Class at the Finnish Society of Art in Helsinki, generally known as the 'Ateneum', she had to exchange the bohemian attic nook she had enjoyed in Stockholm for a platform in the family home. Soon the painter in her was longing for a studio of her own. It was not easy to leave her family but she wanted freedom and independence. Brief stays in various studios and a couple of longish study trips had to satisfy this need until she was able to move into the tower studio in Ulrikasborgsgatan 1 some ten years later.

During her period as an art student at the Ateneum, Faffan's role in her artistic life increased in importance. He had long ago articulated his dreams for his daughter's future in letters to Ham, and after she left Stockholm Tove started, as he had once started himself, in the Drawing Class at the Finnish Society of Art. In

Tove at the Ateneum posing with a portrait of Eva Cederström.

A drawing of the Ateneum with teacher William Lönnberg on the left.
From Tove's notebooks.

this way she followed in the footsteps of both her parents, first Ham's school in Stockholm and now Faffan's in Helsinki, later following both to Paris. Her parents represented two different perspectives on art: Ham sketching, illustration and drawing jobs, and Faffan studio, sculpture and free art. Their daughter was to be neither a 'Ham' nor a 'Faffan'; she became a 'Tove'.

Ham played an extremely important part in Tove's training in drawing and illustration. She acted as a pilot in approaches to editors and publishers, and mother and daughter developed a collaborative solidarity that lasted long after Tove became big and famous. But during her four years as a novice painter at the Ateneum Tove wrote more and more in her notes about the sculptor who was her father. Each was looking for a way of approaching the other, but they weren't finding it easy. 'Isn't it strange that a father and daughter should be going around longing to show affection for one another without being able to dare to do it?' she wrote in the spring of 1935. But just as Viktor had once spoken to his daughter through his sculpture, now art was able to be a shared language for them. They went together to an exhibition at the Konsthallen and continued at a café known as 'Bronkan', where they discussed 'marriage, eternity, art'. It was a precious moment: 'Pappa was wonderful. I didn't recognise him.' Immediately afterwards she met Ham and they talked about the same things.

During her time at the Ateneum Tove established herself as a painter, simultaneously making her name as a draughtswoman and illustrator. She broke off her studies several times, had her doubts about the teaching and felt uncomfortable to be at school – a reaction she had already experienced during her time at Teknis. Her diary recorded every start and every interruption. She began her studies on 18th September 1933 but broke off on 20th March the following year. On 27th September 1934 she started again but stopped on 17th December 1935. Nine months later, on 27th September 1936, she made a new start, this time at evening classes. The following spring she came to a definite full stop, noting '15th May '37 Ateneum finished'. From the first she was keen to join societies that promoted artists, and was elected to the illustrators' association in 1935 and the Artists' Guild in 1937. She was producing figurative art with pencil and brush, and seriously beginning to exhibit. In her self-portrait with a wicker chair (1937) she asserted her identity as a painter – a couple of paintings fill the wall behind the sitter, the outline of an easel can be seen to one side and the artist herself sits, straight-backed and firm, with her eyes on the viewer. In this portrait Sigrid Schauman could see not just Tove's features but also her 'dark moments' as a painter: a 'candid depression' observed with a 'touch of humour'. In particular, she admired Tove's transparency and expressiveness – in other words, the way the artist expressed herself.

Tove continued to keep a diary, but moved towards more reflective and less action-related notes without illustrations. Her notes became full of painting and instruction, of her fellow art students, of philosophy and love. Her ambition to write was subdued, at least in these notes. Already, before her second year at Teknis in 1932, she had made a resolution: 'Time is valuable – first put an end to all writing, all diary writing, which should rightly be restricted to sentimental schoolgirls!' This was when she had one year left in Stockholm and wanted to make the best use of her time. The tension in her between pictures and words was growing, and the more she saw herself as a painter, the less important her writing became – at least this was what she said. Before New Year 1934, after her first term at the Ateneum, she pronounced formally: 'For me, paper is something to draw on, not to write on.' But the same year she started the story that was to be her first to see publication, 'The Boulevard', and in a sketchbook headed 'Spring 1933' there are pages of stories. Quite simply, it was impossible for her to separate words and pictures.

The brief notes she wrote about her first year at the Ateneum have little to say about writing. She had joined the painting class and had gambled all on a single card. But she was unable to stop the flow of words within her. She wrote about herself and about her views on art and made stories out of her experiences and impressions. She wrote about the Ateneum and the painting class – several of these texts became the basis of stories in her last collection, *Messages*. She wrote rhyming verse narratives about her friends and classmates at the school. There are several of these, one titled 'Mauno and Tuomas, a story in six escapades freely after Wilhelm Busch' (extensively illustrated), and one about the young artist Samuel Beprosvanni, titled 'Samuel the little Dyer' (written in the style of the Kalevala). Samuel Beprosvanni, later Sam Vanni, was the object of Tove's passion in the mid-1930s.

In her notes for 1935 Sam continues to occupy an important place for some time. He was five years older than Tove, simultaneously a mentor and a man to love, a classic combination. They grew very close and marriage was mentioned, particularly by Sam. Tove was consumed by love and her wax notebook tells of a speaking man and a listening woman, a man whose art takes up so much room that there's no place for hers. But she was altogether too independent to let herself be totally swallowed up. Sam was the teacher, an artist who knew a lot about light and colour and at the same time a man to be attracted to. Love and art went together. When he was painting Tove's portrait in April 1935, she was thinking about her reading of the Song of Songs and how apt it was for Samuel and herself, but she was also thinking about sketching and about large canvases (at least

'Samuel'. Charcoal sketch of Sam Vanni, 1939.

81 x 65cm): 'It's so hot here. When it begins to get dark Samuel gathers his brushes together and with a joy that hurts I look at his picture, and tell myself it couldn't be so beautiful if he didn't love me.' His portrait shows Tove full face and full length, sitting with sketchbook and pencils on her knee (it is dated 1940). Lightly and lovingly, the picture captures the mix of the ethereal and the powerful in the young woman, the expectant and the decisive. At about the same time Tove did a charcoal portrait of Sam, one of her very best, that captures the man in his pose, pressing into the world of his thoughts and letting them stream out of his face towards the viewer.

She went to the exhibition at the Konsthall to see all the 'greats' of art in Finland – Magnus Enckell and Helene Schjerfbeck, Marcus Collin, Alvar Cawén, Pekka Halonen, Eero Järnefelt and Albert William Finch – but the colours only caused her pain: 'I was ready to burst into tears and it seemed as if I was dragging my own muddy oils with me on my knees from room to room.' But Sam talked of colour and light and how one painted through thought. In her diary she set down what he said. It became a torrent that restored her self-confidence, strong, decisive and boundless. Art was there to be tested; it meant either everything

Painting class at the Ateneum before the ratio of women declined. Tove is far right at the front, next to Unto Virtanen. Eva Cederström is on the third row on the left.

or nothing. 'Enckell and Schjerfbeck don't exist. I have never painted any bad paintings. I shall make a start as a painter for the first time now,' she wrote in February 1936. Sam Vanni was a man to love and a man to admire and respect as an artist. But her notes also could be critical of him. When he went on too long she might be a listener, but one who was capable of going her own way.

The old problem of submitting to a school, of being taught and learning things established by others, returned forcefully during her time at the Ateneum. She was confident in her ability, she knew she had talent and needed to find her identity as a painter, but she was not in tune with the ideals of the school and its principal teacher, William Lönnberg. She missed her vision and imagination and the feeling of being shut in grew ever stronger. Ever since being a child Tove had seen herself first and foremost as an illustrator and artist, not as a girl or a woman, but in the painting class the significance of gender became almost tangible. The female 'embryo artists were a minority', she noted, and they became fewer as time went on. Men dominated. 'The female side of the painting class has been reduced to Eva Cederström and me. And six boys,' she wrote in early autumn 1935. Tove had won 'first prize' in the painting class that spring, but at the December exhibition it was the men who ruled. Runar Engblom and Christian Sibelius 'came top', she wrote on 13th December 1935, followed by Unto Virtanen. Only then did she comment on her own position: 'My work has been placed very low, but I know this is not an accurate picture of my status as an artist. I know I *can* do it, even if my ability is still confined to my heart and my brain.' She went on: 'I've got to get away from the Ateneum, it's doing me no good.'

Along with most of the painting class, Tove left the Ateneum and its teacher, William Lönnberg. This was seen as a scandal and Faffan thought she should stay on for the teacher's sake. But Tove had made up her mind. Together with her male classmates, Engblom, Sibelius and Virtanen, she rented her first studio in Observatoriegatan street. Her only surviving woman classmate, Eva Cederström, rented a room next door. It was like a free artists' collective, with no teacher and in a milieu created by themselves. This new life began in January 1936, and in Tove's case, immediately became a part of her own story. A vivid descriptive passage in her diary brings together her new-won freedom as an artist with her feeling for morning in a deserted city. It begins with her leaving her studio home at Lallukka:

> It was early Sunday morning. I closed the door on the sleeping flat and went out into Apollogatan. Snow shovels were slithering over the pavement but the street lay white and untouched between the high drifts. The Åbovägen/Turuntie road was utterly deserted. A long, long winter road where they have started building a mass of new blocks. Where it narrows and creeps in towards the centre of town a thick yellow fog lay over the city's prickly contours, but higher up the sun was already firing twisted shining flames against all the grey. It was wonderfully beautiful. When I reached Observatoriegatan I stopped and sat down on a bench. It wasn't cold, hardly more than four or five logs were needed in the studio. My first studio. The children have started a slide under the yew-trees and trodden down the ice on the pond.

... Our little hall is dark because we don't think we need to buy a lamp. It smells of liquid glue and formalin. When I open the door to the studio a veil of tobacco smoke is slowly set in motion. The light of day lies uncertain and grey over the soupente platform and it's very cold. Round the walls are our newly-prepared canvases. The easels are stacked together in a corner and on the modelling table are cups and bags from yesterday. ... I couldn't be bothered to sweep up but pulled my easel out to where the light was best. My canvas was half dry and its surface uneven and shiny after too many repaintings. I thought for a minute and then cut out a little bit from the middle and tacked it firmly onto a piece of board. I threw the rest in the fire. It burned well. Then I chose one of the smaller brushes and started work.

'My first studio.' Tove savoured the word and described the way to the studio and its interior, its smells and its atmosphere. The writer in her was present. Her break-out didn't last long, but was an important marker of independence. A class photo from the Ateneum shows a self-confident Tove in the front row. She stares boldly and proudly straight at the camera. She went back to the painting class, but her hopes of learning through schooling had been frustrated. The class had less to do with art than with restrictions and competition. The Finnish versus Swedish language conflict of 1930s Finland affected the atmosphere of the school and its many confrontations between the ideal and reality were summed up grimly by Tove: 'What is the Ateneum supposed to be? Youth, camaraderie, art. Language politics, spite, petty-mindedness!' She did have political views – they would become clearer during the war years – but after a heated discussion about the language problem at the school she wrote: 'Try to understand one another. Be companions. Despite everything. Despite everything? Good God, protect the Ateneum from politics.'

In the background of her reflections on school and painting was Faffan and the free-thinking artistic ideals he had held since his youth. The sculptor Felix Nylund, often a guest at parties, took the same line: 'Bloody hell, girl, what's the point in going to school if you've got talent?' is what he said to Tove, who wrote down his words on 17th September 1935, just when the revolt against Lönnberg was growing. Faffan suggested she might prefer to study with some older painter and mentioned Sam

Vanni. But neither Ham nor Faffan knew anything about the love relationship between Tove and Sam: 'Oh dear, they suspect nothing, nothing,' exclaimed Tove in her diary. They would never approve. Sam was older and he was Jewish. When their affair finally came to light she wrote sadly about her parents' reaction and agitation. But they never tried to stop her seeing Sam.

The year 1935 was an eventful one for the young Tove Jansson. She left the Ateneum for the first time, she got to know Sam and the words in her notebooks formed narratives of herself as an artist: 'Painted. A new canvas of Sveaborg [Suomenlinna]. Full storm. I was *painting* for the first time. With joy and anguish,' she wrote during the landscape course in the spring. A painter was what she wanted to be.

CHAPTER 4

The Travelling Painter

It was such incredible fun to wander about here with Pappa Faffan here. Tomorrow I'm going to paint till the whole thing screams!

Tove in a letter from Paris, 14th February 1938

The spring of 1938 found Tove in Paris. She had won a scholarship and travelled there in January. It was her first really big journey. She had prepared with French lessons at home in Helsinki, and had a powerful memory of a couple of weeks of enchantment from the summer of 1934, when she had gone to the city of cities after spending time with Aunt Elsa and her family in Germany, and returned full of pictures. She had sketched and painted in Montmartre and the Luxembourg area and wandered everywhere and taken in everything she could of art: she had seen, loved, hated and learned. At the Louvre: 'God how I love Rembrandt! Titian's aristocratic painting and van Dyck's. Rubens must have been a sad type (in the judgement of the new generation!).' Often she stopped in front of Degas and 'the others'; she loved the Impressionists most of all. Soon she became a real Parisian, writing down everything she learned about the city and making her diary entries in French; she would return to this practice during her second trip in 1938.

Now she took possession of streets, quarters and milieux again. Paris was a city which had become her own, with Montparnasse and the Left Bank as her headquarters. She drew maps of the delights in letters home to her family, sketching the streets as on the official map of Paris, but adding her own network of places important to her: places where she had stayed, cinema, bathhouse, métro (Saint-Michel), morning café, cheap restaurant, walking routes, meeting places for 'compatriots' and, of course, art schools (see colour plate 6). Her obvious central point was the Luxembourg Gardens where like other Parisians she strolled about, ate a packed lunch or sat on one of the green garden benches, sketching, reading or writing. Guided by Tove's descriptions of her walking routes (Ham followed them in the smallest detail), one can wander with her along windy boulevards and narrow side-streets. She marked the way to the Académie Grande Chaumière where she sketched in early spring, and showed how she strolled from her hotel in the direction of Boulevard Montparnasse: 'The Hôtel des Terrasses is just on the corner down near Boul. St. Jacques which I follow in the morning as far as the beautiful lion statue to continue to Chaumière beside Raspail. I usually walk home via Port Royal because there's such a colourful and lively street market there. The walk takes a good 20 minutes if you go fairly quickly,' she wrote home in February 1938. She was true to her environment, and reported: 'I've nearly got like one of those real Parisians who have never been on the other bank of the Seine. Rive droit' [sic] – why on earth go there when you have everything in your own quarter!' In the spring of 1938 Tove made Paris her own.

The Janssons' Paris

The city became engraved on her heart. This headquarters of the arts, culture and thought was her parents' city. Their studio quarter was one key Jansson place (another was the medieval church where they got engaged), and it was to this area that the young painter first headed in her search for a room. She wrote home to tell the story: 'I first went to rue Moulin du Beurre and knocked on the door of what I thought must be your studio. There was a Frenchman living there, a sculptor, who immediately understood that I was Scandinavian and regretted with countless gestures that "everything was taken, permanently and absolutely".' Montparnasse was synonymous with Paris, and to

The Jansson studio in Paris. Drawn by Tove on the Rue Moulin de Beurre on her first visit to Paris, 1934.

begin with the daughter walked in her parents' footsteps. But soon the tone of her many letters home became ever more independent and self-confident. When Tove had been at Teknis she had faced claims that she should 'help mamma' and contribute to the support of the family. Now she had a scholarship and could support herself.

To begin with she was able to borrow the artist Tyra Lundgren's studio, down in the 14th arrondissement (15 Square Châtillon), but she soon moved to a hotel that was a favourite with Swedish-speaking people from Finland – Hôtel des Terrasses (74 Rue de la Glacière) on Boulevard St Jacques. Here there was an an artists' colony, a crowd of 'compatriots' headed by Hjalmar Hagelstam, Birger Carlstedt and Yngve Bäck. Tove was among the youngest and unusual in the group as a young woman not attached to a man. She soon acquired a 'ward', the even younger Irina Bäcksbacka, who took up a lot of her time. The hotel has been pulled down and the district has changed, but the trains (which Tove mentioned in her letters home) still pass up on the viaduct, and there is a crowded group of buildings in the vicinity that resemble what must have been: a restaurant, a small hotel and several low buildings. It was an entirely peaceful milieu, but the 'Fennoman' colony was not likely to suit the independent Tove. She started thinking about other alternatives right from the beginning. 'You get interrupted all the time by people who want you to listen to their litanies and complaints,' she wrote home in irritation in several letters. She began to take alarm: 'There's rather a smell of burning in this Nordic hotel. I've never before been involved with so much intriguing on all fronts, I feel I'm in a buzzing wasps' nest. Each one comes to me with his grumbles about the others, promises of secrecy, accusations, explanations. Ugh.'

Tove tried several art schools and as always let her own attitude to art be decisive in choosing where to stop and learn. At the venerable École des Beaux-Arts on Rue Bonaparte in the art quarter of the Left Bank it was necessary to take an entrance examination. The place was marked by a studied inhospitality – one must never forget that one was worthless – and the atmosphere was marked by snobbery and bullying. The younger and newer students were expected to wait on the older ones, and pictures were ripped apart by criticism. She described all this in a letter to Faffan in which she described her difficult first days as a pupil (she was admitted in March): 'it isn't easy to be a newcomer'. A student's study of a model might be defaced with green hair and a Hitler bandage round its leg (this happened to Tove), and the young artist might get turpentine in her shoes or be the victim of other tricks. The strict teacher, Guérin, was a naturalist who demanded severe academic studies. But there were some amusing, happy people there too, Tove wrote, and she was in two minds about whether to stay on or not.

In her short story 'Quatz' Arts', which would be published in the daily paper *Svenska Pressen* the summer after her stay in Paris, she formulated her exit. It was a question of attitudes to colour, always very important to her: 'They painted in brown, a brown with indirect light effects, quasi-Rembrandtesque. I could never understand why a background of dirty Pilsner-brown shouldn't be painted a little more attractively on one's own canvas. That's why I followed my own path.' But it was not at all easy to leave Beaux-Arts and the reason is hidden behind the flippant words. After all, it was the school where the great had studied, including her idol Matisse, but nonetheless the atmosphere was for Tove gloomy, dusty and airless.

She got on better sketching at the academy in Rue de la Grande Chaumière, but she found her real refuge in a less prestige-laden place, the Atelier d'Adrien Holy, a long way from the Beaux-Arts quarter. This was a large studio on the first floor inside a courtyard, where it was permissible to paint with more freedom. It was less lively but peaceful. Tove described her first appearance there in a letter to Ham in February:

> Today from 9.30 to 12.30 I had my first day of painting at Holy's, Rue Broca. It's pleasant, just the right number of beginners who interest themselves in the model's pose and busy themselves endlessly over colourful cloths, mirrors and reflected light. The studio is inside an attractive courtyard, and you climb up to it by a long spiral staircase that has been painted blue. You don't have to worry here that someone might make off with your things while your attention is directed elsewhere – as was the case at Chaumière, and the whole atmosphere is more conducive to work.

The artist himself (Holy) fussed about among the easels, called the students his 'children', and at the bottom of the blue spiral staircase there was a studio pathway with daffodils and ancient pieces of sculpture. Here she was able to concentrate on work, she wrote a little later at the beginning of April: 'It is perhaps a bit boring, but I can get on with my work in peace. In three weeks I'll know whether I want to stay there or move back to Beaux-Arts.'

Tove stayed painting at Holy's all that spring. It was her favourite school in Paris. Features of Adrien Holy himself, a Swiss artist who had settled in Paris in 1920, can be detected in a number of her paintings of the period: faceless images and a feeling for the figurative. But in the background was Matisse too. (Later Holy would be best known for theatre decoration, lithographs and posters.) With Holy her transformation into an artist really got started, and her pleasure in producing 'crash-pictures' just to make an impression was blown away, she wrote to her parents. This fitted in with her liberation from the influence of the Beaux-Arts. She was looking for a style of her own and talked about being attracted to what was stylised and striking in its superficial immediacy – 'pure, fresh colours'. She searched for teachers in the museums and studied Matisse and Suzanne Valadon, who painted many still-lifes, often with flowers. Here were colour, strong compositions and themes.

A 'Still-life with shell' (see colour plate 14) she did at Holy's became famous as Tove's best painting to date. She worked on a nude with flower motif, 'woman with lilies', but this met with less favour. She told her parents: 'He liked the flowers and her face very much, but asserted (as Pappa often has!) that the canvas was split between different styles and thus could profitably be divided into two. But I have no intention of doing that, and instead I shall try and find a solution to the problem, even if I ruin the whole thing.' Words that breathe self-confidence and independence. Tove wanted to go her own way, without any

Sketch for 'Still-life with Shell', in letter to her parents, 1938.

father figures. And Holy was happy that his pupil wanted to grapple with a difficult problem.

Tales of a Painter

Her experiences at the Beaux-Arts marked the stories that date from her time in Paris. In one she wrote about the noisy swarming bustle of the carnival atmosphere at the 'Quatz' Arts' school; in another she mocked pomposity and settled her account with false ideals in a parody of an artist. Her story 'The Beard' (1938) demolished the myth of The Solitary (male) Artist. In 'The Violin' (1940) she came to terms with the illusion of the 'great' artist. The sharpest in tone of these stories, 'The Beard' is an utterly merciless portrayal of the male artistic ego that hides his face behind a fashionable beard, paints by the Seine, despises worldly pleasures (cinema, dance, theatre) and regards woman as his 'inspiration'. Man as great thinker and artist (or vice versa) was a type she had many times bravely faced up to and such figures could certainly be found on the staircases of the Beaux-Arts. In this tale she recreates the type in a portrait oozing with satire, and lets his figurative cover (his beard) fall. His hours by the Seine are devoted not only to painting but also to his deep thoughts. He happily lets himself be courted by the young, inexperienced Kristina, who sees him as a 'Great Artist'. The whole thing is basically a parody of Freudian psychoanalysis. Kristina's infatuation with this artist, in which his beard plays a decisive part, is a way of cheating life. She develops 'higher' interests and discusses art and religion with him during their walks along the Seine which, she imagines, are fulfilling her need for spiritual companionship:

> She had completely changed from her old superficial view of things and no longer ever just thought about travel and having little gloved hands. That she had ever had such thoughts was the fault of Life that had never let her be young. This had caused her to have an Inferiority Complex. But her reaction only expressed itself as Sublimation. ... It was a Spiritual Exchange, a Fellowship of Souls that she needed – yes indeed, how could poor Daddy and Mummy ever understand that!

'Hotel Room', 1938.

But when the man loses his beard and his face becomes naked the truth is clear to Kristina: the whole thing was a camouflage for the desires of the flesh. It is not your soul I want, the now beardless artist tells her, but 'the whole you'. It is a fresh and audacious solution that Tove presents in this story, in the roles played by both the man and the woman – six of one and half a dozen of the other – and with the added viewpoint of psychoanalysis.

That spring in Paris was for Tove a time for developing greater depth in her painting, developing her style and accepting pure bold colours. Several of her best paintings from the late-1930s belong to Paris: 'The Hotel Room', 'Blue Hyacinth' and 'The Seaweed Burners'; the last in particular attracted the attention of several critics. The word 'intelligent' crops up in several reviews. Sigrid Schauman classified her as the boldest of three representatives of the new time and its ideals: 'No difficulties frighten her.' This was strong praise indeed. One of those she was considered to have outshone was none other than Sam Vanni; the other was Ina Colliander.

Training in growing and maturing as a person clearly and absolutely fitted together with the art of painting, which also fitted with the art of feeling free. Tove became calmer and more assured every day as she felt her way towards a new independence: 'I need to be free myself if I am to be free in my painting,' she wrote in her notes and letters. She made many similar comments on her time in Paris. Alone and free – that was her ideal. 'Paris is the best place for me to knock on the head the last remnants of my "inferiority complex",' she wrote in one letter. One had to be strong to survive: 'If one is the least bit shy, submissive, apologetic or anxious one will be like a poodle before evening.' When her experience of the city was forced aside by the Fennomanic mass of 'compatriots' in need of a listener, all she could do was escape. She had had enough of the role of listener and comforter. To Ham she wrote: 'You will understand better why I want to be rid of my "compatriots" if you remember that I need to be free of everything old that's hanging round me, everything that reminds me of my years of "dependence".' It was not so much the compatriots in themselves, more what they represented: a Finland-Swedish art ideal, the atmosphere of the circles they moved in in Helsinki and, at bottom, her own family too. At Hôtel des Terrasses a new family had been forced on her in place of her old one. It interfered with her concentrating on her painting, which was the main point of her wanting to be in Paris. Her description of the Fennomane hotel colony has unmistakable echoes in the definition established in the fourth Moomin book, *The Exploits of Moominpappa*. A colonist is a stranger who doesn't like being alone, so he (or she) gets together with others of like mind and spends a lot of time quarrelling. But Tove, on the contrary, was a stranger looking for solitude. She needed space for her own life, to feel free and unfettered. That was the whole reason for her journey.

The escape route passed down Rue St Jacques, towards the Luxembourg Gardens. On the north side Tove found the 'lonely' hotel she was looking for. It is still there today, on Rue Monsieur le Prince, under a new name. As was her custom, she drew her new domain on a map: hotel, morning café, the meeting places Dôme and la Rotonde, the 'honey' of Boudet on Boulevard Raspail and

Pantagruel on Rue des Écoles, the swimming-bath establishment on Rue Pontoise, cinema, métro and exhibitions on Rue de Seine. In her little leatherbound 1938 diary, which she entirely filled during the spring, she described her movements between these various stopping places (and a number of others). When she was not painting, sketching or working on her canvases, she 'did' Paris with both French people and 'compatriots'. She lived a French life and after a month or two she began writing up her notes in French. Struggling with a flower picture at Holy's, she exclaimed angrily, 'Diables anemones!' Men surrounded her, but admirers ('male collars' she called them) could wait. Work came before love and she stuck to her independence. In June she made a trip by herself to Brittany, where she wandered round the villages, painting constantly. She seems to have been very happy there and wrote short poetic entries in her little leather diary on light, landscape, colours and atmosphere. It was like a dream: *'Dans l'obscure je me promène près des roches. Magnifique, comme une rêve. Sauvage'* ('In the darkness I walk near some rocks. Magnificent, like a dream. Wild. Not savage.') She felt free, never mind that the villagers watched her with astonishment. A young woman painter travelling on her own was a sight in herself.

That spring in Paris was the longest period Tove spent abroad in her early years, a time of independence and satisfied longing for freedom. She worked out her own topography, chose her own schools and where she was to live, and when she went to met Faffan at Gare du Nord in May, it was as a young painter in the city where he, in turn, had once met the young Signe. Letters to

A Tove drawing of her father, inscribed 'Faffan'.

Ham from Tove and Faffan tell how 'happy' they are; both use the word. Father and daughter, but also two artists, together at last in the city of pictures.

Faffan 1938 met Faffan 1914 on their very first evening when they walked to his old Paris studio and went into the courtyard: 'everything was as it should be and memories gripped me hard,' wrote the sculptor to his 'dearly loved Signe' back at home. He described what it felt like to be in Paris again; he missed her and the boys, and words had the capacity to fail him as they had twenty years before when he was writing home from the front. Signe and he were never parted for longer periods. But he spent most time talking of his affinity with their daughter and his happiness with his family, his 'biggest asset'.

What Faffan wrote about Tove as 'my best friend' speaks clearly of his swelling fatherly pride in his painter daughter. She was on her way to becoming an artist just as he had long ago hoped she would be, and his comments on her artistic development are all words of praise. His love for Signe lived on in Tove. When father and daughter walked the streets of Paris together it seemed to him as if his wife was walking beside him: 'Tove is my escort, but often I have the feeling that it's you, darling, at my side.' Tove is like a native, he eulogises, and has Signe's ability to arrange and order things. But if it wasn't for her, he would come home. 'That's how it is with me, poor man,' he concluded, feeling homesick – and perhaps a little exhausted from visiting so many museums together. 'Too many sculptures,' wrote the sculptor after a visit to the Rodin museum, 'but there's a wonderful park.'

Longing for Italy

'I've always longed for a real life on the beach,' wrote Tove to her family during her trip to Italy in the late spring of 1939. She followed in the footseps of the Great Masters, from Verona in the north to Naples, Capri, Pompeii and the Amalfi coast in the south. She rounded her visit off with a week in the seaside town of Forte dei Marmi, northwest of Florence. This was the fulfilment of a childhood dream. One day she was the only bather on the whole beach and 'danced' in the powerful waves for two hours. Her journey brought several other dreams true as well, such as picking oranges and flying – which was 'less remarkable than I expected!'

After Paris Italy loomed. Rome and the great works of art of the Renaissance tempted her, and she had won another scholarship. War was clearly on the way and for anyone who wanted to go to mainland Europe there was no time to lose. In April 1939 she took the ferry to Tallinn and proceeded south via Berlin and Munich to Verona. In her usual way Tove often wrote home, a copious documentation of landscape, cities, milieux, people, atmosphere, history and art. She addressed herself alternately to 'Viktor Jansson, Sculptor' and 'Signe Hammarsten-Jansson, Artist', but as always her letters were for the whole family. This time Tove had no other teachers than those she herself chose in museums, cloisters and churches, a free learning exactly to her taste. There were 'glorious' frescoes in Padua and Florence – she naturally wanted to experience Giotto. And she was always equally fond of Renaissance art. The thing was to see as much art as possible in the time available, so she didn't stay long in any one place. She travelled with her eyes wide open, taking in as much as she could. Her programme was full. But there were limits: 'Sometimes one is simply terrified of the whole profession.'

In Italy she felt freer than on her earlier trips; it was a journey of 'healthy egotism' – she wrote a good deal about this in her letters – which like Paris increased her self-confidence. She travelled alone and she travelled light. 'Long live light luggage,' she exclaimed as early as Berlin, blessing the absence of 'unnecessary' paraphernalia. She had plenty of money, everything was new and exciting, and the people she met along the way included everyone from the inevitable compatriots like Rabbe Enckell, Ellen Thesleff and Sigrid Schauman with her daughter, to Italian men and explorers like herself. Naturally there was no great number of women. Her travels in Italy were both bold and adventurous. This time, unlike Paris, she had no headquarters but moved freely according to her own plans. In her luggage she carried a guidebook belonging to her parents – they had been in Rome and elsewhere in 1925 – but after a time she laid it aside. A couple of young Danes ('Jensen and Ferlow') kept her company for a couple of weeks. A single woman's movements could be limited and in Rome she didn't feel able to go out in the evening alone.

She had little to say about politics, though National Day in Italy, when 'the blackjackets' assembled and marched, with women also in uniform, made an ugly impression, and she commented caustically on 'Adolf's speech', an attack by Hitler on Roosevelt. She was travelling on the margin – the storm had not broken 'yet' – and growing with the journey. Her family must not worry, she wrote home reassuringly. 'I manage all right all the time and I know what I'm doing.' Her letters are a story of lack of constraint, of curiosity and openness, and the intrepid young woman who wrote them gave a strong impression of having the love of life in her power. Outside Florence, in the hills towards Fiesole, she admired the landscape and quoted aloud to herself from the Song of Solomon (a biblical favourite in happy moments). She wrote a couple of short stories, one set in Verona and one in Capri; she sketched and painted and – above all – she saw. Her letters are full of word pictures.

Many of her descriptions have a pre-Moomin character. There is a clear connection between the woolly trousers Tove was grateful for in chilly Verona but eventually discarded in Lago di Garda ('I don't think I need them any more,' she announced in high spirits), and the ones Mamma sends with Moomin on his journey in *Comet in Moominland* (and which end up flung into the crocodile's jaws). In fact this comet story, with its dramatic and explosive landscape, carries elements of Italy in it. Nature seems to flourish in the valley which becomes Moominvalley, and the atmosphere of southern Italy was among the most attractive which Tove experienced on her whole journey. On the 1st of June 1939, she wrote home with a powerful description of the view of the hills by the light of Vesuvius from her hotel in Pompeii:

Under my open window lies the garden with dark shadows like holes in the moonlight, while the sky gradually clears. The silhouettes of the trees seem utterly fantastic, some with exaggeratedly broad shadows and some with narrow ones, some shaggy and some graceful, but what interests me most is the orange tree which stands very near the window. I have been given permission to pick its fruit tomorrow. If I go out on the terrace I can see red fire flickering over Vesuvius and the light band of the villages far off among the mountains. This is so intensely Italian, as beautiful as I ever imagined it ...

The summit of Vesuvius. Letter to Ham and Faffan, June 1939.

The experience of seeing the volcano close up a couple of days later was even more powerful and she chose it as the 'climax of what I've seen'.

A picture drawn in the letter is just as expressive as her description of the climb:

> The higher one climbed the wilder and more sombre everything became; the villages, Capri and the sea disappeared in the hazy sunshine till there was nothing but a chaos of gravel and fantastically intertwined streams of lava like a 'snakes' wedding'.

But the real adventure began at the edge of the crater:

> ... in the very cauldron, into the midst of which Vesuvius flung red-hot stones high in the air, and at regular intervals enormous brooms of fire. All over were smouldering cracks yellow-green with sulphur, with rumbling underfoot as it got hotter and hotter. A little newborn crater, four days old, was sending out red streams of lava right to our feet and behind all this the sun was sinking amid the brown fumes. We were able to light cigarettes from the lava, which the guide poked up to us with an iron rod, and we sat and watched the whole glorious show till it was dark and it looked like a natural illustration for Dante's inferno.

The erupting volcano, lava, heat, the picture of the inferno on a Dantesque scale, this is one of Snufkin's set-piece stories in the second Moomin book, *Comet in Moominland*. Moomintroll's and Snufkin's journey to the professors' Observatory in the Lonely Mountains breathes a grandly sombre atmosphere like what Tove experienced so intensely on the edge of the crater of Vesuvius. The letters from Italy evoke Snufkin in many ways: in them speaks the explorer, traveller, lover of freedom and teller of tales. The comet story gained colour and power from the Neapolitan landscape, and at the same time the atmosphere of eruption reflects the threat of war that Tove was trying to distance herself from during her journey. When in the summer after the war she wrote her story of the great comet, the image of the volcano was brooding over her memory. Vesuvius had actually erupted in March 1944, just after the Allied armies had taken Naples.

The Illustrator

During her time at the Ateneum, Tove established herself as a draughtswoman, illustrator and decorative painter. This meant drawing jobs that made money for the whole family. Conditions were hard for young artists and chances to exhibit were limited. The years of the Depression in the early-1930s had made everything more difficult, and it was not until 1939 that the first 'Young Artists' Exhibition' opened at Konsthallen in Helsinki. Tove contributed seven oil paintings, three aquarelles and a charcoal drawing; among them were 'The Seaweed Burners' and a painting from her time at Holy's studio. Her work was well received by the critics.

But endless illustration jobs constituted her grim daily fare, essential for supporting herself. Tove kept accounts of her commissions and her income during the first years is entered in a little cashbook. Her repertoire soon broadened, but it was as a newspaper illustrator that she made herself a name. Notes on 'Fees and Jobs' gives evidence of the varied character of her work:

> Book cover. *Söderström*, Frontispiece *'Christmas'*, Illustr. *Garm*, overtime work, Banknote Press, Frontispiece *'Lucifer'* ... Short story with illustr. *Hels. Journ.*, Decoration for Authors' party ... Shell ad (1934)

> 2 caricatures Garm, ½ p. Garm, vignette and 2 small illustr. Pressen, 1st p. Garm ... Vignette Pressen, Lyckmans ad, story with vign 2 illustr Pressen, Decoration for Fazer on Munksnäs, vignette, 3 illustr for Astra, 3 drawings for Garm, Garm's Easter cover no., Drawing for the tourist association (1937)

Various activities are hidden behind these notes: a cover for Söderströms Publishers, cover pictures for the Christmas papers *Julen* and *Lucifer* (the Christmas journal of the Finland-Swedish Publicity Association), an extra goodie from Ham's workplace, the fee for her first story ('The Boulevard'), decorations and advertisements. In a few years the satirical political paper *Garm* would make a strong entry to her list of commissions, lasting for more than a decade. Now, in the 1930s, she did illustrations for *Svenska Pressen*, wrote and illustrated a story called 'Life on the Landing Stage' for the same paper and drew pictures for the periodical *Astra*.

The signature 'Tove' quickly became well known. A 1938 reviewer in *Lucifer* considered her a 'mighty and monumental figure' among its contributors. She had not only 'illustrated many articles in a striking manner, but also written a picaresque and amusing novelette about the life of artists in Paris' ('The Beard'). The visual world she constructed in her illustrations covered all kinds of texts, literary, factual and political among other things. She illustrated short stories, poems, fairy tales, informal columns, children's stories, reportage, anecdotes, jokes, satires and caricatures.

She sharpened her claws as a humorous and political illustrator in *Garm* and contributed more or less regularly to a large number of periodicals and newspapers. In addition to *Garm*, *Julen* and *Lucifer*, she worked from time to time for cultural and social magazines like *Vår Tid*, weeklies like *Vår Värld*, *Allas krönika* and *Helsingfors-Journalen*, for children's papers and the Finland-Swedish daily press. Among those who employed her were the dailies *Svenska Pressen* (later renamed *Nya Pressen*) and *Hufvudstadsbladet*, and she also did drawings for the Finnish-language press.

She worked with speed and concentration and found many opportunities to express herself. Taking all her drawing and sketching work as a whole, she may be said to have created a school of her own and developed astounding flexibility. As a designer she developed to a very high level her ability to shape a text visually, to illustrate it and to create a relationship between words and pictures. This was the order of events she always tried to use for her own stories: words first, then pictures.

Drawing, Politics, and Trolls

It was in the Swedish-language satirical political paper *Garm* that Tove achieved her greatest triumphs as a cartoonist, and polished her style to become a political artist of high class. At its best, her satire was fearless, sharp and confident. Her disrespectful pictures of Hitler caused anger in Nazi and pro-German circles. There was nothing harmless about this, and she was censured several times. In a memoir, Tove later summarised: 'I enjoyed working for *Garm*, and what I liked best was being beastly to Hitler and Stalin.'

The paper's editor, Henry Rein, waded into the attack in both international and internal Finnish politics in the same 'happy mood'. In fact, he seemed to live entirely in a 'constant state of controlled fury, regardless of whether he was attacking or defending – he was often extremely tired,' Tove remembered, and continued: He made mistakes at times, but was 'honourably and unshakably obsessed with the idea of justice'. She herself was given a free hand and her dialogue with Rein ran smoothly most of the time:

Sometimes Henry came to me with anecdotes that needed illustrating, at other times it was I who thought of the joke. I tried to get him to understand that the best cartoons are the ones that need no text. 'Do as you like,' he would say, 'just make sure you hit them in the mouth.' Gradually I came to draw better.

Garm was not always particularly humorous, but could be 'framed in a bad temper'. Politically it stood to the right, with a dash of liberalism. It had started in 1923 with a stable of well-known artists. Ham was of course one of these, with Alvar Cawén, Hjalmar Hagelstam, Marcus Collin, Antti Favén and Albert Gebhard. It was a firmly Finland-Swedish publication that stood or fell with its editor, Henry Rein. When he died in 1953 it closed, but by then he had long played out his role as a creator of opinion. In the 1920s, Prohibition (in force in Finland from 1919 to 1932) was a favourite target, but the most important thing was the struggle against every kind of dictatorship, above all Nazism. Henry Rein's name seems to have been on a 'black list' during the war, when *Garm* played a part as critic of Finland's rapprochement with Germany. In this connection Tove played a leading role. She became its chief illustrator, often known as the 'court artist', and she used the same fearless pencil to scourge the 'home swine' and the German dictator. What she detested above all was any curtailment of freedom. 'Ribbentrop in Helsinki. Now we've hit the pits!' she wrote in June 1944, and went on: 'The city is seething with German soldiers, machines of war, horses and vehicles. How I loathe them!' She drew many pictures of Hitler, but two became particularly memorable. One referred to the dictator's behaviour at the 1938 Munich conference, and the other to the evacuation of the German army from Finnish Lapland in the autumn of 1944. These cartoons grew into something more than satirical protest. They were transformed into a narrative of the times Tove lived in.

In March 1938 Hitler had united Germany and Austria (the 'Anschluss') and demanded the German-speaking Sudeten areas of Czechoslovakia. Europe was on the brink of war. The supposed aim of the Munich conference was to preserve 'Peace in our time' – but at the cost of the independence of

Czechoslovakia. *Garm* reacted powerfully, not least against the Finnish daily press, which, according to the writer Arthur Ekström, 'kissed Hitler's boots as much as possible'. Tove's cover picture shows Hitler as a spoilt child bawling for 'more cake' and ignoring all the goodies that have already been served to him: the Polish corridor, Alsace-Lorraine, Danzig/Gdansk, Yugoslavia. All around anxious 'adults' are trying to think what to offer him next: a slice of cake from Switzerland, marzipan from the south of Denmark, British colonies (brought in by Chamberlain), and much more. Hitler is the insatiable child who devours democracy. Showing disrespect for power belongs to the oldest traditions of satire and similar portrayals of the Munich conference can be found elsewhere. But this daring comment on Finnish foreign policy threw Tove right into the midst of the political whirlpool. Both she and Henry Rein barely escaped prosecution for 'insulting the leader of a friendly foreign power', as Rein hastened to remind his readers after the war, when he published the picture again in June 1945.

The evacuation of the German army from Finnish Lapland in autumn 1944 was another politically sensitive situation. Finland had ended her alliance with Germany on 2nd September of that year and an armistice had been signed with the Soviet Union on the 19th. The German troops retreating northwards in Finland – they had suffered heavy losses during the summer – tried to collect as much booty as possible on their way out. What they were doing was 'reconstructing' Finland, as the country people sarcastically put it; Hitler had given orders to destroy everything rather than capitulate. Tove's picture, which appeared on the cover of the October 1944 edition of *Garm*, mocked the abuse of political power in exactly the same way as her 1938 cartoon had. Now the dictator was reduced to a ridiculous and self-important fool, fussily hurrying from one activity to another: setting fire to houses, chasing hens, emptying drawers and loading potatoes onto a reindeer, all on behalf of the firm of 'Reconstruction Ltd'. This is a Hitler in multiple editions, not just one but many 'Hitlers', as Tove happily noted in her work diary: 'Garm cover with 10 Hitlers reconstructing Lapland. Good fun.'

She drew for *Garm* for some fifteen years. She was busiest in the 1940s when she was described as 'undeniably Finland's leading cartoonist'. The range of subjects she covered is

Two versions of 'Hitler: The Munich Conference' (Garm, October 1938) and the German evacuation of Lapland (Garm, October 1944). Tove's signature Snork is just visible on the right of the 1944 magazine masthead.

impressive, as is the sheer number of her pictures. Altogether she drew about a hundred covers for *Garm*, the first in 1935, and did nearly 500 cartoons and illustrations. *Garm* was one of the many arenas where she tried out new ideas. Her intensive work for the paper in effect turned its illustrated pages into a pre-Moomin workshop. It was in *Garm* that the Moomin figure made its first public appearance, though it went at the time under the name of 'snork'.

The snork became a picture signature, a means of identification to add to the word 'Tove' in drawings and illustrations. The figure was first seen in 1943 in an illustration for one of the paper's many (and abysmal) alcohol jokes, but there had been earlier examples. The snork was born as if into a delirious world, and grew with pictures for various texts about dreams, hallucinations and fantasies. It had a slender snout, a little mouth, hornlike ears and a long thin tail, altogether an angry image that corresponded with the satirical sting of Tove's cartoons. By autumn 1944 it was being added regularly to Tove's illustrations, both in *Garm* and elsewhere. It had become a signature with an active visual part to play, which imitated or supplemented the action in the picture

Tove hoists the Moomin flag on Bredskär.

in its body language, or suggested possible consequences. It provided a key to the picture and underlined the point of the satire. The snork parodied the content of the drawing as wickedly as he could, as Tove said later: 'His eyes were set close together and were angry.'

'My new title is Mrs Snork,' noted Tove in August 1945. By now her identity as an illustrator had coalesced with her signature and sometimes the figure was enough in itself to identify her in *Garm*. At Christmas 1945 she drew herself as 'snork' on the cover, among such cultural 'Pegasus' figures as Arvid Mörne, Elmer Diktonius and Helen af Enehjelm, Harald Hornborg, Rolf Lagerborg and Yrjö Hirn. In the second half of the 1940s the snork, alias the Moomintroll, became part of *Garm*'s and the illustrator Tove's profile. By the time the first Moomin book came out, the figure was a permanent feature in the *Garm* pictures. In 1946 she contributed to all twelve issues of *Garm* and did the covers for nine: the little signature figure grew larger, changed its appearance and became the illustrator's companion, a figure to identify her work. As a Moomintroll it also appeared in her painting.

There is a drawn self-portrait from this period of her intensive work for *Garm* that is clear evidence of the identification of the little figure with the artist. Tove wears a painter's smock and a knotted artist's cravat, and has a cigarette in her mouth and a palette in her left hand. But it is the little figure near the artist that holds the paintbrush. The text reads: 'Tove and Moomintroll drawn by Her Self'. The year was 1947. In the same year she hoisted a flag on her own island, Bredskär in the Pellinge archipelago. On the flag was a Moomintroll.

CHAPTER 5

A Men's War

The sun is like a red ball among the pines of Rörholm and the south-westerly is roaring off Sandskär.

Letter to Eva Konikoff, 15th June 1941

In the night planes flew over us in even waves and there was shooting over Helsinki from eleven to four.

Letter to Eva Konikoff, 25th August 1942

'The fact is that life is just waiting now, one isn't really living, one just exists,' wrote Tove in a letter to her friend Eva Konikoff at the beginning of July 1941. One tried to hold on to hope. It was the way to connect with life: 'Deep down one firmly believes all will be well – that we'll all meet again, that we'll be able to be happy.' The war was dictating the terms of life, inescapably and implacably. The men were at the front, her brother Per Olov, her lover Tapio Tapiovaara, friends and artists. And Eva had left for America.

It was in June 1941 that the Russian-born photographer Eva Konikoff left Helsinki to cross the Atlantic to the USA. Her story had been dramatic. After the revolution of 1917 and the fall of Petrograd she had fled to Finland with her little brother. The story of their flight to the West – two children crossing the border at Viborg (in Finnish Viipuri) in a snowstorm – was woven by Tove into her late story 'Letter to Konikova', a narrative about friendship, memory, affinity and loss anchored in Tove's many letters to Eva Konikoff. When Eva emigrated, nearly twenty-five years after her flight to Finland, it was only weeks before Operation Barbarossa, the great German attack on the Soviet Union. At this time Finland was neutral, but had looked for support from Germany after the 'Winter War' between Finland and the Soviet Union ended in March 1940. Soviet foreign policy remained a threat and by the time Barbarossa began on 22nd June 1941 there were already large German forces in the north of Finland. When the Soviets bombed a series of Finnish towns, Finland declared war on them on 25th June.

Thus the 'Continuation War' became reality and Finland's defence policy remained as it had been during the harsh Winter War of 1939–40. No armistice was signed for another three years and, when it did happen, as Tove noted sadly in her diary, it was under 'degrading conditions'. Finland was forced to give up the whole Petsamo area in the far north and Finnish western Karelia, while the country's second city, Viipuri, and the district round it disappeared completely from the map of Finland. At the beginning of the 1940s conditions in Finland were far from ideal for a Russian-born Jew like Eva Konikoff; it was becoming an ally of Nazi Germany and her two homelands were about to go to war with each other. The way out was to the West. Eva had relatives in America; she was a free bird and needed to fly on. But her close family, her parents and brother, stayed in Finland.

For Tove that dramatic midsummer of 1941 was a turning point. The war had returned, her brother Per Olov had been called up and her closest and most faithful friend Eva had left for a new land. Would they ever see each other again, be together, be able to be happy?

By autumn 1939, Tove's time for travelling was over for the foreseeable future. Like many other young people she had taken the chance to see what she could of Europe despite uncertain conditions. She longed for Italy and its art. Germany had occupied Czechoslovakia and had its eyes on Poland. Rumours hummed. But in that last summer before the second Great War the borders had still been open and it had still been possible to travel. By September that was all finished. 'England has declared war on Germany,' wrote Tove in a brief diary entry for 3rd September 1939, by which time she had been back home for about a month. Two days earlier German troops had crossed the border into Poland. The war years were to be one of the hardest periods in Tove's life. In page after page of her notebooks she set down her despair and her longing for life to be different. 'It's as if the whole world has become a lump of anguish. I have never seen friendliness so mixed with bitterness, love with hate, and the will to live a good and worthy life so mixed with the pleasure of just getting out of the way and letting go,' she wrote in November 1941, turning into a voice from the depths of a nation at war. One should enjoy life, be happy and meet people. Not that there weren't many wild parties, strange, convulsive events to help people forget the painful present: 'There was a surrealist masquerade with sheet metal, steel wire and sandpaper and belly dancing, all a hysterical flight from reality. The colours screamed and we felt just as much like screaming ourselves.' She organised parties with dancing in her studio. She described the atmosphere to Eva immediately after New Year 1943:

> In the studio the tables are still in the middle of the floor after a series of parties and sequels to parties. Colleagues come on leave, officially not supposed to be dancing, groups forced by the regulations to leave the restaurants earlier than they would like cling desperately to this more or less artificial fun, determined to keep it going. This is when they come to me. I let the rhumbas go, and through my both 'omnipresent and on-the-other-side-of' position as hostess am in a position to observe and understand the undercurrents, the electric atmosphere circulating among · the guests. It's interesting.

They closed the blackout curtains and discussed everything except the war: 'Except when we'd been drinking. Then we talked only about the war.' The urge to live and celebrate in the midst of the frenzy of death becomes life's paradox. A note like 'Cannibal masquerade and bombardment' (20th March 1943) speaks for itself. But most often all Tove wanted to do was to turn to the wall and not see anybody's face. 'If only one could just not live at all so long as there's war.' Tove needed words more than ever.

She did not compromise with her vow to stop writing a diary because diaries were fit only for schoolgirls. Instead she went in for new forms of writing. She transformed one of her old diaries into a sort of logbook, in which short notes on the most personal matters were interwoven with politics and her professional agenda year by year: canvases exhibited, events of the war, love meetings, periods of leave for brothers and friends, criticism and important letters. In the winter of 1944, when hopes for an end to the Continuation War with the Soviet Union disappeared when Helsinki was heavily bombed in February, she makes a note of Per Olov's leave on the 4th, further bombing on the 6th, 16th and 26th, that Lars (Lasse) joined the anti-aircraft defence force on the 25th, that some of her work was rejected for an exhibition in Stockholm on 20th March, and the failure of a peace initiative:

'Peace didn't happen,' she wrote laconically on 22nd March after aborted negotiations with the Soviets. This simple recording of events became important. It was a way of creating structure in chaotic conditions and writing it down. Many of her notes were scribbled down in one go; some were partly inserted later. She also kept more comprehensive books of memoranda in which she collected short texts of various kinds, more or less detailed diary entries, reflections and thoughts. Notebooks and closely written pocket diaries are witness to the fact that she never stopped writing. Some things were published, like the short stories she had written on her travels, but she kept most of the material to herself. In this form her writing became a way of speaking out, a free confession without listeners. It was different with her letters. They show a desire for dialogue, a need for fellowship through words and thoughts. The war must be held at bay and letters streamed from Tove's pen; letters to Per Olov, to her lovers, to fellow artists and friends, and to Miss Eva Konikoff, Philadelphia, USA.

Tove and Eva

'I'm never alone when I'm writing to you,' wrote Tove to Eva in 1942. This was characteristic of their friendship.

Eva Konikoff, called by Tove 'Konikova', had become one of her closest friends, someone to admire and confide in. 'You are vitally important,' wrote Tove, 'as close as Ham, but in a different way.' Eva represented freedom, power and will. The painting 'Eva', which Tove worked on in 1941, shows precisely these qualities. The subject is sitting with her legs apart, her hands firmly clasped and her arms resting on her knees. She is looking to one side and not striking a pose. A free woman, that's Eva in Tove's portrait of her. That she painted her friend in her slip, without the safety net of outer clothing, makes this impression even stronger (it disturbed Eva's family). Sam Vanni's portrait of Eva from the same period (exhibited at the 'Young Artists' exhibition of 1940) radiates the same power but is more conventional in design; it shows a woman in a white blouse looking straight at the viewer.

'Eva', painted in 1941.

Tove's 'Eva' had great importance for the painter, both as an expression of her artistic will and as a memorial to a friendship. She worked on the portrait after Eva left, changing the background and the lighting. She only exhibited it once, at the 'Young Artists' exhibition of 1942. The critics praised it as an 'accomplished' figure study, but this pat on the back was the most she received. She reported to Eva: 'Your portrait was well received at the Young Artists – now you're hanging on my wall.' Then she added: 'Your mother was terribly shocked when she heard I'd painted you in your slip!' It was not for the walls of the exhibition that Tove had painted her friend. She had put a high price on the painting to discourage buyers and, as she told Eva, so as to have something left of her friend. Later she presented the painting to its subject.

Tove and Eva had met in the late 1930s and grew close in the artistic circles they shared. Their common friends included Tapio Tapiovaara, Wolle Weiner, Sam and Maya Vanni, Carin Cleve, Eva Cederström, Ada Indursky, and many others. There was something special about Eva, a feeling not limited by geographical boundaries. It was not a sexual relationship (this was long before Tove's first lesbian experience) but a deep sisterly one, infused with solicitude, affinity and the warmest love. After the war Eva sent letters and parcels of clothes, cigarettes, jewellery and even a new tie for Tove's lover, Atos Wirtanen (his old ones are 'streaked brown with snuff', Tove had observed in passing). Tove was filled with joy by their friendship. Eva had worked out what she needed and what suited her. Eva understood, listened and carried their companionship within her.

The letters Tove wrote her are like a living conversation, strong while looking for reassurances of their friendship. During the war years Tove wrote her two or three letters a month. The post was intermittent and it was always unsure that her letters would reach their addressee safely. Often they were returned unopened and the censor was never idle. Nor did Eva's wartime letters always reach Tove. Months could pass between one and the next. But that didn't matter, even if disappointment at the deterioration of the correspondence into a monologue could sometimes be detected: 'I don't believe you have had any of the letters I've sent you during the last few months – but never mind, it's been a delight for me to talk to you,' wrote Tove in January 1942.

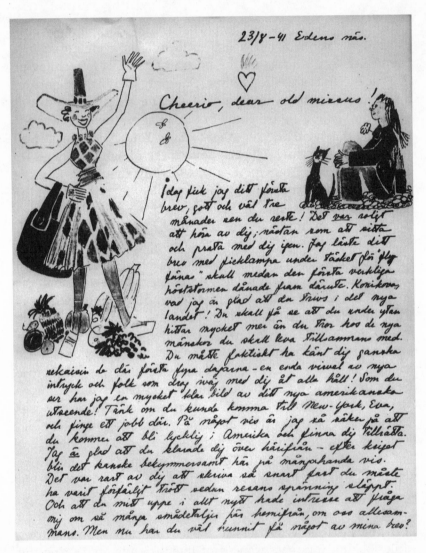

Letter from Tove to Eva (in American dress), August 1941.

The act of writing to Eva became important in itself to the human being and artist who was Tove. The correspondence from Tove to Eva contains about a hundred letters and stretches from June 1941 to the end of the 1960s. It naturally grew less intense with time but the feeling of deep friendship between them lived on through the years. Tove's letters to Eva Konikoff follow her life and transformation from a young painter to a highly respected Moomin author. To Eva, Tove wrote about herself. They became a diary written to 'Koni' (one of Tove's names for her) and through them Tove created someone she could 'talk with'. Tove constantly mentioned how close they were: 'the fact is I talk to you about all my great joy, all my agony, all my thoughts – there's no one else I can talk to the way I do to you. I'm not inflicting you with a burden – am I? I believe, I know, that your constant listening to whatever I talk to you about is like a friendly hug,' she wrote in August 1946. She talked about uneasiness, sorrow and fear and often about the strength of their relationship, that fellow feeling which permitted outspoken and fearless confidence. Tove presented herself from independent positions: her longing for the will to 'be able' to live her own life, and her search for identity as an artist and as a social and sexual being. It is a struggle she carried forward till her forties, when she began speaking of work, life and love from a new changed perspective. The longing to see each other again lived on in letter after letter, but Tove and Eva were not to to be reunited until 1949, several years after the war.

A Men's War

The beginning of June 1941 found Tove in the Åland Islands. She had been appointed commissioner for an exhibition of the work of Helsinki artists in Mariehamn, and she wanted to explore the island as soon as she had done this. The newspaper *Åland*, which interviewed 'Miss Jansson', reported that it was her intention to 'settle down in the Åland countryside' for several weeks 'to busy herself with her much-loved artistic handicrafts'. The very first letter she sent to Eva described how she was enjoying an 'existence fit for paradise' without 'houses or people' – a long-needed solitude she can now make the most of. Like Robinson Crusoe, Tove was making fire, cooking food, painting, bathing and reading. It was an escape from a threatening civilisation, a Moomin existence before Moomin.

The exhibition was not a success. Only one picture by the Helsinki artists was sold. The people of Åland preferred Åland subjects painted by Åland artists at Åland prices. To get sales started, Tove sent the pictures she had painted on the island to the exhibition, bestowing them with 'Åland prices and names' in the most 'shameless literary and inartistic manner', and this, she confided to Eva, made all the difference. She immediately sold a painting entitled 'Mist Rising from the Pilot's Hill at Geta', while another was accepted for the museum's own collection. It is all described in lively style for her friend in America. 'New ÅLAND motifs! announced the newspaper. Direct from our own landscape!' She continued: 'So now I'm all but immortal and the trip has been paid for! The paper wrote most handsomely about how I "practised my dear craftsmanship" on "their dear island". (How sadly easy it would be to get rich.)' The press was not slow to record the donation but naturally chose their words differently. It was proudly reported that the woman artist had presented 'five beautiful paintings, three larger and two smaller, and also a beautiful canvas showing Mariehamn's western harbour'. Finally readers were notified that 'Miss Jansson left yesterday evening on the ferry for the mainland.'

Åland was great fun as an artistic adventure, but the atmosphere of freedom did not last long. The war was getting nearer. There were lots of rumours, and before midsummer in Pellinge with Ham and Faffan Tove was inserting dark atmospheric pictures in her letters. Nature reflected the terrifying uncertainty: 'The sky was as red as copper and the sea yellow-grey, a strange atmosphere of stillness and expectation over everything.' Then war broke out and Tove's words became like a direct report. For several poverty-stricken morning hours they experienced 'the whole glory of summer', but then came the news on the radio. 'Pappa just came in and said "That's that then". Not another word was said. We just went and packed up the things we needed most, each for himself,' wrote Tove on 22nd June 1941, on board the ferry *Lovisa* en route to Helsinki. That evening the air-raid sirens began, and a few days later she counted four alarms before breakfast. 'Everything has really started now, and one waits in terror for the news.'

The war meant separation, disquiet, fear, deprivation, casualties and death. But it was still possible to find moments of peace and places that gave pleasure. When Eva's first letter reached Tove in August, she was back in Pellinge. The summer weeks had been a 'gift of peace and delight after the dismal and hectic time in the city,' she wrote to her friend on 23rd August, and they had been 'necessary before facing everything that might possibly happen to us in the autumn'. She was able to sit for hours in front of the view she so much loved at Laxvarpet, the bathing place of her childhood, writing, reading or simply gazing 'out of my green window at the sea'.

But time was valuable and short. Warplanes, 'flying insects' as Tove called them, droned in the air above city and countryside, and anxiety gave her no peace. Anxiety for her brother Per Olov and for Tapsa, the artist Tapio Tapiovaara, the man she was in love with. Her feelings found expression in letters to her friend in America, and on 24th September 1941 she wrote:

> As things are, anxiety grips me; even though from the outside I might seem to be living an ordinary daily life, working as usual – if I feel happy, there is always a dark, burrowing background of anguish and a mass of gruesomely clear images in the imagination that are not always easy to chase away.

Tove and Tapsa had met at the Ateneum and were lovers during the first years of the war. Their relationship was over by the spring of 1942. It had been stamped by war, by waiting and expectation, short meetings, periods of leave, goodbyes, letters, all in the knowledge that each might be the last. 'Tapsa comes back and Tapsa goes,' she wrote in 1939, and this was the pattern of their love life. It was also made difficult by deceit and unfaithfulness. Tove knew how war can change someone, break them down and transform them. During the civil war Faffan had desperately missed Ham and his little daughter, but as he had explained in his letters, he had been helpless to stop the horrible reality of war affecting him. 'When Pappa came back from his war he was a different person, colder

Eva Konikoff.

Watercolour with black Moomintroll, painted in Germany, 1934.

and harder,' summarised Tove as she reflected on the new war. She was still writing regularly in her notebooks. 'Everyone is changed, and it is important to collect strength, pleasure and confidence. I want to help you to see ahead, to forget the horrible things,' she writes to her lover, but holding the balance became too difficult for her in the long run. His periods of leave became hectic with love, art and hysterical parties, a race against time in the few hours available. And there was something Tapsa wanted and Tove didn't want to 'give' him, at least not for the moment – a child. She wanted to remain independent, she wanted to work and create art. There was no doubt that she loved him, but she hated the thought of starting a classic family. She wanted to share men's lives on different premises.

For Tove the war years were a period of constant confrontation with Faffan. He had been formed by the civil war in which, as a young man, he had fought on the White side; he was a fervent patriot and a blazing anti-Communist. He avoided like the plague anything Red or in any way tinted with the Left. For him Germany was a liberator and friend, and Communism (the

Reds) the greatest imaginable threat to his beloved homeland, his Finland. Nor did he make any secret of his aversion to Jews, which infuriated Tove. 'As you know,' she wrote to Eva, 'any reference to the "Jewish question" is to me "fire and flames".'

Tove's aversion to the idea of having children, and perhaps of marriage in relation to Tapsa, had a basis in her father, men in general and the war. By October 1941 she was 27 years old and the Continuation War had been in progress for several months.

All the reasons I don't want to get married came up. One man after another, and Pappa, Faffan, came first. The whole male solidarity and protective pedestal of privileges, their weaknesses, inviolable and fenced in by slogans, their inconsistency and charming disregard for the feelings of others proclaimed with no trace of nuance as they beat a big drum from morning to evening from the safety of their boys' network of connections. I can't afford it, I haven't time to marry any of them! I'm no good at admiring and comforting. Of course I'm sorry for them and of course I like them, but I've no intention of devoting my whole life to a performance I've seen through. I see how Faffan, the most helpless and instinctive of men, tyrannises over us all, how Ham is unhappy because she has always said yes, smoothed over problems, given in and sacrificed her life, receiving nothing in return except children war can kill or destroy with negativity. A men's war! I can see what would happen to my work if I married. It's no use; I have all these feminine instincts to comfort, admire, submit, sacrifice myself. I would either be a bad painter or a bad wife. *And I refuse to give birth to children who can be killed in some future war.* [my italics]

What Tove wanted for herself was quite different, a vision of another kind of fellowship, a more equal way of being together, a freer love: 'Can we not be together without making demands on each other's work, life and ideas, continue to be free beings without either one having to give way?'

The young artist Tove Jansson stepped forward as a feminist with her own programme, thoroughly aware of the price love demands of a woman. She refused to accept the conditions of the 'men's war'. The thought of giving birth to a child released a flood of reactions against war, the family, and men and women's obviously inflexible roles. A child would restrict her independence and freedom, and above all she was not willing to follow her mother in bringing into the world children who could grow up to be soldiers and be killed in future wars. She had no intention of presenting her country with 'cannon fodder', either now or later – these thoughts came up again during her later relationship with Atos Wirtanen. Men had inflicted death on the life-force and she could never forgive them for that.

To the young Viktor a child had been a promise of the future. For his daughter Tove it had become a promise that the men's war could continue. But the independence of women and the needs of art were equally important. Most important of all was to be a free artist and human being, not under the control of any other person. Painting and love came together repeatedly for Tove during the war years and there was never any doubt about what she wanted for her future. She 'intended to be a painter and only a painter'. Freedom always came first for her.

When she sent her watercolour 'The Solitary Sitter' (1935) as a present to Eva in the USA, it was as a declaration of independence. The picture of the recluse who chooses to remain an onlooker in celebration of freedom and solitude is a portrait of herself. But it must never become necessary to renounce love. Her ideal was a companionship that did not make demands on the other person's life and work. A love that respected the conditions of freedom. Women must be equals in any relationship with a man. After discussing the generally acknowledged inferior status of women, she declared on behalf of both Eva and herself: 'So long as we realise our own value, maintain solidarity and believe in our capacity to achieve things, we shall never fall a step behind men.' A position in which Tove never had any intention of finding herself.

Scenarios of War

During the first half of the 1940s, some of the most dramatic scenarios of the war appeared on Tove's covers for *Garm*. Drawing gave her breathing space, contributed to her daily bread, and at the same time gave her an opportunity to express the despair and anger she felt at the power of the war over life. Her sharp lampoons of the dictators and ridicule of male politics presented one perspective after another on the men's war. In one cartoon two mermaids hold up a child dressed as a diver and decide that he is like his father. Hitler is shown as a spoilt child and Stalin as what was then called a Red Indian. Leading Finnish politicians often found themselves in the line of fire. Her picture of the two faces of Stalin, before and after the day of the Soviet attack on Finland of 30th November 1939, was censored at the time but published later.

In the world of Tove's political satire, Hitler 'reconstructed' Lapland only to end up in a pitiable state himself in his eagle's nest in the spring of 1945. The year 1942 reaches out across the horrors of war as an old man in bandages to the innocent new year of 1943: guns, ammunition, tanks, planes marked with swastikas, ration cards, makeshift substitutes, and so on. Most violent and most explosively dramatic of all was her cover for the Christmas number of 1941, when the Continuation War had been in progress six months. In the midst of the terrible frenzy of war, poor Father Christmas is trying to find somewhere to place his wish for a 'Peaceful Christmas', but the madly fighting inhabitants of the earth literally send his wishes up in smoke. Heaven and earth are a chaos of bombs, falling planes, flames and explosions. Total ruin is near and the angels flee in terror from the sky. This was published a week before Pearl Harbor.

That same autumn she drew the cover for *Julen*, the Christmas paper for the Association of Finland-Swedish Office Staff. During the war years Tove was responsible for *Julen*'s cover every year from 1939 to 1944. Many of these have biblical motifs: the three wise men, the Madonna, angels; one features a V-sign. For pre-war covers she had drawn such scenes as Joseph and Mary's flight to Egypt (1935) and she had also drawn an interesting series of religious pictures with biblical motifs for the same paper. She also found an outlet for such motifs in *Lucifer*, published every Christmas by the Association of Finnish Publicists. *Garm* represented a different sort of arena. From a symbolic point of view, her most remarkable cover was the 1941 one for *Julen*, an example of how biblical material could be used for contemporary political purposes. The picture shows a figure on a sledge in a forest heavy with snow experiencing a revelation, a vision of heaven. He raises his arms towards an

Jacob's dream. Cover for Julen, *Christmas 1941.*

illuminated heavenly staircase on which angels are moving. Jacob's dream from the Book of Genesis has been transformed by Tove into a dream about her own country. About Karelia. Mannerheim had already started his offensive during the summer (Finnish troops had penetrated far into Karelia). The areas lost at the Moscow peace of 1940 had been regained, and more as well. The land had become Finnish again. Tove's picture tells the Bible story in her own way:

> And he dreamed, and behold a ladder set upon the earth, and the top of it reached to heaven: and behold the angels of God ascending and descending on it. And behold, the Lord stood above it, and said, I am the Lord God of Abraham thy father, and the God of Isaac: the land whereon thou liest, to thee will I give it, and to thy seed. (Genesis 28, 12–14, Authorised version)

This is what Tove's revelation was about. The Karelian refugees had returned to Karelia, which was once again populated by Finnish people.

At this time Tove wrote a long letter to Eva. The subject was as always the war and its effect on other people and herself, and most of all how it affected perceptions of right and wrong. She often racked her brains about this and now spoke clearly from a young person's perspective:

> In this time of complete inversion of all moral and ethical concepts, it is difficult for those who have not yet managed to establish an attitude to their environment to find a foothold – I mean for the young. Pressed by the compulsion to keep silent, isolated by anxiety for their own little circle, each withdraws further into his or her shell. The great events around us, instead of broadening our vision, have contracted it to a petty obstinacy; in their panic, people firmly fix themselves to the misguided terminology of nationalistic slogans; boundaries became ever more inflexible and logic goes out of the window. The old principles and prejudices are asserted ever more widely. In this chaos of monologues contact becomes completely impossible with a people who even before were incommunicative and stubborn. You have to either scream and quarrel or keep silent. – I've chosen to keep silent.

But keeping silent was the last thing she did in her illustrations for *Garm* and other publications. On the contrary, she spoke out loud and clear. For her, work was something to cling to, something she could do. And indeed, in another letter she wrote:'

> You can't scream inside yourself. You push things aside, you keep working, but you avoid things that bring the outer world closer to you: newspapers, radio, the telephone, war magazines. They dig up everything that's smouldering and burning deep inside you. Even though one does not bury one's head in the sand but is intensely present, every moment, in every part of oneself.

This was how Tove functioned through her pictures during the war. In them can be found, just as it can in her art work in general, parts of Tove herself, the painter and writer. Her many self-portraits, her letters to Eva, notebooks and diaries are trials in the form of pictures, words and thoughts. The contradiction, the will to act and at the same time to look away, creates a dynamic in her texts and pictures. It is as if we hear a voice speaking to us, a voice explaining her beliefs. There is an intensity and a presence in her illustrations of these difficult times in *Garm* and elsewhere that also speaks to the children of later generations. Tove never let go of her dream of peace and brought it to the fore whenever the political situation demanded it. The illustrator in her interpreted events and at the same time expressed her self, her own special mark and her presence through the picture, whether it was political, humorous or reflective. The most pregnant mark of this individuality was of course her snork signature.

One of the most important peace initiatives during the Continuation War was the letter the opposition peace movement wrote to President Risto Ryti in August 1943. The thirty-three signatures included the writers P.O. Barck, Ragnar Olander and Atos Wirtanen. Tove gave her version of this budding hope for peace on her cover for the September 1943 edition of *Garm*. The angel of peace comes forward against a dark background of war machinery at a point where two searchlight beams cross over a blood-red sky. A year later, before the armistice negotiations with the Soviet Union (19th September 1944), she placed the angel on a great question mark.

War was always a time of uncertainty, and uncertainty characterises the pictures that appeared over the signature Tove during the time she always called the lost years.

The Family

During the early 1940s Tove worked on her large canvas 'The Family', which measures 116 x 89 cm. Figurative pictures were as important as they were sensitive. This was a portrait of a family she loved, but equally of a family she felt imprisoned by. It is a picture of *her* family, of the Jansson family and their home at Lallukka. But it also illustrates the *concept* 'family', a group of people of varying ages who are clearly related to each other. The family as idea, much as Tove was later to work with her Moomin family, if with different means. Tove returned to 'The Family' in letters and notes, discussing it and analysing it, sketching its arrangement (in letters to Eva), describing the subjects' expressions and the thoughts behind them. Her plan was to show the painting for the first time at the 'Young Artists' exhibition of autumn 1941, but it wasn't ready in time and she held it over till the spring exhibition of the following year. (See colour plate 22).

'The Family' is at the same time a self-portrait and a portrait of the artist with her family. It is also a portrait of the war. The family caught in a frozen instant, a version of the constant anxiety Tove describes in her letters to Eva. Stiffened poses, downcast eyes, people with no mutual closeness. She has abstracted her anxiety for her brother into an idea, she wrote to Eva, and that

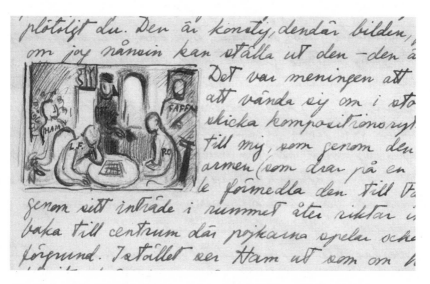

Sketch for 'The Family'. A letter to Eva Konikoff, December 1941.

thought and feeling flows into the painting. The uniformed Per Olov is as if surrounded by light, his look is dreamy and a halo seems to glow round his head. He has the role of a saint. He is youth, he is the future and he is a picture of Finland. And he is a much-loved brother, only 22 years old. Opposite him with downcast eyes sits Lasse, still a schoolboy. Two years later, at the age of eighteen, Lasse was to be called up but he never saw active service. The brothers are the family's participants in the war; behind them stands their sister Tove, who writes letters to the soldiers at the front and waits on the platform when the train brings them home and waves them off again at the end of their leave. On either side of the siblings are their parents: Faffan their father, warrior of an older generation, to the right and Ham, their mother, to the left. On the table in the middle, where the brothers sit facing one another, a game of chess is in progress. It's a men's war.

Tove watched over her brothers, virtually watched over the whole family, like a mother. She was the central point that held brothers and parents together. Faffan has the newspaper under his arm and Ham has a smoking cigarette in her hand. Lasse is looking down at the chess game. Per Olov is looking away. Tove herself is dressed in black and looks as if she is on her way out. This was how she painted her family and the concept of family, as part of the 'collected anguish of the world' that she described so vividly to Eva in December 1941 (there are similar descriptions in notes she made at the time). She wrote of silence, feelings, pain and of the members of a family setting off in different directions:

> War everywhere, the whole world at war. What can I say? I don't say very much these days (maybe that's not how the poor censor sees it?). I don't think very clearly either, it's all just feelings. Sometimes it feels as if something of the collected agony of the whole world has been weighing heavily in me like a lump and threatening to burst apart. Never has sympathy been so mixed with bitterness, love so mixed with hate, and the will to live – and despite everything to live rightly and worthily – with an urge just to creep away and let go.

These are moods she paints into 'The Family'. The brothers' game of chess may seem peaceful, but it casts a heavy, ominous

Tove painting in her cold tower studio.

atmosphere over the whole picture. The war is a game with life as the stakes. The picture is vibrant with symbolism and art-historical references, not least to the fifteenth century, which was so important to Tove. Death playing chess with a knight is a famous scene by the Swedish painter Albertus Pictor.

Tove places her game of chess slap in the middle of her country's political history. The chess pieces are red and white, the colours that, at an earlier time, placed the very existence of the family at stake. Ham could easily have lost her husband then and Tove her father. Now the family is again in danger, a family which has lived on and developed, a family which could lose sons and brothers. And a family where Red and White can be in conflict. They are all marked by their anxiety about Per Olov. It was while Tove was exhibiting 'The Family' that he was on the northern front. In January 1942 Tove told Eva:

> In his last letter Prolle wrote that they were on the alert and since then there have been battles up there. Days of anxiety like these

are gruesome. Ham goes about stiff and slow in her movements, Lasse hides, Faffan goes about everywhere being contradictory and I paint and paint. Do anything. Write verse – scrub the floor!

The most important place in the artists' home is the one that until now has been the least noticed: the hall mat. The place where letters from Prolle land.

It is a picture of the Jansson family and at the same time the picture of a typical Finnish family during the war years. It represents the Janssons and at the same time any family, anywhere in Finland. Everyone had some sort of relationship with someone who was at the front: a son, brother, husband, fiancé, friend, colleague, lover or relative. Women were participating in the war too, in the Lotta organisation or involved in medical care. Anxiety could quickly turn to loss and grief. The Janssons' good friend, the artist Hjalmar Hagelstam, was killed in 1941, friends of the brothers went missing and the Collin family, also fellow artists and good friends, lost their son. Busy at her easel, Tove wrote to Eva in spring 1942:

> In the north constant battles, with no chance of any post arriving during the thaw. As I paint I hear at regular intervals – and so frequently! – the salute of honour from the cemetery, and it makes me shrink together inside. The Collins have lost their boy, and so many of our friends have gone. At home it's like water flowing silently from a spring, everyone has withdrawn into their own thoughts.

In the event Tove's family did not have to make the supreme sacrifice: Per Olov came back, Lasse was never sent out to battle and no harm came to anyone at home. It was cruelly different for many others: nearly 50,000 Finns died in the Continuation War and 22,000 in the Winter War. And memories of the war and constant confrontations within the family marked all the Janssons deeply. Tove's painting 'The Family' became her image of the sadly flowing spring.

'The Family' is also an image of the breaking up of a family. Tove and Faffan had grown further apart, the war and politics the constant subject between them. She could not accept her father's authoritarian attitude, manic patriotism and political rigidity, locked as he was in positions that derived from the war he had once fought himself. To him, alliance with Germany was

Finland's only chance of salvation. Everything for the country, as Tove put it. While she was working on 'The Family' she confided to Eva:

Now the great crash I feared but expected for so many years has come. No doubt about it this time. Faffan and I have said we hate each other. I'm so sorry for Ham. But otherwise I feel no guilt, no sorrow, nothing. I feel like a stone. It would be nice to stop living but one goes on all the same. It's hell to be still living at home here, but for Ham's sake I must at the very least come home to dinner. Damn the war.

Later the same year (1942) she moved out of Lallukka to a studio of her own. But the political quarrels which had wrecked the peace at home continued for the whole war and became a deep wound between Tove and her father. 'Dinnertime clash with Faffan,' she noted in her diary after an argument about the armistice negotiations in September 1944. The subject was 'nationalism'.

Tove and Faffan did come closer again after the war. The love between them survived the discord, and their happy weeks in Paris in 1938 stayed fresh in her mind. A moving letter from Tove to her father the year before he died (1958) talks of a special kind of closeness and respect, of an understanding which had always been there and had grown deeper with the years. 'Dearest Faffan,' she wrote, 'I think I understand you better than you've ever realised. All I can say is that I'm hugely fond of you, more for every year that passes.'

Tove wrestled with her painting 'The Family' for a long time. It's so 'clear', she told Eva, but hesitated to expose it to a judgemental public. But she did exhibit it all the same in the spring of 1942 as her only contribution to the 'Spring Exhibition'. Its reception was disappointing, 'wishywashy', as Tove herself put it. To the critic Signe Tandefelt it was a demanding major work, but she had reservations. One can't pull off such a challenging task at 'the first attempt', she felt, but one can learn from it. The composition was approved and the motif was described as 'freer and more simply perceived' than in earlier works. Others too praised the composition, but the critics were lukewarm and not even her colleagues showed any enthusiasm. 'It's a diligent piece of work, but with no self-esteem,' Ina Colliander told Sven

Grönvall. Tove's self-confidence was severely shaken and she refused to exhibit the painting again. Instead she would 'paint calmly, stubbornly, try to get somewhere'.

But 'The Family' would not let her go, and she never finally abandoned the subject. A couple of years later she was working on a 'new Family', in charcoal this time, and in the last days of 1944 she set the painting up on the easel again: 'I painted most of "The Family" again. Better.' By this time she had written her very first story about a family of Moomintrolls.

I Just Paint

Tove worked hard during the war years, intensively and productively as always. In the autumn of 1941 she exhibited six canvases at the Konsthall autumn exhibition, bought a blue fox cape and drew war horrors for the cover of the 1941 Christmas issue of *Garm*. Any number of drawing jobs was available, she told Eva, and she was particularly busy during the autumn with book covers and illustrations especially for the Christmas editions. She drew advertisements, not least for a fizzy soft drink, designed textiles and postcards and was given her first commission for official public decorations, including paintings, some of them on glass, for a restaurant, a school and a student hostel. She deputised a couple of times as a teacher, at the Central School for thirty adult students of drawing and for art students at the Ateneum, but this didn't last long. 'It was terrible to criticise others,' she wrote, 'and I'll never do it again.' At the Ateneum her teaching was interrupted within half an hour by an alarm and she took advantage of this to leave the teacher's desk for good.

Work was the remedy during the difficult years, a way of keeping alive the creative flame. Tove was in a strong position, both as draughtswoman and painter. With a couple of illustrations in the Christmas issue of *Folket i Bild* in Sweden, in 1941 she was presented as one of the few women cartoonists in the Nordic countries. Series of drawn postcards of various types – greetings cards, animal cards, and so on – gave her a decent income (they sold in Germany too), and she began dreaming of journeys to Italy, Brittany and America – as she told Eva in 1942:

I have a new series of Christmas cards behind me – The Centre for Art Cards raised their original offer of 300 marks each to 1000, so I could not refuse. Four series a year, Koni, that means 40,000 marks. And, quite apart from what I get from painting – it means both Brittany and Italy – America! – perhaps Bali sometime … if the money retains its value. I can do a card a day if I work non-stop, calmly – and one and a half if I work non-stop wildly. I've just done two a day for the last week – by the end of which I was seeing trolls and angels everywhere as if in delirium!

Working wildly, that was Tove's style, and the tempo never slowed. Literary writing, textbooks and children's books landed on her drawing table, everything from provocative novels like *Black Eroticism* to textbooks for beginners in English and relatively modest children's books. Commissions for covers and book illustrations flooded in. Among the children's books were *Little Olle and the Baby Hare* (1943), *A Fly Called Maia* (1944) and *Nalle's Journey* (1944), written by Brita Hiort af Ornäs, Martin Söderhjelm and Solveig von Schoultz respectively.

The painter Tove was busy too. The blackout limited the time available for painting, but she could still spend her evenings on illustrating jobs. She exhibited at salons and elsewhere and took part in collective exhibitions of modern Finnish art in Gothenburg, Stockholm and Oslo in 1940 and 1942. She sent three of her 'best things' to the second of these exhibitions, and was granted a position as an official assistant to the Post Office. This brought her a travel permit and a chance to end her isolation with a trip to Stockholm. But she didn't feel up to it: 'Just now I can't face making uplifting statements to relatives and friends about the fighting spirit, Nordic solidarity and ration cards. When I'm not working I drill my way through one book after another,' she wrote in January 1942. She wanted to be alone and silent and please herself by speaking through art. Her painting 'The Air-raid Shelter' went into the first exhibition and was well received by the critics. An able painter, no question, wrote a Swedish reviewer when it was exhibited in 1940, but mistook the painter's gender, referring to the artist throughout the notice as 'he'.

Tove had had no less than ten works in the 1939 'Young Artists' exhibition at the Helsinki Konsthallen. The following year she exhibited at the gallery known as 'Stenman's Daughter' with four colleagues as 'The Five Young Artists'; the others were Ina Colliander, Sven Grönvall, Erkki Talari and Nils Wikberg. Her career as a painter was really taking off. Sigrid Schauman pointed out that her canvases stood apart from the rest and added: 'Tove Jansson must be allowed to go her own way, even if this is not the same way as most of the others in the group.' Signe Tandefelt took the same line: 'Tove Jansson has had more opportunity than the rest to escape the isolation and the handicap of lack of instruction that so impedes our young artists.' She was critical, but at the same time praised Tove for technical control, speed and a rich freshness of ideas. Three years later Tove presented her first one-man show, which she had already been planning for several years.

Times were hard but the art market was lively. The value of currency was uncertain and art had become an opportunity for investment. Tove sold more than eighty paintings during the war years up to 1944. Her income was relatively good – at least as she saw it – and she had become a name in the new market arena. In a letter to Sven Grönvall (who was at the front) in May 1943, she described a visit by the art dealer Assendelft to the studio and his choice of pictures: 'several tranquil blue-green canvases to prime the public before he goes over to entirely modern painting. He was much cheered when he realised I had no idea what the commission was for anything and he reduced his prices at once. Each of us tried to deceive the other as ingeniously as possible, but I'm afraid he won! He was extremely agreeable.' This agreeable art dealer was to become Tove's future agent. Several times she sold several pictures together and did well financially, in her own view. She sold one to the writer Mika Waltari, while her 'self-portrait smoking', known as 'Smoking Girl', was bought by the businessman Artur Nyman, to be used in his shop as a 'cigarette ad', she told Eva (February 1942), adding a string of exclamation marks.

Sometimes she used pictures in payment for dentist's fees, tobacco or heating fuel. In autumn 1946 she gave a self-portrait in exchange for forty sacks of peat and the repair of a window, a transaction also marked with lots of exclamation marks in her diary. By now she had moved into her studio on Ulrikasborgsgatan, which got desperately cold in winter. But an artist's income was always uncertain. Her second one-man show

'The Air-raid Shelter', oil painting, 1940.

after the war, in 1946, 'brought in only 7000', and she was forced
to turn to more lucrative sources of income. Hence: 'Sold my
soul for ten advertisements.' She was better paid as an illustrator
than for her painting. She illustrated one whole edition of the
cultural periodical *1946* and noted: 'I delivered 1946 and they
were very satisfied. 10,000!' She had worked hard on these
pictures, redrawing one of them fourteen times.

During the dismal war years Tove developed and made
a breakthrough as a painter. 'Tove Jansson is one of the most
noticed of our young artists,' wrote Sigrid Schauman in *Svenska
Pressen* after her first one-man show. Admittedly there were
not so many artists around; the men had been called up and
many of them had been killed, but the female contribution was
unusually strong, in the opinion of one writer on art. The war
years had given women a chance to become more visible as

artists, as was also the case with several other professions. But the typical representative artist was a man, twenty-five years old after the war, and it was men who would claim the top places in the history of local art. In the chapter on painting and graphic art 1918–1960 in the general review *Konst i Finland* (Art in Finland, 1978), the only women listed, besides Helene Schjerfbeck, are Sigrid Schauman, Ina Colliander and Tuulikki Pietilä (the last two in picture captions). Tove Jansson appears only as the author of *Sculptor's Daughter* in the section on her father, the sculptor Viktor Jansson. In the revised edition of 1998 she is allowed a short section on her own as an internationally known illustrator.

By the time Tove celebrated her thirtieth birthday in August 1944 she was able to look back over many years' experience of exhibiting and being assessed by the critics. Her journeys to Paris and Italy had introduced her to new worlds. She had gone to look for the sources of painting and fallen in love with the

'Evening Interior'. The studio in Fänrik Stålsgatan, oils 1943.

Impressionists, and a little later Cennini's book on the art of painting had made him into a household god. But during the war years her painting was at times heavy, slow and intermittent. Her love of canvas and colours went together with doubts about her own ability and anguish at the realities of war. Tove looked for incentives to hope, life and meaning, but her pictures did not measure up to her needs. Dark shadows fell across any pleasure.

> If only painting could help me. I believe all art should be the irresistible expression of delight and insight, a liberation and a need. Never a heavy duty, never a path to success. Sometimes a canvas may be hasty, out of tune and almost ugly, but even then – I do see that – it can be art. It happened when I was very happy, very expectant, or very full of grief – and I had to paint what I felt quickly. But too many canvases are 'able', or forced, or 'artificial'. Depression arising from misgivings, disappointment, or brooding over the organisation of a whole world, that cannot be painting, it is sterility. Only fresh, sharp pain can achieve anything. My greatest asset should be painting, but either it is failing or I am failing.

This is what she was writing in 1942. When the world is in chaos still-lifes, portraits and interiors can have no valid existence.

Liberation and necessity are two concepts that recur in the aesthetic discussions she constantly had with herself in her notebooks. The judgement 'able' or 'capable' had been inflicted on her, as it had been in other circumstances on many women, as a criticism of her portrait of Eva. In her letters Tove returned to her hard-won concept of pleasure, whose implication and meaning for her work she was to wrestle with all her life. She worked hard to change the way she expressed herself as a painter, seeking for concentration, and was disturbed by the tension between her drawing work and her painting.

'Sometimes I feel like an "Indian ink machine", she told Eva in the early 1940s, and it really hurt when her old flame Sam (Vanni) let slip that he believed her drawing made painting graphic. It was a cruel comment. Painting was her very identity as an artist, and her 'drawing jobs', however ably executed, were merely work she had to do if she was to make a living. They also brought her closer to Ham, but she longed for something more as well. Tove had a deep need to air her thoughts about art with someone who could understand *her*, a woman like herself. And it was Eva who came to play this part.

Her craving for a new freedom away from the artistic ideals and traditions of her family and the studio at Lallukka grew ever greater. In the summer of 1942 she decided she must leave home, and on 30th August she ceremoniously noted the beginning of her 'independent existence'. She had previously spent short periods in other studios in various places. But this was the real thing. At the age of 28 she moved, not for the first time, to Fänrik Stålsgatan 3. The time had finally come for the emancipation she had dreamed of so long. Now 'at last' she could paint, both in her studio and out of doors, in the morning and before dusk. 'I don't know whether what I'm doing is good or bad. I just paint,' she wrote and 'backed out of' all her drawing commitments. Now she was able to concentrate as she had longed to do. She enjoyed the solitude and silence, the freedom from the need to discuss pacifism, internationalism and tolerance. The atmosphere in Lallukka could be oppressive in the extreme: 'You try to hold your own and read the papers without having to take refuge in the bathroom to cry or throw up. Perhaps one has become harder. I listen to Faffan without contradicting him and I don't think I'm yielding in any way, it's just a healthy instinct of self-preservation.' She was driven by a new freedom: a matter of really living, not just continuing to exist.

She wrote happily and passionately to Eva about how she was setting up the studio. It was 30th August 1942. The city was being bombed and sixty planes had come over the night before. But she had found a kind of peace: 'They are wild now, the Russians. But how calm it seems here. In my own studio, with my work round me. All my things from Lallukka have been dragged round and the place is chock full. How shall I cook – where shall I put my clothes? It'll sort itself out. Everything will sort itself out. O Konikova, I'm free, free!'

Self-Portraits and One-Woman Shows

During the 1940s Tove painted many self-portraits. She painted herself in a fur cap, in new hats, sometimes smoking and in various furs. She worked on presentations of herself, created new

'The Lynx Boa', oils 1942.
(See colour plate 15).

identities and individualised herself in a new way. Once she had moved away from her family it was time for a self-portrait in lynx boa (she had bought the boa in a reckless mood, she wrote, and Ham got a squirrel cape). 'The Lynx Boa' is a demonstration of her new freedom, Tove Jansson both as individual and painter. Here were the animal features she liked to display in a number of self-portraits. She likened herself to a cat with cold oblique eyes. She had no intention of letting herself be hampered by feelings of guilt. The family's valued doctor, Rafael Gordin, had played an advisory part in her liberation and advised her to break away.

Next year the new studio became the basis for a one-woman show. With this she confirmed her new independence. On 2nd February 1943 the final decision was made. 'It's a memorable day today because it's thawing and dripping, and seduced by some kind of spring-feeling substitute I went to Bäcksbacka's place and asked him if he would like to mount an exhibition of my work in the autumn. A one-man show, about as important as preparing for marriage!' Leonard Bäcksbacka owned one of the best-known galleries in Helsinki and he was particularly interested in contemporary Finnish art. He had started his gallery as long ago as 1915, and the prospect of exhibiting with him was a spur. Tove wrote that 'Bäxis' was the only art dealer who had never offered her his gallery: 'In fact, he's pretty careful about what he exhibits and he never minds if the place stays empty for a few months. When I'd got a little more stuff together he came to the studio to give his opinion.' It went all right and in the autumn the painter Tove Jansson held her first one-man show. Thus at long last she made herself one with her art. She returned to 'Bäxis' in 1946 for her second solo exhibition.

In the summer of 1943 she did some voluntary national service and looked after sixteen hectares of lettuce for three months, developing into 'an extremely effective farmer'. She was worried about her one-man show, which she had been working on during the spring. Several of her canvases had been coolly received at the Konsthall and she was in a bad mood 'for a whole day'. Bäcksbacka had a French exhibition on: 'With easy, obvious taste, bold yet soft colours, charming, free and refined. Oh, the softness.' She did not write so many letters to Eva that year. The censor seemed uncomfortable and few of her letters were delivered: 'Most of the letters I have written to you have been sent back to me. I ought to have persisted anyway, but I lost courage.' She didn't even write about her vernissage on 3rd October, or about the generally positive reviews of the exhibition.

There was great expectation and her regular critic, Sigrid Schauman, spoke of an impressive boldness. 'The painter Tove Jansson accepted no limits in her choice of subjects,' she wrote, but 'romped about' on large canvases with rich, complicated motifs. The exhibition 'confirmed Tove Jansson's position as one of the most reliable and talented of the younger painters,' stated Brita Y. Gustafsson in *Nya Argus*. She praised Tove's French training, saw her as genuine, even brilliant, but also considered her to be inhibited. 'One wishes she could break out,' concluded Gustafsson. Similar comments came from other critics. For Tove this process was well under way. Her self-portrait with lynx boa was evidence of one aspect of her liberation. She was 'an artist who knew where she was going,' as Wolle Weiner wrote in his article on the exhibition.

The Studio in the Tower

It was in the tower studio at Ulrikasborgsgatan 1 that her free life really began. Fänrik Stålsgatan 3 had been on a corner near Lallukka, but now she achieved a liberating geographical distance. When she had the offer to take over the new studio from Olga Nordström in the late summer of 1944 she didn't hesitate for a second. The studio was well known and had once belonged to a war victim, the late Hjalmar Hagelstam. It was like a dream come true. Here was a different atmosphere and even the ravages of war could not destroy it: 'It looks dismal after the bombs: no windows, cracks everywhere, large sections of the wall fallen down, stove and radiators wrecked. But it's still my great dream – huge – 7.70 square. *And* with a little room alongside to live in.'

It was love at first sight and Tove stayed faithful to the studio for the rest of her life. The tower became yet another new beginning for her identity as an artist. Excited and relieved, she told her diary: 'I *am* getting her studio, the fine big one! Thanks to the good God. Perhaps I shall even yet come to be able to paint.' At last somewhere to exist, paint, live, and in her delight she made a drawing of the studio in a letter to Eva with her plans for painting and fitting it up. That autumn and winter were extremely cold. Minus-17 degrees Celsius outside, four degrees in the studio and seven in her room, she noted one day in November, and the sacks of peat she had exchanged for a self-portrait really turned into a bargain for the freezing painter. During the first year Tove lived by grace and favour and after a couple of years was threatened with eviction. A hotel and restaurant company wanted to convert the top floor of the building where the tower was, and she wrote desperately to Eva in August 1946:

There's nothing I can do, but I hope Atos can help me – or maybe a lawyer I know. Though it's not very likely – I once hit him on the nose when he tried to kiss me at a party. It's dangerous to own things, to be attached to things! If all they can give me is an ordinary little room in place of my castle – where shall I put my enormous work table, my newly prepared canvas, my pieces of sculpture, the massive bookshelves I was so proud of, and – I have to smile – my heavenly bed? I have tried to build up a home, an ideal studio in the tower I've been dreaming of all my life and have been thanking the Muse for every morning. And then I get a torn-off scrap of paper telling me I can go wherever I like on the first of September. *This* is the collective life of society, the civilised city life I have always felt so negative about.

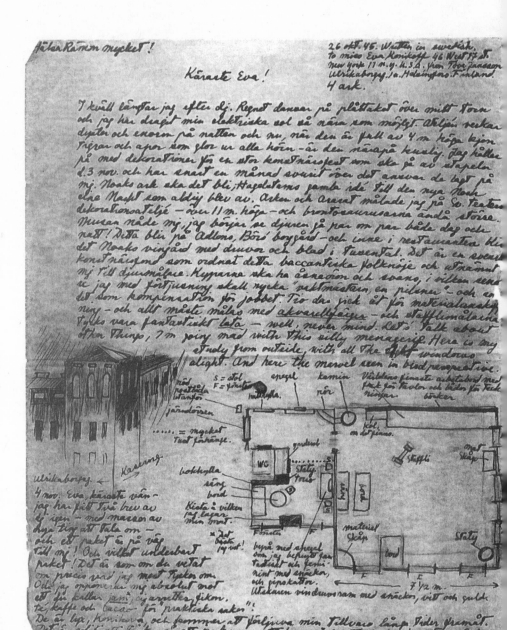

The tower at the corner of Kaserngatan and Ulrikasborgsgatan, with a plan of the studio. Letter to Eva Konikoff, autumn 1945.

It got no further than a threat, but she was given notice several times over the years and it took a full decade before the tower became her own. She grew into the studio with her body and her art, converting it and making it into a living environment. It was a studio to work on throughout a whole life: 'It's magnificent, isn't it?' she wrote to Eva just after she had moved in:

A tower room, as high as a church, nearly eighty metres square with six bow windows and above them little rectangular windows like eyebrows up under the ceiling. Piles of rubble and cracks here and there because it hasn't yet been completely repaired after the bombing, and in the middle of all the rubbish an easel. A huge grand decorated stove in Jugend [Art Nouveau] style and a funny old door with transparent green and red glass in it. A studio one could spend a lifetime perfecting if one wanted to. And alongside it an asymmetrical whitewashed room where I can keep all my feminine nonsense, all my soft, playful, showy and personal things, with two windows under the ceiling.

The studio has naturally changed since Tove's death, but it is still full of her atmosphere. The square studio with a light space consisting of high walls and a total of twelve windows, with space for storing pictures high up along one wall and long bookshelves on another, easel and palettes, sculptor's stand and Faffan's sculptured women, the zebra skin, the giant French posters, the model ship, the elegant carved cat – many things had their places there from the beginning. The doors with panes of coloured glass separate off the 'asymmetrical' room with its divan, green lamp, wardrobe and mirror, low bookshelves and spiral staircase leading to her sleeping platform, a *soupente* as in her childhood home.

Before Tove moved into the tower studio she had already met the philosopher, politician and journalist Atos Wirtanen, 38 years old, in 1944. He was a Member of Parliament for the Social Democrat party (from 1936), later for the People's Democrats (Communists). He was editor-in-chief of the newly founded leftist paper *Ny Tid*, having earlier worked for *Arbetarbladet* (Workers' Daily). Politically, Atos was 'incredibly' active, a 'parliamentary enfant terrible', as the besotted Tove told Eva, describing him as a life-loving philosopher with a passion for parties, like herself. Atos was 'more or less' the man she had been longing for. He came from the Åland Islands, sprung from a wild stock, who 'fight and abduct each other's women'. Atos was the only intellectual in a large family. From the moment their paths crossed amid a 'swarm' of actors, politicians, artists and writers at a party at the villa he rented in Grankulla (in Finnish Kauniainen) outside Helsinki, things developed quickly: 'it was obvious we belonged together'.

Atos awoke new feelings, a proud affinity that for Tove stood above gossip and slander. But it was not possible to live together freely without legalising their relationship. People 'were talking'. Sigrid Schauman (giving her opinion unasked) strongly advised Tove to get married. But she held firm from the beginning: 'For the first time I can't be bothered to hide and sneak away – I am proud of him! Of course I must pay – but I can afford to. (Such pathetic little hyenas people can be – some of them.)' Atos was the missing friend who was like Eva, and Tove's lovesick description fastens precisely on their common features:

> You would like Atos Wirtanen. He is as full of vitality as you are yourself. Full of an unruly feeling for life and with a flashingly clear mind. I have seen him angry, but never depressed. He is no taller than I am, a tousled and crumpled little philosopher with a smile even broader than yours. Ugly, happy and full of life, ideas and utopias. And self-esteem. He is calmly confident that he is the most intelligent person in Finland at the moment (why not in the whole of the Nordic countries, he sometimes wonders!) His great prophet is Nietzsche, whom I have heard analysed countless times, and whom I am beginning to be a little tired of. But at the moment he is busy with a book on the said hero, in which he replaces Wille zur Macht with Will to Form. Hopefully this – the book – will help free him from his great ideal so that he can create more freely himself.

To create freely. Tove returned to this again and again during the war years, and Atos's work became meaningful in this context. She took his self-esteem more lightly, with a roguish glint in her loving gaze. She saw clearly and loved at the same time.

Atos's circle mostly discussed politics, minor literature and art, but anything could be included. It included Eva Wichman (later a friend of Tove's), Olof Enckell, Gunnar Björling, Tito Colliander,

Anna Bondestam, Ralf Parland, Eric Olsoni and sometimes also his daughter, Tove Olsoni. Miscellaneous guests might include 'disciples' of the poet Björling. It was obvious that Tove and Atos would stand close politically. As an opposition figure on the radical left – he was one of the thirty-three members of the so-called peace opposition – he was forced to go underground on a couple of occasions. 'Dinner with Atos. Must organise a refuge for him if there is a right-wing coup here. Walked around Brunnsparken [Kaivopuisto] late. It was horribly sombre with ruins, ice and searchlights. Wanted to get away so I could fall apart'; these were her despairing words on 27th March 1944. This is the most expressive of all the notes Tove wrote during the war, from a desert land one could only want to escape from.

Atos and Tove first met in 1943 and their relationship became important for Tove's writing. Their intellectual common ground was the written word; they seem not to have discussed painting to any great degree. During her years with Atos, Tove wrote her first Moomin books and her first Moomin comic strip. Atos was one of the exclusive circle who were able to read the early Moomin stories in manuscript. During the 1940s Tove also wrote poems and verse-texts and made collections of them, but she

Atos Wirtanen. Tove wrote: 'he has a big, generous smile'.

kept them to herself (they have never been published). As a poet she was traditional and wrote 'in verse' about the hated war to which she had, as it were, had to pawn parts of her life. Her poems have titles like 'On Leave', 'Anguish', 'Guilt'and 'After the War'. A few years later she wrote 'love poems', but these belonged to a completely different time and another love.

Colonies for Artists and Forests of Dreams

The war and its 'lost years' gave rise to dreams of something else, another time, other places. 'Perhaps we have loaded peace with too many hopes,' wrote Tove in her notes. 'Then and not before will be the time when we shall want to work, when we shall understand each other, when we shall talk, travel, build and learn to love. All our misfortunes are simply the fault of the war. What shall we do when we can no longer blame the war?' Visions of another world proliferated during the war years and took various forms: building a house, furnishing a cave, constructing a model of a lightship. She wanted to construct a world of her own, create a space free of everything from outside. There were dreams of an artists' colony in warm, colourful Morocco, of another society and a peaceful existence in her philosophy. When painting gets difficult, one way out is to escape 'into something else', as she put it in June 1943. Inspiration failed her while she was working towards her one-man show. Words again became a tool for artistic self-analysis and 'escape' began to play a bigger part.

> I was beginning to get started again with my painting but now it's all gone wrong again. The main thing is not to be afraid. The pleasure will return, and the colour. It may be that I had too good a start, too much success too early, and now this has led to a block. It's easy to escape into something else. I escaped into a childish watercolour landscape, a dream-forest of forbidden possibilities. Neither better nor worse than the grotto I discovered and filled with white sand and surrounded with an unnecessary fence. Or the model ship I bought and rigged out.

She retreated through words to her childhood and a time of terror and safety, colour and sharp details. This was the fundamental material she would introduce to her tales of the

The studio canopy, 1956, with Tove's drawing of Sam Vanni on the right.

Moomin world and later transform into an aesthetic programme in her essays, especially 'The deceitful writer of children's books'. She was astonished at how, when she wrote, the 'back door' proved to be still open 'to that creepy yet secure world with red and green skies and a violence of details'. Her 1943 artistic self-analysis was also an escape from another form of writing that had not yet taken form: 'I had tried to write about the grown-up world and it didn't work. My desire to express myself was pushed aside by the desire to make an impression. I wanted to write a story about a family split. ... I couldn't be impartial and objective.' Here was a tension between child and adult that would recur repeatedly in her writing. It was not yet time for her to write directly for adults about the family she had painted. It was to be through her Moomin characters that her family narrative would develop.

This 'delayed' childhood was what was brooding at the bottom of her desire to creep behind reality, as she told Eva in June 1942. To be able to be really happy after 'this long rotten time'. It was a creative need that had to find expression and release. It was connected with the urge to create a world of her own, to transform the landscape and her surroundings. This was a very powerful urge in Tove all her life. She built houses and she built a Moomin world. She pulled things down and built them up again and asked herself: 'What are these atavistic home-seeking instincts that constantly beset me? However childish it may be I really enjoy this kind of work, sawing, pulling things, building, nailing things down, digging. Perhaps because – unlike painting – it always becomes what you expect, you get a considerably quicker result.' This was how she described her 'latest flight from reality' and the details of its intricate construction (in front of a cave): 'It is built so that the cave opens out like an inner room ... its back wall is not covered but you look up to see the mountainside and a patch of sky.' The walls are lined with pitch and the ceiling is made of pine.

> Under the ceiling runs a primitive multicoloured thorn, with a window of plaited osiers, and outside a totem pole carrying a wildly grinning goat's head with horns made from twisted roots. Similar twisted roots are set up on poles at the entrance. The palisade will be of light-grey branches dried by the sun. I have made steps all the way up to the top of the mountain, and on the right I'm in the middle of creating a particularly promising ravine. Inside there's an earth floor with flat stones and a stair up to the cave on whose white sandy floor I have strewn shells and on whose walls I am busy carving mammoths and other animals faithfully copied (from ancient discoveries). In the cottage there's a comfortable wide place covered with my big goatskin where I can sit, with raffia mats on the walls. My porcelain Madonna is trying tactfully but in vain to feel at home in this wildly barbaric atmosphere, right inside the cave. The people think I'm nothing – but they're interested.

She constructs herself backwards into a 'primitive' world of adventure where one communicates through totem poles, goats' heads and palisades with a 'wildly barbaric' atmosphere, linked by a Madonna to the everyday world. 'I want to be a wild thing, not an artist,' she wrote in her early diary entries, and her longing for the wild was simply a way of everyday life. 'Creeping behind' reality was a process that carried new creativity within itself. She wanted to preserve this reality within herself, even if it meant clinging to her 'delayed' childhood by means of decorative details and being busy establishing herself 'in reality', as she wrote to Eva. The dreamlike watercolours of her Teknis days many years before were exactly the sort of 'melancholy, wild fantasies' that she wanted to preserve in herself.

A joint Tove and Atos project was a colony intended for writers and artists who (in Tove's words) either couldn't work or couldn't work in peace. It was to be in Morocco or in the Basque district of Guipúzcoa. They played with the idea of buying the Finland-Swedish philosopher Edvard Westermarck's empty

An escape from the reality of war: the house by the cave. Letter to Eva Konikoff, 1942.

The dream artist's colony. Letter to Atos Wirtanen, August 1943.

villa near Tangier. Tove wrote a lyrical description in some notes from March 1945. It 'lies on a hillside near the sea, high up, surrounded with mimosa – a sandy beach down by the bay.' She had already elaborated the architecture for the colony in a letter to Atos from the summer of 1943. In the middle there would be a tower for Atos, with a hanging garden on top so he could write out of doors. She herself would have a large studio in a neighbouring house, but no plants. Or perhaps grapevines round the windows. Plotting colonists would hold sway in the vicinity and there would be a little house to accommodate 'anyone who was homesick'.

This project lived strongly during the war years, one of many that helped them to survive. Never, wrote Tove to Eva in October 1944, 'have I dreamed and planned so much as during these years. Not as a game, but as a profound necessity. I've travelled the whole world over and come to rest in Morocco where Westermarck's villa lies by the sea. Warmth and colour, Eva! This is where Atos and I would found a colony for artists and writers and perhaps only travel up here for the lovely pale summers of the north. And to America, Koni!' They saved up money for the colony for several years, but the day came when the cash box (kept by Tove) was empty. Its contents had been diverted to fund a strike in the north of Finland.

There were also plans for a settlement in an old pilot's cottage on Äggskären in the Pellinge archipelago. 'I have such a strong desire to build,' wrote Tove to Eva after the war in the summer of 1946: 'Work, home, atmosphere, a relationship with a loved person.'

Peace

'I shall soon be thirty years old. Time to assess my attitude to life and know what I want and what I believe in,' Tove wrote in spring 1944. She had been busy with her attitudes all through the war; quarrels with Faffan, constraint with Ham, moving from home, her relationship with her childhood – it was all to do with liberation and independence, both for Tove the individual and for the painter Tove Jansson. The same applied to her relations with men. To paint freely and independently was the main thing. Illustration jobs and fairy tales, as she called the first Moomin books, were secondary.

She believed the dreary years of war had reduced the value of humanity. She had no sense of war as a natural part of history:

> One day people will say that we lived in interesting times, in a great period. But I think the great events around us have only diminished us. People cannot manage to be magnificent in a long-lasting war. They become more and more diminished and see less and less, clinging to the phraseology of nationalism, to slogans, ancient prejudices and principles, to themselves. Or they creep into something and hide.

When peace finally came, her first thoughts were for her brothers, then for all the others who had 'fought out there for more than four years' and could now come home. Happiness came over her 'like a wave', but inside herself she promised she would never forget.

Words and pictures had been Tove's defence against the war, a way to illuminate it and hold it at arm's length. She moved into her new studio a month before the war ended. It became her guarantee of survival. Art gives life, just as her father once dreamed. Once Tove had taken possession of her tower, her art had found a home and she herself a place to build. This was the start of a new era: 'The first time I came into the new studio there was an alarm and the artillery gave me a salute of welcome. I just stood and looked, and was happy. The wind was coming in through the broken windows and chimneys, and big piles of rubble were lying under the cracks in the walls. Twelve windows reaching out to the light and as high as a church. I planted my easel in the middle of the floor, I was utterly happy.'

CHAPTER 6

Moomin Tales and Monumental Paintings

At last they came to a small valley that was more beautiful than any they had seen earlier in the day

The Moomins and the Great Flood

'Moomintroll's Strange Journey' is the title Tove gave to the first Moomin story in her notes in the difficult spring of 1944. She had written it during the 'Winter War' of 1939–40. When Finland was attacked by the Soviet Union on 30th November 1939 she drew a double cartoon for *Garm*: the good Stalin with friendly smile and sheathed sword, and the wicked Stalin with angry face and drawn sword. It was censored and never appeared in the magazine. Stalin's features were retouched to show an (anonymous) Russian soldier, a version which was not printed until March 1940, in the double issue that introduced the new year. (In fact, the original Stalin version was not published until 1988, in Sweden in *Dagens Nyheter*.)

Around 1940 Tove became more politically involved with *Garm*. The Stalin picture was a brave expression of its fierce scorn for dictators and for the absurd idea that a nation could be suppressed. When the dictator draws his sword, it is seen to be half-size. The peace terms exacted by the Russians were severe, but their territorial demands were toned down. The war

The censored double picture of Stalin. From Tove's notebooks.

no longer threatened the very existence of Finland, only her boundaries.

In her story, Tove passed over the realities of war for the little person: discord, loss and sorrow, but also the hope of a change for the better. Moomintroll and his mother are looking for a home for the winter. During their travels they adopt an abandoned 'child', the little animal 'sniff' (he still has no name), and in this way a little family is formed. The father and husband has disappeared, and it is uncertain whether he is still alive or whether he has been lost for ever. The breaking up of a family, the search for a home, the threat of annihilation and longing for a safe place. This was the substance of war that Tove was constantly referring to in her letters to Eva. During the last year of the war she lost her desire to paint. In October 1944 she wrote:

> For a whole year, Eva, I've not been able to paint. The war finally destroyed my pleasure in painting. But perhaps it was even more that I had suddenly lost my goal: honour. It took time to realise that what matters is a path, not a goal. Now I want my painting to be something that springs naturally from myself, preferably from my happiness. And I am determined to be happy, and I will be happy. I *am* happy just at the moment, Konikova. I have often wanted to live these lost years again. They were terrible. But now I don't want to think about them, or write about them.

Happiness had replaced honour. The two concepts were not interchangeable, but there were new strains of humility in the way she formulated them. The direction of her impulse towards art had changed. In spite of everything, she went on writing but transformed what was terrible into stories from a world of her own. Her inclination lay towards warmth, colour and beauty, she often talked of it in her letters, and she steered her story of Moomintroll's strange journey towards the fulfilment of a longing of this kind, towards a beautiful place of sunshine, flowers and fruit. She called it Moominvalley.

Moomintroll's Strange Journey

The Moomin story is not mentioned in notes and letters from the beginning of the 1940s, though the snork-figure appears in *Garm* in 1943. But when Per Olov is at home on long leave in late spring 1944 the story comes to life: 'I felt I wanted to write a fair copy of Moomintroll's Strange Journey and change it,' wrote Tove in her diary on 6th May. This desire took in not only Moomintroll but 'every possible thing'. Life was worth living – now happiness had taken over again – and she got 'the Moomintroll book' done in a couple of days. Atos read it, thought the story 'good', and one fine May day of 'glorious sunny weather', Tove handed the manuscript in at Söderströms Publishers. She celebrated with a flowery blue spring hat – 'my first really feminine and idiotic one' – and started on a new self-portrait. She proudly wore the hat out walking with Atos. Her investigation of herself harmonised with her new mode of expression. Now Tove Jansson was a writer too.

It was a family tradition to offer manuscripts to Söderström & Co. Publishers, and their editor, Bertel Appelberg. He was in practice the firm's head illustrator (having succeeded his *Garm* colleague Topi Wikstedt), and he continued to push illustration jobs Tove's way, including covers for publishers' lists and catalogues. Tove had done a selection of fairy tales by Zachris Topelius (1936) and a filling-in book for babies called *Jag* (Me, 1937), the last in collaboration with Ham. But the summer was passing and the publishers took their time to respond. The political situation was locked in stalemate, the peace negotiations aimed at ending the Continuation War dragged on and Tove lost hope: 'they don't care about my Moomintroll now when our war's going to hell!', she wrote in despair in August.

She looked for new illustration work and was commissioned to do the pictures for a new children's book, *Nalleresan* (*Teddy's Journey*) by Solveig von Schoultz. At this time many writers and journalists were writing children's books: Viola Renvall, Martin Söderhjelm, Eirik Hornborg, Harriet Clayhills – a new market for many of them. Tove did as many as fifty illustrations for *Teddy's Journey*, drawn in a month of working at breakneck speed during weekends and evenings. At the same time her new studio was being repaired, while Tove was simultaneously preparing contributions to exhibitions and sketches for commissions in a new field, for public paintings on the walls and glass of public buildings. Her diary records a couple of typical Tove days from the end of September 1944:

> Worked all day. Bouquet needed for Guild exhib. giving trouble. Fiftieth and last illustration for *Teddy's Journey* finished. – Pooh! *Garm* drawing. Sketch for round glass window for K.a.s. (21/9); took 1 canvas to Konsthallen. ... delivered *Teddy's Journey* illustr. (22/9) Helped Ham with addresses. 3 illustr. for von Numers. (23/9) Delivered Numers pictures, got new one from Stenius. (25/9); Illustr. for Stenius. Handed in 'Twilight', still-life and Bouquet to Guild. (26/9)

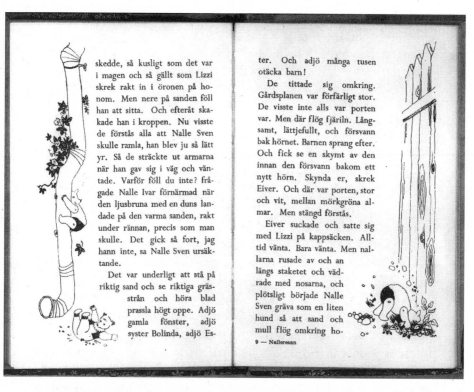

Illustrations for Solveig von Schoultz's Nalleresan (Teddy's Journey), *1944.*

The reference was to an exhibition at the Artists' Guild, the painting of a glass window for a girls' school in Apollogatan, illustrations for Lorenz von Numers's *Ordkynne* (The Nature of Words), and a 'Pooh!' on completing *Teddy's Journey* as an oblique tribute to A.A. Milne's *Winnie the Pooh*. A 'quiet' day might involve 'a little work' and designs for shelves, cupboards and the work table for the studio, but her circus of illustration was soon in full flow again. The atmosphere she worked in was turbulent. She went in search of furniture and equipment, exchanging some for 'art', and herself transported one of Faffan's plaster women to the studio on a cart. She dreamed of a great golden canopy to go over her bed, which she planned to pay for with twelve pictures (it did become hers). The studio needed painting, new windows had to be fitted and money was constantly needed. 'Collected payment. Broke!' she noted in October 1944. And so it went on all through the autumn while she made the great studio her own. It represented a new life. She told Eva:

I've been so happy all autumn, Eva! I've moved to an enormous, beautiful studio with a room beside it – my great dream has come true. I haven't been able to work since my one-man show last autumn – this has been quite the ugliest year of the war. But now things are getting going again, and I'm full of confidence. I have an intelligent, happy and lively person at my side; the philosopher and Member of Parliament, Atos Wirtanen. With him everything goes easily.

She had already explained about Atos, but in letters that never reached Eva.

Teddy's Journey is an excellent example of the pattern of blending text and illustration that became one of Tove's specialities. She would work with the text's graphic possibilities and let the placing of the pictures grow together with the visual aspects of the text. This is a method with old traditions, used for example in E.H. Shepard's illustrations for *Winnie the Pooh*. The Finland-Swedish *Teddy's Journey* with its cast of dolls and teddy bears is a relative of *Pooh*, but the story is set in a political present: it tells about Finnish war children evacuated to Sweden. The aesthetic graphics developed by Tove for her illustrations would also be used for her forthcoming Moomin books, especially *Comet in Moominland*.

At the same time, she was busy with illustrations for Martin Söderhjelm's picture book *Om flugan Maja* (*Maya the Fly*). This might seem a harmless story about small insects, but the tension between fly-gobbling sparrows and their victims is a matter of life and death. Like *Teddy's Journey* the book belongs to the time when it was written. The author's stated purpose is to talk about peace (with the fly Maya as an envoy). The progress of the pictures (there were thirty) was fully recorded in Tove's diary, but there was certainly no peace in sight outside the studio window. It was during the bombardment of Helsinki in spring 1944 that the fly pictures were created. The work helped Tove overcome her depression, but the war refused to relax its grip. 'Maya the Fly all but finished. Very sad,' she wrote on 25th March.

The picture books came out that autumn, but Tove's own book was delayed. But she planted her Moomin figure on the teddybear and fly illustrations as she waited for the beginning of her own 'strange journey'. It finished up on the cover of the fly book too, also in the black and white version. The following

The original Snork on the toilet wall in Pellinge archipelago.

spring (1945) found her working on the pictures and make-up for her own book. At the same time she was preparing a collection of pictures for the spring exhibition of the Artists' Guild. She searched for a spring hat (a repeated ritual) and indulged herself in an extravagance in black velvet and tulle. The next day she drew the last five Moomin pictures, and later started on a self-portrait. It was time for yet another new presentation of herself.

By the stage that the proofs arrived, the expression 'Moomin book' had found a place in Tove's vocabulary: 'Received the proofs of *The Moomins and the Great Flood* and made a sort of start on the next Moomin book,' she noted in her diary on 28th June 1945. At the publishers publication was not formally announced till later, in the form of 'publish Tove Jansson: Moomintroll', as written in the directors' report of 2nd July. An abbreviated version was also published in Sweden by J. Hasselgren's Publishers' Bookshop, which had a good many books from Finland on its list. She was granted a 15 per cent royalty in Finland and would get '10 per cent for printed edition sold to Sweden'. It was important that the book should come out in Ham's homeland. But the Swedish publisher considered the book expensive, so Tove waived her ten percent. In Sweden there was also 'trouble' over the text to appear on the cover, which was not cleared up till October. Publication was further delayed and by the time *Småtrollen och den stora översvämningen* (*The Moomins and the Great Flood*) finally appeared in late autumn 1945 Tove was already well into her next book.

Writing to Eva, Tove made no great fuss about her debut. She mentioned the various books published by the Jansson siblings in spring 1945, but put herself last in the list. Per Olov brought out a book of stories (*Ung man vandrar allena – A Young Man Walks Alone*), Lasse was busy with a 'stone-age book' (*Härskaren – The Ruler*) and she herself was publishing a 'fairy-tale book'. But the next year the friends were concocting American plans for the newborn Moomintroll. By now Eva had received the book and Tove was writing happily (June 1946): 'Do you really believe, Eva, that the Moomintroll could come out in the USA? That would be enormous fun. And there's going to be another troll for Christmas. Imagine, Lasse could translate them and then someone in America could ginger up the language a bit. Tell me what you think.'

There were to be no American adventures for Moomintroll in the 1940s, but the third Moomin book, *The Hobgoblin's Hat*, was published in the USA as early as 1951, under the title *The Happy Moomins* (it was later retitled *Finn Family Moomintroll*).

A Moominological Story

With *The Moomins and the Great Flood*, Moomintroll was born as a literary figure in words and pictures. When Moominmamma draws a Moomintroll in the sand (for the deaf-mute Hattifatteners), she does the same as Tove Jansson had done herself: she shows what a Moomintroll looks like.

The expression 'Moomintroll' already existed in the exhibition world during Tove's time at Teknis. In any number of interviews about the origin of Moomintroll, Tove established his birth as having occurred sometime in the 1930s, when the figure was given its first visual form, and the story of his birth is neatly summarised in her workbooks. He came into existence as a visual response during a discussion with her brother Per Olov on the toilet wall at their summerhouse. The drawing still exists and beside it Tove engraved the first words of Bishop Thomas's song of freedom: 'Freedom is the best thing'. It was part of a discussion about Kant. The name Moomintroll came from Sweden (according to the official genealogy) and inventive Uncle Einar. When he discovered that his niece had a habit of raiding the larder at night, he warned her to beware of 'Moomintrolls'; these were figures that may have lived behind the stove and could come out and strike the miscreant's legs with

— Då jag sprang in i mitt rum och låste dörren, tyckte jag mig känna Vivianes husspöke blåsa mig i nacken. I förskräckelsen vred jag av nyckeln på mitten, hoppade isäng som ett skott, och hörde ända till morgonen mumintrollena dra mina tofflor fram och tillbaka under sängen.

The ghostly inspiration for Moomintroll. Tove's diary, 1932.

their snouts or blow on her neck. J.O. Tallqvist, an early writer on the Moomins, asked in a 1947 interview for the periodical *Vår Tid*: 'How on earth did you come to invent Moomintroll?' Tove's explanation was 'psychological': 'When I was a small child I used to steal food from the larder. And then my uncle said, "Watch out for the cold Moomintrolls. They rush out of their hideyholes the moment a larder thief shows herself and begin to rub their snouts against her legs and then she begins to freeze so that everyone can see that there goes someone who's been stealing jam and liver pâté."'

In her diaries of the early 1930s 'Moomintroll' appears as an invisible being, who can attract attention when one is ill: 'I lie on my bed emptying an endless succession of bottles of mineral water and babbling about Moomintrolls with Sun-Maid eyes,' wrote Tove in the spring of 1931. A year later she described herself as 'a prey to colds, angry hosts and Moomintrolls.' No neck-blowing trolls would ever appear in any of her own stories, but the troll turned up again after a storytelling evening with a fellow artist who had a lively supply of ghost stories. This artist told of a 'house ghost' whose habit was to 'puff' on his neck, a story that made an impression on the young Tove. 'Fortunately we didn't meet any of his house ghosts,' she wrote afterwards, but as she reached home she became aware of the breath of the ghost on her neck. 'Terrified, I turned the key in the lock, jumped into bed like a shot, and all that night I could hear the Moomintrolls pulling my slippers backwards and forwards under my bed.' She 'babbled' of trolls, recognised them under her bed and had them on her mind. This was where the story of the 'Moomintrolls' began and the myth of their origin was created. There are several theories about where she got the prefix 'moomin' from. One of the more imaginative is that it comes from the Arabic 'Mumin' (meaning 'Believer' or "Good One'), but no clear etymology for the word has ever been established, either by Tove or anyone else.

The early Moomintrolls are visually related to the Hattifatteners, and the description of these 'troll-creatures', as the Hattifatteners are called in *The Moomins and the Great Flood*, is clearly reminiscent of the ghostly Moomintrolls in the attic lair at Norr Mälarstrand. They keep their distance and like ghosts and the gnomes of folk belief, draw attention to themselves but cannot be seen: 'sometimes they can be found under people's floors, and you can hear them pattering about in there when it's quiet in the evenings', as it says in this first book. Moomintroll and the Hattifatteners are as if descended from the same original figure, but divided into two species, one with snout and tail and the other without snout and tail, one able to talk and the other mute. The troll was slender to begin with, with a long snout and horn-like ears like the signature-creature in the *Garm* drawings. In the background is another troll, a shadow of the white one, a black figure that embodies what is dark, gloomy and fateful. The diaries also speak of 'Moomintrolls' as frightening figures from the subconscious, ghostlike figures of the dark that move in secrecy, beings from another and alien world.

In the early 1930s the young Tove painted these dark troll figures in a series of watercolours. These were dark Moomintrolls,

Lighthouse with black Moomintroll. Watercolour, undated.

placed in expressive landscapes of boulders, seas, dark islands and deserted roads, fenced around with agitation, uncertainty and anguish. One painting shows a group of troll figures on a wintry island, seen as if from above, dark and shadowy. Another shows a little island with a lighthouse tower, surrounded with greenish-yellowish-grey water. In the open door can be glimpsed a dark Moomin figure, while another is rowing away in a red rowing boat. In Velbert in Germany in 1934, when Tove was staying with Ham's sister Elsa Flemming and her family, she made a third picture, with a dismal, fate-laden aura: the body of the black Moomintroll with its long slender snout and markedly pointed ears is completely formed. Its mouth is open, its eyes shine red (as in the lighthouse picture) and it has no tail. There are many pictures of black trolls, but the Velbert watercolour transforms the troll into a figure of darkness, an ominous creature associated with dreams, confusion and emptiness. The picture is loaded with tense anxiety, with the black figure in the middle of an empty road, on the way between light and shadow to an unknown landscape.

There are many versions of the black Moomintroll, which may be found in various visual contexts. One troll watercolour finished up – minus troll – on the cover of B.E. Colliander's novel *Månens horn* (*The Horns of the Moon*, 1943). The troll had first been deftly removed by the painter herself. The black troll came into existence long before the war, an early sign of the dark currents behind the family of Moomintrolls that developed in the first books. The trolls would never leave Tove in peace. Their figures would vary from snork to troll, from slim to fat, from white to black, and take various forms. The first representation of a 'snork' in *Garm* (1943), the group of ghostly figures in an illustration for *Julen* 1941, the figures worked into illustrations and cartoons, the black Moomin figures in the watercolours – all foreshadow the image that became a (white) Moomintroll in the first book, in which there is never any doubt of his true identity: 'I am a Moomintroll,' he declares confidently when a little animal wonders who he is. No further introduction is necessary. In her next book, which Tove began working on in the summer of 1945, the concept becomes even clearer. A 'real' Moomintroll is always white.

The Creation Story

'*The Moomins and the Great Flood*' is the creation myth of moominology. It is introduced by a basic image, a mother's symbiosis with her child. Moominmamma and Moomintroll are searching for a place to build a house for the winter. Moominpappa has gone off with the Hattifatteners, and their search for a home is soon combined with a search for the vanished father. This leads to the discovery of Moominvalley, born as a result of the Great Flood.

All day they walked, and wherever they went it was beautiful, for after the rain the most wonderful flowers had come out everywhere and the trees had both flowers and fruits. They only needed to shake a tree slightly, and the fruits fell down among them. At last they came to a small valley that was more beautiful than anything they had seen earlier in the day. And there, in the midst of the meadow, stood a house that almost looked like a stove.

The book tells of the origin of the Moomintrolls, their early dwelling places and their deep-rooted traditions, such as the custom of going into hibernation from November to April: 'This is a good idea, too, if you don't like the cold and the long winter darkness', as it was put later in *The Hobgoblin's Hat*. As a basic moominological text, *The Great Flood* explains why the Moomins like to live in tower-like structures (earlier they lived behind tiled stoves) and it explains Moominpappa's eternal longing for adventure, two fundamentals of deep-rooted importance for the Moomin works as a whole. Moominmamma points out that Pappa is an 'unusual Moomintroll' in that he is restless and likes to move from one stove to another. Their symbiosis with humans can be broken by electricity (i.e. by modernity), which forces the Moomintrolls to take flight. This is the background narrative.

A third fundamental is the creation of Moominmamma. She has a mother's whole arsenal of strength, looks after the Moomin child, is ready to accept and look after the foundling Sniff and courageously saves a cat with kittens from the flood, a 'mother' like herself. She represents the life force and her central position is made clear. Her handbag is there from the beginning and symbolises her power. Inside it she carries a corkscrew which can be used to open Moominpappa's floating bottle-post and with that the way to reunify the family. Pappa seems adventurous, but it is typical of him that his escapade with the Hattifatteners ends in Mamma's arms. The story of the family in the valley starts with Mamma.

The Moomins and the Great Flood ends as it begins, with a Moomin mother who takes her son by the 'hand' (the Moomin terminology is not yet fully realised in the two first books) when she steps into the rooms of the Moomin house. The theme of the family that is divided and reunited, and of homelessness and return, appears again in various forms in the later books. The family as an institution can be altered and called into question, but is always accessible in various combinations. The generous collectivism of the early Moomin books – you just bring in new beds and make the dining table bigger – can be narrowed down to minimalised family images, as in the late book *Moominpappa at Sea*, in which the basic cell of mother, father and child has its corrective in Little My.

As yet the literary Moomin language is not fully developed, but the fundamental scenario is complete and ready. Already we have a typical Moomin catastrophe and rescue, and the distinction between chaos and paradise which distinguishes life in Moominvalley. The style moves from fairy tale to action and, in her letters to Eva, Tove calls her narrative a 'fairy-tale book'. Her debt to such classic authors as Jules Verne (*Captain Grant's Children*), Carlo Collodi (*Pinocchio*) and Hans Christian Andersen (*Thumbelina*) is only lightly camouflaged in the search for a father (Jules Verne), the girl Tulippa who lives in a flower (Andersen) and her shining blue hair (the fairy in *Pinocchio*). Mother and troll are threatened by gigantic mud-snakes and terrifying bog-lions, are carried over tempestuous seas and wander through a hot landscape full of cacti. The finale is the flood, which in a Janssonesque paradox prepares the way for the family's happy reunion. In the manner of Noah stranded on Mount Ararat with his ark, the Moomin family finds its way to Moominvalley, to where the flood has carried the house that Moominpappa built. It is the very simplicity of the story that is such an important part of the enchantment of the perspective as seen after the event. The adventurous expedition also reflects Tove Jansson's own journey to Moominvalley.

Part of the enchantment is the pictures, powerfully expressive yet at the same time restrained. The tinting was achieved by drawing in Indian ink, a mixed technique Tove abandoned after her first two Moomin adventure books. This made possible

45

ut över vattnet. Bredvid sig hade han bundit fast en nödflagg. Han vart så häpen och glad när marabuherrn slog ned i trädet, och hela hans familj klättrade ner på grenarna, att han inte kunde säga ett ord. »Nu ska vi aldrig mera skiljas», snyftade mumintrollets mamma och tog honom i famn. »Hur mår du? Är du förkyld? Var har du varit hela den här tiden? Var det ett mycket fint hus du hade byggt? Tänkte du ofta på oss?»

»Det var ett mycket fint hus, tyvärr», sa mumintrollets pappa. »Min kära lilla pojke så du har vuxit!» »Jaha», sa marabuherrn som började känna sig rörd.

»Det är väl bäst jag sätter er iland och försöker hinna rädda några till innan solen går ner. Det är väldigt trevligt att rädda folk.» Och så förde han dem tillbaka till stranden medan de allihop pratade i munnen på varann om allt hemskt de varit med om. Utmed hela stranden hade folk tänt eldar där de värmde sig och lagade mat, för de flesta hade blivit av med sina hus. Vid en av brasorna satte marabuherrn ner mumintrollet, hans pappa och mamma och det lilla djuret, och med ett hastigt farväl flög han ut över vattnet igen. »Godafton», sa de två marulkarna som hade tänt elden, »varsågod och sitt ner, soppan är strax färdig.»

»Tack så mycket», sa mumintrollets pappa. »Ni har ingen aning om vilket fint hus jag hade före översvämningen. Byggde det alldeles själv. Men får jag ett nytt är ni välkomna där närsomhelst.»

»Hur stort var det?» frågade det lilla djuret.

»Tre rum», sa mumintrollets pappa. »Ett him-

Extract from The Moomins and the Great Flood. *A stranded Moominpappa and homeless creatures with bonfires (tinted wash).*

gloom, darkness, twilight and light phenomena, something she made the most of in *The Great Flood* and *Comet in Moominland*. Nowhere else are there pictures so openly full of anguish and fear as in these two stories, both conceived in the shadow of war. This tragic tone has no parallel in her later books. These first two contain pictures of homeless refugees, of hopelessness and desolation and a wet, sorrowful Moomintroll and Moominpappa stranded up a tree. On the shore the homeless warm themselves around fires and prepare food. These were contemporary scenes. Tove noted in her diary on how 'hordes' of people bombed out of their homes gathered in Atos's villa in February 1944. When Tove was illustrating this first book in spring 1945 she was simultaneously working on a mural, commissioned by the Strömberg factory (in Sockenbacka outside Helsinki). She described the work for Eva:

It's the workers' canteen that must be decorated, which gives me an unusually free hand. I'm covering my wall with everything as far as possible from the closely confined work of a factory full of machines, putting in roads and horizons, ships, birds, wind and flowers. The shortage of painting materials has been wretched, and I've spent a lot of time worrying about how to produce anything worthwhile from all the nasty substitutes.

The Moomin story was interwoven with painting on both walls and canvas, a sort of combined work that was to continue on into the 1950s. But her mural for Strömberg's turned out to be altogether too full of fantasy for the taste of those who commissioned it. What they wanted was subjects related to work at the factory. Tove had to start again, the year after she had her second one-man show. This was a more comprehensive collection than before, with oil paintings, fairy-tale illustrations and drawings. She wanted now to integrate her work as an illustrator with her paintings, especially in relation to her own stories, and to be able to demonstrate the breadth of her art.

The Original Manuscript

The surviving manuscript has been handwritten in pencil on thick sketchbook paper and is covered with alterations and corrections in blue ink. It has no title. Its corrected text agrees to a large extent with the printed book, though the published text has been filled out. The manuscript version begins in the conventional and economical style of fairy tales: 'Once upon a time a Moomintroll was walking with his mother through a very strange forest', while *The Great Flood* as published goes straight into the middle of the action: 'It must have been late in the afternoon one day at the end of August when Moomintroll and his mother arrived at the deepest part of the great forest.'

As printed, the story turned out to be 48 pages long with 47 illustrations of various kinds. Its four gatherings were bound together with two central stitches. Production was simple, with no cardboard used for the covers, but the cover illustration is two-toned – green and pink – and the shifting perspectives of the illustrations make the little volume gleam. The great forest

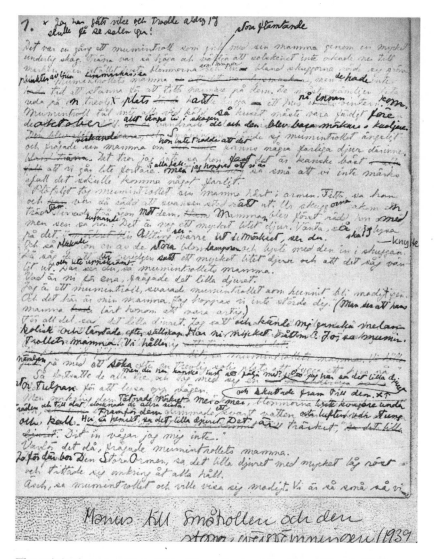

The original manuscript of The Moomins and the Great Flood, *1944. Pencil with ink alterations.*

shines like a thick dark jungle in the manner of Henri 'Douanier' Rousseau, with the little Moomintroll and his mother wandering through the shifting green and black shadows on the way to their unknown goal. This is how the 'strange journey' begins in the first book.

The publishers were to a large extent responsible for the book being given the title *Småtrollen och den stora översvämningen* (literally, 'The Little Trolls and the Great Flood') rather than 'Moomintroll's Strange Journey' or some other title. But Atos had his doubts too. No one had ever heard of Moomintroll, he argued (Tove herself had suggested 'Moomintroll and the Great Flood'). So many others missed this chance to meet Moomin for the first time. In effect, the book passed unnoticed. It achieved only one review, in *Arbetarbladet* (January 1946), written by Gudrun Mörne. 'Tove Draws and Writes', read the headline. At the age of fourteen, Tove had illustrated one of Mörne's fairy tales and the reviewer was naturally aware of her visual work. But the main reason why *Arbetarbladet* reviewed the book at all was that its editor was Atos Wirtanen.

Mörne wrote appreciatively of 'keeping company with Tove Jansson's little troll even through a flood comparable to a deluge of real Old Testament proportions', and continued in the same positive style:

> The Moomintrolls, hattifatteners and snorks or whatever they're all called are extraordinarily human even if they possess the genuine troll quality of being able to survive absolutely anything. And what sort of a fairy tale would it be unless absolutely anything could happen! Tove's drawing skill needs no introduction, not even when it comes to illustrating fairy tales. She has already given so much proof of her ability in this field. She now has the ability, in the simple bending of a line, to make a comic point – or a moving one – at will. Her Moomintroll, followed by the blue-haired Tulippa and the little animal together with all the unusual personages they meet on their travels or during their splashing about in the waves of the great flood, show amusing personal traits that move us and make us laugh.

Mörne went on to criticise the fast tempo of the story, and inconsistencies in the characterisation: Pappa's habit of tucking his tail into his pocket is mentioned several times, but no pockets can be seen on 'the moomin profile'. (The first books contain a good number of inconsistencies of this kind.) But, all in all, the reviewer found the book original, more profound than it might seem at first glance, and captivating, a story to be put into the hands of the youngest reader.

In Sweden the appearance of *The Moomins and the Great Flood* passed completely unnoticed. It came out late, on the cusp of New Year 1946, but that wasn't the only reason. 1945 was the year of *Pippi Longstocking* and a new wave of Swedish children's literature. The Moomin story had its roots in another tradition. There is no trace in these books from Sweden of the reality of war that lurks in the shadows of the great forest in *The Great Flood*. But it does have one thing in common with *Pippi Longstocking*: a new perspective on the family. Tove Jansson writes of a divided family and widens the concept of family; Astrid Lindgren presents a child who creates her own 'child-home', as Pippi at one point describes Villa Villekulla.

The World of Peace

By the time the *The Great Flood* appeared Tove was a well-known figure in Helsinki cultural circles. She was regarded as a promising artist who might go further. She was constantly looking for new directions to take. The winter of 1944 had been difficult. The despair which had characterised her notes during the late winter is extremely moving; the hopes for peace of the February to April period (Mannerheim was conducting the negotiations at this time) were brutally destroyed by Russian bombs on Helsinki. Her laconic notes on people, the city, the atmosphere and 'the bombardment' in February speak for themselves: 'How nervous people are! How tattered and torn we have all become!'; 'Bombardment. Horrible. ... The city's burning. Another alarm – at 5 in the morning.' She watched the fires with Faffan and her brothers, 'uncanny, magnificent'. Next day the windows of her studio were blown out. 'I knocked slivers of glass out of the windows. Three more alarms.' Dinner with Atos a couple of days later was accompanied by 'bombardment till 11', and no sooner was she back home than a 'new bombardment' followed, going on till six in the morning. During the worst of the bombing she was with Atos in his house at Grankulla: 'alarm at 7', but she wished she could have been with her family in town. A 'magnificent hell,' she noted in her diary.

Her visions of artists' colonies and forests of dreams gathered strength as the spring progressed. Together with Sam and Maya Vanni she planned to 'construct a happy society and peaceful world' (March 1944). The aim was to 'lower a curtain on the war', she wrote on 11th March, but there seemed no prospect of any end to it. One lived with war and politics whether one wanted to or not. At the same time, Tove was working for *Garm* and politics was part of her life with Atos. On one occasion she acted as a courier and carried 'a secret paper to him', an event noted in her diary. More and more frequently references to herself would be restricted to laconic comments like 'gloomy' and 'very gloomy'. It was difficult to work. The artists' colony was 'the dream' that kept her going during the war, she wrote later to Eva.

'It was the utterly hellish war years that made me, an artist, write fairy tales,' she told J.O. Tallqvist a year after the publication of *Comet in Moominland*. Her identity as a painter was fundamental, but when she lost her desire to work with canvas and brushes she looked for other outlets. The Moomintroll stories gave her a new vent for expressing herself and gave material form to dreams and melancholy, hope and despair, desire and lack of desire. She later described the process as an escape to a world where everything was 'ordinary and not dangerous', a flight from reality to the world of childhood. But in fact it was something bigger. The Moomin stories became an act of protest, an expression of her need to get away from the hard realities of war that she was drawing and writing about all the time.

Flight, catastrophes and homelessness are powerful themes that directly connect the two first stories with reality. The war left no immediate traces on her painting; no bombs, no ruins, no escapes. One of her few paintings with a war motif is 'The Bomb Shelter' (it exists in various forms, sometimes with the title 'Alarm'), which portrays people inside a shelter (a motif that also occurs in her pictures for *Garm*). But paintings like 'The Family' say more about the war than they might appear to on the surface. This remarkable mix of strength, helplessness and proud resignation gave her no peace.

Snork in Garm, 1943

The story of the family in the valley was a realisation of the idea 'of a happy society and a peaceful world', a fiction sprung from the dreams of the war years and a longing for something else. A dream oriented more towards the future than the past. It was rooted in her childhood and family, with Ham, Faffan and her brothers in the principal parts, but it grew and freed itself from reality. The family was there, more or less disguised, a bigger or lesser part of the characters, like the summer landscape of the Pellinge archipelago and the big house with attics and tiled stoves in the little valley at Blidö. They are there as a family whose life and its contents have helped to create the moominological lifestyle. A happy, peaceful society that exists in symbiosis with nature and other powers, and is threatened by comets, floods and storms, a society constantly forced to revise its view of itself. The Moomin family is not the same as the Jansson family and the Moomin books are not about writing up her own childhood. Her project is greater, but visionary. It is a narrative about the conditions of life which soon develops a life of its own.

The Moomins and the Great Flood became a 'shelf-warmer', which sold only 219 copies in 1946. More than 2,800 were available. The following year, 183 were sold. Naturally it was not reprinted. Today the first Moomin book is a bibliographical rarity and in bookshops in Sweden it sells for several thousand kronor. When the book came out in Finland it was priced at 41 Finnish marks. The royalties earned by the author after its first year on sale amounted to 1,346 marks and 85 pence.

CHAPTER 7

The Time of the Apocalypse

The world could have split apart without him having noticed it in the least.

Comet in Moominland

The Moomins and the Great Flood had scarcely been printed when Tove started on a new story. She was burning with the desire to tell stories. The Moomin tales demanded to be set down on paper and to come out into the world. The manuscript of the new book, *Kometjakten* (*Comet in Moominland*), developed at high speed in the summer of 1945. The entry 'wrote Moomintroll' occurs frequently in Tove's diary and at the end of July she noted, 'Moomin book finished.' During the autumn she worked further on the story and in the spring of 1946 came happy news from the publishers: 'Moomin book accepted!' She immediately started illustrating and at the same time yet another Moomin story began growing inside her. Before *Comet in Moominland* reached the bookshops in the autumn she was already working on the third book, *The Hobgoblin's Hat*. The craving to 'write Moomintroll' was so strong in her that she had to urge herself to 'leave Moomin' – she had to prepare her second one-man show that autumn – but, quite simply, she couldn't stop. She was building a world of her own in words and pictures in a way different from her painting and drawing. The Moomin world was forming itself into a picture of life and the creator was becoming one with her fictive world. There was no other power but herself: 'a fine evening in the studio alone with the Moomintroll,' she wrote in November 1946 while working on *The Hobgoblin's Hat*.

After the war the painter in Tove Jansson regained her love of colours and a desire for canvas, palette and brushes stirred in her again. Her relationship with Atos Wirtanen had been important. Her two years with him, she confided to Eva in a letter written on Midsummer's Day 1945, had made everything 'richer, warmer and more intense ... My love for him has so changed me that I would even happily marry him.' But there was one requirement she could never give up: her freedom to work. She must keep her studio, just as he would keep his workroom in the house at Grankulla. They would not marry, but the subject would often come up between them.

In the summer of 1945 she went to the district where Atos had spent his childhood, in Saltvik, north of Mariehamn, to meet his family and experience Åland with him. His six brothers were known in the locality as 'the Terrors of Saltvik', and she was astonished at the difference between them and her Atos: 'great wild laughing men with dark hairy chests and red cheeks and an uneven numbers of fingers, eyes and noses as a result of battles fought in their early years'. What 'remarkable chromosomes to have been able to produce a philosopher on that hill!' she wrote to Eva. She was moved that Atos had been named after one of *The Three Musketeers* – his mother had been impressed by Dumas's novel – it was a name which suited him.

But the journey was just as much marked by a need for solitude. She wanted to be free to work and tour the island by bicycle, set up her easel, paint, bathe, live an outdoor life, pick mushrooms and pickle them. And she wrote intensively, almost passionately, for days on end. It was in the landscape of Åland that her new story, 'Moomintroll and the Creepy Comet', as it was called in its first draft, took shape. It followed her wherever she went; she wrote on the rocks after bathing, in her room, on her easel, on the boat home. Her lonely adventures became the Moomintroll's adventures. She used her experiences of the Åland hills and of rolling stones down gaps in the hillsides with Atos. The manuscript contains notes on how he taught her this

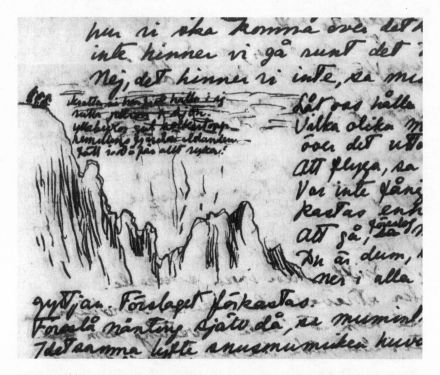

On the edge of the abyss. Sketch for Comet in Moominland. In the published scene (opposite) the group has grown to four.

art. As a philosopher and great lover of life, he obviously had a part in the adventure, and of course he was one of the first Moomin readers.

Her illustrations for *Comet in Moominland* developed during an intensive two weeks the year after, in May 1946. Tove started in the dark atmosphere that had so often afflicted her during the war. 'Gloomy. L.[Lallukka] Started illustrating Moomintroll 2. Grankulla [Atos's house]'. But work went well and the proofs of 'Moomintroll 2' reached her at the end of June. Now she needed to link text and pictures together on the pages, as she had done for *Teddy's Journey* and other books she had illustrated. This time she herself was responsible for the text. This work was fundamental. The text was pasted into a dummy and formatted page by page, and the pictures were numbered, given a size in centimetres and placed in their context. In a proof she sketched in the pictures and designed the layout of pages, text and empty surfaces. Symbols became part of the illustrations, while she worked out her graphic

aesthetics, relating text and pictures to ancient traditions in book design, illustrated poems, emblematic scripts, calligraphy, and so on. She made use of many examples from children's literature, including Lewis Carroll and John Tenniel's *Alice in Wonderland* and, as already mentioned, A.A. Milne and E.H. Shepard's *Winnie the Pooh*.

Tove was responsible for everything: she was the author who wrote the text, the artist who drew the pictures and the designer who gave the book form. *Comet* established Tove's practice as a double artist. First she wrote the story, then the pictures followed. One might suppose that, as a visual artist, she might have done things the other way round, but with Tove the words nearly always came first. When putting *Comet* together she occasionally sketched subjects for pictures in the proofs (Moomintroll, Snufkin, Mamma), but more often did no more than give a verbal hint like 'The Bridge', 'The Monkey', 'He is diving', or 'the Muskrat in the rain', etc. The illustrations come after the text is finished. But some scenes and characters needed to be thought through as pictures from the start. In *Comet* a couple of illustrations were sketched in this way: one of Moomintroll with his walking stick, and one of Snufkin, who makes his literary debut in this story.

In practice, the most highly developed illustrations in the manuscript went almost unchanged into the finished book and were kept in subsequent editions. This is proof of the seriousness of the story and provides an indisputable visual key. The sea has disappeared, and Moomintroll and his companions are seen silhouetted on rocks high above the dry seabed. This can be glimpsed between the black peaks of cliffs and steaming vapours. In this dramatic representation of the individual's meeting with the forces of nature lies the kernel of the story: the threat of annihilation and the vulnerability of man's existence on earth. But it also gives an image of the will to challenge these powers, of the capacity to look for salvation on the edge of the abyss and to survive the comet's scalding breath.

The Comet and the Prophet

Tove Jansson's catastrophes are a thematic marker in her Moomin world. Security and terror, vitality and chaos clash both in the diaries of her childhood and in the Moomin books. Thunder and general bad weather in Pellinge are transformed into adventures. 'The water is rising! The landing stage is being carried away!' wrote the thirteen-year-old Tove in 1928, in lively illustration of the power of weather. Faffan's passion for wild weather interrupted the peace of their summer lives and reshaped it. This passion reappears in many of her texts – Moominpappa entirely shares it – and when Tove's eye sweeps across her father's wild landscape the result can be utterly enchanting:

> Every time there was severe weather Pappa would take us out in the boat, he loved storms. We would sail to ever wilder and more uninhabited islands and spend the night at sea in thunderstorms much greater and more dangerous than they are now; the tornadoes were fiercer then, and when we got lost in the mushroom forests the autumn darkness was blacker. We rescued shipwrecked smugglers. Pappa was capable of waking us in the middle of the night to put out forest fires many miles from our own island, and when the water began to rise he would look happy and say, 'I fear the worst.' The storm would

intensify reality and deadly danger for the whole family, most of all for the children.

She used such situations in her stories. The power of catastrophe made life changeable, unpredictable and new. *The Comet* begins with mystic signs, ants and gulls in formation like a star with a tail. A communication from a higher power, God granting humanity (the troll) a portent of danger to come. The world suffers agony, bad weather strikes, an uneasy wind gets among the trees which sigh and turn away their leaves. The event is described in the fateful biblical language (in this case Romans 8:22) that typifies certain parts of *The Comet*. It was during her period at Teknis that Tove made her first deep study of the Bible, and one of her diaries is full of quotations from Psalms, the Epistle of James, Ecclesiastes, the Song of Solomon, Luke's Gospel and many other passages, mostly from the Old Testament. Proverbs was a favourite. Here is an entry from Tove's diary in 1932, when she was eighteen:

> When your fear cometh as desolation, and your destruction cometh as a whirlwind; when distress and anguish cometh upon you. Then shall they call upon me, but I will not answer; they shall seek me early, but they shall not find me.
>
> Proverbs 1, 27-28.

Bad weather, storms and distress recur in the catastrophes of the Moomin world. The Bible is particularly important for the early Moomin books, up to and including *Moominsummer Madness*, but nowhere is it more pervasively important than in *The Comet*, both for subject matter and language; the book describes apocalypse and catastrophes on a biblical scale – complete with Egyptian plagues of grasshoppers and dry seabeds – and places a comet with a glowing red tail heading for Moominvalley on Moomintroll's blue sky. 'The children of the world may

Moomintroll deep in thought.
From Comet in Moominland.

The Jansson family enjoy a storm (Tove in middle, Faffan on right).

lament and fear,' declares the Muskrat faced by the threat of a falling star with a tail. Revelation, the Books of Moses, the Gospels (the falling star is mentioned in Mark, Matthew and Luke); these lie behind the comet story.

The comet, dating from Tove's 1930s reading of the Bible, appeared early in Tove's phenomenological world as a heavenly object that could bring destruction. In her notes the young Tove talks of destruction as God's punishment for human hubris. If humanity 'dares to research into the infinity beyond the planets', for example, by colonising the moon and initiating regular traffic to Mars, this would arouse the wrath of God: 'then God will be angry, and send a comet, of a sort which would fall more or less every other minute but never actually hit the earth. But now it is on its intended course, heading straight for our world, when we are at our most arrogant and sure of ourselves. We shall be burnt to atoms and vanish with everything around us, before the comet even reaches us. It distresses me to imagine how it will be.' This is the thought she was to dramatise much later in *The Comet*, but in a different key.

A collision between the comet and the earth, Moomintroll explains, would mean that 'Everything will be smashed to pieces.' But when the comet comes it lashes out towards the valley with its tail before disappearing out into space again – a comet that alters its course. A parallel in real life is Halley's comet (known since 200 BC), and scientists calculated that the earth would 'find itself inside the comet's tail' when it approached the earth in 1910. Scientists also play an important part in the story of the Moomin comet. It is at their observatory on the Lonely Mountains that its time of arrival is established: according to the professor's calculations it will touch the earth 'on the seventh of October at 8.42 in the evening. Possibly four seconds later.' In her picture of the comet Tove wove the Bible, folk wisdom and astronomy together into a fateful philosophy of existence, but gave her story a life-affirming end.

An important role is played by the comet's herald, the gloomy Muskrat who appears at the door of the Moomin house one rainy evening. He knows how to interpret signs and believes the end of time is approaching. His reading reinforces his status as a prophet of ruin: he is reading Oswald Spengler's famous book about the destructive cycles of Western civilisation and

The Muskrat meditating on Spengler. From Comet in Moominland.

cultural organisms, *Der Untergang des Abendlandes* (*The Decline of the West,* 1918–22), a work that enjoyed huge popularity. An illustration shows the Muskrat philosopher in a hammock (his favourite place), his head propped on his hand in a thinker's pose while his copy of Spengler lies on the ground, stuffed with bits of paper marking important places in the text. In her comic strip 'Moomintroll and the end of the world', published the year after *Comet,* Tove gives the complete title of Spengler's book. Like many others with an interest in philosophy, Tove had read some parts of it. The Muskrat accepts science but appears as a fatalist; whether or not the comet will arrive cannot be of any significance to a philosopher who believes in the 'pointlessness of everything'. A conversation between the Muskrat and Moomintroll sets the story's conflicting attitudes to the comet against one another. In fact, the thinker is not indifferent to the power of the comet; he just has no idea what action to take. On the other hand, he lights the path to science, to the observatory on the Lonely Mountains. The same is true of the professors in the observatory, their ivory tower on top of the highest mountain, where they live in 'isolation together with the stars'. They have not thought of what will happen when the comet comes, but they will 'record the course of events in great detail'.

Comet again and again sets out a critique of isolated intellectualism, which it sets against practical action based on intuition and directed towards the present. Its philosophical antithesis has its roots in both Henri Bergson, whom Tove read in summer 1945, and in Spengler. It contrasts a scholarly approach to life with practical experience of life, the mechanical with the organic, the intellectual with the artistic, like a tug-of-war between fate and causality. Intellectualism is set against a living life force (*'élan vital'* in Bergson's term), which is represented by the family in the valley and their friends. The entomological Hemulen who has specialised in butterflies is a typical example of isolationist science. He interprets the world through science and when Snufkin talks about comets the Hemulen thinks he means moths. The later meeting with his postage-stamp collecting cousin gives even greater evidence of the detachment of science from real life. The postage-stamp Hemulen has broken off his relationship with his entomological cousin:

'He had no interest in anything but his old butterflies,' said the Hemulen. 'The earth could crack under his feet and it wouldn't bother him.'

'That's exactly what's going to happen now,' said the Snork. 'To be precise, at 8.42 tomorrow evening.'

'What?' said the Hemulen. 'Well, as I said, there has been a tremendous fuss going on here.'

In *The Comet*, Tove presented a sharp critique of isolationist science, the inability to see beyond the boundaries of one's own subject and to have any sense of proportion. The adventurers who persist in their hunt for the comet as far as the Lonely Mountains are the book's real heroes. But they are also capable of analysis. After a conversation with the Muskrat, Moomintroll sinks into deep thought and is shown (with an emblem of the comet behind him) in a pose closely reminiscent of Rodin's famous sculpture 'The Thinker'.

Tarzan and Atos

Tove Jansson devoured adventure books when she was young: 'I have longed for adventures ever since I was a little clapper of a bell,' she wrote in her diary in 1929, and she pursued her fantasies by reading L. Rider Haggard, Karl May, P. N. Krasnov

(*The Amazon of the Desert*), Jack London, Jules Verne and Edgar Rice Burroughs. Tarzan was a great favourite and Tove's and Per Olov's Tarzan games were part of summer life in Pellinge. Tove's adventure stories from that time – neatly written up in black notebooks – also have clear traces of the aristocratic jungle hero's life and adventures.

Tarzan became part of the Moomin culture. *The Hobgoblin's Hat* has to do with play, and the roar of the ancestral forest sounds happily in the overcrowded living room of the Moomin house. But in *Comet*, play has a different significance as Moomintroll assumes the role of Tarzan and rescues his beloved Jane (Snork maiden) from the arms of a monster. The giant ape that Tarzan fights has been transformed into a poison bush of the 'Angostura' variety, and the jungle knife has shrunk to a penknife. But at the same time the scene parodies the gender-coded ideals of the adventure story. The illustration presents Moomintroll as hero: his hackles have risen, he tests the blade of his penknife on his paw and drums impatiently on the ground with his foot. The Tarzan of the Moominworld is ready to attack and the Snork maiden later dubs him her saviour with a medal (a Christmas-tree star). But she too stars in a heroic role through her clever rescue of Moomintroll when he is threatened by a gigantic squid. She captures light from the comet in her mirror and blinds the monster, and Moomintroll is filled with admiration: 'Snork maiden, you saved my life, you know! And in such a clever way too!'

This is a feminism that seizes upon the ability to take action, the quality that for the most part marks out the adventures in *Comet in Moominland*. (In *Kometen kommer* [*The Comet Comes*, 1968], the third and last version of the comet story, the rescue happens by chance and the Snork maiden's role becomes traditional.) But in *Comet in Moominland* there are traces of the young Tove Jansson's personal feminism. She (and the Snork maiden) also effectively puncture the long-winded style of speech beloved of male meetings. The Snork maiden's brother Snork calls a meeting about the comet: 'but one thing stands out as clear as the nose on my face, and that is that we must find a sheltered place to hide in,' he says, and his sister answers: 'You make such a fuss about it all.' She goes on: 'It's quite simple. All we have to do is to creep into Moomintroll's cave and take our most precious belongings with us.'

Atos and Tove kicking up dirt.

The situation was all too familiar to the woman painter. In her notes Tove makes no bones about her opinion of men in meetings. Is there anything more idiotic than assembled men being formal?' she wrote after a meeting of the committee of the Illustrators' Association on the subject of buying in art in February 1945, and after a later meeting the same spring she recorded in exhaustion that they went on for 'five hours' with 'their diaries and protocol'. She was the only woman present, like the Snork maiden in the hunt for the comet. It is a woman's voice against men that we hear in *Comet*; what the woman talks about is what matters most: how they can all survive the great catastrophe.

The 1940s were a period when Tove developed her interest in philosophy, to some extent inspired by her association with Atos Wirtanen and the writers of his circle. But she read

Schopenhauer (whom she didn't like) and, earlier, Nietzsche and Bergson. She returned to Bergson in the late summer of 1945, when she was working on *Comet*, and celebrated her 31st birthday alone on Åland by reading the French philosopher. Atos was somewhere else.

The philosophical Muskrat is related to Atos and her depiction of the male thinker, but it was not so much Wirtanen as a person that the Muskrat personified as the idea of a philosopher. There was also a Muskrat in a marsh near the Grankulla house and this became a place for reflection on both Moomintrolls and philosophers: 'Atos went to the muskrat swamp and pondered upon Nietzsche,' wrote Tove in her diary on 10th May 1945. Atos was working on his book on this 'Great Idol', as Tove often mentions in her notes. He read Spengler, but could not have been less of a prophet of ruin. There was a strong love of life in Atos; he had a 'positive charge' and was easy 'to be happy with'. His vitality became important during the dismal years of war and played an important part in Tove's love for him. This could also be found in one of her new characters, Snufkin. Snufkin has a need for a free life and the strength to cut loose from things. He has no hesitation in pushing his tent and other necessities over a precipice. For his part, Atos was happy to talk about 'the idea, the inessential feature in every superficial course of events'.

When Tove explained Atos's nature to Eva, it was as something 'comet-like and absolute'. He related to what was sudden, incandescent and shining, never to catastrophe. He was a 'unique figure' with no need to 'continue himself' and his only desire was to 'complete his thought-life'. There was no one else she would rather have at her side. Atos was absolute, quick, intensive, glimmering. And he had a wide, generous smile.

They were alike in their strict attitude to work, but their attitudes to the nature and character of love were different. 'I know he is scarcely capable of love,' wrote Tove to Eva, 'at least, of what we mean by love.' Atos was fond of her in the same way as he was fond of the sun, the earth, laughter and the wind. 'More fond but in the same way.' When she wanted a ring he bought her a ceramic brooch in the form of an ox. 'Darling donkey,' was her only comment. The question of marriage came up several times. Their open way of living challenged conventions and the subsequent gossip affected them both. He was the first to mention engagement. They thought of children but, as before, Tove had serious doubts and for the same reason. In summer 1945, while she was working on *Comet*, she wrote to Eva in America: 'This war has taught me one thing at any rate. No sons. No soldiers. Maybe it's become an idée fixe – but I've seen too much to dare.' If she must have a child, she hopes it will be a girl.

Comet in Moominland as a Children's Book

Comet is a book unique in its time. It depicts a threat to destroy the world, and the ultimate horror: the annihilation of life. As Moomintroll gloomily puts it: 'It's all falling apart.' The comet may be seen as an image of the terrible atomic bombs that were dropped in August 1945. Tove had lived through the bombing of Helsinki and in Pellinge the bombers had swept low over sea and islands. But her story was as good as finished by early summer and she had been illustrating the bombing in *Garm* throughout the whole war. When in late summer 1946 Tove drew together the tensions between war and peace on one of her covers for *Garm*, she gave the scientists power over life. The angel of peace (on a plane) is greeted by a neat little man with the formula for the atom bomb in his briefcase. 'Uran 135' is written on it. The atomic bomb was war for the new age. There is no depiction of catastrophe to match *Comet* in the children's literature of the Nordic countries at the time. But when Tove wrote her comet story in war-ravaged 1940s Finland, she was describing conditions people had lived with every day.

The war was a nightmare for a colourist like the painter Tove Jansson, a threat to the desire and will for colour. One art critic feared she would become a 'lady in grey', but felt reassured by her second one-man show in autumn 1946. Yet her pale metaphors broke through in *Comet*. When Nature had been emptied of life, it had been deprived of colour. The sun vanished, the moon became pale green and faint, the blue sky was tinted red and at night the stars were hidden. Already in an early sketch for a short story (1933) she had written of 'a dried-up seabed, illuminated by the eye of the devil, tragic and strange'. The eye of the devil illuminates the landscape in the comet story. From the chasms between ancient mountains the mist rises, 'icy cold and greyish white like the breath of death'; everything is inconceivably old, gigantic and 'fearfully lonely'. The seabed the characters wander across is full of hot vapour and black fissures. The climax of all this is the dark red arrival of the comet which lends a nightmare illumination to Moominvalley:

> It was gloomy and desolate on the shore with the great gap that had been the sea in front of them, the dark red sky overhead, and behind, the forest panting in the heat. The comet was very near now. It glowed white hot and looked enormous as it rushed towards Moominvalley.

> In the red gloom under the trees not a breath of life stirred: all the small creatures had hidden themselves underground and were cowering there, silent and afraid.

'*Dyster*' (gloomy, dreary, sombre) is a recurrent adjective, both in *Comet* and in Tove's diaries of the war years. In her next book, *The Hobgoblin's Hat*, the word doesn't occur at all. In *Comet*, whether deliberately or unconsciously, Tove was in a literary sense on the wavelength of existentialism and 1940s modernism, a period when it was possible, in her own words, to exchange greetings like 'anguish to you'.

She had wanted to write the war out of herself and started with *The Moomins and the Great Flood*. But that story wasn't enough. The comet represents the greatest of all our fears, and as a symbol represents more of a long-term threat and is more intensely laden with meaning than the flood rains. It also reinforces a sense of life triumphant. Tove Jansson's glorification of the fury of natural elements has clear features of the Nietzschean song of joy. The parties of the war years, when people danced, drank,

ignored the bombs and lived for the moment, were also staged under the comet's red sky.

In *Comet* this feeling is incarnated in the life aesthetic of living in the present. The seductive show of the dance floor affirms the joy of life; disaster will not strike for a few days more. The comet summons up the fundamental urge, the will to live. This is also the message of the story. It is about the little person's challenge to the great powers, about having the strength to live and the ability to manage. But it also celebrates the natural changes in the life of a young person, the need to leave home and experience love outside the family. In one of his darker moments Moomintroll comforts himself with the thought that Mamma certainly knows 'how everything can be saved' – that is to say, as in *The Great Flood* – but this time she has no answer. Instead the answer is with the new woman in Moomintroll's world, the Snork maiden. But the basic thinking is the same: women control the source of life. When the family takes refuge in the cave by the seashore to escape the catastrophe, they return for one night to life and security with mother. With its smooth, slightly uneven rock walls, its sandy floor and its inner rooms, the cave is a fine image of the protective womb. In front of the opening to the cave hangs a blanket that has been made fire-proof by some underground sun-oil. This has been provided by Snufkin.

The morning after the catastrophe the family finds a new-made world. The sky is blue, the sea returns, seaweed reaches towards the sun, fish slip out of hidden holes and from the horizon a flock of seagulls fly screaming in over the shore. They creep out of the cave as if born anew.

Publication

Söderströms also published *Comet*, and the blurb on the back cover of the first edition presented its author as a 'talented and imaginative woman who knows just what children like to hear'. The fact that she had illustrated the story herself makes it into 'a complete little work of art'. But *Comet in Moominland* was no more of a commercial success than its predecessor. It was given a few reviews in the Finnish press, but in Sweden this second Moomin book disappeared, leaving as little trace as the first.

Tove's covers for Comet in Moominland *in their original Finnish (left) and Swedish (right) editions.*

The Finland-Swedish reviewers were for the most part positive. They talked of 'the most wonderful story book' (*Västra Nyland*), and called it 'enormously penetrating and inventive' (*Nya Pressen*), while Gudrun Mörne in *Arbetarbladet* detected 'nuggets of golden wisdom' and glimpses of 'enchanting poetry'. The story was compared with *Winnie the Pooh* and Disney and, particularly interesting, it was already being spoken of as a book with appeal for children and adults alike. (*Nya Pressen* recommended the book to a 'multiplicity of ages'.) The publishers also encouraged this line. The blurb on the back cover claimed that the author was so versatile as a storyteller that she was capable of entertaining 'full-grown children as well as younger ones'. This is of course a publisher's cliché, but comments of this kind would follow Tove Jansson as a writer. From the beginning people were aware of this double quality, and from the beginning they talked of both children and adults as potential readers.

But there were limits. The power of Tove's imagination made a strong impression on all the reviewers, but it is interesting that the apocalyptic subject matter excited no reaction at all. The comet was seen as an adventure and even dismissed as 'miraculous' in one headline. In other words, *Comet in Moominland* was published as a book for children and was most often seen as just that (even if it did also have the power to 'entertain' adults). Tove herself saw the matter differently. In the blurb she first planned for the back cover the comet itself took the leading role as a matter of course: implacable, burning red-hot and with a tail of fire. She left any interpretation of the unprecedented events to the reader.

> Far out in space the comet started out, burning and alone, followed by a tail of fire. It relentlessly approached the valley where Moomintroll lived with his father and mother. In the observatory in the Lonely Mountains they estimated that it would hit the earth on the seventh of October at 8.42. This is a book about the exciting time before the catastrophe, days when the sky became ever redder over Moomintroll, the little animal Sniff, Snufkin, the two Snorks, sister and brother, and the Hemulen. Extraordinary things happened to them on their dangerous journey, things that were terrible and yet at the same time fun, as they often are when we are little. Worst of all were perhaps the octopus on the dried-up seabed and Moomintroll's struggle with the poisonous Angostura bush. Or perhaps the lizard defending the garnets. And the most fun was perhaps the pearl-fishery and the great party, but you must decide that for yourself when you have read the book and know how everything went.

The Moomin books were published simultaneously in Finland and Sweden, except *Comet* and *The Hobgoblin's Hat*, which both came out a year later in Sweden, where *Comet* was published by Sörlins Publishers in Norrköping (Hasselgren was out of the picture) under licence from Söderströms. As had been the case with *The Moomins and the Great Flood*, the formal decision to publish was taken extremely late. The production of the book had already been completed when the directors at Söderströms officially decided at a meeting on 2nd December 1946: 'Decision to publish the children's book *Comet in Moominland* by Tove Jansson. Royalty 15% for Finland edition. In Sweden Karl Sörlins Publishers will take 3,000 copies at 55 öre per copy.'

The cover illustrations for the Moomin books were partly altered for Sweden. This applied particularly to the early books but there were changes later too. *The Great Flood* was identical in both countries, but a new cover was designed for *Comet*. The picture for Finland shows the dried-up seabed, the great comet in the sky and the adventurers on their high stilts as small silhouettes. This emphasises the threat to Moomintroll's beloved earth and skies: it is the changed landscape that dominates the picture. The cover for Sweden places the individual in the centre of a crowd of refugees with several of the principal characters, Moomintroll, the Snork maiden and Snufkin, in the foreground. This emphasises evacuation, as if from a war. The comet story also uses the word '*landsflyttning*', implying the removal of population from town to countryside, a word scarcely in use today. On their way home to Moominvalley the adventurers meet great crowds of refugees. All who can are leaving: 'They met masses of refugees on the road. Most of them were walking, but some were driving carts or wagons and some had taken their whole home with them. They were all casting frightened glances at the sky, and hardly any of them were ready to stand and talk.'

This description hints at the realities of war. It was in similar words that Ragnar Ölander remembered the evacuation of Helsinki in 1939, a compact stream of fugitives heading northwards: 'There were old and young, mothers carrying small children in their arms or pushing them in prams. There were old people moving with slow, tired steps and lively youngsters. Some had their belongings piled on handcarts and others were carrying suitcases or bags.'

There can be no doubt at all that *Comet in Moominland* was a book written in the shadow of war.

CHAPTER 8

Moomin Passion

'You see, you must always have something to dream about.'

Letter to Eva Konikoff, 14th August 1946

I long to unfold a 'happy new forcefulness in colour', wrote Tove
to Atos on December 1947. He was in Warsaw at the time, she in
Helsinki. She described herself as 'charged with a forceful new
means of expression', watching ideas grow 'like trees through
him'. Forcefulness was the new keyword, for painting, colour, expression, for everything that was coming back after the war. Things
had to be bigger and simpler than before. Ideas were growing like
trees for Tove too. She was changing. 'Painting and thinking. Perhaps I'm still busy catching up with myself so as to be able to sur-
pass myself. Perhaps I'm out on altogether new paths and won't
even know when I've passed beyond the old boundaries.'

She now made a fair copy of *The Hobgoblin's Hat*, which she
had been working at on and off for almost a year. She described
herself as a 'proud Moomin scribbler', perhaps en route to
America and Eva. The manuscript was with her new publisher:
'The next Moomin has been delivered to Schildts; Warburton
has read it through and according to Ham he seems positive.'
During the autumn Tove had also started on her first strip series,
'Moomintroll and the Destruction of the Earth', for Atos's newly
founded *Ny Tid* (*New Time*). It ran as a weekly serial in the
children's corner of the paper from October 1947 to April 1948.
Moomin's fame was growing and the books already had devoted

A previously unknown MS page for The Hobgoblin's Hat (Finn Family Moomintroll), *in which Thingumy and Bob make their entrance.*

fans. According to Tove: 'Yesterday a tiny little lady came to me and said she was circulating a publicity list in a school: 'Why was there no new Moomin coming out?' So I went to see Söderströms. I hope this made an impression on Appel [chief publisher Bertel Appelberg], it did on me!'

Writing had become part of Tove's identity, and Moomintroll was now living alongside the artist in her. As we have seen, he was taking up so much room that before her second solo show in autumn 1946 she had to make an effort to control her urge to write. She forced herself to hide the manuscript: 'now I must paint, just paint', she promised her diary on 6th October. She got together a collection of pictures for the 'Young Artists' exhibition and in no time at all it was time for the vernissage at the Bäcksbacka gallery on the 19th. The exhibition swarmed with visitors and she recorded happily that she had sold two small canvases and one drawing. The party in the studio went on till nearly six in the morning, very much in the manner of her famous house-warming a couple of years earlier, with dancing, 'glorious dancing'. 'All went well,' she wrote, apart from the fact that Maya Vanni fainted and 'that skunk Lilja disturbed us again'.

There was much to celebrate after the vernissage: 'The recapture of the tower' (she had been under notice to leave), 'the expulsion of my neighbours, the inauguration of my sky-bed' (she had found a frame for it), 'and selling my pictures. The exhibition went well.' It had been a success, but the critics were getting more severe. Sigrid Schauman let it be known that her notice contained 'grave criticisms', though these took into account her respect for the artist's individual character. She drew attention to worked surfaces and spoke of a neglect of form studies, a criticism which Tove instantly dismissed as 'idiotic'. Time to get back to writing the Moomins. She completed the cover for *Comet in Moominland*, which was in the process of being published, and within a few weeks she and Moomin had the studio to themselves. *The Hobgoblin's Hat* was going well and as early as January 1947 she was able to write to her new love, Vivica Bandler:

The Moomin book's finished. Thingumy and Bob have now run riot at the end and definitely overcome the Groke. They are inseparable and sleep together in a desk drawer. No one understands their language, but that doesn't matter so long as they themselves know what it's all about. ... Do you love me? Of dourse you coo! Sanks and the thame to you!

In the late autumn of 1946 she had met the trainee theatre director, Vivica Bandler, and they had fallen violently in love. 'Thingumy' and 'Bob' were codenames for Tove and Vivica, and the enemy of their love went under the name of the Groke. 'After a long break I've started a new chapter in Moomin 3. It's about Thingumy and Bob. And the Groke. And I've been making good progress with this year's Moomin 2', wrote Tove to Vivica during work on *The Hobgoblin's Hat*. The Moomin story was well able to put love into words. She was writing about affinity and close identification between two creatures who have a language of their own and wander into Moominvalley one August day bringing a mysterious suitcase. In her notes Tove described their symbiosis (in the same words as she used in her letter to Vivica): 'Thingumy and Bob have defeated the Groke, they are inseparable and sleep together in a desk drawer No one understands their language, but that's all right so long as they themselves know what it's all about.'

This description was carefully tested and transferred almost word for word into the book. Love had to have a language of its own that others could not understand. 'We have to be careful,' urged Vivica in her letters to Tove. Censorship was still active and homosexuality was illegal (the law was not changed till 1971). Both were also committed elsewhere. Vivica was married to Kurt Bandler while Tove had Atos, and with time more complications with partners developed. But it was difficult for Tove to hide her new bliss. 'I'm full of happiness – that's the truth – but it breaks me up to be so lonely,' she wrote to Vivica.

Falling in love with a woman was shattering and boundlessly different. This new love evoked new colours, thoughts, ideas and feelings that came to have enormous importance for her both as an artist and as a human being. It was heart and mind together. 'I'm in love with your mind too,' wrote Vivica. This was how Tove had earlier described falling in love with Atos. The changed roles had great significance for her self-esteem. 'Now I'm the sun shining,' wrote Tove happily. But after three hot weeks of passion, Vivica went abroad. Their intense correspondence tells a convoluted and passionate story of longing and expectation

Tove and Vivica Bandler on Bredskär.

and, gradually, disappointment. 'It's as though you have made me new,' wrote Tove, aware she had been transformed: 'How can I explain how everything has changed since I met you! Every tone is more vivid, every colour cleaner, all my perceptions are sharper – my happiness is stronger, my despair more powerful.' Tove's letters were like literary narratives as she surrendered to the yearnings of love, with its tension between her new happiness and the constant reality of external control. Vivica's letters were full of declarations of love, but shorter, more restrained. Between them germinated the 'boldness of happy self-esteem', as they constantly urged each other on in their letters. But their infatuation was feeding off its practical impossibility.

They talked of meeting in Paris but this remained only a dream. When Vivica came home there were others in the picture and Tove was hurled into a maelstrom of feeling. Her letters tell of a confusion of relationships, a love-carousel that turned spring and early summer into an emotional hell for her. Her beloved Vivica had made her feel proud and natural, and she had ignored anguish and thrown her complexes overboard, but the cost was too great. By midsummer 1947 she was writing to Eva: 'Before the war I used to think the purpose of life was to act as justly as possible; after the war I thought the purpose of life was to be as happy as possible. Perhaps one should just work and try to live as worthily as one can.'

All that spring she was working on two great murals in the cellar of Helsinki Town Hall. She painted Vivica, herself and Moomin into one of them. With this mural she was making a statement, publishing a new portrait of herself. New figures began appearing in her pictures for *Garm*, too, together with large and small Moomin characters, including a Thingumy and a Bob. She was growing closer to her characters now, deepening her perspective and penetrating further into her fictive world. *The Hobgoblin's Hat*, published in autumn 1948, would be her first literary success, both in the Nordic countries and further afield (it became *Finn Family Moomintroll* in Britain).

Moomin Summer

The Hobgoblin's Hat is the summer book of the Moomin world. It presents Moominvalley as an epic setting. The charged August days when Mamma and the Moomintroll saved Moominpappa from the flood and found their way to the Valley was how *The Moomins and the Great Flood* started, followed by the dramatic October weeks when the apocalypse threw its red shadow over the Valley. *The Hobgoblin's Hat* begins with a prologue set sometime in November, when the family hibernates. Snow falls and time stands still, but in Chapter 1 a cuckoo flies through the Valley and wakes it to life again.

In *The Hobgoblin's Hat* the writer clears the stage both for herself and for her readers. In Tove's studio I found a detailed sketch for the map that comes at the beginning of the book, in which she fixes the story's time and place. In the middle is the tower-shaped Moomin house with its veranda, and round it the Muskrat's hammock, the tobacco patch, lilac and jasmine bushes,

The Hemulen with Thingumy and Bob. From Finn Family Moomintroll.

the woodshed and a flowerbed with crocus, lily and hyacinth. By the river is Snufkin's tent and beyond that the Lonely Mountains, while nearer the sea lie the forest, the mountain with the Hobgoblin's hat, the cave and the landing stage; even the cuckooing cuckoo is marked. Beyond the coast is the Hattifatteners' island. The Moomin house is shown in cross-section, complete with room plans and furnishings: fireplace, tiled stove, cupboards, desk with mirror, sofa, and so on. One room had been reserved for 'the Hemulens aunt', though she disappeared from the story while it was being written, only to return in the next book.

The flood of ideas rushed as strongly as the river in springtime in Moominvalley. The result was such a long manuscript about the Moomin summer that the publishers stipulated that two chapters should be cut out. On her way to Italy in April 1948 Tove wrote to Eva about this new Moomin story she had just finished: '*The Hobgoblin's Hat* is coming out from Schildts at Christmas with 40 plain black-and-white illustrations and no tinted drawings. A new, smaller format. I had to cut two chapters so it would be cheaper to publish. Really hectic getting it finished before travelling.'

In *The Hobgoblin's Hat* Tove Jansson the writer enlarged her Moomin world, sharpened her aesthetic, honed her vocabulary and anchored the codes of her fictive world to a firm foundation. She worked on the personalities of her characters, refining their characteristics and use of language. Moomintroll is characterised in a sketch with the words 'Goodness gracious me! That's what Mamma said. Pee-Hoo!'; Sniff has his favourite expression: 'Evil or lack of judgement. Good Lord!'; the Snork uses characteristic phrases like 'Absolutely! Strict order. Yes, but!'; Moominpappa's exclamation is 'Bless my tail.' The Hobgoblin has 'white gloves' and Snufkin 'no possessions'. As for the Moomins as a biological species, they were white with 'noses' that could cause tactless folk to liken them to hippopotamuses, and small friendly eyes, a long tail and round attentive ears. Tove summed up: 'He's really not a troll at all, or an animal – he's a being.' This third book saw the foundation of Moomintroll traditions and customs like hibernation and using rope ladders, and Tove noted down expressions and turns of phrase typical of Moomin language, such as 'With this I baptise you for time and this' – a 'Moomin expression' used at baptism.

One new feature was the introduction of narrative chapter titles in the style of novels from earlier times, such as Swift's *Gulliver's Travels* and Cervantes's *Don Quixote*. The Moomin version summarises the chapter in short sentences, often linked by a repeated 'In which' or 'Which is' to connect unexpected turns of thought. Apparently separate events are linked together in a chain, as in the title of the last chapter: 'Which is very long and describes Snufkin's departure and how the Contents of the mysterious suitcase were revealed; also how Moominmamma found her handbag and arranged a party to celebrate it, and finally how the Hobgoblin arrived in the Valley of the Moomins.' In the earlier books the chapters were divided only by ornamental capitals and lack titles.

A new illustrative technique is also introduced. *The Great Flood* and *Comet in Moominland* contain a number of tinted pictures, but this time Tove restricted herself to pen and Indian ink. A step forward, she reported to Eva during spring 1948: 'The illustrations for my Moomin book are finished, 44 pictures. They are better than the ones in "Comet" – nothing tinted, only black and white. Using a new technique. What fun it'll be to send you the book next winter!' Only black and white. She stuck to this technique throughout her Moomin books, though working with varying emphasis, nuances and contrasts between the black and the white. The number of pictures eventually stopped at forty, inclusive of the cover for the first edition.

With *The Hobgoblin's Hat* the atmosphere changed and apocalyptic threats to life were removed from the scene. In the newborn universe of Moominvalley one exists as a Moomin,

Moominpappa tries on the Hobgoblin's hat.

intensely, sensually, in body and mind, from one's ears to the tuft at the end of one's tail, as if dropped into the middle of a sparkling intoxication with life. Bathing at dawn in June in the breakers off the Hattifatteners' island is enough to make anyone long to be a Moomin: 'O, to be a newly-woken Moomintroll dancing in the glass-green waves while the sun is rising.' For the Moominvalley community, transformation is one of the most basic principles of life. With the Hobgoblin's hat, initially used as a wastepaper basket, the principle is developed to the utmost in a succession of 'magic and peculiar events'. The hat produces a cloud of eggshell, a jungle of cryptogams turns river water into fruit juice and transforms Moomintroll into a 'ghost-animal'. In the crowded house in Moominvalley everyone does what they like and seldom worries about the morrow: 'Of course upsetting things could sometimes happen, but no one ever had a boring time. (And that was a great advantage.)' In Snufkin's newly winged words: 'Life isn't peaceful.'

Love of life leavens *The Hobgoblin's Hat*, containing melancholy, unease and longing too. Change is inevitable, transformation part of life. The long final chapter begins on a note of poetic melancholy:

> It was the end of August. The time when owls hoot at night and flurries of bats swoop noiselessly over the garden. Moomin Wood was full of glow worms, and the sea was disturbed. There was expectation and a certain sadness in the air, and the harvest

moon came up huge and yellow. Moomintroll had always liked those last weeks of summer most, but he didn't really know why.

The wind and the sea had changed their tone; there was a new feeling in the air; the trees stood waiting.

The Moomin summer carries everything within itself. When the end of August nears Snufkin moves south, and after the great party cool autumn moves into the valley, 'for how else can spring come back again?' With these words Moomin summer takes its leave.

The Golden Butterfly

For *The Hobgoblin's Hat* the painter Tove Jansson took up her palette, spread out her colours and let them shine through the story. The butterfly that announces the Moomin summer is not yellow (which would mean a 'happy summer') but golden. It stands for a happy new power that revels in warmth and colour, in everything that Tove was sick with longing for during the war.

She had always been fascinated by colour, ever since as a fledgeling artist she had avoided fashionable combinations of yellowish brown and pinkish grey – 'modern, for heaven's sake!' – and had looked for contrasting images in 'natural' blue in the young artists in Paris who were on a collision course with the brown ideal of Beaux-Arts. 'There are so many lovely words,' exclaimed Tove in notes she made at the Ateneum in 1935. 'Naples blue, burnt sienna, cobalt, ultramarine, March violet. Use them! They won't turn to ashes in your mouth!' Colour was expression *and* material, idea and material at the same time, and it demanded careful planning. Preparing to work on her murals for the Town Hall cellar, she made a thorough study of fresco technique and made notes on 'unusable' and 'virtually reliable' colours. She had to learn these things in any case, but for Jansson the colourist the heavily laden significance of colours was a matter of life and death.

She thought in colours, the critics wrote, and colour treatment was said to be her most important means of expression. They discussed her awareness of the expressive possibilities of painting and the art of warm and cold colours, of balancing one colour against another, of seeing 'things in colours' and working for 'colour agreement'. Sinikka Kallio-Visapää, writing in *Panorama* in 1945, after the 'Young Artists'exhibition at Konsthallen, was the most interesting of this chorus of colour-conscious reviewers. She identified an important development. 'Tove Jansson's predilection for ash-grey had shackled her natural talent for colour,' she wrote, commenting that elegance had now been replaced by a 'cultivated richness of colour'. In the artist's still-lifes a 'refined' use of colour had been preferred to the use of colour as an end in itself, and one of these (the most beautiful, in Kallio's view) was built up from 'white, cowslip-yellow, ultramarine, bottle-brown and deep green'. In another example she fastened on 'the velvet-heavy, dark and juicy colours of several flowers in the foreground – against a rain-grey background'.

Tove's use of colour language in the three first Moomin books developed in the same way. The flood in *The Moomins and the Great Flood* is melancholy grey and the forest full of shadows and darkness; in *Comet in Moominland* the landscape is dominated by grey, white, black and the red of the comet. But in her transformation book the artist in her let the whole scale go. The flowers on the Hattifatteners'secret island are quite different from the flowers in Moominvalley: 'Heavy silver-white clusters that looked as if they were made of glass, partite wonder-flowers in twilight shades and crimson-black chalices that looked like the crowns of kings.' The Moomin summer is irradiated by the shifting of colours and light; it is a time when sea and skies combine in a 'shimmering pale blue surface' in the June night, when the gardens are 'gaudy as an engagement bouquet' in the 'deep colours' of late summer, and the Hattifatteners' island lies as if on fire in the sunset while the swell is 'coloured' in gold and green fading to blue and violet. Impression and experience, power and creation, can all be brought together in colour. It became a keyword in her later essays on the prerequisites of writing, in which a fairy tale might be described as 'a gaudy bouquet of many colours' and the world of a child as 'a landscape with strong colours'.

The story the 'Moomin scribbler' delivered to Holger Schildts Publishers is full of pleasure and love, loss and sadness, warmth and colour, everything that can be found in the Nordic summer. When Thingumy and Bob come to the Valley, the cold grey

Groke follows them. The result is a conflict between warmth and colour, a struggle that is really about love.

The Magic of Love

The relationship between beauty and ownership is one of the book's themes, and magical transformation is another, but more important than anything else is the theme of love. The great symbol is the King's Ruby, hidden in Thingumy and Bob's suitcase. The Groke is after it, as is the Hobgoblin who makes his entry in the last chapter. There is an obsession with precious stones in the Moomin stories. Garnets sparkle, opals glisten like moonlight and the eye of the King's Ruby glitters out into space from the August darkness. It is 'as big as a panther's head, glowing like the sunset, like living fire and glistening water', a ruby compounded from various colours: 'At first it was quite pale, and then suddenly a pink glow would flow over it like the sunrise on a snow-capped mountain – and then again crimson flames shot out of its heart and it seemed like a great black tulip with stamens of fire.'

Precious stones evoke whatever is most sublime for the observer: the most beautiful, boldest and finest in thought or experience. Pleasure and colour. The King's Ruby is a metaphor for the elements, the beautiful and the wild, a work of art whose meaning is different for different viewers. But above all it is a picture of love, arousing longing, desire and delight in a Hobgoblin, a Groke, or a Thingumy and Bob. The right to own the ruby is the key point in the court case conducted in the Moomin garden one beautiful summer day. A complication is that, while the suitcase belongs to Thingumy and Bob, its secret 'Contents' are the Groke's. The problem seems solved, until the Hemulen intervenes:

> 'It's not clear at all!' cried the Hemulen boldly. 'The question is not who is the *owner* of the Contents, but who has the greatest *right* to the Contents. The right thing in the right place. You saw the Groke, everybody? Now, I ask you, did she look as if she had a right to the Contents?'

> 'That's true enough,' said Sniff in surprise. 'Clever of you, Hemul. But on the other hand, think how lonely the Groke is because

nobody likes her and she hates everybody. The Contents is perhaps the only thing she has. Would you now take that away from her too – lonely and rejected in the night?' Sniff became more and more affected and his voice trembled. 'Cheated out of her only possession by Thingumy and Bob ...'

What the Contents are is not revealed, only what they represent to the interested parties, at which point the court case is transformed into a lesson in ethics. For the Groke the Contents are the most valuable thing, for Thingumy and Bob they are the most beautiful and the fact that in effect they pinched the Contents from the Groke becomes meaningless. ('They were born like that and can't help it.') One knows from the start that the Groke is in the right. Everything in its right place, says Snork. But before the judge (Snork, of course) is able to deliver judgement, Moominmamma solves the problem. 'The Contents' are exchanged for the Hobgoblin's Hat, an agreement that confirms the philosophy of the justice of there being a right place for everything. Thingumy and Bob keep the suitcase with its Contents (the King's Ruby), while the Hobgoblin's Hat goes to the Groke. That is to say, only those who are worthy of the Contents (love) can own them. The proceedings do not end so uncompromisingly. When Mamma puts a couple of cherries into the hat to demonstrate its magic powers, they are transformed into small rubies. The Groke's longing too is a matter of love, warmth and colour.

When Thingumy and Bob unlock the suitcase they disclose the luminosity of love to the world. It has no price. 'Bind your own mizness!' turns out to be their tough answer to the Hobgoblin's proposals, and his offer to exchange it for 'two diamond mountains and a valleyful of mixed precious stones' is answered with a vigorous 'No!' Instead they tell him their desire and conjure up a ruby similar to their own. This way they fulfil his greatest longing.

The most important thing of all is for them to open their suitcase and show its Contents to Moominvalley. The light from the ruby (and from love) is so strong that it reaches far out into the universe. Even the moon loses its brilliance. Love no longer needs to be hidden inside a suitcase. And the Groke can no longer threaten it.

The Publisher's Smile

Tove remained faithful to the publishers Holger Schildts for the rest of her career. As before, she had first offered her new manuscript to Söderströms, but *Comet in Moominland* had not sold well, only 246 copies. At New Year 1948 there were still 2,443 in the warehouse. Söderströms did not want to invest in more Moomin books. So Tove took her manuscript to the head of Schildts, Thure Svedlin, who read it and passed it to his young English editor, Thomas Warburton. Warburton was new with the firm, as he recalls in a recent memoir, and he doesn't now remember all the ins and outs with the manuscript. But he does remember the expression on Svedlin's face when he handed it to his editor. Svedlin was a man who seldom smiled, but 'when he did his smile was strikingly beautiful', and he smiled when he handed Warburton the manuscript of *The Hobgoblin's Hat*.

The Hobgoblin's Hat contains seven chapters plus an 'Introduction', and the action runs from early spring to late August. But there were two more chapters in the manuscript Tove delivered to Schildts. The 'odd' proportions of the book had been a stumbling block with Söderströms. The young Irmelin Sandman Lilius, who with her sister Heddi had become friends with Tove, remembers that a description of a dam structure was cut, also an excerpt in which Moomintroll, Snufkin and Sniff jump on icefloes, and an episode with the Hemulen's aunt. The aunt survived for a long time in the manuscript – as did several other rejected passages – but she was eventually shelved till the next book.

The original manuscript is lost, but during research for this book I found in Tove's studio several previously unknown manuscript pages and sketches. A couple of these relate to the sections cut. They concern the damming of the brook (shrunk to one sentence in the published version) and how Moomintroll and Sniff carve out a great block of ice to enable the water to flow freely. 'The brook gave a leap of joy – then it was free, and threw itself forward and roared on in triumph. Moomintroll and Sniff danced a war-dance, each on his own bank. "Down with winter!" screamed Sniff above the roar of the water.' After which they start fighting because Sniff tells Moomintroll he's fat: 'Actually, the worst thing you can say to a Moomintroll is to tell him he's

The piano crashes down the attic steps. Illustration for the omitted section of Finn Family Moomintroll.

fat. He *is* in fact quite fat. So sparks flashed in Moomintroll's eyes and he threw himself on Sniff with a hiss.' The battle is fierce: 'Moomintroll was on top to begin with, but then Sniff got in a good bite on his nose' (Tove didn't write 'snout'). 'They rolled over and over in the wet moss snarling and yelling, till the ground suddenly gave way under them and they sank up to their ears into a snowdrift.' They come together again and climb to the top of the hill (to build a cairn, just as in the published book) and find a tall black hat. Snufkin is not yet in the picture. In the published version the three make an expedition together to the top of the hill to build their cairn, find the hat and return to the house to have coffee, while the battle between Sniff and Moomintroll is expanded into a struggle between Moomintroll (transformed into a ghost-animal) and the others.

Tove did not tell Eva what the cut sections were about, but Irmelin Sandman Lilius remembers a 'wonderful chapter' describing Moominmamma spring-cleaning. Furniture was moved out of the way and rubbish was dumped in the Hobgoblin's hat. Irmelin has written: 'Fog rose from the Hat, filling the house and the whole valley, so that when it was time to bring the furniture in again, the family could not see to find the right places for it. They couldn't find the living room at all but struggled together to get the little piano halfway up the attic stairs until it tumbled down again.' One of the four pictures cut shows the family and the piano falling down the stairs. In the finished book the spring-cleaning has been reduced to an anxious reassembling of possessions which have been spread about the place (including the Hemulen's cryptograms), resulting in a jungle growing over the entire house. The cuts were made at a late stage, Tove told Eva, but traces survive in the final text. For instance, the Snork maiden thinks of both floe-jumping and damming when she wants to impress Moomintroll.

With this manuscript that made its publisher smile the Moomin world became an accepted concept. Tove came to be known as a visual artist for children who could write. These were artistic children's books. Solveig von Schoultz, in a comprehensive survey of children's books for Christmas 1948, devoted by far the greatest space to *The Hobgoblin's Hat*. She was impressed by the way the writer encouraged the reader to take part in the narration. The subtlety is that nothing is explained: 'a Bob is self-evidently a Bob and is accepted as a Bob: the reader is allowed to take part in the creative process. Pictures and text belong organically together and have the same qualities; one can't talk about illustrations in the normal sense, but rather of an artist with two native languages.' This was a far-sighted analysis. It is precisely as a double artist in words and pictures that Tove makes room for the reader and when she came to put her theories of writing for children into words it was exactly this combination that she focused on. In places where the 'self-centred writer' skips over something so that it will not disturb his text, the illustrator can fill the gap. The illustrator can leave out pictures that might disturb the child's imagination, but sometimes 'lines and surfaces can say more than words' (Tove in *Nya Argus*, 1966). The reader is invited into a world that can be developed in several dimensions.

The new book brought a change of publisher in Sweden too. Schildts worked there with Hugo Gebers, who brought out the new Moomin book. According to Gebers, the reason *The Hobgoblin's Hat* didn't appear in Sweden until autumn 1949 was confusion caused by the bookbinders, but in fact it was not much delayed. When it did come out Gebers took a realistic attitude and invited the children's book reviewers to pay it special attention. 'We attach great importance to it, and don't want it to drown in the flood of Christmas books,' wrote chief publisher Nils Wikström, planning to increase the print run later. By this time Tove was already flying the flag for her next Moomin book, *Muminpappas bravader* (*The Exploits of Moominpappa*), and her first Moomin play which was due to have its first performance at Christmas 1949.

In Sweden she was introduced as a 'young Finland-Swedish storyteller and painter from a richly artistic background', and as one of 'the most promising of Finland's young artists', known to the public for 'her original books from the world of the Moomintroll'. For Tove, what mattered was to be presented first and foremost as a visual artist. The edition for Sweden had a different cover illustration, on the same principle as *Comet in Moominland*. The version for Sweden shows Moominpappa wearing the Hobgoblin's hat in front of a mirror. The version for Finland has Moomintroll himself in the centre.

Nils Wikström must have been very satisfied with the book's reception. All the most important children's book reviewers wrote about it – Eva von Zweigbergk in *Dagens Nyheter*, Greta Bolin in *Svenska Dagbladet*, Jeanna Oterdahl in *Göteborgs Handels och Sjöfartstidning*, Lennart Hellsing in *Aftonbladet* – and they all reacted in much the same way. Von Zweigbergk talked of the 'stamp of artistic originality', Bolin of 'artistic touch', Hellsing of 'a trail-blazing book of international class' (though he didn't like a touch of 'poetic overcolouring').

Happiest of all was Jeanna Oterdahl, who found it 'unusually great fun' and praised its language for showing genuine artistry. The publishers prepared a special advertisement with Tove's portrait, collected the

The botanising Hemulen is approached by menacing Hattifatteners. From Finn Family Moomintroll.

reviews and reported the encouraging opinions of the critics. But the highly praised trail-blazing author herself had to wait before she could read their appreciative comments: 'At the end of the year when we no longer need the reviews for advertising purposes we'll send the originals over to you so you can enjoy them too,' Wikström told Tove.

The Hobgoblin's Hat came out in English in 1950 as *Finn*

Family Moomintroll; a literal translation would not have helped introduce Moomintroll to a new audience. There was a network of friends behind this debut on the overseas market. In the summer of 1949 Tove had rented out her studio to Kenneth Green, an English artist in Helsinki, to paint portraits. When she returned from her island to the studio he was quite simply still there, and she hadn't the heart to throw him out. For a time they camped in the studio together. She sent an English translation of the book to London to Ernest Benn, who had earlier published a children's book of Green's. In spring 1950 Tove discussed publication in Britain and the USA with Benn's director, K.E. Hughes. She stated her terms frankly and they were promptly accepted: a royalty of 10 per cent on the first 3000 copies sold, then 12½ per cent between 3001 and 5000 copies sold and 15 per cent for any sales beyond that for editions sold in Britain.

The initial translator had been Elizabeth Portch, a teacher working for the Finnish-British Society of Helsinki; she had wanted to practise her Swedish on a literary text. But *Finn Family Moomintroll*, being full of Moominis terminology, was unusually difficult to translate, so the English text was checked and edited by Margaret Washbourn (wife of the British Council representative in Helsinki). This gave Tove two versions with different characteristics: 'Margaret's version was more fluent but also more commonplace,' while Liz's, though a bit awkward and topsy-turvy, was more 'personal'. Together with Lasse she went through the text and met the translators but there were too many cooks involved in this English broth, as she told Eva in February 1950. In consequence there were a number of oddities. Perhaps it would have been better if Thomas Warburton himself had done the job in the first place, but Tove did not like to go back on her word to the others. One typical adjustment to the text has survived successive English editions and is still there today. In the Swedish edition the Muskrat goes out to pee, but in English it is to look at the stars.

Benn's edition prepared the way for the international circulation of Moomintroll and for the forthcoming Moomin strip series. Tove had long had plans for launching the Moomins abroad. She had already discussed possible opportunities for the Moomin stories in the USA with Eva after the first book was published, and was fully aware of the commercial strength of the Moomin characters. During the 1940s she wrote four Moomin books, one strip series and one theatre adaptation. Atos was researching possible opportunities for the first strip series to be launched in overseas newspapers, perhaps in the USA. It could be a wonderful opportunity for Tove to go there and meet Eva, whom she was missing badly.

> Atos has great plans for the Moomin strip, even if he is always so wildly optimistic. He's in the middle of trying to get a Swedish newspaper to take it – and I think he'll succeed. He wants to place it in America or England too. Sometimes he really does make his utopias come true, so there's a chance, Eva. Just think, we might both come over. I keep that plan permanently in view, because I want to see you again. I need you and long for you, and I'll do anything I can to give you a little happiness.

Thingumy al Fresco

'What a painting I could do of you,' wrote Tove to Vivica. In her notes she continued to write constantly of work and love. 'We'll find all the most important things, work, love and play. All year long, and every year,' she wrote in December 1946. The Moomin book, Thingumy and Bob, and her murals, were all things they shared. Vivica for her part was 'preparing' a little Tove Jansson exhibition in Denmark. When Tove wasn't painting she was able to hesitate between either 'finishing the Moomin chapter about Thingumy and Bob or drawing a map of the house they're going to have on Kummelskär island,' as she put it in the first days of January 1947. She saw their future in terms of work. 'Writing and drawing. Signed: Thingumy and Bob. On Kummelskär and Saaris [the Bandler family's summer home]. How well the work of each fits the other,' she wrote in 1947.

Just after New Year 1947, Tove was asked to paint murals in Helsinki Town Hall. The commission had come from Vivica's father, District Director Erik von Frenckell. She wrote exhaustive notes on the work: planning, composition, themes, colours and execution, in letters to both Vivica and Eva. She measured the surfaces (5 m x 3.13 m) and decided to cover them completely. 'For the present it all seems like a hopelessly tangled spider's web. All I know is that one picture could show a society reception on a balcony overlooking the chestnut trees in the street (opportunity for long lines and colourful clothes) and the other a country breakfast scene,' she told Vivica on 6th January.

Painting a fresco was a new experience. Sam Vanni came to have a look and thought she was 'mad' to try to finish two murals in one spring. This 'wasn't the greatest encouragement', wrote Tove, but Sam's views no longer mattered. She had a new self-confidence, not vulnerable to male commentators, and her sketches and choice of colours were immediately approved by both the architect and the man who had given her the commission. But it was essential that Vivica should follow her ideas, thoughts and alterations, and Tove 'talked' (i.e. wrote) to her constantly. Propping her sketches against the walls, she wrote in detail to 'My darling Bob' about her new composition:

'The Breakfast' has become simply 'Joy of Life'. The girl in the tree leans down to kiss the boy who has become younger and shyer. He's no longer a 'he-man' strong enough to lift her up; his raised arms express tenderness rather than power. But the fiddler is bolder, and the dismal breakfast table has had to make way for a buxom woman with a bosom full of garlands who, severely foreshortened, is stretching her arms straight out to the centre, towards a youth in the background who is throwing himself forward towards her. Among the branches and flowers water and bathing bodies can be glimpsed. Both compositions now have have eleven figures. 'The party' has been going on so long by now that those taking part have lost their stiffness and are kissing each other on the cheek instead of the hand and are gesturing more freely and are dancing at the very least the polka. Now I'm busy with two details in natural size, the cartoons are 1m. x 75.

She painted herself and friends into the pictures. One was Illo (Camillo von Walzel), the model for Vivica's dance partner; another her fellow artist, Unto Virtanen. 'Bob, I want you as a model for the lady in the yellow dress. I won't do her face till you come. Bob full-size on the wall of the Town Hall!' These paintings were undoubtedly part of the change in Tove. Her new love had transformed both her life and her work. 'I feel as if I'm suddenly a calmer and happier person. My work has become richer and my ambitions are no longer pursuing me so ruthlessly. Even my bitterness towards Faffan has entirely disappeared, and I'm getting over my nervous obsession that "everyone's hounding me". It's as if you have created me anew.'

She wrote of the growth in her of a 'new boldness and self-confidence', 'a wonder she hardly dared believe in'. As she did with Eva, she used her letters to Vivica as a route to intimacy. 'It's childish to write you a letter a day just to tell you how fond I am of you,' she wrote just before Christmas 1946, but 'it's my way of talking to you. While I'm writing I have you here.' Writing gave her access to emotion, to belonging together, to everything the twins Thingumy and Bob stand for in *Finn Family Moomintroll*. One of her most expressive letters presents in word and picture a Moomintroll working at his art, longing passionately for his 'Sweet Bob'. She called it 'A Letter from Moomintroll' (3rd February 1947). Now it was 'Moom' painting frescoes, planning her working time and promising new paintings. It's 'Moom' too who is going to read about Thingumy and Bob on the radio and 'hopes that Bob is as deeply in love as Thingumy is'.

The frescoes were a big job, two murals in six months. She started the work with Niilo Suihko, who had studied in Italy. But soon there was endless 'bother over materials and models', so she did the second fresco on her own. 'I work best by myself,' she told Eva, and this applied to all her artistic work. She read up about technique and wrote page after page on method and procedure in her notebooks as a preparation for painting everything directly onto the wall. This was bold, but among other things she was able to rely on the help of the Ateneum's specialist teacher on materials, Johannes Gebhard. 'This is a once in a lifetime chance for you to create a real fresco,' said Gebhard, and it was not an opportunity she was prepared to miss. A great deal depended on it. To Vivica she wrote: 'These frescoes could be the most important work I've ever done; I must succeed with them. I've discovered people are angry I got the commission without doing a painting first, but they aren't making open trouble yet. I have to show them I *can* paint a fresco. And to do that I need time, and peace and quiet.' Now work had to come before love. 'Can you wait for me?' she asked, signing herself 'Thingumy al

'What a painting I could make of you': the fresco depicting Vivica dancing (with dark hair and white gown), 1947.

Fresco'. She saw the future as a happy springtime of work and love: 'You shall be the model for the woman with blue hair who is dancing in the middle of the ball on the balcony. You shall meet my friends. You shall come with me to Kummelskär in the new sailing boat and show me Saaris just as it is without fog and grey weather.'

When Tove painted Vivica and herself into the fresco, she did what Thingumy and Bob do in *Finn Family Moomintroll*: she opened her suitcase and displayed her love to the world. Her relationship with Vivica was to be short but heart-rending. Vivica was away in France and impatient. Tove in Finland was vulnerable and loving and moving forward in a way that affected her work for both good and ill.

> I know the whole of my painting is going through a process of change just now, becoming stronger and more alive, and this is thanks to you. Lines and colours aren't enough if there is no expression and sap and intensity in them, even if it's the intensity of despair. If I can't immediately find the form for what I want to paint *now*, it doesn't matter. It'll come. So you mustn't be distressed, sweetheart, because of the frescoes. Both of them are you – and it's not at all certain that the best you have given me is in the first.

The two frescoes (see colour plate 16) were a task where she staked everything on a single card: her identity as an artist, the forms of her painting, responsibility, integrity and love. 'My yearning can paint any walls in the world so long as it keeps away from wounded vanity and exaggeration,' she wrote to Vivica. When the relationship ran into difficulties her feelings found additional expression in poems (she also called them ballads or songs): 'I'm writing poems to you that are perhaps quite strange and I'm drawing you – if not as a terribly good likeness! And in the hope I can manage a little music I've set myself confidently and optimistically to write a song in your honour!'

These poems are distributed among her waxcloth and other notebooks, beautifully inscribed by hand. As with her war poems, she had plans to publish a collection of them but 'Songs to my Beloved' (there are a couple of notebooks with different titles) never saw print. It was simply that they didn't seem fully formed, even if she did let friends read them. There was a place for Eva in them. Several poems belong with the fresco. The picture is transformed into words, as was love:

> Blue, blue I painted the sky
> sun-yellow your skirt
> lovely your smile.
> I painted you most sweetly
> I painted you on the wall,
> there you will stay
> just as you were
> when you loved me.

She called one of the poems 'Al Fresco' and wrote to Eva about it:

> Who is that who dances with smiling mouth
> and yellow roses on her foot?
> My darling dances with smiling mouth –
> smiling to me.
>
> Her dress was painted bright and fine
> as the sweet time was.
> But all around is dark carmine
> and the darkest colour I have.
>
> Morning shines with greater glory
> on rising from night
> And I am grateful night was
> there for me too.

The frescoes really were finished in six months. Tove had shown what she was capable of as an artist. Nothing could stop her, not Sam's disbelief, not the trouble with Niilo Suihko, not envious colleagues. She had been given an opportunity and she had taken it. 'They're finished now – a week ago – and I think it went well,' she wrote to Eva in the spring of 1947.

Windrose House

In the summer of 1947 Tove built a log cabin on Bredskär, the island in Pellinge archipelago that after many years of stress and disappointment had finally become hers and Lasse's. But it was Kummelskär, an island with two small beacons on it, which she had dreamed of since childhood. During the spring she hoped to get permission to build there, her boat was ready and she had obtained the necessary nails from Sweden. Timber was the problem. You couldn't buy it without a building licence. 'But that'll sort itself out. If you keep dreaming and negotiate ruthlessly enough it's *bound to* happen!' she assured Eva in March 1947.

But there were so many obstacles. All the local fishermen and farmers firmly said no to any building on Kummelskär. 'Because they fish for whitefish and salmon round there,' Tove's representative, Alex Karlsson, told her after a meeting. So there could be no question of granting a building lease. He went on: 'Perhaps a cabin or shack on such a large island would not get in their way,' he went on, 'but any serious boat traffic to and from the island could frighten the fish.' Tove then suggested two other islands, Tunnholmen and Äggskären, but these were also vetoed for fear of disturbing the seabirds. Alex Karlsson had yet another island to propose: Klovharun, which had a fine harbour for boats, though he was afraid the fishermen would also want this one protected. As it turned out, one day Tove would build her second log cabin on this very island. But now, in the spring of 1947 she had her eye on other islands. Gradually a new alternative entered the discussion, an entirely undisturbed island which had never even been any use for growing anything on. She was welcome to build there. So she signed a fifty-year lease for Bredskär on 26th June 1947.

There, while living in a tent and working on her next Moomin book, she built 'Windrose House' (a 'wind rose' is a diagram that shows the relative frequency of wind directions at a particular place). 'I'm building a house to entertain my friends and protect my solitude,' she told Eva. Thoughts of her lost love were thrust aside by thresholds, roof-trusses, joints and calculations. 'I was utterly exhausted by dragging about stones and boards day after day, clearing up, tacking pieces of flotsam together, sawing and hammering ... The house stands on the furthest rocks out to sea, measures 4 metres by 5 and consists of a single room with three windows. In fact I'm building two houses,' she reported to Eva that summer, 'an outer one, and an inner place of peace and indifference.'

Much of the Moomin summer in *Finn Family Moomintroll* was distilled from Tove's archipelago summers, from Blidö, from Pellinge and not least from Bredskär: a sailing trip to an island, or a storm that forces the family to camp out for a night and use the sail as a tent. Happy moments of this kind are captured in *Finn Family Moomintroll*: a tablecloth held down by stones, butter buried under the cold sand, a storm that turns dawn phosphorus-yellow, thunder and lightning that transform sky and horizon into a flaming theatrical drama. Writing about real landscapes that she had made her own, she placed them in a different world with different topography. On 19th August she wrote to Eva from her tent:

This is the first night I'm sleeping alone in the tent on Bredskär. Through my insect-net the crowberry and pine twigs look like infinitely fine lacework against a stormy violet sea. An enormous red new moon is sticking up like a horn from the sea. The beacons we used to see on Sandskär are shining, strong and friendly now in the August darkness. And there stands the house.

She was working on her Moomin strip for Atos's paper. She was enthusiastic, unable to say no. Drawing, getting 'the house ready', cutting wood among the trees, all in the solitude she had needed to be able to write 'poems and Moomintroll'. She stayed on the island till October. It had become a place of

Endless peace and a certain desolation – especially in the evenings. It's been stormy nearly all the time and out on the point the house has been thoroughly ventilated. Breakers all round and the weirdest illusory sensation of voices, steps and music in the wind. In particular, the acoustic phenomenon of rhythmic violin music when I want to sleep has been a bit disturbing. You become different and think new thoughts when you live a long time alone with the sea and yourself.

She carried this experience into the Moomin story, in which Snufkin listens to the orchestra of the storm, which for him articulates the eternal longing of the world wanderer: 'out there the storm increased. Strange sounds slipped into the thunder of the waves. Voices and running feet, laughter and the tolling of great bells out at sea. Snufkin lay still and listened and dreamed and remembered his travels round the earth. Soon I must start out again, he thought. But not yet.'

In her third Moomin book Tove's subject was love: love for Ham, for Vivica, for Atos, for her family, for the islands, the valley and the sea. 'No one can understand me as Ham does,' she confided to Eva, and this ability emanated from love: 'Ham can see through every disguise, because she loves me.' Ham was a prototype mother; she could always recognise her children, just as Moominmamma can recognise Moomintroll inside the ghost-beast's grotesque body in *Finn Family Moomintroll*. Tove's love for Vivica was the exact opposite. Their intimacy was completely over by the summer of 1947, and Windrose House marked the beginning of a new life. Once her feeelings had cooled a bit and her relationship with Vivica had settled on an even keel, she decided almost in passing to marry Atos. Being married to him could be part of her transformation, another way of crossing old borders.

Tove had never experienced anything like her passion for Vivica before, but it was time now to move on. For her, work had always been intertwined with love, a processing of mental and physical emotion. Making life into pictures and words. Now she was planning a future with Atos, who was still there in the background. 'If he asked me to marry him I'd say yes,' she had told Eva in March 1947, but without her earlier sense of joy.

They had certainly changed positions in their relationship. 'I'm no longer anxious, waiting and preparing and adorning myself. I'm not so poor that every time I see the sun rise, I wonder that such a thing can happen for my benefit.' But at the same time she felt she was 'hanging in the air' between woman and man.

Tove in front of the Windrose house on Bredskär.

Tove's courtship of Atos in mid-December 1947 was hardly conducted in a state of passion, rather in one of calm camaraderie. She wrote: 'Then I wonder if you think it might be a good idea if we got married. I don't think it would affect the way we live. If you don't want to, we'll talk about something else when you come back. There are plenty of other things, aren't there?' But above all she wanted to close the door that led to the 'other side' and restrain her longing for 'la rive gauche'. Atos represented safety from devastating passion, a way of being together without extravagant demands and overwhelming feelings. With a man like 'Sopher' (one of her pet names for him) there could never be any question of the humdrum home life she so dreaded. She would be able to keep her freedom. Atos agreed and the wedding was planned for spring 1948: 'He answered my proposal as only he could have done: "Tove, is it true we aren't married yet? I thought we already were, we've definitely been neglectful. It's certainly no more than a formality. We absolutely must clinch the matter soon. Or people will start thinking we aren't enjoying each other's company any more."'

Tove planned the wedding, a ceremony in the presence of the Mayor, with Ham and Lasse as witnesses and perhaps a dinner for four at the Kämp restaurant. Banns, rings, a certificate from the church registry, she went through all the formalities and suggested various dates. But Atos felt there was no need to hurry, better to wait till after the Parliamentary Elections (as elsewhere in Europe, there was a serious East/West political crisis in Finland). For him the idea of marriage was the thing; the timing was less important.

In the event there never was any wedding, either before or after the elections. 'Philosophers have their own yardsticks,' Tove wrote, disappointed but not particularly upset, suffering mostly from wounded vanity.

At the same time she was completing the pictures for *Finn Family Moomintroll*. In it, the Muskrat-philosopher's book 'The Uselessness of Everything' was magicked away and immediately replaced by 'The Usefulness of Everything'. In April she went with Sam and Maya Vanni to Italy and Brittany to paint. It was her first long journey after the war. She wanted to find landscapes which had warmth and colour.

CHAPTER 9

Trolls and Humans

You never know with words,
at least not on a Sunday afternoon.

Stenåkern (The Stony Field)

'Two letters from Ham! I'm so happy! Painting like the deuce!'
Tove had been waiting impatiently for letters from Finland and
had at last heard from her family. She had lined up her canvases
in her chilly pension room just outside Florence, with its con-
vent-like furniture and black stone floor. She did not yet know
what to think of these canvases, beyond the fact that Italian
painting had inspired her to continue with 'a new way of seeing
and a longing to be bigger and simpler'.

This was what she wrote to Atos and what she was writing
now, at the beginning of May 1948, to Eva. She was standing
among the avenues in the hills sketching in charcoal, drawing
voluptuous pines and the 'succulently black' shadows of houses.
The result was pictures with new nuances. The whole landscape
was like a colourful 'horn of plenty', but could at the same time
seem static in its perfection and unattainable, causing a painter
to despair. In June, after a week in Paris, she went on alone to
Brittany and the fishing village of St Pierre Phar Finistère. There
the landscape was the exact opposite: wide open, peaceful and
solitary, suggestive of contemplation and alive with seemingly
mysterious and enigmatic colours.

Perhaps nothing during this powerful journey has affected me so much as the flat land here ... a succession of white and slate-grey houses huddling over the sea, the sun-bleached grassland chequered with stains of cadmium-coloured moss ... And a belt of seaweed with every nuance between purple, black and honey-yellow, grey-white sand, endless ebb-marks in sienna and green earth and, further out, blue, intense blue. There are grey days too with bellowing foghorns and storm and rain – but I love it all.

For Tove, the colours expressed the landscape. She drew a woman in a black Breton dress with high headgear. This was how the Breton women had dressed when she came here before, after her six-month stay in Paris, and now, ten years later, they were still dressed in the same way. It was as if time had stopped. Tove wandered along the coast with her sketchbook from one village to the next, giving perspective in black and white to places like St Guénloé, Kerity, Penmarc'h and Guilvine – she drew a whole series of them – and living 'more intensely than ever'. A powerful lighthouse swept its light across the wall of her room at night. 'I don't think, I hardly speak to anyone,' she wrote. 'Everything is like a parenthesis between one sentence and the next,' and with what coming next, she wondered. For the moment her writing could offer her no answer. But in the longer story of her life there would be only one answer: the Moomins and fame.

Between One Sentence and the Next

With *Finn Family Moomintroll*, Moomin and his world really began to spin. Now Tove was working on her fourth book, *Muminpappas bravader* (*The Exploits of Moominpappa*), the great memoir about Moominpappa's origins and stormy youth before he met his lifelong love, Moominmamma. It would be a success with the critics. After Christmas 1949 her first Moomin play reached the stage. Moomin was spreading in every direction. Murals, picture books, strip series, new storybooks and, little by little, as she herself put it, trolls and other figures in both possible and impossible materials. Only four years after his literary debut, Moomin was well on the way to becoming a multi-media celebrity.

After her trip to Italy and the calling off of their marriage, Tove and Atos drifted apart, though a 'warm companionship' survived and Atos remained a really good friend, as Tove told Eva in June 1949. The plans and dreams they had shared never became reality. Politics was what mattered most to Atos, and it took up more and more of his time. Tove developed in other directions. But they still had one project left, a last attempt to come together as a family. They thought about buying a houseboat together with Lasse, and Tove wrote a good deal about this in her letters to Eva. Like the artists' colony and the villa in Morocco, it represented Tove's permanent longing to get away and find something else; not least, something of her own. This plan would never become reality either, but the houseboat idea survived in Tove's diaries where it went for a long time under the codename 'Christopher Columbus'. She and Lasse also made wilder and more secret plans, such as emigration to Tonga. The idea was Lasse's, but Tove was ready for change. Apart from Ham, she told Eva, there was nothing to tie her to Finland, and she could paint and write anywhere. The thought of such a change of perspective tempted her. She asked Eva to research possible routes and tickets, and in her letter of thanks for the 'Polynesian plans' she wrote: 'They have been lying there growing deep inside me and in a strange way have started to transform the way I look at many things.' Later that summer (1949) she took the idea further:

> As for Polynesia. Of course you're right that each one of us is an island; a beautiful thought that can be developed. And to say that freedom can't be affected by external arrangements, but only by an inner process, designed to set free our relationships and attitudes to people and things. I've gradually come to understand this.

> If this journey is a flight from responsibility, it's capitulation, an absurd and meaningless romanticism. I really don't know yet whether deep down this is the truth about it – what I thought was that it represented a liberation from misdirected ambitions, from the love of possessions, from the convulsive need for surroundings where one is 'known'. I don't for a moment believe in Hula-hula romanticism, I got rid of that long ago. But at least it'll be warm there. And no Helsinki painters unlike in France and Italy. And plenty of colour. And that's where Lasse wants to go. We'll talk more about it later.

Warmth, colour, freedom, it sounds like Gauguin. Their secret plans – which were clearly worrying Eva – were serious in intention. Whether Tove would really have left Ham, her beloved tower, her work and her family and friends, is unclear, but there can be no doubt that both she and Lasse made preparations. It was a project to plan for, a thought to develop, an idea to dream of together with her dearly loved brother. Lasse wrote to the governor of the island they had in mind, but when the governor answered they finally shelved their plans. 'He writes very politely that Lasse and I can't settle there because of a shortage of houses (and building materials); they don't want more people living there. But of course there are other islands ...'

The project formed part of the permanent debate between pleasure and duty that Tove carried on with herself: 'I have tried on my own to find the root of the "pleasure v duty" problem, because that is where everything must have got into such a mess.' She tried to find new ways to deepen her insight into herself. Tonga would have been an opportunity to separate the person she was from her signature 'Tove'. She longed to get away: 'Nothing can happen to one except what is already similar to oneself. Till one changes.' After the murals she did in Kotka in the late winter of 1949, she had gone back to painting in oils. 'I'm in some way stuck in an inconvenient fix in which everything I've done up to now seems to me bad and alien, and I want to find my way out to bigger, calmer surfaces with less emphatic lines.'

She was still stuck between one sentence and the next.

Moomin on the Wall and on the Stage

In autumn 1948 Tove went back to the Ateneum to learn how to paint *'al secco'*. A new commission 'for murals in a lighter style' awaited her in the Helsinki University student hall of residence known as 'Domus'. As always she started from the beginning, documenting technique and the learning process in her painter's notebook. Soon she was summoned to Kotka, a town on the coast east of Helsinki, to paint murals for a kindergarten. She was glad of the job. It made a welcome contribution to her miserable finances. No one was buying art any more the way they had during the wartime investment fever. She was saddled with unpaid taxes and debts going back several years, even with demands for church tax. No scholarships or grants were available and this state of affairs lasted well into the 1950s. 'They think I'm rich,' she remarked bitterly. Of course she had lots of 'drawing jobs' and was working as hard as she always did, but she was not well off. Her Moomin books were not yet providing any income to speak of. She was simply happy that publishers were accepting them at all. The first thing to help relieve the economic pressure was her first Moomin comic strip series.

'I wonder very much what you'll think of my fresco *al secco*,' she wrote to Eva when she had been painting in Kotka for a month. She longed for others to see her new art, especially those closest to her. 'It's seven metres of a wall in a kindergarten in a building built by the Gutzeit factory for their workers. A place where they deposit their children (about eighty of them) when they go to work.' She never had any doubt about her subject: a mixture of trolls and humans, of fairy tale and reality. By presenting her teeming Moomin world in the form of a large painting to a young audience, she would conquer new territory as an artist. She

Tove with the secco *mural in Kotka, 1949.*

had drawn countless illustrations, for children's books written both by herself and other people, but she had never *painted* for children in such a form as this. 'It has moved me very much to be painting for children,' she wrote, formulating some basic theoretical principles for what for her as a painter was a new group: 'I have tried to set myself in their world, which I imagine to be a mixture of fantasy and everyday life, of romance and humour, of splendour and simplicity.' When a couple of years later she won the Nils Holgersson plaque in Sweden for her picture book *Hur gick det sen?* (*The Book About Moomin, Mymble and Little My*), she referred to this in her speech of thanks. Most children, she said, 'live in a world in which the fantastic and the matter-of-fact have equal value'. This was a belief she retained in later expositions of her aesthetic principles. It is also what gives the Moomin books their strength.

It was something new for her as a painter to work with gilt ornamentation; she described her technique in her letters. I work 'on wax and coloured stones set into the wall, based on a 500-year-old formula. I'm sure it'll make the Artists' Guild rear up and foam at the mouth.' The ancient formula came from her household god Cennini whose *Treatise on Painting* held an important place in her thinking at this period. It contained instructions on the use of colour and above all maxims on the fundamentals of true art: 'The master will teach, but the artist must guide himself according to his own ideas and feelings.' One result of this is Tove's Kotka mural for children. A passion for what is golden, glistens and glimmers, whether sparkling garnets, flaming rubies, shining gold ore or fragments of shimmering green glass (*Moominpappa at Sea*) lives strongly in her books. When she painted beautiful things on the wall she inserted gold and glistening colour, working stones and glitter into her *al secco*, mixing in trolls and humans, painting herself and issuing a challenge to the sort of art represented by the big beasts of the Artists' Guild. One colleague did bridle at the sight of this glittering fantasy. This was the painter Unto Koistinen, who was known as a regenerator of national painting. It is said that he looked in and remarked, 'Sheer crap.'

In painting this monumental *al secco* kindergarten piece and creating a narrative mural, Tove cut herself off from her time and from masculine modernism. Working from her own ideas she combined expertise and emotion and – just as Cennini had advised – allowed herself to be guided by pleasure. Her creative imagination combined the real with the fantastic, intersecting the world of trolls with the world of humans. At Kotka, Moomin, imagination and fairy tale came together as *her own* art, in a major expression of the painter and artist Tove Jansson herself: 'It seems beautiful to me with these glittering stones and pale gold against the surface of the wall – in the crowns, in the bridle of the grey-white horse, in the folds of cloaks and treasures spread over the ground.' She had swept aside all thoughts of criticism and prestige and it was for this very reason that the 'result' was liberated.

Tove discovered new powers of concentration in creating this mural. For the first time for ages she was able to concentrate on a single work without splitting herself apart. Individualism had become her guiding star and art a part of herself, while at the same time she had left a path open to the viewer: 'It's sublimated flight. Sublimated because it leaves something behind for others.' She had chosen her position and made a personal statement in favour of personal will. 'Dearest Eva, I'm afraid that all my life I shall be an unpolitical = asocial painter, a so-called individualist depicting lemons, writing fairy tales, collecting weird objects as a hobby and detesting associations and societies. It seems rather silly, but that's the way I want my life. And if I fight, it's only so as to find peace,' she wrote in February 1949.

If this seems oversimplified, it should be seen in relation to Tove's own position at that moment – she had just spent an evening at a meeting of leftist writers who worshipped society and collectivism – but it was also an honest declaration of her own position. To her, independence could only be freedom from imperative artistic and political ideals, from unwanted collective organisations and social obligations. An independence that was her own, not dependent on artistic currents, lovers, friends or family. She needed to be a loner, retreating into herself, working from her own ideas and guided by her own requirements and emotions. 'Even Faffan can no longer stop me creeping into my tower and painting unpolitical still-lifes,' she wrote in a letter. If she wanted to paint in gold and set stones into an *al secco* mural, then that was what she would do, irrespective of who might be expected to foam at the mouth.

The painter was seeking expression in her own individuality rather than in artistic fashion. Ideas might come and go and canvases might be covered with a succession of still-lifes, but Moomintroll was and would remain an expression of the Tove Jansson ideal: expertise and joy in work. Now she could see her Moomin stories through the eyes of others, gaining a sense of proportion and adjusting her perspective. When the father of two Moomin-besotted children came to her studio with a book full of copies of her illustrations, she was deeply moved. 'I've been feeling a bit stupid with my fairy tales,' she wrote late in November 1949, but a visit of this kind 'helps me to see things in perspective'. Painting and Moomin could combine – as in Kotka – and she did not need to feel constantly forced to keep her artistic identities apart. At the same time it was precisely this double identity – painter and Moomin creator – that would remain the major conflict for Tove through the whole of her artistic life.

The year 1949 also found her working on her first piece for the theatre, 'Moomintroll and the Comet'. The basic idea was the destruction of the world, as it had been for the strip series in *Ny Tid*. At the same time the action of the play was also rooted in the magical transformations of *Finn Family Moomintroll* and was also related to her forthcoming book, *The Exploits of Moominpappa*. Roles are changed, individuals change places and episodes are transformed. The magic is organised by Snufkin (with a magic wand), while the Groke has a ruby set in her head and is later trampled flat by a 'dodo' or Booble and the comet has the power of speech. New figures appear (such as the ominous herald of misfortune, 'Härmasken' or 'Hairworm') and others have disappeared – though Thingumy and Bob remain. The Hemulen's aunt, who will appear in *The Exploits of Moominpappa*, teaches

Images from the programme for 'Moomintroll and the Comet'.

among other things 'opinions' to Moominvalley's (frankly unteachable) inhabitants. A magic 'troll ring', which can only be controlled by Moomintroll, and a shining fairy bring together the threads in a happy ending. The play is a real mishmash and clearly required adaptation for stage and audience as a dramatised version of the prose narrative. In her script Tove attached the utmost importance to clear presentation, but she was capable at the same time of hurling all her theories on the subject of understanding children across the footlights. To Bob's question, 'Are you kafking moffee?' Snufkin answers: 'What? Kafka?' The Muskrat's reading of Spengler in the comet story works in the same way. (In the original Swedish version of *Finn Family Moomintroll* the Muskrat is studying that once popular work of philosophy, Spengler's *Decline of the West*.)

The theatre attracted Tove, who had long made use of it in her repertoire as a painter, a fine example being 'The Theatre Studio' (1943). It was the palace of possibilities, the place where everything could be swapped and transformed and stand for something else – a perfect setting for Tove's never-ending search for new means of expression. She had attempted a few short dramatic pieces in her childhood and adolescent writings; definite attraction to the scenically dramatic can be detected in the heroic 'James Roadville' and his struggle against the scoundrel 'Wawatam', in what had been judged by its fourteen-year-old creator to be a 'terribly exciting' story.

'Moomintroll and the Comet' had its first performance on 29th December 1949 at Svenska Teatern (the Swedish-language theatre) in Helsinki, directed by Vivica Bandler. It had been Vivica's idea that the play should be written. As with Atos and the strip series, work and love were inseparable. But it had initially been refused by the theatre's commissioning committee. It was not that they were unwilling to try anything new (they were in the middle of a season of new Finland-Swedish drama at the time) and they admired the 'eccentric-looking figures' that 'carried their creator's personal signature'. But they decided it wasn't suitable for children, and clearly not for adults either. Their report went on: 'It seems scarcely likely that children will understand and appreciate this bizarrerie any more than an adult judge would.' They don't think it's 'traditional enough,' was how Tove herself summed up their response, though she hoped for an

Ghosts, trolls and humans at a rehearsal. The director has the script under her arm, the author grasps a broom. Drawn by Tove for the newspaper Nya Pressen, *1949.*

experimental production for Easter the following year. Then, after a series of protests, the committee did a volte-face and Moomintroll was able to make his first stage appearance after all.

Like the Kotka mural, the play created new surfaces and connections around the Moomin characters. The stage demanded a new way of working with form, space and text. The trolls, with their long snouts and fat stomachs, became figures of sculpture, trolls that could be heard to speak and be seen to move on a stage. Presenting three-dimensional Moomintrolls demanded special preparation, and the effect of the drama would stand or fall by their masks. It was of course difficult to speak through a snout, and in later versions the action was adapted to the circumstances, with the snouts taken off at the beginning of the performance.

Tove worked hard, editing her script and toiling over scenery and costumes; for months before the first night she spent nearly every day at the theatre. She was determined to experience everything, from script to performance. After the dress rehearsal she reported to Eva: 'It was so appallingly awful that there must be a good chance the first night will go well. Snufkin overslept after a party and didn't turn up at all, the lighting was all to hell, some of the props were missing and everyone gave a feeble performance.' She would later turn this theatrical chaos to good artistic effect in her book *Farlig Midsommar* (*Moominsummer Madness*), the great theatre story of the Moomin series (1954), in which the dress rehearsal of Moominpappa's tragedy is full of vocal and scenic errors. It is claimed in *Moominsummer Madness* that a disastrous dress rehearsal guarantees a fine first performance and with Tove's first Moomin play this was what happened. The critics praised it for imagination and individuality, in a word for originality, but it also caused surprise. A strange story of terror and the conquest of terror, 'lively cascades' of games as the comet approached 'with its threat of destruction', wrote one reviewer, reporting on an audience of children with huge eyes 'who rather warily allowed themselves to be carried away'.

Some reviewers also wondered how far children could be expected to understand a play about the destruction of the world. But the greatest commotion (moral panic, we might call it today) was caused by a letter to *Hufvudstadsbladet* from a 'bewildered father'. This writer complained of the destruction theme in passing, but what really disturbed him was the play's 'strong language'. Fortunately, this father wrote, such expressions as 'begrowled' (*förmorrade*) and 'hell's growl-jumps' (*helvetes morrhoppor*) passed his three-year-old son by, but they still remained essentially unsuitable. 'Moomintroll could have been a pleasant piece for children, if only the author had taken the trouble to make some use of the power of judgement she undoubtedly possesses. But in its present form, with its boozing prophets and strong expletives, I cannot recommend it.' This started a debate, and Tove made notes about some of the shocked parents who wrote to her. One complained that their little son was demanding 'mahogany-grog' and had started to swear, while another reported that her son was running round their flat with outstretched 'paws' claiming to be a Hattifattener and mumbling, 'O horizons, O horizons.'

Tove replied in the newspaper, counter-attacking sharply with both word and picture. She informed the 'bewildered father' that 'hellfire' [*helveteseld*] is a harmless expression and 'Groke' [*Mårran*] is just a name; both of these happen to occur in my play, while 'hell's growl-jumps' [*helvetes morrhoppor*], as an expression, seems to me only mildly vulgar. If you are really determined to, you can read an ugly meaning in any word you like. If 'begrowled' is a 'terrible' [*förfärligt*] expression, then the very word 'terrible' must also be a damned [*förbannat*] expression. The prophet in the play drinks wine mixed with mace; as his creator, I am utterly bewildered to learn that this makes him a boozer.

The problem of what is and what is not permissible affects all writing for children. 'Can one exclaim "Hell!" in respectable children's books?' wondered a (gushing) publisher's reader in Sweden after reading the *The Exploits of Moominpappa*. This put the problem in a nutshell. The 'bewildered father's idea' of a pleasant piece for children was typical. He wanted a text free from 'unsuitable' expressions (i.e. purified); if he had been transported to the Moomin world himself, he would undoubtedly

Premiere of the first Moomin play, 24th December 1949. The author has been called on to the stage.

have been a Hemulen. In Tove's forthcoming *Moominsummer Madness* there is a disappointed Hemulen policeman who mutters about a princess he saw in a children's play long ago, while the Moomin family is concentrating on the alarming events happening on stage.

Tove couldn't be bothered with the question of suitability in her answer to the offended father who had written to the paper. Expressive power was what mattered; interpretation could be left to the audience. The interesting thing is that she bothered to write to him at all, a very rare occurrence. But the father had not only inaccurately quoted her play, but interpreted it wrongly as well. Yet there could be no doubt that it had excited emotions – the essential ingredient in all artistic endeavour, according to Cennini.

The Queen of Surprises

'It would be lovely to paint a peaceful old-fashioned still-life,' wrote Tove to Eva once the first night was over in December 1949 – 'but how I'll miss the theatre!!!' Writing for the stage whetted the appetite and there were to be settings, play-scripts and stories related to drama, the stage and role-playing in the picture book, *The Book About Moomin, Mymble and Little My*, in *Moominsummer Madness* and in the Moomin play 'Troll in the Wings', a great stage hit of the late 1950s.

But first came the last Moomin book from the 1940s, the story of Moominpappa's stormy youth 'Written by Himself'. This was shaped like a picaresque *Bildungsroman*, an autobiography with the future Moominpappa as narrator. The life-story of his early years begins on the steps of a Hemulen Home for Moomin Foundlings and ends one stormy autumn night, when the sea flings the future Moominmamma straight into his powerful paws. She is the Aphrodite of the Moomin world, born of the spray (on a plank with her paws in the air). It is love at first sight. This is how 'The most wonderful of Moomins' makes her appearance, and the consequent description makes clear that she is the great love of his life. What he meets is his own reflection, 'a Moomin, like myself, but still more beautiful'. He finishes his memoirs in the healing sign of love and is transformed into a mature and full-grown Moomintroll: 'Since then my follies have been supervised by her gentle and understanding eyes, and thereby transformed into sense and wisdom.' We are not given Mamma's impression of her future husband – he is wielding the pen – but the look she gives him as she blushes at his first compliment is (so Moominpappa says) 'unfathomable'.

Tove left a first draft of the story with Schildts in June 1949, but the publishers had their doubts. Moomintroll was not yet standing firmly on his own legs, and was clearly something of a risky project. They 'don't want to accept it straight off', was how Tove put it; they preferred to wait and see what the reception of *Finn Family Moomintroll* would be in Sweden in autumn 1949. But after that the way was clear. Much had been staked on *Finn Family Moomintroll* and comments on it in the Swedish press were rich in words of praise such as 'fun', 'profound', 'fantastic' and 'exciting'. In fact there was only one objection. How could parents reading aloud to their children get through such long chapters at bedtime? Fortunately it could be divided into episodes 'after these dramatic denouements a line could be drawn,' according to an enthusiastic lecturer called B. Kleingaard. Her new book, which was to become *The Exploits of Moominpappa*, was a long-term project, and during the autumn Tove revised the manuscript she had delivered to Schildts in the summer. I'm busy rewriting 'the Moomin memoirs', she told Eva in November, 'and it's almost more of a chore than writing a completely new book. *Finn Family Moomintroll* seems to have been astonishingly successful in Sweden – now the thing is not to let what comes next be an anticlimax.'

The Exploits of Moominpappa is, with *Comet in Moominland*, one of the most rewritten of the books, and was published in three different Swedish-language editions, in 1950, 1956 and 1968. Three manuscript versions written before the first edition also exist, more or less complete and more or less alike. One of them has no title, but the other two are headed 'A Moominpappa's Stormy Youth: Memoirs' and 'My Stormy Youth, the Memoirs of a Moominpappa' respectively. Tove replaced these with 'The Memoirs of Moominpappa'; the publishers changed this to 'The Exploits of Moominpappa'. The word 'memoirs' was not considered suitable for a book aimed at children, while 'exploits' was familiar in that context: more playful, not so grandiose. It

The Aphrodite of the Moomin world. From The Exploits of Moominpappa.

was not until the third edition in 1968 that the book was given the title Tove had originally wanted for it: 'Moominpappa's Memoirs'.

The story of Moominpappa's young days ·was an urgent project. The Moomin story needed to be developed further, and *Finn Family Moomintroll* needed a sequel. But there was also the problem of the author's identity. When Tove made Moominpappa into a writer she identified him with herself and her own writing. Like Tove, he practises various literary genres and later was to appear as a dramatist (*Moominsummer Madness*), as a novelist (in the comic strip series *The Moominfamily and the Sea*) and as a scientist (*Moominpappa at Sea*). Pappan (the father) is identified with what is written and writing is identified with masculinity. In the memoirs Tove gives him her own birthday, 9th August (an identification cut from later editions). *The Exploits of Moominpappa* is an expert identification with the male writer of memoirs and his way of writing about himself. But the project is also an account of building up one's own identity as a writer. This was something Tove really enjoyed. She enjoyed illustrating the book almost as much as she had enjoyed building a house, as she wrote to Vivica in February 1950.

Becoming a writer, being literary and becoming famous were themes on Tove's new Moomin agenda. In the manuscript Pappa as a youngster is already dreaming of becoming a writer, when a culturally sophisticated hedgehog gives him tips on how to reach the 'crème de la crème', where he will be able to look for answers to his existential questions. '"What deep things these Moomintrolls must deal with in there! Will I finally find answers to everything there?" reflected Pappa.' The entrance ticket to the place where they live, states the hedgehog, is to have an interesting identity and the part of 'poet' will fit the young Moomin like a glove: 'You are a young poet nobody understands, so naturally it would be really good to understand you. All you have to do is let your hair grow a bit.' He goes on: 'Let's say, for example, that you've written a poem with the title "That Never To". Then everyone will know what it's about.' The satirical pieces, aimed at a modernistic, Björling-like kind of poetry, never came into the book (and besides, Moominpappa is bald). But the reference to the Helsinki poet Gunnar Björling (who, unlike Moominpappa, was not bald) survived: the Muddler's father who disappeared during a spring-cleaning with his collection of poetry, 'The Ocean Orchestra'.

With *The Exploits of Moominpappa,* Tove was transformed into the queen of surprises. She had changed genre and narrative viewpoint and now presented writing thematically as process, memory and individual characteristics. Underlying memory became the principle of narration, parody became narration's new tool and exaggeration (hyperbole) became one of its new means. In Moominpappa's description of his stormy youth she displayed her belief in fantasy and her delight in writing and in spinning tales. It was a matter of creating *credible* fiction. When Moomintroll questions the authenticity of the memoirs, Moominpappa answers with the authority of the true storyteller: 'if a word has been a trifle *emphasised* here and there that naturally just makes the whole thing more convincing.' Tove's model was the Renaissance artist Benvenuto Cellini's famous *Vita. Scritta per lui medesimo* of 1558–66 (*Life. Written by Himself*), often regarded as a masterpiece of early autobiography. Cellini, like Faffan a sculptor, became an easily parodied exemplar of male writing, one of the Italian artists Tove most admired. She let Moominpappa himself hold the pen from the first page (the memoirs are stated, like Cellini's, to have been 'Described by Himself'). She makes no claim herself to be the publisher, discoverer or collector of the material (though, in the second edition she does claim to be the person who wrote the memoirs down.)

The Exploits of Moominpappa came on the cusp between the war-torn 1940s and a new, visionary, forward-looking time. In writing Moominpappa's memoirs Tove was looking backwards in Moomintroll's genealogy, but at the same time she was setting the family in a wider context, writing a story on which the young Moomintroll and his friends would be able to build – seen from the perspective of an outspoken father. Also, Moominpappa's memoirs are not just the story of *one* father, but of three. (His companions, the Muddler and Joxter, are later revealed as the fathers of Sniff and Snufkin respectively.) In extension the memoirs constitute a narrative about Moominpappa as individual, character and species: 'And you, foolish little child, who think your father a dignified and serious person, when you read this story of three daddies' adventures you should bear in mind that one daddy is very like another (at least when young).'

FÖRETAL

Jag, mumintrollets pappa, sitter i kväll vid mitt fönster och ser eldflugorna brodera hemliga tecken därute i trädgårdens sammetsmörker. Förgängliga krumelurer av ett kort men lyckligt liv!

Moominpappa the writer. From The Exploits of Moominpappa.

Book 44 from Tove Press,
1925. [1]

'The Adventures of Prickina and Fabian', serialised in *Lunkentus*, 1929. [2]

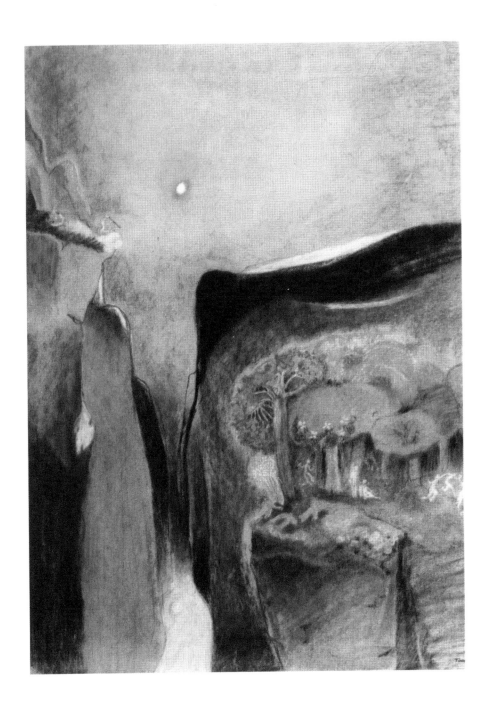

'Ensittaren', 1935. [3]

Journey to Stockholm Technical School from 'Homecoming', Autumn 1930. [4]

Walking home at night in Stockholm. From diary, 1931. [5]

en med allt måleri. En mural exposition emellertid, väldiga saker som staten beställt av några av de bästa moderna må-larna under det senaste året, gjorde mig mycket liten och full av beundran. Vid rue de la Seine ligger alla de små konst-salongerna, ständigt nya vernissager, färg butiker, antikvitets-handlare, här och var ett grönsaks stånd, en bistro. Här ritar jag upp planen över de gator jag vanligtvis går – jag har nästan blivit som en av de äkta parisare vilka aldrig va it på andra sidan Seinen. Rive droit – vad skulle man gö ra där när man har allt i sitt eget kvarter!

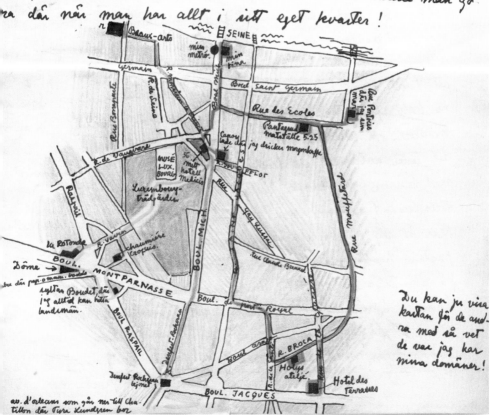

Tove maps her Parisian domain, 1938. The Holys studio and Hôtel des Terrasses are bottom right, the 'lonely' hotel is by the Jardin du Luxembourg (centre) and the Beaux-Arts college is top left. [6]

Three takes on Rembrandt. Tove's 'Self-Portrait with Fur Hat' from 1941 [7]; Rembrandt's self-portrait on which it is based [8]; and Moominpappa in Rembrandt-pose, from the original cover of *The Exploits of Moominpappa*, 1950. [9]

[8]

[9]

'Hotel Room', 1938. [10]

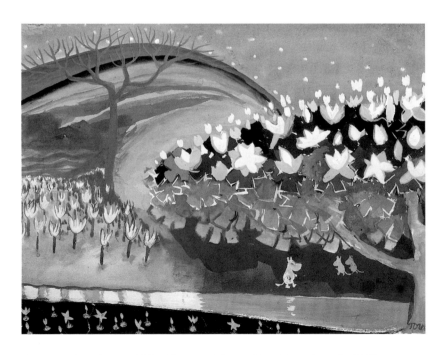

A watercolour from 1930 with one of the earliest Moomintrolls. [11]

Tove's densely written diary from 1944, with her pen from the period. [12]

Sam Vanni's portrait of Tove Jansson, 1940. [13]

'Still-life with Shell', 1945. [14]

'Loboan' (The Lynx Boa) self-portrait, 1942. [15]

Two frescoes for the Town Hall of Helsingfors, 1947. [16]

'Red Cape', 1964. [17]

'Still-Life', 1966. [18]

'Temple', Crete, 1959. [19]

Scene from *What Happened Next? (The Book About Moomin, Mymble and Little My)*, 1952. [20]

Scene from *Who Will Comfort Toffle?*, 1960. [21]

'The Family' , 1942 – from left, 'Ham', Lasse, Tove, Per Olov, 'Faffan'. [22]

Sketch for 'The Family' in a letter to Eva Konikoff, 1941. [23]

The magazine *Garm* published more than 600 of Tove's illustrations over a fifteen-year period. This was for the cover of the July 1941 issue. 'What I liked best was being beastly to Hitler and Stalin,' Tove recalled. [24]

Moomintroll ideas are developed in a letter to Vivica Bandler, February 1947.
[25]

The kiss scene in 'Moomintroll and the Comet', staged at Helsingfors, 1949. [26]

Muskrat and Moomintroll sketched for *Comet in Moominland*, 1949. [27]

Sketch for the Snufkin (*Snusmumriken*) character for a dramatisation of the Moomins in Stockholm, 1982. [28]

'The Graphic Artist' – Tooti at work in the studio in Paris, 1975. [29]

Too-ticky and Moomintroll in the snow – a cover design for *Moominvalley Midwinter*, 1957. [30]

'The Hobgoblin's Hat' mural for Pori kindergarten, 1984. [31]

Tove with her 1975 self-portrait. [32]

It is a story of male adventures in a closed circle, the Muddler is the cook, Joxter is the lazy one, Hodgkins (Moominpappa's best friend) the technical genius. When the adventurers settle down and a colony is built, it is time to pair off. The male memoir perspective emphasises two qualities in a woman: fruitfulness and beauty. If beauty is represented by Moominmamma, fruitfulness is represented by the well-rounded Mymble ('everything's round about her'), mother to Mymble's daughter, Little My, Snufkin (as is revealed later) and an unknown number of mymble-kiddies, eighteen or nineteen at each birth. Mymble is eroticism incarnate: to 'mymble' was a codeword for making love among Tove's friends, and a 'mymble' could be a lover of either sex. But even if gender roles may seem fixed in the male narrative, other forces are at work too. Like Pappa and his companions, mymbles are full of a passion for exploration. This is based on their need to leave childhood behind and free themselves. The story has no particular gender for its author, Tove Jansson.

Imagination

Moominpappa's book follows the pattern of genre memoirs and autobiography. To write the story of one's own life one must be able to see oneself, as narrator, at the centre of important or historic events and meetings with memorable people:

CHAPTER ONE

In which I tell of my misunderstood childhood, of the first Event in my life and the tremendous night of my escape, of the building of my first Moominhouse and of my historic meeting with Hodgkins.

The technique of adjusting memories to make them more favourable to himself usually plays an important role for the writer of memoirs, as does the pleasure of making up stories. Moominpappa is no exception. 'My memory used to be excellent, but it is now undoubtedly rather poor. Yet, leaving aside a few small exaggerations and misunderstandings (which I'm sure merely add to its liveliness and local colour), this autobiography will be entirely truthful.'

Mominpappa's memoirs are naturally based throughout the story on parody; his memoir writing is motivated by the 'words of wisdom' he has discovered 'in the memoirs of another remarkable personage', i.e. Cellini: 'Everyone, of whatever walk in life, who has achieved anything good in this world, or thinks he has, should, if he be truth-loving and nice, write about his life, albeit not starting before the age of forty!' Everything derives from Moominpappa, at least in His Own Opinion. Statements like unusual, intelligent, significant and exceptional recur in his characterisation of himself. He polishes his character as his story proceeds, but remains basically the same. This is the important thing. I used to be a great 'Moomin-fan' when I was young, he remembers, adding: 'And I'm not so bad now either.' And when he puts his memoir pen down it is in the assurance that he will be able to go on to have 'a hundred' even greater and more varied 'new adventures'.

It all has to do with the desire to tell a story. Beneath the surface of the memoir lurk the possibilities of imagination. The memoir itself expounds the play between memory, narrative and (fictive) reality. Moominpappa as a writer represents pleasure, poetry and imagination, all the things that mattered most to Tove Jansson as a writer. The fact that it is Moominpappa (together with Mymble's daughter) who wins the prize for imagination in the Autocrat Daddy Jones's Royal Lottery is clearly significant. His memoirs are a defence of the possibilities of imagination, but you have to have the right faith. And if you do everything can happen over again but in a new way: that's the bottom line. In telling his story Pappa encourages the young and recreates his friends through his memoirs. He makes them live again. The writing author and the storytelling imagination can always create themselves anew and are always accessible.

The Exploits of Moominpappa is a narrative about the self and basic personality. When Pappa thinks he must 'yield to Moomintroll's persuasion and to the temptation of talking about myself' he puts into words the impulse to expose himself that lurks inside the soul of every potential writer of memoirs. The book's original cover (see colour plae 9) bears witness to the player of the principal role. A young Moomin poses as if for a photograph, one paw against a pillar and the other by his side – there are traces too of a Rembrandt-style self-portrait in this picture. In the garland that surrounds him crowd the companions and friends of his youth, those who literally adorned his young years (Moominmamma not yet one of them). Tove used this composition on her much-used 'ex libris' from 1947. Moomintroll as a figure has now set himself firmly in the centre of the picture, surrounded by his story, his relations and his friends.

Through Moominpappa's self-centred memoirs, Tove Jansson the writer was able to exercise her need as an artist to create self-portraits, examining her ego in detail from different angles and presenting herself as she herself wished to do, without subjecting herself to other people. Ever since the diaries of her childhood and adolescence she had been accustomed to describing herself from various perspectives in words and pictures. Moominpappa the writer is her portrait of herself as creative writer. There could be no doubt of her need to make up stories.

A New Age

To be famous you need to have done something no one else has ever done before, according to the *The Exploits of Moominpappa*. In the Moomins, Tove Jansson had discovered something new, with no earlier parallel. What fame brought with it and what this would mean would set its stamp on her work over the next decade. For Tove as artist and writer, a new age had arrived. Her time of hesitating between one sentence and the next was definitely over.

Even before the memoir book was published, various 'Moomin duties' had begun to make demands on Tove's time, and the Moomintroll figure had begun to live a life of its own outside the books. Celebrity was becoming ever more of a factor, affecting her life and work in various ways. During the spring of 1950 she was fully occupied with theatre work (sketches and scene designs for a revue for writers), she was busy with any number of illustrating jobs (her finances were still a problem) and she was in the middle of drawing some forty pictures as illustrations for Moominpappa's memoirs. In February she told Eva:

> I've been thinking about you all the time and 'talking' to you, have wanted to write but no peace and quiet. These Moomin duties seem to be swamping me. Thank goodness I no longer need to

defend myself in public in newspapers, but there are constant interviews and arrangements to do with the books, I do stupid things in connection with business deals which then have to be sorted out and the whole thing is getting out of hand. Moomin ceramics and Moomin slides you look at through special viewers and whatnot. And then the Moomin opposition, help! – all those aggressive people who scold me about the poor troll. And hordes of children ...

The fourth book had not yet come out, but Moomin was already well established. The overheated debate about the play had helped, as had the strip series in *Ny Tid*. This came to an end when readers angrily criticised Moominpappa's reading matter ('The Royalist News'). Tove's troll signature loomed large in *Garm* and appeared in other publications too. Two short Moomin stories appeared in newspapers, 'Moomintroll's Christmas Eve' and 'Moomintroll – the Escalator'. Tove was invited to exhibit Moomin illustrations in Norway (something the painter in her at first objected to), while ideas for the commercial exploitation of Moomintroll streamed in from friends, businesses and entrepreneurs both large and small. For Tove what these 'stupid things' implied was learning how to negotiate and say no – this last a quality Moomintroll himself finds very difficult – and it created complications in her relations with her environment. So many people wanted a share in Moomin for themselves.

This was paralleled in the USA. Through Eva, who had plans for launching Moomin there, Tove got to know the figure of 'Shmoo' in Al Capp's series *Li'l Abner*. A Schmoo is everything and nothing, it simultaneously has form and no form. It likes being eaten and can taste of whatever one would like it to taste of, it can be a universal scapegoat or stand for all the desires in the world. First appearing in 1948, Schmoo became enormously popular and was soon featured commercially in dolls, toys, glass, wallpaper, belts, jewellery, etc. In July 1949 Tove wrote to Eva: 'Schmoo was an excellent animal. Thank you very much! I'm not surprised the Americans are entirely disarmed. What if I could pinch the idea for one of my own animals.' She added in English, 'I am the one who is to blame ...,' before reverting to Swedish again: 'There could be money in it, maybe. But it's hardly likely to work.' Nonetheless she sent a copy of *Finn Family Moomintroll* to Al Capp to show that 'there's a sort of Schmoo in Finland too'.

In autumn 1949 Eva visited Finland for a couple of months. Tove was overjoyed to see her much-loved friend again, and later exclaimed: 'It may be you don't understand what it meant to me that we could meet and talk and just be together with each other. So much happened to me while you were here and you being near me made it easier to solve problems and interpret everything in the right way – or at least better than I did on my own.' Despite the years (Eva had emigrated in 1941), her importance to Tove had not changed. She could expect Eva's support and encouragement. The plan to take Moomin to the USA was like a proof of their friendship: 'You're a brilliant friend, Eva, to be doing this for me,' she wrote in February 1950. 'I kiss and hug you! May it all go well!' She went on in English: 'All right. Let's see to the facts.' Then followed three pages larded with facts about the artist, the characters and the books.

Description is one of the earliest forms of self-presentation, interesting because of the unlimited opportunity it gives for detail. Tove was describing herself in anticipation of meeting a new audience in a new country, so she presented herself as a painter with a broad repertoire: exhibitions, frescoes, cartoons and illustrations. Moomintroll's origin and visual form were described right from his birth in Uncle Einar's kitchen in the 1930s: 'When I was very young and was living at [my uncle's] home in Sweden, I used to help myself to food from the larder at night. He fooled me into believing that there were "Moomintrolls" who might blow on my neck – they lived behind the tiled stove in the kitchen. I took Moomin's appearance from a tree stump in the forest that was covered with snow hanging down from it like a great round white nose.'

This last comment was no doubt intended to give the figure an exotic Nordic touch, since in actual fact the earliest Moomintrolls have narrow snouts – frankly, an attempt to create a market. She offered a detailed background to her writing, a story she later was to alter any number of times:

I began writing the first Moomin story in 1944 [crossed out and changed to 1938] when I was feeling sad and scared of bombs and wanted to get away from gloomy thoughts. (A sort of escape from reality back to the days when Ham used to tell me fairy tales.) I would creep into an unbelievable world where everything was natural and friendly and possible. Then I would continue to write whenever it amused me, to amuse myself – but mostly when I was feeling light-hearted and happy. The books are not in any way intended to be educational or anything else – nor was my children's play about Moomin – despite masses of angry letters accusing me of a tendency, namely that it was 'demoralising for children!'

'Better to say too little rather than too much,'Tove exhorted Eva, but their plans never came to anything. *Finn Family Moomintroll* was published in the USA in 1951, but this happened through other channels.

The Project had also been intended as a reunion 'over there'. Establishing Moomintroll abroad might help towards a steadier income too. In the early 1950s Tove's finances were giving her a lot of trouble: the words she used most often to describe them were 'wretched' and 'catastrophic'. In her worst moments she was ready to take on any job whatever 'for mammon'. As far as Moomintroll was concerned, the situation was two-edged. The fuss over the characters was increasing and commercialisation was in full swing. Tove wrote to Eva, in a mixture of Swedish and English, in February 1950: 'although "I'm terribly fed up with the critter" I can think of nothing that would give me more pleasure than that he should find a foothold in America. And his "mistress" would gradually follow him ...'

But Tove never made it to America to see Eva and introduce Moomintroll.

CHAPTER 10

The Wild 1950s

I'm aiming at deeper pleasure, love and progress in my work.

Notebook, 1955

The Moomin books of the 1940s tell how things were and how they could have been, with themes like apocalypse and resurrection, youth and adventure. In the new decade Tove began writing about illusions, change and what was still to come. Her journey to the Moominvalley of the future began at dawn one August day when the amphibian pointed its snout toward new adventures, the amphibian being the houseboat, the ship from the time of youth and adventure in *The Exploits of Moominpappa*, cast in a new body and with a new range. In the book's final words: 'A new door to the Unbelievable, to the Possible, a new day that can always bring you anything if you have no objection to it.'

The door to the unbelievable was now open for the Moomin writer and painter Tove Jansson. The next years would be a vertiginous period of new projects, connections and experiences. It was now that the story of Moomin's success began to be written. The tug of war between pleasure and duty, which had marked the war and the years after it, was temporarily over. Pleasure was in the ascendant and it was fun to work. Tove's finances were often 'wretched', but she was still able to pick and choose her commissions (when not entirely broke) and to set her own conditions for work: 'If sometimes I work hard it's on my *own* work,' she wrote firmly. The reviewers were enthusiastic; the books were being published in Sweden and being discussed – a good gauge of success – but they hadn't yet broken through on the market. She invested her royalties in equal proportions in art and living, using advances on the wall paintings at Fredrikshamn (1952) to cover debts and unpaid taxes, spending 20,000 marks on canvases for paintings done in the studio, then cutting loose on a fine bag and a new dress: 'now, for the foreseeable future, I'm poor again!' she wrote happily enough on 17th January 1952.

The spring was set aside for the wall paintings in the club building at Fredrikshamn; she made a sketch for a new mural for Kotka and corresponded with the *Daily Mail* in London about her planned strip series, while at the same time her picture book 'from last summer', *The Book About Moomin, Mymble and Little My,* was being printed. Next day it was time to hand in '6–7' oil paintings for a general exhibition at Konsthallen. This felt like a comeback and she was nervous. 'There's a lot happening all at once. But it's fun to work – at last, after so many hellish and unproductive years of failure.' This was her employment situation in February 1952. In the summer she was to design decor and costumes for *Pessi and Illusia*, a ballet for the Finnish National Opera based on Yrjö Kokko's 1944 bestseller (known in Swedish as *The Earth and the Wings*, 1945), which was due to have its premiere in the autumn. In the middle of this hectic spring, a syndication manager from London called Charles Sutton arrived to draw up the contract for a Moomin strip series for Associated Newspapers. This was an opportunity she had no intention of missing, she assured Eva. She worked night and day to prepare a synopsis for the meeting, writing the last line the very day Sutton set foot in Helsinki.

She was not one to miss a deadline and the intensity of her work is clear from her notes. In a letter to Vivica Bandler, she summarised: 'I finished the Fredrikshamn paintings at the last minute and have set them up. The Kotka mural has been drawn ready in the studio on a scale of 1:1. The premiere of Pessi and Illusia at the Opera will be on 23rd October.' She had originally declined the Opera commission but, she wrote, could not resist her 'perverse' weakness for fairy tales. Like Tove, Kokko had mixed fairy tale and war in his story, but his tone was quite different from hers. An elf-girl and a troll-boy meet in a Finnish forest near the wartime front line. Forty-two thousand copies of Kokko's tale were printed in its first year of publication and in 1945 he was awarded the Finnish state prize for literature. A family man in battledress who wrote his story during lulls on the front line, Kokko achieved something much more than an 'imaginative children's story and a beautiful picture book' (illustrated with photos by Kokko himself), as the back cover of the Swedish edition puts it.

Tove devoted the summer to her strips and sketches for the ballet. 'I'll get through all right so long as I keep calm,' she wrote in May, and she certainly did manage. But her fairy tale job for *Pessi and Illusia* proved a great disappointment. Her thirty-five fantasy costumes clashed with Kokko's ideas – truly a political matter – and the month she spent working on the ballet was pure hell. She could not take responsibility for the costumes, she regretted, since 'the author, Kokko, arrived at the last minute and made such ugly "national" alterations that I asked to have my name taken off them.' When imagination turned political and her work was misrepresented, no other outcome was possible.

Murals, stage scenery and costumes, comic strips: Tove's artistic range and energy for work were remarkable. After war, isolation and the increasing pressure of her need to paint freely and be free to travel, after her drudgery as an illustrator for *Garm* and others, after her years with Atos and her heartrending romance with Vivica, it was now time to create the world and Moomin anew. Change became the guiding star of her work. She wrote stories about inner revelation and personal impressions. The Moomin books that began taking form now demonstrated how environment can change perspective and transform life: going out to buy milk for Moominmamma can involve an expedition full of danger, a flood can cause the Moomin family to find themselves on a theatre stage, an unfamiliar season of the year can create an environment for individual change. The 1950s would see the publication of the pictorial *Book About Moomin, Mymble and Little My*, and two new stories that would take the Moomin world by storm: *Moominsummer Madness* and *Moominland Midwinter.*

The first Moomin strip. From the book edition of 1957.

Starting as a not particularly remarkable painter and writer of children's books in Finland, Tove Jansson was transformed in a few years into a star author and glittering creator of comic strips, published in an ever-increasing number of languages. When after years of correspondence and discussions between the London syndicate and Tove's Helsinki studio, the first Moomin strip finally got under way in England in 1954, it was a smash hit. At the time, the London *Evening News* was the world's biggest daily paper (with a circulation of twelve million) and the series soon spread to other papers. The Moomin strips turned their author into a worldwide household name and the Moomin world became popular with both children and adults. 'How strange,' Tove commented to Eva; after the worst thing she knew, politics, had cast a shadow over the first part of her life, 'is commerce, the next worst thing I know, about to dominate the second?' There was some reason for this anxiety, but for her, in the end, it was always her own work in words and pictures that came first.

At first the craving for Moomin astonished her: 'I'm sending off business letters right, left and centre and I'm amazed how far the Moomin business seems to reach,' she wrote in June 1952. By this time the picture book was on its way, the Lindström publishing company was delivering posters for children's rooms to the bookshops and she had been in correspondence about the Moomin strips for about six months. Barely a year later her tone had changed: 'I'm happy to have work at last – but it leaves me so much less time to myself. Everything connected with the fairy tales takes an enormous amount of time and worry and these days that mostly means business letters and meetings with firms and publishers. My royalties are mostly stuck abroad and it needs endless transactions to get hold of the money and I still lose most of it. Now there's a plastics company after me. What d'you think of the idea of rubber tubes shaped like Hattifatteners?' she asked Eva in January 1954.

As the 'Moomin business' steadily grew, Tove was forced to turn quickly into negotiator, lawyer and businesswoman. Of course this affected her life in many ways. The 1950s saw a radical transformation in her letter writing. She who had so loved writing to friends and family, chatting, telling stories, describing characters (her letters abound with fine examples), had to restrict herself. Moomin's fame was demanding more and more of her writing time. Increasingly, her letterbox was concerned with questions of guilty conscience and with enquiries, requests and obligations, even if this (sometimes horror-laden) access to her studio also brought her letters of happiness, friendship, love and happy work.

When on 19th January 1952 Charles Sutton first wrote (in English) to 'Dear Miss Jansson' to suggest the idea of a Moomin strip for the *Daily Mail*, it was the beginning of a long correspondence. Tove said yes at once. She would love to make a strip series, she already had plans for one, and the prospect of being published internationally was much more interesting than the world of local publicity. It could help her books (which were not circulating as widely as she would have liked): 'Besides it would probably give our Moomins more publicity,' she wrote in her answer to Sutton. This proved an understatement. A spotlight fell on 'Moomin' as soon as the strip started; there was masses of publicity. Tove herself became a living advertisement for her work and her correspondence increased to unimagined dimensions: to syndicates, publishers, agents, the press and media, translators, lawyers, Moomin manufacturers of all kinds, advertising agencies, entrepreneurs, interested parties in general and, of course, streams of readers and admirers. Her correspondence relating to the strips alone amounted to hundreds of letters and continued into the 1960s. Those she communicated with in London were Charles Sutton, Julian Phipps and Gerald Sanger, but there was only one correspondent in the Helsinki studio – Tove Jansson herself.

A Theatre of Pictures

The Book About Moomin, Mymble and Little My was the first Moomin picture book. Its title in Swedish is *Hur gick det sen?* ('What Happened Next?'), a question relevant in a more general sense to Tove in the 1950s. She was exploring a new landscape, feeling her way in expression, emotion, work, pleasure and love.

The Book About Moomin, Mymble and Little My is a speaking theatre of pictures that blends traditional and modern concepts of literature and art. The theatre offered many opportunities for both the scriptwriter and the designer of costumes and sets. It was a hand-in-glove fit for a double artist in words and pictures like Tove Jansson. She began working on the picture book the year before doing the strips became a reality. The idea was to build on surprise, she told Eva in autumn 1951:

Last summer I made a new book, for very small children this time, a picture book in colour with a few lines of verse on each page. Mostly about Mymble. It's coming out next year, and I shall try and place it with Benn's. The idea is great fun. Each page has a hole in it, representing a door or the entrance to a cave or a tiled stove or something else that fits the context. The characters crawl through and are met on the next page by the most surprising things. I think the moment of astonishment is vital when you are trying to capture the interest of small children. You see, looking through each hole (backwards and forwards through the book) you catch a glimpse of something tempting and strange that when you turn the page turns out to be not at all what you expect.

Illustration from The Book About Moomin, Mymble and Little My.

The queen of surprises had spoken. Her theory could not have been clearer. She had tried the story on little children, who liked the idea. The ideas for the pictures became scenes and the landscapes interchangeable theatrical wings, while the book's red cover acted like a curtain, or like a door opening onto the scene of the story and presenting those involved in the production: the stage hands, the leading actors (Moomin, Mymble and Little My), the scriptwriter (Tove Jansson) and the director (the publishers). The closed door to the Moomin house on the back cover of the book indicates that the play is over, but also, like every piece created for the theatre, it can be performed again: 'Back in a minute,' says a notice on the door. The whole adds up to a play conveying a direct experience as if to the audience in a theatre.

She had created it on Bredskär in the summer of 1951 and her thought processes during the preliminary work were extensively documented. Six or seven mini-models exist together with notes on the presentation process, including possible combinations of printed colours, and the conditions necessary for binding the pages together and for printing and photo technique. Any mistake in assembling the book could destroy the whole concept, she told her editor, Svedlin at Schildts: I know it's 'rather a bother with all those holes'. So she would send an 'explanatory' schedule and give detailed instructions for printing:

> The book must be printed on two eight-page sheets. The colour distribution has been calculated to give each sheet its own combination of colours, with the same for the covers. So when after printing the sheets are divided into octavos [two four-sided sections] and fastened together, there will be a richer variety of colour than would have been possible if we had printed in three colours throughout. I have tried to arrange it so that each page as it were 'borrows' colours through the holes from the preceding and succeeding pages. Thus a blue and red opening can give the impression that it has also been printed in violet and gold.

Here spoke an artist who was used to making her own decisions. The picture book had become like a painting, with herself in complete control of the canvas. Her correspondence with her publishers – both Schildts and Gebers – is ample evidence of the strong will behind the book. 'What I most need to know is whether you will be able to carry out the idea on which I base the whole picture book,' she wrote to Nils Wikström at Gebers. 'That is to say, that the cover and every page (except the title page) is pierced with a hole.'At this point the picture book as yet had no title, just that it would be a 'simple' story based on a deliberate idea. Tove made a careful study of the printing possibilities for her 'breakthrough': roughly circular holes, with both straight and uneven edges. The text, in an enhanced version of her own handwriting, must be visually expressive and calligraphic in the manner of her first comic strip ('Moomintroll and the End of the World', created for Atos Wirtanen's *Ny Tid* in 1947–48). She visualised the story in lettering alone. This was the embryo writer of comic strips in action, but offstage in the wings behind this exhibition of mature graphic art the experienced illustrator could also be found.

The book had its roots in imaginative nineteenth-century picture books with their fold-out and stand-up pages, threads linking ideas, cut-out holes, moving figures, and so on. Tove herself gave various literary and artistic clues when she answered questions about the book's concept and origin. One clue led back to Elsa Beskow's *Tomtebobarnen* (*Children of the Forest*, 1910), in which the horrible troll who looks out from behind a stone frightened the little Tove so much that Ham stuck a piece of paper over it. When this was lifted to reveal the troll, the little Tove was even more terrified. Another clue led to a book with cardboard trapdoors which could be raised to reveal wild animals. 'No other book was such fun as that one,' she wrote in a note. 'I mean, that you could *look in*, and if you made yourself very small you could look out too.' There were many books of this kind in the nineteenth century, with titles like *Picture Book of Surprises*.

She blended the traditional with the modern. 'I love Matisse,' she wrote in February 1952. Her one-man show several years later carried traces of this beloved painter, not least in Tove's use of colour. The reviewers noticed. Then there was Matisse's own work with scissors, in his 'découpages' (cut-outs), not least in his book *Jazz* (1947). This is a picture book whose coloured pages are combined with a handwritten text, just as in *The Book About Moomin, Mymble and Little My*.

'Working with scissors' was something new. 'I had lots of fun,' wrote Tove, reproducing the scissors on the title page of her book.

Longing for Mother

Tove's picture book is set in the present but its basic story is traditional: a tale of homecoming. Moomin is on his way back from the dairy when he meets Mymble and Little My, and the three pass through a series of adventures in a variety of dramatic landscapes. *The Book About Moomin, Mymble and Little My* is a psychological thriller about being tied to one's mother's apron strings and suffering separation anxiety, with Freudian overtones. Lines like 'He shouted through the gunge and fluff,/"Oh, Mother, help, I've had enough!"' speak for themselves. The story is in fact constructed from holes, openings and grottoes combined with phallus-shaped environments and objects: tunnels, vacuum cleaners, cans, and so on. The oblong milk can links mother and child (though the milk goes sour) and is transformed into a symbol of incipient (male) independence. Moomin's terror of the unfamiliar landscape beyond Mother's control is tempered by his urge to explore it. The pictures expressively depict childhood nightmares, in which the fear of being abandoned by Mother is reflected in the dreamlike colour combinations of the landscape. Gold and violet, black and blue, red and grey; a colour scheme far from Elsa Beskow and the cosy fidelity to nature characteristic of so many picture books of the period. *The Book About Moomin, Mymble and Little My* contains not a single calming green place on which to rest the eye. It's as if nature as we know it didn't exist.

Moominmamma challenges the sombre images of motherhood so common in children's literature; she is a counterblast to all those absent and dead mothers. There is no other place in the Moomin literature where she projects such a powerfully mythological maternal presence as in this book. Her entry as a beautifully rounded goddess (she can even be compared to Aphrodite) is like an illumination of life and sensuality. Berries, shells and roses surround her body with a symbolic world of fruitfulness, birth and love. The sun shines in brilliant glory behind her head, there is a rose behind her ear and beside her stands her big handbag marked 'M.M.' The only sign of Moominpappa, elsewhere prominent as a writer of memoirs and adventurer, is the hat that holds the berries (the hat was introduced as one of his attributes in the strip series). Mother *is* love.

The text that acts as an infrastructure to these words and pictures is a mid-nineteenth century Christian children's song, 'In a dark unending forest', by Carl Olof Rosenius. It describes how we are all like little defenceless children before God and need our great Father's home and comforting embrace.

In a dark unending forest
where black clouds and thunder threatened,
a little child once walked
the livelong day.

Oh, that day was ever so long,
the sky was dark and the forest dense.
Lonely and weeping
the child walked on.

Weeping to think: I shall
never more see my father's home.
Here in darkness, cold and want
I shall die.

Then in deep despair as he wept
the clouds parted, the sun shone through –
and there brightly lit
in the sunshine stood his Father's house!

This song was in Ham's repertoire. Tove wrote it out in a childhood letter and quoted the verse about homecoming in her 1931 diary, when she was studying at Teknis in Stockholm and longing for home. The text belonged to her childhood. But the version in her diary, like the later picture book, is not about a great Father but a great Mother. Rosenius wrote, 'I shall never more see my father's home,' but Tove changed 'father' to 'mother': 'Moomintroll feels extremely glum./He wants his home, his bed, his Mum.' The same reversal occurred when still later she included a couple of verses in *Sculptor's Daughter*. In the chapter 'The Dark', the narrator speaks of her fear of separation from her mother and happiness at being reunited, with other words about the symbiosis between mother and child. In this context Rosenius's text enters the narrator's story in compressed form and without quotation marks: 'Through endless forest dark and drear no comfort near a little girl alone did roam so far from home the way was long the night was cold the thunder rolled the girl did weep no more I'll find my mother kind for in this lonely haunted spot my awful lot will be beneath this tree to lie and slowly die.'

In the picture book Moomin takes the place of the child and wanders through a dark unending forest, but the female text has a different purpose from the male one. When the sun shines through in Moomin's world it shines directly on his mother's house. *The Book About Moomin, Mymble and Little My* pays homage to motherhood, but it is above all a story about growing up and approaching adolescence. After Moomintroll's expedition, the time of milk and childhood is over (in any case the milk has gone sour) and Mother forcefully asserts: 'Now we've all got a great excuse/For drinking sweet pink berry juice!'

The picture book was widely and very favourably reviewed. In particular, the cut holes and colour combinations attracted attention. The powerful Eva von Zweigbergk nominated it in *Dagens Nyheter* as the most original new picture book of the year, and spoke lyrically of the tension between its 'peaceable verses' and 'dramatic theatre decor'. This was no picture book for colourless people, she concluded, but a glorious surprise for everyone else – just as Tove had intended it to be.

The Book About Moomin, Mymble and Little My won Tove her first prize for a children's book, the Nils Holgersson Plaque, awarded by the General Association of Swedish Libraries. It may be worth noting in this connection that the book had earlier been given the thumbs-down in the same Association's periodical, *Biblioteksbladet*, where it was dismissed as uninteresting and tedious and not worth buying (readers were even warned against its characters' 'strange, unreadable and incomprehensible names'). Any embarrassment this might have caused was obliterated by the prize, whose citation speaks a different language: 'a picture book shaped in a strongly personal manner, which combines humour and imagination with lively dramatic power' – qualities nearly always associated with Tove as a writer of children's books. Imagination was the theme she chose for her speech at the presentation ceremony, when she elaborated on her theoretical ideas about writing stories for children (the mural in Kotka). 'I believe,' she said, that 'most children live in a world in which the fantastic and the matter-of-fact have equal force, and this is the world I have tried to describe and reconstruct for myself.' She expressed similar views in an interview for *Svenska Dagbladet*, which awarded her its own 1952 prize for picture books.

Public appearances often terrified her. A couple of hundred people listened to her at the presentation of the Nils Holgersson Prize. 'I've never been so nervous,' she wrote, 'and I had to take to my bed with stomach pains.' But at the same time the prize, a glass plaque 'with a goose on it', as she described it to Eva just before Christmas 1953, shone a new light on her books. In passing she regretted not being able to wear the plaque on her chest. But these awards for *The Book About Moomin, Mymble and Little My* were to be no more than a beginning.

This was the first of her books to come out in Finnish in the same year as its first appearance in Swedish. It was not until 1955, ten years after Moomin's debut, that any other Moomin books were published in the majority language of her home country. In the spring of the same year a strip series in Finnish appeared for the first time in *Ilta Sanomat*, and there could be no doubt that the strips and the books attracted attention to one another, as Juhani Tolvanen has pointed out. But there had been plans for Finnish-language editions of her books as early as 1950. The interested translator, Jarno Pennanen, sounded out the Otava publishing firm but the project came to nothing.

Private Changes

Tove's fortieth birthday on 9th August 1954 found her roughly halfway through her life. 'A day like any other day. I'm forty years old and have had a certain success, I'm tired of many different things and at the same time tired of monotony,' she noted. She was now old enough to write her autobiography, though she gave it no thought. But her personal writing was intensified in diary notes, sketches for stories, dialogues with herself and transcriptions of letters that she collected in exercise books. Her letters to Eva were still important to her, even if time and distance were having an effect on them. She still wrote several a year, insightful narrations and reflections on work and love. On the other hand, important new series of letters developed with Tuulikki Pietilä and Maya Vanni. She also wrote to her family when she was away travelling, and to friends. And her business correspondence was getting even heavier.

Old relationships were settled. Atos disappeared from the limelight after years of intimacy. When at long last he decided in 1952 that he did want to marry her after all, it was Tove who said no. She felt 'happy not to be in love'. At the same time an urge to move over to the 'rive gauche' or 'spook side' (code words for lesbianism) began to surface and gain strength. She had felt emotionally homeless, and longed to find the right way for herself and see herself clearly. She elaborated her thoughts to Eva, who had been worried when Tove began falling in love with women:

> Now at last I think I know what I want, and since my friendship with you is so important to me and honesty is vital, I would like to talk to you about the matter. I haven't finally made up my mind, but I'm inclined to believe that the happiest and most genuine solution for me will be to go over to the spook side. It would be silly for you to be upset about it. But I myself am very happy and feel a strong sense of liberation and peace.

Meanwhile she had found a new love.

> For the last few weeks I've been spending nearly all my time with someone I unfortunately only discovered just before she was due to leave for France. We are both equally happy. At the same time I'm working like a madwoman – among other things, on a couple of portraits and naked studies of her. She won't be coming back here, but I've decided that this time I'm not going to entomb myself in any kind of grieving.

Tove's relief was great, her happiness liberating. She had made her choice: 'The most important thing is stay at peace with oneself and to know what one wants,' she told Eva. It seemed simple, but in practice it was difficult even so. She was entering a little world that was even more restricted than the close and introverted world of Finland-Swedish cultural circles, whose cramped and overcrowded artistic universe she analysed:

> One runs into old mymbles [lovers of either sex], friends and enemies everywhere. It's so unbelievably small – and

the Swedish-speaking intellectuals and artists in particular constantly stumble over one another. And get helplessly entangled with each other. We are so few! And another group who are few are the lesbian 'Spooks', as we call them.

'We are so few,' declared Tove, defining her identity both as a Finland-Swedish artist and as a lesbian woman. The world was shrinking and expanding at the same time. She settled down with her new love, the goldsmith Britt-Sofie Foch (who had returned from France after all), and their relationship gave new impetus to her oils and pictures. She made many paintings with 'Bitti' as model. In the studio she constructed benches so they could both work. As always, love and work were mixed together. She was happy, but it was impossible to live openly as a lesbian. Neither society nor her family would allow it.

It was a real torment not to be able to discuss her new love with her parents. But even if people didn't talk, they knew. 'Such a pity one has to sneak and conceal,' she wrote: 'I've got a feeling Ham knows, but she will never mention the matter before she herself is ready to.' As it turned out, it wasn't Ham who asked the question, but Faffan. Gossip and rumours had reached him, but he couldn't bring himself to get the 'difficult word homosexual' across his lips. She could not discuss the subject, either with him or Ham. Tove noted: 'Ham said nothing. She never says anything. I think she knows. But she doesn't want to mention it. I can accept that this is right and more elegant. But it feels lonely.' Thus their daughter adapted herself to accept the code of silence. She could not speak to either her mother or her father.

Tove believed her acceptance of this silence was respect for Ham's integrity, but it was respect at the cost of loneliness. And it was a great sorrow. It was a place where they could not meet. There was no definite assessment, no open repudiation, but there was no connection. Any intimacy between them had to exist under new conditions. Thus this 'elegant' silence was never entirely broken, not even when Tove met Tuulikki Pietilä, who was to be the love of her life.

In the early 1950s the studio at Ulrikasborgsgatan 1 finally became Tove's own, after years of precarious renting arrangements. A sewing studio and a kindergarten were just two of the threats it had suffered. She loved her tower, but sometimes felt like a 'visitor' in her own home. It was difficult to work, paint and live when prospective buyers of the studio kept knocking on the door to be shown round. She had long relied on illustration jobs to pay the rent, but every so often threats of terminating her tenancy and selling the premises recurred. During the late winter of 1952 the tower had been up for sale for a year and the owner, 'a great scoundrel' in Tove's eyes, had deceived her into thinking that he had sold the studio to a printing business. She called his bluff and grabbed the chance to buy it herself.

This threw everything in the air and the conditions he demanded were severe. She must act at once, but if she could 'put half a million [Finnish marks] on the table' the next day (the full price was one and a half million), the tower would be hers. After paying all her taxes she hadn't 'a penny' left in her purse, but against all the odds she managed to raise a bank loan to tide her over for the next twenty-four hours. Such was the dramatic story she told Eva in June 1952.

Her conversation with the bank manager had revealed that her name had a power she had not been aware of: 'To my astonishment he said my name was worth half a million (they are not giving *any* loans at the moment, and if I could collect two rock-hard names [as guarantors] I could have the rest too.' So she rushed off to the owner, whose name was Westerlund, and told him it was all settled: 'Then the pisspot said he must have 100,000 in cash, or he might give the studio to the printers after all while I was away in the country! At the last minute I remembered that for once in a while I could also make profitable use of my old paintings. And the bugger agreed to accept them in pawn!'

It was a triumph in several ways, both for her pictures, which had long been difficult to sell (art breeds new art), and for herself as a negotiator. At long last she really had a place of her own. 'They were exciting days, having to get there ahead of others, haggling and being diplomatic, lawyers and paperwork and guarantors – and in the end I was able to unlock my own door and close it behind me, conscious of the fact that I no longer needed to let anyone in except those I wanted to. The mortgage is for ten years – and I shall pay it off.' The purchase of the studio was a huge victory.

Midsummer Night's Dream

'It was a short but happy summer. I wrote a new Moomin book that I'm thinking of calling *farlig midsommar*. The new book's title translates as 'Dangerous Midsummer', and in English it was to become *Moominsummer Madness*. In late 1953 Tove summarised the plot for Eva:

> After a natural catastrophe the family gather round a theatre, without understanding that's what it is. The only survivor from the previous life of the theatre is the old theatre rat Emma. On midsummer night they are dispersed in various directions and after a muddled series of wanderings they finally come together again in the first performance of a play. All ends happily of course. I'm in the middle of illustrating it and hope to be able to send you the completed book before the summer.

'You come out of the theatre to find life still going on outside it,' Tove said in an interview before the first performance of 'Moomintroll and the Comet'. Life as theatre is the time-honoured theme that cuts into the Moomin play, both on the real stage and in the books. Theatre is the arena for role-playing and changing identity, somewhere it's possible to be 'someone completely different', as Misabel aptly puts it in *Moominsummer Madness*.

Dress rehearsal. From Moominsummer Madness.

But Moomin theatrical practice demonstrates even more clearly who one really is, a maxim formulated by Emma the theatre rat: 'Theatre is the most important thing in the world, because that's where people show what they could be, and what they long to be even though they can't be, and how they are.'This was a literary self-description. Tove had shown who she was, both for herself and for the rest of the world. *Moominsummer Madness*, which came out two years after the *Book About Moomin, Mymble and Little My*, makes play with identities, errors and life roles, with dreams, longing and existence. It is also a happy book, full of the joy and high spirits of comedy. *Moominsummer Madness* is a comedy of errors, inspired at a remove by Shakespeare, a midsummer night's dream full of surprises and transformations and containing a play within a play – Moominpappa's blank verse tragedy, 'The Lion's Brides or Blood Will Out' – a direct analogy with the amateur theatricals in Shakespeare's play.

The question of the distinction between what actually is and what merely seems to be is the key problem behind the action. Behind the scenery at the theatre there is no firm reality, everything can stand for something else. A tiled stove is painted on the back of a paper door, a stairway ends in thin air, and Whomper (a new character) reflects:

A door should lead somewhere and a staircase too. What would life be like if a Misabel suddenly behaved like a Mymble, or a Whomper like a Hemulen?

He's looking for the order of things as he knows it, but theatre shows what is unknown – it shows what might happen if a Misabel did behave like a Mymble, or a Whomper like a Hemulen.

Theatre is the accepted setting for role-playing, error and shifting scenery and it structures *Moominsummer Madness* from beginning to end. The magic atmosphere is called forth by midsummer, in popular belief the traditional time for witchcraft and dangerous dreams. The principle of the story is scenic and the manuscript includes a page with short character studies of the actors like a cast list. Three parallel courses of events intertwine in the story, as they do in the stage comedy, and the manuscript material includes an illuminating sketch of the direction in which the courses of action move. They circle around each other, eventually to come together and unite. Entrances are replaced by sudden exits, disappearance is transformed into meeting, confusion leads to complications. The unities of time and place are inscribed through midsummer and the theatre. And on the stage a great dramatic finale introduces the great resolution of the comedy's errors and complications – a 'Happy End'.

It is when the floating theatre runs aground that the real comedy begins. One course of action follows the theatre company, which consists of Moominmamma and Moominpappa, Whomper, Misabel, the Mymble's daughter and (soon) the theatre rat Emma; another follows Moomin and the Snork maiden who are separated from the family and join up with a Fillyjonk; and a third follows Little My, who has fallen out of the theatre into the water through the prompter's box but saves herself in Moominmamma's  work basket. This eventually gets caught on Snufkin's fishing hook. Then the author appears as prompter in the style of a classic novel, and serves up a surprise, in much the same way as in the picture book:

> Dear reader, prepare for a surprise. Chance and coincidence are strange things. Without knowing anything of each other and each other's business, the Moomin family and Snufkin had happened to arrive at the same little inlet on Midsummer Eve.

At midsummer the border between dream and reality disappears. When theatrical performances that play with time are united with the laws of the Moomin world, what was merely magical is transformed into 'troll' material and constructs its own mythology. Only on Midsummer Night can Hattifatteners be summoned up from the earth, and only then can their seed be sown and begin to grow. The fact that Little My was born on Midsummer Night, as we are told in *The Exploits of Moominpappa*, has its own obvious significance. 'The troll-bewitched night,' as it says in a note with the manuscript.

The Nature of Theatre

Connected people separated by fate only to be happily reunited are one of the fundamental patterns of literature, not least in comedy. The Moomin family has been broken up; Moominmamma longs for it to come together again, Moomin longs for Snufkin, the Fillyjonk longs to have relatives and company – they all long for family bonds. This is the subject of both the book *Moominsummer Madness* and Moominpappa's play. The theatrical performance is the peripeteia (turning point) of the story and it is transformed into a display of dreams, longing and meetings both for the actors on the stage and their audience. In time-honoured idiom, Moominpappa's play comes to frame the real performance that takes place on the stage. At the beginning, form is the most important thing. Emma the theatre rat acts as instructor:

'But you must write it again, in blank verse! Blank verse! Rhymes won't do!' said Emma.

'What do you mean, blank verse,' asked Moominpappa.

'It should go like this: Ti-dum, ti-umpty-um – ti-dumty-um-tum,' explained Emma. 'And you mustn't express yourself so naturally.'

Moominpappa brightened. 'Do you mean: 'I tremble not before the Desert King, be he a savage beast or not so savage'?'he asked.

'That's more like it,' said Emma. 'Now go and write it all in blank verse. And remember that in all the good old tragedies most of the people are each other's relatives.'

'But how can they be angry at each other if they're of the same family?' Moominmamma asked cautiously. 'And is there no princess in the play? Can't you put in a happy end?? It's so sad when people die.'

'This *is* a tragedy, dearest,' said Moominpappa. 'And because of that somebody has to die in the end. Preferably all except one of them, and perhaps that one too. Emma's said so.'

Lion, tragedy and complicated genealogy mix ancient drama with Shakespearean comedy and tragedy, with in the margin an old broadside ballad called 'The Lion Bride'. The title of Moominpappa's play is 'The Lion's Brides or Blood Will Out'. The

Shadows from the world of illusions. Moominmamma, from
Moominsummer Madness.

popular ballad (based on a poem by the romantic poet Chamisso)
deals with the unfortunate daughter of a lion tamer forced to
marry a man she doesn't love and then torn apart by a lion. A
similar fate awaits the Mymble's daughter in Moominpappa's
transformation-rich piece. Dramatisation takes the form of
two parts which are performed in succession. One chapter
describes the dress rehearsal, another the first performance.

We see the dress rehearsal from the point of view of the actors on stage, but the first performance from the point of view of the audience beyond the footlights; this includes Snufkin, the woodies and the Hemulen policeman. Thus we are able to see two performances of the play, one from either side of the footlights, and so experience both the actors' and the audience's experiences and feelings. Snufkin (who knows something about theatre) sees Moominpappa 'declaim something peculiar about a lot of his relatives and a lion' while the Hemulen (who once saw a play when he was a child) expects something with a princess in it. Neither of them can feel he is living in the play, but for open-minded children theatre is pure reality. Little My can't understand why Moominpappa is scolding her sister and the woodies are frightened of the lion. They see that 'the lion is chasing the Mymble's daughter all over the stage' and that no one is coming to her rescue or killing the lion. Then My leaps onto the stage and bites the lion on the leg. It shrieks and 'breaks in the middle'.

My's leap destroys the boundary between theatre and reality and demonstrates the strength of the bond of kinship. She makes the connection between theatre and reality comprehensible; at the same time reality becomes the true theatre. No one recites any more blank verse; they speak 'quite naturally' and the audience 'at last' understands what the play is about. 'It was about someone who had floated away from home, and had awful experiences, and now found her way home again. And everybody was marvellously happy and going to have a cup of tea.' The festival of theatre is transformed into a carnival in which all swarm round each other; the audience as community is also an ancient constituent of comedy. When Moomin, the Snork maiden and the Fillyjonk enter, the play continues in the midst of reality. Life really is theatre. The mingling together of illusion and reality is not over and the question is, is it possible?

The actual premiere brings together the various strands of the action and reunites the bonds of kinship cut off by the midsummer adventure. Now Moominmamma's deepest wish comes true – everyone comes home and all is well. The framework for this is the staged script, the play written and directed by Moominpappa, but the person really responsible for staging and directing the action is Moominmamma. She encourages Moominpappa to write ('Of course you could, dear'), keeps him going when others begin to criticise ('Dearest one – We think it's wonderful. Don't we?'; 'Of course,' everybody said.), and supports his favourite character ('Of course there must be a lion, dear'). Her method is a skilful combination of encouraging pushes and attentive urges to rewrite: 'Everybody likes it. You just change the style and the plot a little. I'll see to it that you're not disturbed, and you can take the whole bowl of candy with you.'

In this text is the kernel of the midsummer adventure, which is to accept dreams and longing as reality, and find ways of being oneself. The family moves off towards the Valley, leaving the others in the theatre. Perspective is adjusted. June nights are never dangerous, Snufkin tells Moomin. The pale, dreamy night of enchantment has gone. But life has been changed. The shadows that came from the world of dreams and illusions will always remain with them.

Jansson the Moominist

Summer 1953 found Tove in Österbotten – in the province of East Bothnia, in Western Finland – painting an altarpiece for a new church at Övermark. She went there at the end of May to make a preliminary sketch al secco. Her subject was the 'fool-ish and wise virgins', she wrote, and she had toiled away at it all spring, genuinely moved by her first sacred commission. Al-though religious pictures were, generally speaking, not her style, she had produced a good many for Christmas magazines during the 1930s and 1940s. While working at Övermark she was read-ing 'the Psalms of David' but she was finding them rather mo-notonous,' she confided to Vivica Bandler: 'The psalmist spends most of his time just quarrelling with his enemies and begging God to destroy them.'

In the evenings she was working on the Moomin book, editing it in accordance with Vivica's directions. Busy, as always, with several different pieces of work at the same time. It wasn't just the altarpiece and the book that became *Moominsummer Madness*; she was also working on comic strips. It was a good time for fitting together words and pictures of more than one kind. Her

Secco *altarpiece in Övermark, 1953.*

reading of the Bible left its mark on the Moomin book. Little My in her floating work basket relates to Moses in the bulrushes, Moomintroll's homecoming recalls the Prodigal Son, the floating theatre is an ark that runs aground, and the the initial flood is of course as an image of the end of the world – which Little My wonders about. 'Try to be good now if you can find the time, because in a little while we're all going to Heaven,' her sister the Mymble's daughter warns her, to which My answers: 'Heaven? Do we have to? And how does one get down again?'

Choosing a suitable title for the book had bothered Tove. There is an allusion to Steinbeck's novel *The Wayward Bus* in the title she gave it in one nearly complete version of the manuscript ('The Wayward Theatre'), but she changed her mind. She made a note that the first page had been partly withdrawn and rewritten, while a longer section in which an excited Moomintroll describes a boiling sea, the eruption of a volcano and the appearance of a tidal wave was struck out altogether. There is a good deal more destruction in the manuscript than in the finished story – perhaps she was haunted by her reading of the Psalms.

The critics completely capitulated before *Moominsummer Madness*; even previously critical voices, such as the reviewer in *Stockholms-Tidningen*, were won over. *Dagens Nyheter* published an advance excerpt from the book (this differs to some extent from the final text), illustrated by Tove with a large coloured picture. Her writer-colleague Bo Carpelan started his career as a Moomin critic with his article 'Jansson the Moominist' written as an academic parody for *Hufvudstadsbladet*. Later he would write a similar piece about *Moominland Midwinter*. He dealt with

Jansson's shorthand terms 'Moomin psychology' and 'trollology', and analysed her concept of style and the theoretical foundations of her work. Altogether, he found it a 'horribly amusing book that all children can profitably give to their parents'. This was a constant theme with the reviewers: they saw it as a book for everyone. Gudrun Mörne, after a rewarding read over a cup of tea and a 'good cigarette', asked herself whether it was likely to amuse children as well as adults. Not surprisingly, her answer was yes.

Moominsummer Madness was dedicated to Vivica, Tove's theatrical consultant, who had checked the manuscript. The same year (1953), Tove was asked by Gothenburg municipal theatre for permission to stage 'Moomintroll and the Comet'. This was to be the very first staging of a Moomin play in Sweden, though the production has been entirely forgotten. Tove's requirements were harsh. It was self-evident to her that Vivica must direct it, but the director of the theatre, Karin Kavli, had other plans. Gothenburg has a large theatre with a permanent professional staff (one of the best in Sweden) and Tove's questions about decor and sketches were waved aside. The theatre had its own studio and scene-painter. Kavli's stiff letters (she was clearly afraid of extra expense) discouraged Tove from co-operating. No notice was taken of her wishes relating to the aesthetic requirements of the piece, and she was afraid the whole thing would be a 'débacle'. Kavli knew nothing whatever about the Moomin books.

The script's progress onto the Gothenburg stage is shrouded in darkness. 'You ask me where I got hold of "Moomintroll and the Comet,' wrote Kavli. 'I found it here in the theatre. How it got here and who left it here I don't know. It seemed to me an excellent piece for children, but on the other hand I don't know the Moomin books and would be grateful if you could lend copies of them to the theatre, as this would be of some help to the director [Nils Ahlsell] who is to stage the piece.' No more detailed information was given, nor did Tove herself return to the matter.

The reviews of the production were reasonable, but the public did not flock to it and it came off after eleven performances. Yet Tove was relieved. She told Eva, 'I knew the piece was weak and its fame undeserved. It was with great hesitation that I signed the contract, and it's an enormous relief that it wasn't an absolute fiasco.' She never saw the production. The concrete result from her point of view was a cheque for a thousand Swedish kronor. According to the theatre's accountant the takings were 12,208 kronor, of which the author got eight per cent, to be exact 976 kronor and 69 öre.

A couple of years earlier, Dramaten (the Swedish national theatre in Stockholm), which had read the play, planned a production for Christmas 1951, but this came to nothing. (They were 'enormously' slow about returning the material to me, commented Tove in a letter.) It was only with the staging of the second Moomin play, 'Troll in the Wings', that Moomin really made a hit on stage in Sweden.

Dear Mr Sutton

It was with the strip series that 'Moomin' won international recognition and fame on a wide front. The first of the international strips started in the London *Evening News* on 20th September 1954, and within two years they were running in twenty countries. By 1955 Moomin had reached most of the leading Nordic newspapers, like *Politiken* (Denmark), *Svenska Dagbladet* (Sweden), *Ilta Sanomat* (Finland, Finnish-language) and several Finland-Swedish and Sweden-Swedish papers. Norway said no, thank you. The editorial board of *Aftenposten* (Norway) was against the idea; it isn't clear why.

It all started with a couple of letters. Tove's English publishers suggested a Moomin strip (they were even thinking of a television production), and in February 1952 an initial letter from Charles Sutton slipped through Tove's letterbox. *Comet in Moominland* (published in English in 1951) had aroused interest with its 'charming' story, characters and illustrations. The idea was an adult readership and a story containing social satire, not 'necessarily' aimed at children. Sutton gave a short introduction to the structure of newspaper comic strip series and invited Tove to London to discuss the subject. She wasn't free – that spring she was busy with murals – but she fired off several questions. Most important was: what exactly was a 'strip'? She wrote in English: 'I suppose you with this strip intend a continuing story

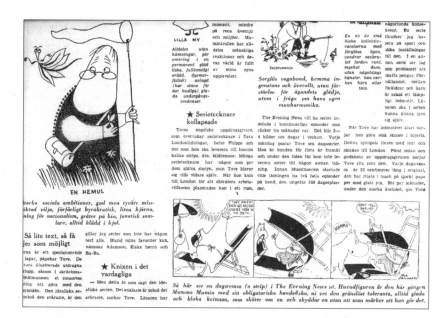

The new comic-strip artist interviewed in Nya Pressen *in November 1954.*

which appears in the paper every day. How many pictures are there generally in a daily strip – and which size are they? Well, I will wait with the questions until you have developed the suggestion you hade [sic] made further.'

This was the beginning of a correspondence that was to last more than ten years, sometimes involving two or more letters a week. In the folders of letters and drafts of answers in Tove's archive we can follow the work letter by letter, from beginning to end. Charles Sutton became a partner in discussion, and it was he who laid down the conditions. The strip series should be a deepening of the books. Unlike many critics, he made a distinction between a child audience and an adult audience: 'We like the figures because we think they would appeal to adults. Would it therefore be possible to invent something new as you suggest, which would be a little more *sophisticated* than your books?'

At the same time he was anxious to get the commercial side of things going, and the existing Moomin artefacts would have little appeal to adult readers. He was soon suggesting himself as an agent. There are American series, he wrote, with 'characters' that have been manufactured as toys, pieces of soap and sponges, and 'if they catch the public eye, they sell widely'. Tove was amenable to products that could support either books or strip series, but they must be of good quality. She was also seriously in need of money and had of course taken out a large bank loan to buy her studio: 'A permanent job – the first time in my life ...' she wrote in excitement in June 1952. The market for merchandise was gigantic and rejected proposals fill folder after folder in her archive. The Bobbs-Merrill Company (which was publishing the books in the USA) wanted exclusive rights to the word 'Moomin' and the illustrations, but she was never interested in holding a clearance sale. She also rejected Walt Disney.

Tove was in full flow with her murals for Fredrikshamn when Sutton, 'my Moomin agent' (as she described him to Eva), came to Helsinki to sign an agreement. It proved an intensive twenty-four hours:

> In the evening a Mayday-Eve party for him in the studio with 20 people, guitar and vodka, angry caretaker, balloons and intrigues and dancing and morning coffee and all the paraphernalia. And then on 1st May itself on top of that a business breakfast at Kämp – disturbed to some extent by the restaurant being full of students singing, dancing and climbing up the pillars, and children playing, together with most of the people who had been there all night. It may have given Mr Sutton a slightly misleading impression of how we celebrate in Finland, but he certainly had a good time.

They wrote the contract, but Tove had cold feet, checking it from a legal point of view (I am 'mistrustful', she wrote) and detecting a trap connected with a percentage. 'The clever wording, when one read through it quickly, made it look as if I should get a certain percentage for strips sold to other papers, whereas in actual fact it only referred to television, broadcasting and cinema rights. And these are hardly likely to have much relevance to strips. So I got Sutton to add a clause about rights of percentage on publication in other newspapers.' But she failed in an attempt to increase her royalties. The 'clever' contract with its clause about TV, radio and film showed that the Moomin series was something for the future. In fact, it soon did become topical when a Finnish company expressed an interest in filming, and a few years later (1957) Europafilm wanted to make an animated film of *Moominsummer Madness*. None of these projects came to anything. The literary Moomin merry-go-round was also in action. Benn's brought out *The Exploits of Moominpappa* in the USA and a publisher in Switzerland expressed an interest in *The Finn Family Moomintroll*.

Years of correspondence and negotiations followed before the Moomin strip series was ready to make its debut. Everything was ready for the *Daily Sketch* when the editor backed out, but at about the same time the *Evening News* (which had backed out earlier) came back into the picture. 'It really seems as if the Moomin were getting popular at last,' wrote Tove to Charles in February 1953. Finally the moment came for her to make a trip to London to fix the final arrangements: 'It is really fine things are working out this way; I'm going to see you again, see London (or the glimpse of it my work will permit) for the first time, and finally come to a conclusion concerning the matter of Moomin.' In fact, in the spring of 1954 Tove made two trips to London. She described her experiences for Eva:

> A month ago my strips agent rang from London and said if I could go there in a couple of days at their expense we could place the strip in the *Evening News*. I left everything in chaos, not least the mural for the bank Nordiska Föreninsbanken that I'd promised to finish this spring, and rushed off. So I had two busy weeks in London with work and conferences all day in Fleet Street, restaurants, excursions, masses of people and strong drink and theatre in the evenings – constant excitement with new people and a new language, standing up for my rights, making sure in a polite way that I wasn't being taken in. Oh well, *you* know.

With the strip 'Moomin' about to be launched on the world, Tove and Charles joined forces as its parents. 'If I'm Moominmamma then you're Moominpappa,' Tove wrote in September 1954, and Charles answered immediately, 'I like the thought of being MOOMIN'S pappa.' The first instalment of the strip on 20th September 1954 was preceded by a launch offensive, and in 1955 its parents were able to celebrate its first birthday. It proved demanding both as baby and child, demonstrated in the intensity of their correspondence. 'This is no bit of fun on the side,' wrote Tove during their preliminary work in 1953. The illustrated strip series was a huge job that developed simultaneously with her murals, books and paintings.

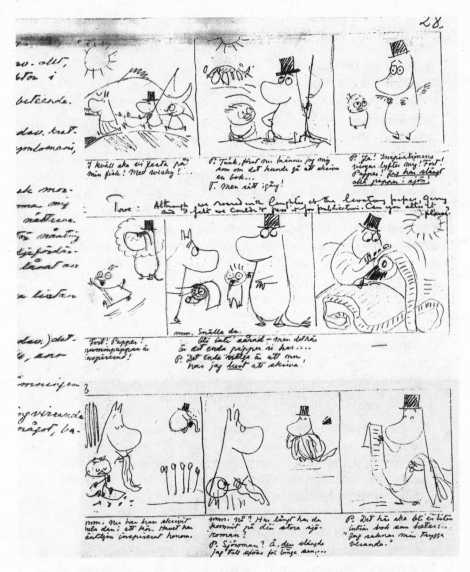

Sketches for the comic strip Moomin and the Sea. *The unconventional writing paper was rejected by the syndicate in England: 'We could never pass this for publication'.*

In their letters they discussed synopses, proofs, rejected episodes and shared ideas in a constant dialogue. 'Moominwinter' made an early entry into the ideas bank and was one of Tove's first suggestions. The strip 'The Dangerous Winter' was published in 1955. Sexuality could scarcely even be hinted at (Sutton was firm about that from the start): 'Always bear in mind that we want no emphasis on sex, only the sort of harmless aspect of it we get with the Snork maiden.' Flirtation, which comes up in a number of the strips, became Tove's way of presenting the 'harmless' aspect of sex. Nor was Sutton happy with the Hattifatteners' uninhibited life and oblong form, and he suggested relaunching them as 'poor relations'. Traces of this idea can be found in the first strip, in which Moomin's home is invaded by hungry guests, including a large number of Hattifatteners. Anything that might be thought in bad taste was firmly censored. The most famous example is the toilet paper in 'Moomin and the Sea', on which Moominpappa decides to do his writing. This was changed to kitchen roll (still retained in the versions used in Sweden). On the other hand there was no problem over Moomintroll going naked except when bathing (any more than there was with Donald Duck).

An interview Tove gave after the series had started in the *Evening News* gives direct insight into how she saw her strip drawing in its early days. The story's content was just as important as its form, she said. She had chosen an intimate style with the sort of events that could happen to anyone. The thing was to find 'the curtsey in everyday life', and she wanted to build on 'psychological moments, rather than pure adventure and environment. The Moomintrolls have entirely human reactions and their world is full of my own experiences.' This interesting statement shows how close she liked to keep to her storytelling. That she used her own experiences did not mean that she was writing about herself. The 'curtsey in everyday life' referred to her aim to make personal use of private things by transforming them into something her readers could recognise and feel they could share. Most of all, it was necessary to make the most of one's material:

> Every idea may be embroidered, but not at too great length. Each episode should have a leading motif which is in some way consistent. I may base one strip on sport and various attitudes to it. In another I may take up the problem of making money. Another suitable key theme could be the relations between parents and children. Readers should be able to recognise themselves in the strip.

The ideal strip, in her view, had from two to four pictures at a time forming a complete whole. 'The drawing must have movement and a lively rhythm, it must avoid repetition and be clear, without too many details, preferably line-drawing with black surfaces placed in alternation. Each picture should contain something of what went before and something of what is to come next, and events must follow consistently.' In fact, 'The strips I like best are those that have no text at all. Among my favourites are Adamson, the Wicked Gentleman and Ba-ba.'

She was commissioned to provide strips able to be divided into 'suitable episodes, each strip to last three months'. She would make small sketches in pencil, add a text synopsis and send the whole to London. Once the strip had been approved she would make a fair copy. Each week she posted off six daily episodes. It was hard work, and in time it came to dominate her life and artistic activity. It wasn't the technical aspects of drawing, but she needed an unending supply of new 'stories'. The constant search for new ideas eventually became painful, as Tove acknowledged in many interviews. On her very first visit to London she worked in an office in Fleet Street haunted by a previous occupant, a creator of strips who had suffered a melancholy fate. She summarised: 'He is now in a rest home and in the office you could still sense the distress of his desperate search for new ideas.' Much later she was to write a short story, 'The Cartoonist', in which she developed her experiences of comic strip work, fame and this troubled office.

A couple of strips came to serve as synopses for her books. One of these was 'The Dangerous Winter' (*Moominland Midwinter*), the other 'Moomin and the Sea', a story about living in a lighthouse (*Moominpappa at Sea*). Otherwise her main aim was to link Moominvalley to the wider society: for example, by living according to the teachings of a guru, imagining an invasion from Mars or by experiencing the meaning of wealth. Tove returned to her fundamental themes of the comet and the flood, and set the Moomin family in the context of such basic happenings as being crowded out by visitors, building a house or falling in love. The strips also helped to refine her characters and provided the members of the Moomin family with visible features to make them easy to identify. It was now that Moominmamma got her apron (an idea of Sutton's) and Moominpappa his top hat, while

'It was like crawling up a hairy mountain, without a ladder unfortunately.'
On an elephant in London Zoo, 1957.

their son came to be the eponymous Moomin himself. In the pictures for *Moominsummer Madness* (1954), these identifying features are nearly complete.

But after some years the pleasure Tove had taken in creating the strips diminished. They took time and energy and she felt imprisoned by the work and emptied of ideas. The contract had been exhaustively discussed to and fro by lawyers and employers. It was a contract for seven years, a slave-contract, according to one of her Swedish agents. The Bank of Finland demanded a statement of accounts and an agreement, and relations with Sutton began to grate. The year 1957 came to be a big one for the discussion of contracts, products and rights, and Tove's desire to give notice to quit (as she often wrote) got stronger and stronger. I need a change of scene, she explained to Tooti, and from London, where she was working on the strips in April, she envisaged a Toveless future for Moomin: 'If everything goes as I hope and believe it will, I shall work with him [Moomin] for two more years, and then be just as free and penniless as I was before. For ever!'

But during 'complicated business' and contract discussions with 'well-dressed Fleet Street gentlemen, all in Moomin ties', it was decided that the momentum of the comic strip series must be kept going. It was in this context that the photograph of Tove sitting on an elephant was taken for the *Evening News*: 'It was like crawling up a hairy mountain, unfortunately without steps. I still smell of elephant,' she told Tooti, who for her part was full of admiration. But you did it, she answered.

She agreed to continue with the strips for two more years, exactly as she had planned, after which a successor would have to be found. Associated Press had the right to continue the series with a different artist, while Tove had some say over the choice of her successor. But basically there was no problem. Tove and Lasse had already worked together, he writing texts and she making drawings. All it needed was for a synopsis he had written to be approved, and in 1960 Lars Jansson became the artist for the series. He had no great experience as a creator of pictures, but had worked at drawing and nurtured plans of being a sculptor in his youth. Working together with Lasse also involved a change with the working practices of the 'Moomin business'. He now became responsible for developing Moomin projects and took over the financial side of things. They founded a company, 'Moomin Characters', to look after rights and production.

Altogether Tove created thirteen Moomin strips, plus eight more in co-operation with Lasse, a total of twenty-one. This involved more than 10,000 individual drawings. Eventually she began to calculate the time still ahead of her on the strips by counting the drawings, and sometimes used these calculations to date her letters. For example, a letter to Tooti in the summer of 1956, when she was drawing her latest and still nameless strip, was numbered 10,242.

At its peak the series circulated in some 120 daily newspapers and soon appeared in book form too. Many longed for new Moomin stories. In February 1956, Gebers's editor, Brita Odencrantz, suggested a selected edition for 'Moomin-hungry young people'. Sörlins Publishers had already had the same idea, but had envisaged something a bit bigger. Then Brita went straight to the point: 'Not that I could imagine that you would let us down, but it gave me an idea (with the help of one of my colleagues here): would it be possible to think of bringing them out in the form of a volume of strips for Christmas? I'm sure lots of people, both children and adults, would think it a great idea to get several series together.'

Tove was naturally loyal to her publishers and took it for granted that Gebers should have first refusal, but she 'suspected the Evening News would have some rights in the matter'. She had already written to them about it. Meanwhile, what really worried her was that new and time-consuming work might be expected of her. 'Have these strips got to be in *colour*?' she asked. 'Brita, Brita, I couldn't bear going through the whole lot *again!*' It would be a nightmare. So colour was restricted to the cover, and the first volume, *Moomintroll 1*, containing three strip stories, came out in spring 1957.

For the little troll who had started life as a mere signature in *Garm* and made his literary debut in *The Moomins and the Great Flood*, this period as a strip character was full of change and turbulence. His world was endless, with words and pictures intersecting one another. Tove made new drawings and revised text in an almost hectic way. Moomin was now reliving his life on the pages of newspapers, in his own story, drawn as a comic strip at a rate of three frames per day.

The Moomins Grow

Celebrity came at a high price. 'It's going so well I can't help getting rich even if they keep cheating me,' noted Tove ironically. At first, the strips had been a guarantee that she could keep the studio and work freely, but the relationship between storytelling and business soon became complicated and eventually difficult to control. Tove often remarked how drawing the strips had

Tove studying a sea chart, on Bredskär.

become an artistic straitjacket, turning pleasure into duty, into something that had to be done and delivered by a deadline. What should have given her freedom to do the work she wanted in time became a job that restricted her freedom. Naturally, she began to experience deep ambivalence in her relationship to the 'Moomins'. It grew sharper with the years, a conflict between pure storytelling on the one hand, and on the other what the stories generated: contracts, negotiations, correspondence, appearances, public and social duties; things that killed freedom for someone who would sometimes have liked to shut herself up in her tower and just paint still-lifes. In November 1955 she wrote: 'Fifteen degrees of frost and ice flowers on every window. And the strips and business letters and lawyers and endless bother with everyone wanting me to sign contracts and trying to do each other out of agency work and production rights.'

By the second half of the 1950s her notes were becoming increasingly frustrated and angry with this *phenomenon* which was beginning to live a life of its own outside her words and pictures, beyond her full control. Storytelling had been a way of 'abreacting' – an expression that occurs more than once in her notes – a way of recapturing her childhood and holding despair at bay; this had been its function during the war. 'He has done so much abreacting for me,' she wrote of the figure of the Moomintroll. 'But he's in the process of changing. I'm becoming unable to escape any longer to the security of my secret cave, it's beginning to shut me in.' The struggle between work as pleasure and work as duty was coming back in new forms. Her characters were literally beginning to tower over her head. 'I could vomit over Moomintroll,' wrote Tove in one of her self-analyses.

At the same time, the Moomin world was alive deep inside her and she had not finished with it. She still had several major narratives to write, but she dismissed out of hand all those (and there were many of them) who begged her to write shorter stories to order. 'I write for pleasure,' she told one newspaper; 'in the little free time I have available I want to paint,' she told another. With few exceptions (a strip for Save the Children was one) she kept commerce and her stories strictly apart. It was only much later, when she had left the Moomins behind her, that 'new' Moomin books were written, drawn and produced by others than Tove herself.

Once Moomin had become a megastar, his figure grew physically in the pictures she drew for the books and strips. The small-snouted Moomin of the first Moomin book had put on weight, and he reached his roundest in the illustrations for *Moominsummer Madness*, which was published in the same year as the first strip began to appear in England. He grew in circumference as he became more famous, and for a time seemed almost obese. This visual change was like a metaphorical gauge of celebrity. In the strips Tove later worked on the physiology of the trolls, making them bigger or smaller, as in 'Moomin and the Martians', the synopsis for which she was working on in summer 1956. These experiments with the characters' bodies became a way of communicating about herself and her Moomin creation, and finding release for her mixed feelings. The troll had become a figure that could take on almost any form (like the character Schmoo she had once discussed with Eva). It could even become invisible, as in the story with the Martians, or disappear altogether.

In the last strip story she worked on (together with Lasse), Moomin literally returned to his prenatal form, formless and unborn. He is diagnosed as full of complexes by the former psychiatrist 'Dr Schrünkel', is prescribed tranquillisers with iron and chromosomes, and rapidly begins to shrink until he dissolves into nothing at all. 'I hope he'll be the same as he was before when he turns up again,' says the distressed Snork maiden as she pours a life-restoring drug (also from Dr Schrünkel) over the chair where Moomin was sitting. Tove thus killed off her Moomin, but at the same time promised he would be resurrected. The next year Lasse took over the series and Moomin reappeared. More than fifty more stories appeared up to 1975.

An important book for Tove during her strip work was Göran Schildt's *Cézanne*. This had been sitting on her bookshelf at Bredskär for several years, but when she finally came to read it it had an effect on her strip work as well as her painting. It suggested new words for the constant struggle between pleasure and duty. She transferred this tug of war to stories in strip form: work on new projects, synopses, delivery, discussions about demands and contracts; these things lie like an invisible subscript behind several of her strip stories. Even in the very first one Moomin practises saying no, as he tries to escape from his unhappy tendency to fulfil only the demands of others. He is invaded (and eaten out of house and home) by demanding visitors and ends up in the claws of Sniff, obsessed with fame and fortune. The story is a parable on the futility of pursuing the mirage of celebrity, rather than living properly. How can you ever expect to get rich and famous if all you can do is just exist, says Sniff to Moomin, who wants to do nothing but plant apple trees and catch slugs and snails.

This problem recurs in the last of the strips Tove created on her own. In it she deals with the demands of fame, not least in relation to her alter ego. 'Moomin and the Golden Tail' is a rather merciless story of vanity and will, innocence and split personality when faced with celebrity, wealth, personal change and the demands of the marketplace. The symbol of celebrity is Moomin's shining gold tail, with its multiple functions as parasol, curtain fastener and lamp. Golden Tail Products or Moomin Products, the phenomenon is the same.

Moomin Business

The first Moomin advertisements appeared as early as 1947 after an agreement with the drinks manufacturer W.W. Salenius. These promoted a whortleberry juice drink, low-alcohol beer and soft fizzy drinks, with two pictures and a little verse. Tove produced a dozen or so of these, the pictures featuring Thingumy and Bob. Their career turned out to be short, despite Salenius's hope for a 'vein of drawings that can never run dry'; the drinks didn't sell particularly well.

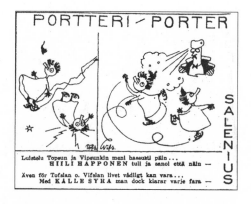

Thingumy and Bob
advertise Salenius drinks.

I dag:

Tove Jansson

och hela hennes Mumin-familj
drar in på NK!

*"Mumin-Huset" på NK-Leksaker • Tove Jans-
son signerar sina böcker • Ritar för
barn och vuxna på måndag
i Lunchrummet m. m.*

Redan i höstas började Tove Jansson roliga och skarpöglade Mumintroll med familj, vänner och "vedersakare" i olika former sitt segertåg i Stockholm via NK. Mumin — det är inte bara figurer och hastig underhållning, det är sällsynt klok livsfilosofi baserad på verklig människokännedom, som slår an lika mycket på barnen som på oss äldre. Det är inte utan att vi känner igen oss själva i de små sagorna, i böckerna och i de dagliga serierna i SvD och i andra svenska tidningar. Du har också hört marken för den långa rad Mumin-saker som NK under hand presenterat sedan i höstas och som på kort tid blivit så oerhört efterfrågade, att du nu alla har sammanförts på en plats, NK-Leksaker, där de fått sin egen avdelning, det hastigt uttermade "Mumin-Huset". Premiär i dag, då Tove Jansson själv besöker Stockholm och NK...

**Författarinnan-konstnärinnan
signerar sina böcker
kl. 14—16**

En nyhet är här presens Mumin-serier i bokform, som startar med "Mumintrollet I" och som innehåller "Mumintrollet", "Muminfamiljen" och "Den farliga resan". Pris häft. 5:75 och inb. 7:75. Dessutom övriga Muminböcker "Hur gick det sen?", inb. 9:50, "Trollkarlens hatt", inb. 6:50, "Muminpappans bravader", inb. 6:75, och "Mumintrollet på kometjakt", inb. 5:75. Så finns där också de trevliga "Mumin-tavlorna" i förfärgerycek: "Den hemliga ön" (36×39 cm) och "Karusellfen" (30×39 cm), som per styck kostar 3:75, med glas och ram 16:25, samt "Regnbågshuset" (39×46 cm), 3:75, med glas och ram 18:25.

Mumin gänge-handduk

är en annan nyhet, handtryckt, i tjusigt gjord komposition och två olika färgställningar, som säkerligen blir mycket populär. Storleken är 47×75 cm. Den kostar per styck 4:75

**Mumintrollet i plysch —
och annat**

Muminpappan, Muminmamma, Mumintrollet och Snorkfröken finns originalmoget gjorda i plysch och ea 12 cm höga. Pris per styck .... 9:75 Desstom finns Pussel med Muminmotiv, ea 100 bitar, 9:50, askdukar per styck 65 öre, ritblock 2:50 och 1:50, överfärgningsbilder med 4 figurer 75 öre, ljus 3:75, papperskorgar från 12:50 och Mumintrollet, Muminpappan och Muminmamman som små lustiga broscher i gullmetall, per styck 2:75.

P. S. På måndag em tidag ritar Tove Jansson för barn och vuxna
i Lunchrummet, 4 tr., kl. 16.

**Muminfigurerna i glaserat
lergods**

finns med följande motiv: Mumintrollet, Snorkfröken, per styck .... 2:45 Muminmamman, Muminpappan och Lilla My, per styck .... 2:95 Mymlan och Snusmumriken, per styck .... 3:65 Bisnavern med Muminmotiv, 3 delar, i flintporslin, per sats .... 6:75 Ny är NK:s Muminfjärdesas i modell Muminpappan, 22 cm hög. I eglaserat lergods .... 4:50 Ditto i glaserat lergods 6:75

Muminhavet, NK-Leksaker, 2 tr.

**Nytt för dagen —
Mumintyger!**

Tove Jansson har gjort en charmfull komposition för dessa tyger, ett stycke bomullstyg, som är lika användbart till småbarnskläder och förkläden som till gardiner och kuddar m. m. Tyget ligger på en bredd av 80 cm och kostar per meter .... 4:00 Säljes på

NK-Bomull, 1 tr. och
NK-Gardintyger, 2 tr.

*Alla barn till NK i dag
och träffa Tove Jansson
personligen i*

Muminhuset, NK-Leksaker, 2 tr.

Telefon 23 00 00 • Riks 23 63 00

Nordiska Kompaniet

The great Moomin market got under way in the mid-1950s. The record of promotional campaigns at Stockmann's department store in Helsinki gives a revealing picture of the whole process. For sale were trolls and other figures in various forms: ceramics, cloth, wall hangings, handkerchiefs, aprons, brooches, crockery sets, Easter cards, curtain fabric, albums for cuttings, sketch pads, skirts, etc. etc. In Sweden Moomin commerce was looked after by the NK department store in Stockholm and included pictures for children's rooms, puzzles, figures, towels, Moomin pens, ties, piggy banks and waste-paper baskets, with a special Moomin area opened in connection with the toy department in 1957.

According to Stockmann's advertisements, the Moomin family could be bought in three forms for Easter 1956: marzipan (in the delicatessen department), ceramics, and toys or mascots 'made in white leather with bodies in pastel-coloured plush'. In the case of the latter, individual family members were available at two price levels (425 or 510 Finnish marks). The Moomin books were also for sale but the main focus was on the merchandise surrounding them. During the autumn an event was also arranged with 'Moomitrolls

*Moomin merchandise is launched at NK
in Stockholm in 1957.*

on the loose'; this was such a sensation that it disrupted a mannequin show featuring children in 'Moomin skirts'. The campaign attracted 50,000 people to the department store in ten days, was reported on in many newspapers and magazines (*Life* ordered material) and the exhibition hall was redesigned as a 'Moomin Hill'.

In the succinct form favoured by advertising, the offer of edible trolls in a variety of shapes (Mamma, Pappa and child) seems absurd, as do the leather Moomins with pastel-coloured bodies, but otherwise this first generation of Moomin products was tasteful enough. Ham made ceramic figures (today these are sought after as collectors' items). The whole repertoire was controlled by Tove herself, whose exhaustive lists document a growing and increasingly motley supply. There were fine wallpapers stamped with Moomin figures, printed textiles and pictures for children's rooms, crockery services, wrapping paper, cards, writing paper, calendars and diaries, puzzles, bookmarks, braces and suspenders, ties, mugs, and even hairbands. The production of these objects stretched like a serial from file to file. One such file is divided into sections marked 'plastic', 'ceramic' and 'Moomin dolls and cloth'. Letters with enquiries, propositions, demands and claims and the answers they received tell stories of the background and ideas behind all this activity; about putting things into effect, rights, remuneration, royalties and agreements.

As long as she could, Tove tried to supervise production and control artistic quality – this would continue for a long time into the future. A letter addressed in English to a Mr Vyvian Bell of Associated Newspapers gives an idea of the process. The subject is vinyl dolls, and Tove demands unconditionally that her detailed requirements as to size and colour be passed on to the makers, Mettoy Playcraft: the dolls must be small, to make them more pleasant and intimate for a child: 'Say, about 5 to 6 inches for Moomin and Snork maiden, and 6 to 7 for the parents (possibly 6½ for mamma and 7 for pappa as he has his hat on).' As for colours: 'I propose that Moomin and Snork maiden be entirely white, Mamma *very* pale blue and Pappa pale grey.' Also, she insisted on seeing the models before they went into production, and, above all, the 'design' of the trolls had to be consistent with her latest illustrations. This letter was dated 29th

Moomin wrapping paper at Stockmann's, Helsinki, 1956.

May 1966. Tove had just published *Moominpappa at Sea* and was preparing for an art exhibition.

A few years earlier, in 1963, an Italian firm of fruit exporters wanted to print pictures of Moomin on tissue paper as a wrapping for oranges. No, said Tove, suggesting Little My as more suitable for this purpose, though without explaining why. Tove's fee was not important, but the fruit firm would not be granted any rights. On the other hand, some products were rejected out of hand, among them crispbread, margarine, jam, fruit juice, marmalade and soap. When in 1962 she was asked to allow a sanitary towel specially designed for young girls to be called 'Little My' because the name was 'neutral' and suggested a 'vision of something nice and soft', Tove's negative reply was carefully impersonal:

'Since I try as far as possible to avoid the use of my characters in connection with advertising, unfortunately I am not in a position to accept your offer.' But she filed the absurd proposal in her archive and it appeared much later in her short story 'Messages'.

These examples are just a fraction of the whole. Folder after folder document the huge variety of the streaming torrent that the Moomin market became. 'My troll has already appeared in far too many connections,' wrote Tove to some people who wanted to use him on soap, adding that she thought the public must be getting tired of seeing him in 'every kind of material'. So she decided to restrict him to the existing copyrights she had 'unfortunately already gone so far as to grant'. Or that was what she said in the mid-1960s, before Moomin's breakthrough in Japan and before the films and TV series and the Moomin boom they precipitated. Today Moomin Characters, which controls copyright and artistic quality, is one of the most profitable companies in Finland.

Painter and Author

Moomin pushed Tove Jansson's work as a painter into the shadows. Her original professional identity was as a painter, but the entry of the Moomins into the book, picture and comic strip markets had reduced the time available to her for free creativity. I want to paint, she would repeat like a mantra in interviews during the 1950s; writing about it in her letters and introducing herself as a painter. She only staged one private show during this period – in 1955 – and ten years had passed since her last before that. People have wondered why it took so long for Tove to move towards abstract painting, when contemporaries like Sam Vanni and others had started much earlier, at the beginning of the 1950s. But unlike them Tove could never fit her 1950s into a world of pure art. She was too much taken up with other work, and this separated her from her colleagues. She painted what she wanted to paint (there were ten still-lifes among the twenty-nine exhibits in her 1955 show), strongly asserting her independence. At the same time her painting was becoming more sculptural, with thicker brushstrokes and stronger lines, as in 'Model' and 'Woman Reading', two of her 1955 exhibition paintings.

Tove Jansson in furs at a private viewing, late 1940s.

When her Moomin celebrity expanded beyond all borders, her agony intensified. What had happened to the relationship between pleasure and work, and would it ever be possible to combine the two again? She repeatedly returned to this question. It wasn't only Moomin that was getting in the way. In June 1955 she wrote: 'I can't recall exactly *when* I became hostile to my work, or how it happened and what I should do to recapture my natural pleasure in it. At one time I thought the strips would help me. They would raise Moomin, a pleasurable half-forbidden hobby, to the status of a new responsibility.

And thus the pleasure would go over to my painting. The devil only knows where it has gone, but it isn't in my painting.' Her one-man show did nothing to liberate her; on the contrary, it increased her pressing sense of responsibility: 'Not even the exhibition could lift the curse. I thought that once the pressure to exhibit had been taken off me for several years to come, I would begin to delight in my work again. Nothing of the kind happened.' She wrote with ironic despair of the figure who had started the merry-go-round of fame: 'He's the only thing I never forced myself to create, he's the only one I like. Really that is right and makes sense.'

As a painter, Tove Jansson was now almost entirely hidden behind the writer of children's books and 'troll-mother', despite her monumental murals and the exhibition. In earlier interviews she had been presented as 'a painter who wrote', with oils and Indian ink as her natural elements. When the Moomin books started to be well known, she began to get headlines like 'Painter in Her Twelve-windowed Tower Invents Amusing Trolls for Children' (*Svenska Dagbladet*, 1952), and 'The Painter with the Moomin Family' (interview in *Astra* 1954), but soon she was just Moominmamma or Trollmamma to everyone. 'Moomintroll's Mamma Lives on an Island' (*Vi*, 1956), 'Moomintroll's Mamma' (*Folket I Bild*, 1959) and 'Mamma to Moomintroll' (*Arbetaren*, 1960) are characteristic. Her image as author became stamped with an obstinate 'mammaisation', a fate that often afflicts children's writers. They are transformed into a mamma or a pappa and can thus be loaded with responsibility for the reader's happiness or lack of it. This may explain the moralising panic that can break out when writing for children offends convention – Tove had come up against this when the 'hell's growl-jumps' debate had blown up in *Hufvudstadsbladet* in 1950.

The solo exhibition was a comeback for Tove as a painter, but it was hedged round with considerable suffering. She had drawn comic strips and worked to launch Moomin in various dimensions, sizes and materials. The exhibition went well, it had a good reviews and she sold a good deal. But Göran Schildt's book on Cézanne touched an old sore when she read 'that anyone who tries to make a work of art out of his life seldom achieves really good art'. But, she argued, 'it's rather that in my case, emotions

Glass and bottles as a recurring still-life motif. 'Still Life with a Grey Background', oils, 1959.

that should have their natural productive release in painting are immediately transformed, sublimated and compensated for; they enter my life as nourishment or are recycled and enclosed as if dangerous or superfluous. I understand my material.' And further:

> It happens automatically, it's only later that I understand what has happened. I am incredibly good at taking charge of what affects me and finding a place for it in my life and my world of perception. Every emotion is thoroughly exploited and anything negative is rendered harmless as quickly as possible. Not always with success. But this machinery goes into action and prevents the only sublimation that is really fruitful and positive: the transformation of experience and suffering into art.

She would return to this subject of sublimation and transformation. It was a question of fulfilling expectations, particularly of living up to what she expected from herself. Deep inside her there seemed to be hesitation and uncertainty – her search for an answer applied not only to pleasure, but to will and responsibility too. That was what Tove had imagined should happen: that pleasure and responsibility should be able in some way to change places with each other.

CHAPTER 11

The Troll Who Stepped Out in the Cold

Sometimes I read to small children and then
I choose the winter log fire and Sorry-oo's wolves.

Letter to Tuulikki Pietilä, 20th November 1957

'To My Mother', reads the dedication of *Moominland Midwinter*, which came out in 1957. Tove and Ham had taken Moomintroll with them on a couple of business trips together to England. On the first occasion (spring 1954) they discussed the Moomin strips in London, where Tove had two weeks of intensive work in Fleet Street. Then they moved on to walk the streets of Jansson memories in Paris before settling near Juan les Pins on the French Riviera. A little villa, as if 'cut out from a picture book', became their home, with green shutters on the windows and a garden with palm trees, oranges and yellow roses and cypresses in the corners. 'Everything is exactly as I planned it when I was a young girl and first planned this journey with Ham.' Faffan, who always suffered from severe homesickness, hadn't wanted to come with them. So it was mother and daughter, just as Tove had dreamed for so long. A mural she was working on for the Helsinki bank, Föreningsbanken, in the spring of 1954 helped pay for the trip, but since she only managed to finish no more than two-thirds of the mural before it was time to leave, she had to be content with two-thirds of the fee. A 'gift of money', awarded by the state to Ham for her contribution to the cause of 'making Finland known', supplied the rest. So off they went; it was May 1954.

At a distance were millionaires, casinos, luxury shops and mile after mile of hotels and private beaches. Tove took the chance to write a synopsis 'about Moomin accidentally getting caught up in the whole show here and misunderstanding everything'. This became the strip 'Moomin on the Riviera'. She couldn't just push useful ideas out of the way when they came to her, even if she had planned not to work. She looked at the fashionable life of the Riviera from a sort of 'superjanssonesque' perspective, and her experiences immediately went directly into the strip. Long sections of the coast were fenced off for private use, and after searching fruitlessly for a beach mother and daughter returned in a state of 'near-communist fury' to the solitary strip of accessible beach near their picture-book house. Moominmamma and Moomin were to face similar experiences during their time as penniless guests in a large luxury hotel.

The Moomin strips started in early autumn that year, and the years that followed saw in succession 'Moomin and Family Life', 'Moomin's Desert Island', 'Moomin's Winter Follies', 'Moominmamma's Maid', 'Moomin Builds a New House', 'Moomin Begins a New Life', 'Moomin Falls in Love', 'Moominvalley Turns Jungle', and 'Moomin and the Martians'. In the middle of all this, Tove altered and 'corrected' some of the Moomin books: *Comet in Moominland, Finn Family Moomintroll* and *The Exploits of Moominpappa* would come out in new editions in 1956. The most revised of these is *Comet in Moominland*, which was given a new title in Swedish. The other two retained their titles, but changes were made to both books, particularly to *The Exploits of Moominpappa*.

The alterations were conditioned by the requirements of publishers. Sörlins, who had published *Comet in Moominland* in Sweden, wanted to bring out a new edition and add *The Moomins and the Great Flood* as well; in this they had a gold nugget on their list that was not available on the market. It was an ideal opportunity: the new Moomin strips were rocketing in popularity and Tove Jansson had become an internationally famous author. She herself didn't want her first books printed again in their

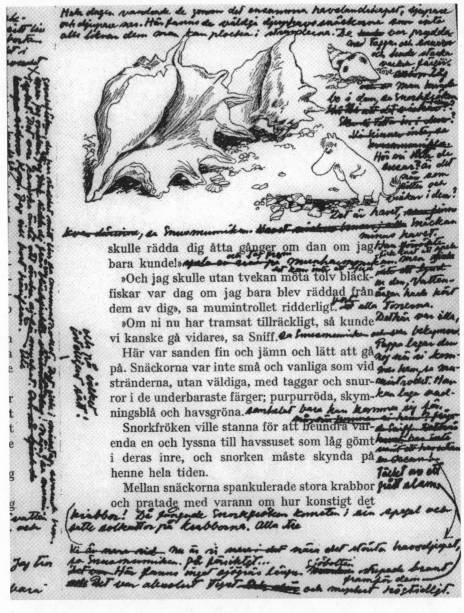

skulle rädda dig åtta gånger om dan om jag
bara kunde!»
»Och jag skulle utan tvekan möta tolv bläckfiskar var dag om jag bara blev räddad från
dem av dig», sa mumintrollet ridderligt.
»Om ni nu har tramsat tillräckligt, så kunde
vi kanske gå vidare», sa Sniff.
Här var sanden fin och jämn och lätt att gå
på. Snäckorna var inte små och vanliga som vid
stränderna, utan väldiga, med taggar och snur-
ror i de underbaraste färger; purpurröda, skym-
ningsblå och havsgröna.
Snorkfröken ville stanna för att beundra var-
enda en och lyssna till havssuset som låg gömt
i deras inre, och snorken måste skynda på
henne hela tiden.
Mellan snäckorna spankulerade stora krabbor
och pratade med varann om hur konstigt det

How Comet in Moominland *was reworked. A page from Tove's annotated copy of the first edition, which she entitled 'The Great Comet Version 2'.*

existing state. So she started reworking them, but in the case of *The Moomins and the Great Flood* she never finished the job, nor did the book reappear in its original form either.

The question of rights seemed complicated. Söderströms had published the books in Finland, while in Sweden Sörlins had *Comet in Moominland*, but Hasselgrens had *The Moomins and the Great Flood*. For *Finn Family Moomintroll*, Tove had switched publishers in both countries, in Finland to Schildts and in Sweden to Gebers. The question of who had the rights to *Comet in Moominland* became a moot point. Tove was worried. She valued loyalty to her publishers, as the head of Söderströms, Bertel Appelberg, explained to Hands Küntzel, head of Gebers, in May 1956 and 'wouldn't like to be disloyal to Gebers who had launched her so successfully in Sweden'. But the uncertainties over rights in Sweden were more apparent than real. Sörlins brought out a revised version of *Comet in Moominland* in Sweden in 1956. At the same time Söderströms took the opportunity to bring it out in Finland (a third edition was published as late as 1961). In this way Söderströms got hold of another Moomin book, despite losing *Finn Family Moomintroll*. For their part, Schildts and Gebers were able to bring out new editions of *Finn Family Moomintroll* and *The Exploits of Moominpappa*, at a time when the strips were appearing in full in the newspapers of both Sweden and Finland. *The Moomins and the Great Flood* stayed out of the picture, but Moomin addicts were fed several tasty morsels as they waited for the next new book.

Before the publication of the revised *Comet in Moominland*, Tove gave detailed instructions to her publishers about design, the placing of pictures and the format of the book. A 'more cheerful' cover was needed, and also a new title (its original 1946 Swedish title translates as 'The Hunt for the Comet'). Tove now suggested 'The Comet Comes' but said she would be prepared to settle for 'Moomintroll Hunts the Comet'. She didn't want any blurb on the cover, just a few words to say it was 'an exciting children's book'. The publishers immediately went for 'Moomintroll Hunts the Comet' – it was important to name the main character in the title – and decided to concentrate strongly on bookshop presentations, advertising and activities for children. Plans were made for an exhibition with children's theatre and a picture-tape with sound. The reviews were excellent and the advertisements were given good space by the press. A first edition of 10,000 copies was printed and altogether *Comet in Moominland* achieved an edition of 30,000, which made it one of the most widely circulated of the Moomin books during the 1950s.

'As you see, I'm very interested in presenting the Moomin book as a real comet in the children's book heaven,' wrote Bo Sörlin from Sweden to Tove, as he arranged for everything to go ahead at enormous speed. There was no time for Tove to read the proofs. Sörlin had this done through 'an academic at the university library in Uppsala', as he told Tove, so any further changes would have to be made in the second edition, already planned.

This was a great mistake. Tove always wanted to control every detail in the production of her books from manuscript and illustrations, through proofreading and placing of pictures, to the final printed text, so Sörlin's Moomin plans for the future were coldly received. I feel 'an obligation as if for home' towards Gebers, she told Sörlin sharply, and 'I shall offer all my new work in the first instance to them'. In fact this was what happened with the publication of the current series of Moomin books and she put an absolute stop to Sörlin's hopes of bringing out her first book, *The Moomins and the Great Flood*. Her revision of it had come to a halt, and if she was to ever to finish rewriting it at all, it would be for Gebers:

> My way of working has changed so much over the last fifteen years that it would be impossible for me just to tidy the book up. It needs to be rewritten from start to finish. And if I were to write an entirely new book I should scarcely choose the great flood as a subject, and in any case, out of loyalty I shall give first refusal to Gebers.

Her relations with Sörlins became distinctly frosty, especially when they were exceptionally slow in answering her request for a financial statement. 'Has the book been going well, and were those alterations to the text ever introduced in the second edition? It was brought out so quickly I didn't even have a chance to see the proofs,' she wondered after four years, and a couple of years later still she withdrew all her rights from them. When in the end she did get an answer, it was to say that the new edition had been printed – 20,000 copies, which had all been sold – and no further edition was planned. They sent her 5,750 Swedish kronor, and that was where their connection with her ended. The next time *Comet in Moominland* was printed, it would be under the title Tove herself had wanted ('The Comet Comes'), and the publisher would be Gebers.

Moomin did rather less well in the other Nordic countries. The Danish edition of her books was, in the words of its publishers (Eiler Wangels), the worst fiasco in the firm's history. They had decided to publish the books in succession and had begun by printing 10,000 copies. But the reviews were bad and they sold virtually nothing. This was announced in 'harsh' words and all too terrifying events, according to Tove's uncommonly active agent and translator, Børge Bavngaard. He told Tove that contemporary Danish publishers were mass-producing poor, unimaginative and sentimental reading matter. Quite simply, Denmark wasn't ready for Moomin, and after long-drawn-out negotiations between Tove, Bavngaard and the publishers, her agreement with Eiler Wangels was terminated. By then Tove was already corresponding with another Danish firm (Hansens Music Publishers). At the same time, she was working towards publication in Norway via Thure Svedlin of Schildts. This led after a couple of years to an edition of *The Book About Moomin, Mymble and Little My* in 1957 and *Moominland Midwinter* in 1958, but it was really only when the Moomin play reached Oslo in 1960 – by that time her breakthrough book *Finn Family Moomintroll* had been translated into Norwegian – that the Moominworld became better known there.

Publication of Tove's books in Denmark had begun as early as 1954, the year before Moomin's international breakthrough, so that the books came before the strip series started in *Politiken*. The fact that there was never any link between the Danish books and strips may have contributed to the fiasco there. Publication started with *The Moomins and the Great Flood*, the only translation of this book before the 1990s, which in any case is far less sophisticated as a narrative than the strips. Then serious trouble broke out between Tove and her Danish publishers, when she found out that they had divided the second book, *Comet in Moominland*, into two stories, published separately, an event Tove only discovered through a newspaper clip. Also, the vignettes and colours for the cover had been chosen without any reference to her. They are so harsh and coarse they give 'an almost evil impression', as Tove angrily complained to Bavngaard. Having to communicate for so long through an agent was causing her too many problems. There was some talk of publishing *The Book About Moomin, Mymble and Little My* in Denmark, but it was decided it would be too expensive.

When Tove finally wrote directly to the Danish publishers herself she expressed her views on a number of subjects, but the real misfortune was the splitting of her books into two parts. 'I do realise it was done to help them sell better and be cheaper, and I accept this so far as the *Comet* is concerned.' Like her first book, it had been built on 'childish suspense', using adventures that led from one to the next, and for this reason it didn't lose so much by being cut in two. But the books that followed the *Comet*, to which she 'attached much more importance', had been constructed 'organically' and would suffer enormously from being 'mutilated'. She was not ready to negotiate and didn't mince her words when writing to her Danish editor, Torben Monberg, in February 1955: 'They weren't written to be cut in two!! Would you cut paintings in two and assess the composition separately from each half? The only possible result would be hostile criticism, leading to poor sales.' She told them that if they persisted in cutting her books up, she would withdraw her permission to publish them.

'I feel like the mother in the Bible who was ready to give up her child rather than let it be cut in two,' she declared, adding in brackets to be on the safe side, '(see Solomon)'. Quite simply, Denmark wasn't ready for the Moomins. It may well be, she continued acidly, that the Moomin books are not 'suited to Danish children'.

Too-ticky

By the time Tove began writing *Moominland Midwinter* she had years of hard work on the strips, on new editions, and on translations, and Moomin business behind her. The German edition of her books, which began publication in 1954 (two books), proved exceptionally tiresome with a firm that took upon itself to cut

Och hän är ett nytt litet djur som inte är riktigt rä- kert på att det får komma in !

Din Tove.

'My Too-ticky'. Letter to Tuulikki Pietilä, summer 1956.

and change the texts, making Moomin god-fearing and devout, and introducing an evening prayer before hibernation.

She was longing for something new; she wanted to change things, shake them up, write greater, deeper things. 'I want to write something new instead of tidying up,' she told Tuulikki Pietilä. Tidying up or 'further tidying up' was her term for revising and correcting her books. Against her principles she had promised *Svenska Dagbladet* a 'dreadful' article on 'what it's like to write for children', a subject and a task that caused her 'a long period of disinclination'. She described the text to Tuulikki in June 1956: 'I've tried to spice it up with young people's own fresh feelings for the macabre, the matter-of-fact and the healthily spontaneous and tried to write as little as possible about myself and my blessed old troll.'

In addition, she had promised a new Moomin story for the paper's 1956 Christmas supplement, and this was causing her even more anxiety. She cobbled it together in a state of 'unprecedented disinclination', but observed in passing that it should be illustrated in two-colour printing. This was the short story, 'The Spruce Tree', which was later included, in a slightly revised version, in *Tales from Moominvalley* (1962). Her feeling of disinclination was cleverly transferred to those who attach importance to the curious rituals of Christmas (stressed Hemulens, Gaffsies and aunts), whereas all Moomin wants is to be allowed to sleep on as he waits for spring. She was more enthusiastic about forthcoming strips. She was on the island, 'making strips' and thinking about a synopsis to feature Moominpappa as a lighthouse-keeper. It was to be a story about 'sea and loneliness and everything you can experience round the shore', elements close to her all her life: lighthouses, the sea,

The striped cat, Tuulikki's Christmas card, 1956.

the shore, the islands. A new character, Too-ticky, was to enter the Moomin world in this forthcoming lighthouse-keeper strip. But Tove had not yet planned the story.

Tove's meeting with the graphic artist Tuulikki Pietilä was a turning point in her life. They met over the gramophone at the Artists' Guild 1955 Christmas party. They had both brought their best 78rpm records with them and were unwilling to let anyone else meddle with the music. Tove asked Tuulikki for a dance, but Tuulikki didn't think it suitable – on that occasion. But soon a Christmas card reached the studio: a striped cat, signed 'Tuulikki Pietilä'. It hangs there on the wall to this day. A little time passed, they telephoned, and when, a little after New Year, Tove set out from her door on Ulrikasborgsgatan and headed for Tuulikki's studio at Nordenskiöldsgatan 10, in 'further Tölö', she knew what she wanted.

Their paths had crossed several times before. They had both been studying at the Ateneum in 1938, but belonged to different generations, while the 'language war' between Finnish-speakers and Swedish-speakers also divided the school into two camps. But 'Tuulikki' does figure in one of Tove's verse-stories about the students of the time. One hot evening in 1952, in their favourite city, they found themselves at the same Montparnasse nightclub when Tuulikki was living in Paris and Tove was on her way home from a trip to North Africa and Italy with Vivica Bandler. But it was during the cold Finnish winter in March 1956, in the studio on Nordenskiöldsgatan in Helsinki, that the love between Tove and Tuulikki really began. Tove's road there was full of winter poetry and expectation. It was sparkling cold and snow was lying in huge drifts. Tuulikki took a bottle of wine from behind the curtain and played new records from Paris. They talked about life, longing and dreams, everything people talk about on a profound first occasion. They drank the wine and listened to Tuulikki's music. Then Tove walked the long distance home again. Her journey across Helsinki became a journey towards Moomintroll's winter.

It was in Tuulikki's home that autumn that Tove wrote her winter story. The name Too-ticky was very soon invented and shortened for private use to Tooti. That summer Tuulikki had been invited to Bredskär. When the ferry *Lovisa* eased into the bay and Tove met it with her rowing boat, it was as if time stood still. In that moment they came together for life. 'I've finally made progress with the person I want to be with,' wrote Tove when Tuulikki had left the island to work and teach at an 'artists' colony' in Korpilahti. She felt a new sense of peace and expectation. Soon 'a new little animal' had been drawn in one of her late summer letters of longing, and Tuulikki had been transformed into 'My Tootikki!' 'Love needs to be allowed to take its time and grow like a blossoming garden,' wrote Tove, as the letters darted between Bredskär and Korpilahti. 'I love you, enchanted and at the same time in great peace, and I am not afraid of anything that lies before us,' wrote Tove, and Tuulikki answered: 'Tove, you can have no idea how much I love you.'

Like Tove, Tooti was a builder, and when much later she was looking for a new studio, she found an empty flat at Kaserngatan 26c, just round the corner in the same block as Tove's studio. This Tooti built up to be her studio and home. So they lived in the same building separately but together – just as Tove had imagined work and love could be when she loved Atos.

Tooti and Tove, 1962.

Tove's summers were filled with relatives, friends and preparing food. And, as always, masses of work. She drew advertisements and strips. But she was now 'calm and happy' and in control of her time. 'You understand,' she told Vivica, 'it's not so bad now I'm calm and happy and don't get nervy and I've gradually taught myself how to be honest. I work at what I must for a certain number of hours each day, and ruthlessly force my friends to fit in round my work.' She was waiting calmly for Tuulikki. 'For myself, at long last I'm deeply at peace with my world.'

According to Tove herself, there are two characters in the Moomin world that have prototypes in real life: Moominmamma who is bound up with Ham, and Too-ticky who is related to Tuulikki. The relationship between the person Tuulikki and the character Too-ticky is clear to all who can and want to see it. For a general reader it may make no difference whether or not a real person is written into fiction, but for the Moomin books it affected both text and pictures. The story lives through its own power. Fiction and personal reality are not the same, but they can *resemble* each other and work together. Life can become part of fiction and fiction part of life. That's how it was with Tove, Tuulikki and the enchanted winter. 'That I was able to write *Moominland Midwinter* was entirely due to Tooti,' asserted Tove in her last letter to me (March 2000). That is 'an important thing', she said, going on:

> Exactly as she does in the book, she taught me to understand winter. I abandoned the Moomin family's terribly hackneyed summer veranda and stopped writing about what was deeply loved and guaranteed to continue the same and tried to write a book about how *hellish* things can be. And the result was a winter book! Moomintroll was just as distressed by winter as I was by the newspaper arts people fussing over deadlines and royalties and about my always being just a little bit late, no matter how much I tried not to be. So Tooti made me write that book about what it's like when things get difficult, and I believe that here, at last, Moomintroll was able to break free and become something like his real self.

Tove wrote elsewhere, too, about how Moomintroll was transformed in *Moominland Midwinter*, and about how he came to have a 'face' of his own. It was as though he had been shackled to the forced permanence of summer but had now cut himself loose. The secret cave, which she had written about in her notes the year before *Moominland Midwinter*, had opened again and Moomintroll had been freed to become once again a tool for Tove's 'abreacting'. Liberation needed to find the right words.

Moominland Midwinter

A snow-covered stump in the forest: that was how Tove had described Moomintroll's original form when she'd been thinking of launching him in the USA in 1950. She returned to this image when she set him in a winter landscape. The vignette on the title page (moved in some editions) shows Moomin looking at a tree transformed by snow, a tree whose rounded form resembles himself. *Moominland Midwinter* introduces a new Moomin, a winter troll with a new shape and new skin, both inside and outside his body. In the midst of the first cold snap, his velvety skin decides to grow, so as to become 'by and by, a coat of fur for winter use. That would take some time, but at least the decision was made. And that's always a good thing.' Moomintroll becomes more individual, growing and being transformed in a series of awakenings. This transformation is described metaphorically through time, from the blue-black winter darkness immediately after New Year to the first budding signs of spring sometime in March. 'Now I've got everything,' Moomintroll tells himself near the end of the story; 'I've got the whole year. Winter too. I'm the first Moomin to have lived through an entire year.'

Moominland Midwinter further developed the stories of *The Book About Moomin, Mymble and Little My* and *Moominsummer Madness*, especially the process of breaking away from Mother. When Moomintroll wakes from hibernation one winter night, his first thought is to wake his mother (if she doesn't respond he sees no reason to try any other members of the family), but she turns away from him in her sleep. The door is blocked, the windows have sunk underground, everything is buried under the snow. When he emerges headfirst through the trapdoor in the roof from the white cocoon of the house (actually a tower), he is reborn, this time through his own efforts. New smells fill his snout, the air is full of silence and his eyes meet a landscape clad in white. The troll has stepped out in the cold.

This winter book began to take shape as Tove's work on the strips stopped being a pleasure and began to be a duty, with her way to the easel literally blocked by business correspondence and the studio transformed into an office: 'I'm always behind myself,' she wrote in March 1957, the year that saw the publication of *Moominland Midwinter*. Her whirling circle of work on the Moomins had caused a depression bordering on despair in her notes – 'I'm never done with my work and with what others expect of me' – but she had no thought of giving up. She kept looking forward to a little empty space, a little respite to enable her to work at something that might bear some relation to pleasure.

> I toil away in the constant hope that in the end, if I work fast enough, I may begin to win a few free days. A few days for myself, maybe even a few weeks for myself and the work I long

to do. In terror. But every time I think I glimpse a ray of hope, a new avalanche of things needing attention descends to block the light. Time after time.

This avalanche of 'things needing attention' was a consequence of her work on the strips, and it seemed virtually impossible to solve the problem of how to set herself free in the way she wanted. The painter and human being Tove Jansson had vanished behind a screen of Moomin celebrity and descriptions like painter and artist no longer had any place in the vocabulary that described her work. 'I go round and round with the strips; a strip-illustrator, a fairy-tale auntie, a person with a certain quiet fame that has gradually become fixed in commerce. Sometimes I want to bite.'

It was a difficult state of affairs that left Tove nothing at all for herself. She could and did talk about everything she would have *liked* to do – biting the people who manufactured foam rubber and sweets, shocking the demanding parents of comic-strip-drawing children, yelling at gentlemen who came to see her with binding contracts from London – but 'naturally' she did none of this. Her work demanded a never-ending stream of responsibility, duty, consideration for others and endless politeness. One might perhaps be permitted to snap at one's friends, she wrote, but never at journalists. 'You smile and say, yes of course I find time to paint. Of course I love children. It's such tremendous fun

Moomintroll and Too-ticky. From Moominland Midwinter.

Painted letter-card, late summer 1957. Tove writes to Ham about
Moominland Midwinter.

answering their letters. Oh yes, it's quite true, you can get even
my characters in marzipan and candlewax these days. Isn't that
wonderful?' She further developed this ironic view of herself
in a bitterly satirical summary of the interviews that had been
inflicted on her as Moomintroll's mother, together with articles
on Moomintroll's popularity and all the opportunities offered by
the media:

> Oh yes, the strips are running in twelve countries and hundreds
> of different newspapers. Hundreds of people write to me.
> Enormous interest, it's true. Oh yes, radio, television and theatre
> too – and maybe film as well, that would really be fun.

Behind this façade can be glimpsed other descriptions of
an endless stream of meetings, engagements, appearances
and correspondence. Words were becoming her enemies, and
moments of solitude no more than a dream.

Onsdag. Älskade Ham – nu är jag ute på ön igen och ligg i sängen med dina karameller bredvid mig. Kom hem sent och styrde efter lampan i atuljfönstret, Tooti hade Te' få dig. Vad här är höstligt redan. Man doppar sig bara om men än ändå och nätterna är kalla och sotmörka. Här är de andra två korten, vad tycker du om dem? Vet du, jag blev så rörd över att ni alla försökt hjälpa mig med bokens titel. Flera av förslagen var ju Tynis ha för idégivaren! Tack och lov att saken är ordnad nu och att du gillade det slutgiltiga. Svedlin ringde omedelbart och var riktigt nöjd och hemskt vänlig Kan du tänka dig att Maya ska läsa kom. på den. Jag sänder Thure mitt kort med not om att dina invändningar blir de avgörande – det kan ju hända att vi fäst oss vid olika saker. Jag är också tacksam att du sett igenom korret. Onsdag vill jag nog gärna att du gillar förat. Få se om jag får ihop något Till söndag. Var det inte bra med Associatedes försäljning Vissavi Lasse! Hoppas han går med på det. Skriver

Newspapers, telephones, telegrams, post post post in heaps, stacks, avalanches, strangers, lectures, conversations, conversations, masses of words and myriads of children. And never alone.

Never ever really alone.

Desperation reaches in every direction from these lines. Tove Jansson, the disciplined worker, who had coped with the most difficult problems and never stopped working, knew deep inside herself that she was now near breaking point, had almost reached the limit of what she could take. The balance between need and will, between desire and fulfilment, was becoming ever more fragile. Her 'old' self was meeting a 'new' self and keeping the balance between them was difficult. The dam was near to bursting. She was working hard at presenting herself in words and pictures and in her own image, but the trolls and the people around her did not always fit together. It was obvious she must keep working, but she had lost her motivation. She longed for a life which combined pleasure and responsibility, but this longing bore not the slightest relation to reality. She was an artist longing for solitude who could never be alone again. Even her island was no longer a refuge. 'I've even let people interview me about the island, a well-known place that is now old hat to everyone. People can come there to stare at me.'

She studied the situation, analysing her responsibility to her work, cutting everything into pieces which she turned this way and that, passing judgement on herself. The result was a settlement of accounts that she set down with self-lacerating irony and sheer fury:

> Is this nice Moominmamma's fairy tale world?
> *How* can you get into Moominvalley?
> Just step in – no problem at all.
> It's soft and pleasant, padded with foam-rubber and
> marzipan and decorated with percentages.
> It's my office nowadays.
> I've forgotten the other valley.

This was March 1957. That autumn her new book, *Moominland Midwinter*, came out. It was a huge success, won her more prizes and had an enormous first printing compared to her earlier books: 25,000 copies. The reviewers chorused their congratulations in words like 'classic', 'unity', 'artistry' and 'depth', and articles on the book made a big splash in the newspapers in Finland and Sweden.

The Painter

Between *Moominsummer Madness* and *Moominland Midwinter* Tove held her third one-woman show. Nine years, four books set in the Moomin world and a mass of comic strips had passed since her last exhibition in 1946. 'That's a long time for a painter,' she noted. Letters, interviews and self-searchings all breathed her craving for colours, paintbrushes and canvases during those productive comic strip years. She told Eva she was dividing her time between painting and the strips. When she was painting her altarpiece with the foolish virgins at Öster-mark in 1954, her letters revelled in descriptions of colour, technique and theme.

'Today I've painted a cobalt-blue dress and a dark carmine cloak,' she told Vivica Bandler, describing the dramatic requirements of mural painting and gold leaf – a kind of work she continued to love against all the odds. The sanctuary wall was stained with damp and, after scraping, scratching and brushing it, she could only 'pray to heaven' that the stains would not reappear. The windows of the new church had not yet been fitted, so that winds of storm strength blew freely through it. In felt boots and with a winter scarf round her head, she had to chase the gold leaf backwards and forwards over the scaffolding. 'You understand,' she told Vivica, 'the pieces *ought* to be transferred onto the waxed wall with cotton, but all you can do is hold your breath, throw them up in the air and slap them into place wherever you can – if you can grab hold of them at all.' One day the tabernacle was blown in – it had been used to stop up the sanctuary window – and planks and Masonite fibreboard came crashing down on top of both the artist and her work. 'The whole tracing-paper pattern got splattered all over with paint. I was so angry that they promised to phone the nearest market town for a more heroic glass-fitter.' But she loved gold leaf: 'I feel I've really achieved something when I apply the gold. It's instantly bright and beautiful and doesn't fool you. Not like paint!'

Tove the painter wrote her longing for colour into *Moominland Midwinter*; she had had to hold it back during her work on the black-and-white strips. The very first sentence brings colour to the reader: 'The sky was almost black, but the snow shone a bright blue in the moonlight.' The colour setting fixes the image of enchanted winter in the reader's mind, and speaks frankly of winter's changeable nature in Too-ticky's simple expression: 'Nothing is certain.' Winter changes the colour of the landscape from green to white, a transformation that even extends to the interior of the Moominhouse, where the furniture is hidden under white winter covers. *Moominland Midwinter* works with both the warm and the cold aspects of colour, but alters their meaning and deepens the colour-scale. Moomintroll remembers summer as hot and green with a striking blue sky, but in winter green becomes the colour of cold, while the snow turns blue in the light of the moon. A sentence like 'The evening sky was green all over, and all the world seemed to be made of thin glass' is typical of this book. But the most beautiful play of colour comes when Moomintroll sees the northern lights for the first time. 'You can't tell if it really does exist or if it just looks like existing,' says Too-ticky, staring up into the black night sky as she puts winter's mystical aesthetic into words: 'All things are so very uncertain, and that's exactly what makes me feel reassured.' But Moomintroll, who sees something 'white and blue and a little green' draping 'the sky in long fluttering curtains' keeps his faith intact when he says: 'I think it exists.'

I long for warmth and colour, wrote Tove again and again in her letters to Eva and Moomintroll's longing in *Moominland Midwinter* points in the same direction. On the way it is moderated by Too-ticky's cool matter-of-fact attitude. He learns to live with what is, rather than with what was. *Moominland Midwinter* is a story about balance; balance between greyness, darkness and cold, and balance between colour, light and warmth. The seasons present a play of pictures that step by step reveals Moomintroll's deepening experience. When spring has returned and the rest of the family has woken up, he voluptuously evokes the image of winter etched on his consciousness. The end of the book is as visually expressive as the beginning. Moomintroll sits alone on the bathing-house steps listening to the spring sea rolling in. He closes his eyes and tries to remember 'the time when the ice had stretched away and melted into the darkness of the horizon'.

The Enchanter

Too-ticky is the one who analyses winter. The picture on the cover of the first edition shows Too-ticky and Moomintroll meeting eye to eye in the blue-shadowed winter valley by the bridge over the river. Moomintroll with his paraffin lamp, Too-ticky on the railing of the bridge with a great shining moon behind her, each with his or her own source of light but different assumptions. This image reveals the narrator's heart, the growing connection between Too-ticky and Moomintroll. There are other covers, but this first one carries the book's message: Too-ticky is at the centre of the picture. She is the enchanter in the story (the Swedish title *Trollvintern* can mean both 'Troll winter' and 'Enchanted winter'). It is Too-ticky who tells about the northern lights, the Great Cold, death, the night animals of winter and all kinds of other things not known to Moomintroll, but she is also someone who never fully explains anything. Nothing is certain, everything is in a state of change, a perspective that also applies in *Moominsummer Madness*. It's all about learning a new way of seeing.

Tove made many sketches but decided to suggest only one cover. This she sent to her mother when the book was at the proof stage. If Ham didn't like the picture, she had a couple of reserves, the Ancestor in the drawing-room lamp and Moomintroll in the open door facing the winter, but these were only to be used in an 'emergency'. It was important for Tove that her mother should approve the cover picture with Too-ticky, but in fact she had already made up her mind. In her letter (a postcard featuring Too-ticky in a Hamlet pose), she mostly talked about setting the text, printing and the basic colours round the edges of the picture. The cover was important: 'they're going to print 20,000 copies of the book!' As a textual expert, Ham was invited to improve its execution. 'If you like the white text more,' wrote Tove, 'can you remove my name in yellow from next to the moon and put some ultramarine there instead?'

Moomintroll and the Ancestor. From Moominland Midwinter.

'The Enchanted Winter' was one of many alternative titles Tove worked with, and her correspondence with the publishers became quite heated before they fixed on *Trollvinter*. This title killed several birds with one stone. Readers could mull over the various possible meanings of the combination troll plus winter and interpret it in any way they liked – Moomintroll's winter, the winter's Moomintroll, enchanted winter, winter's enchantment, and so on – or they could concentrate on the new wintertrolls, those to be found beyond Moomintroll himself, light-fearing and mysterious and living their own lives unseen by him. It was figures of this kind that Tove had drawn in her black trolls of the 1930s, figures that crowded into her illustrations for *Garm* and other papers. In the Moomin texts, the word 'troll' relates to metamorphosis and transformation, as for example with the Hobgoblin and his magic hat, or the dream-pale enchanted arts of midsummer. In the darkness of the trollwinter the unreal can be found; those no one believes in, as they are described in a typical expression. Moomintroll's own experiences of the nature of winter are transformed into a journey into the interior of his self, an exploration of his dark and unknown sides. One of the most important of these is his meeting with his Ancestor. This is the turning point of the story.

By opening the cupboard in the bathing house and releasing his Ancestor, Moomintroll opens the door to his own dark past. The family portrait album, hidden away in the attic, shows page after page of 'worthy' Moomintrolls, most often posing in front of porcelain stoves or on verandas. But none of these are like the troll in the cupboard. Behind that door is the ultimate Ancestor and in him is what is dark, hidden and strange.

It is all fundamentally genealogical. The fluffy troll from the cupboard whizzes past his descendant 'like a draught', just like the trolls Tove talks of in her diaries and that Moominmamma describes in *The Moomins and the Great Flood*. Now Moomintroll meets the basic material of history and thus himself too. Their communication is wordless (the power of speech has earlier let Moomintroll down), and this happens in one of the most ritually significant places in the Moomin tradition: the drawing room where one hibernates, where the cut-glass chandelier ('a family piece') can be found together with the porcelain stove – another link with the past. 'Mother has always told me our forebears lived behind stoves,' remembers Moomintroll once his Ancestor with unerring accuracy has found his home. The illustration of this meeting of trolls outside time shows the present in the form of the white Moomintroll with his lamp, a connection with the past through the porcelain stove with its damper cord, and a historical past in the form of the black Ancestor in the gauze-wrapped cut-glass chandelier, all illuminated by the light of the paraffin lamp. The Ancestor has the body of an earlier form of troll, as Too-ticky puts it: 'A troll of the kind you were yourself before you became a Moomin.' Moomintroll sees himself in a living distant past. The bond of family relationship, so essential in the Moomin universe, connects through time and space.

Transformation

Tove made an unusually large number of illustrations for *Moominland Midwinter* – seventy-one in all, compared with a mere 60 for *Moominsummer Madness* – and about forty-five for *The Exploits of Moominpappa*. She also introduced a new illustrative technique. Scraperboard (or 'scrape-paper' as Tove called it) involved scraping or engraving the subject of the picture out of a dark background, working from black to white. She had used this method before (in a couple of illustrations for *The Exploits of Moominpappa*), but here it became an integral part of the story, working together with the content, ensuring a correspondence between text and pictures. The pictures are strikingly graphic in their interplay of darkness, light and shadow, and it is no coincidence that Tuulikki was a graphic artist. The tension between the various shades of darkness has been literally scraped into the pictures. This makes possible a finely tuned aesthetic with space for unspoken things.

Not everything should be illustrated and not everything should be explained: this was a principle that Tove early wrote about and analysed for herself. Just as the writer and illustrator can make herself visible in the text with commentaries and pictures, so she can render herself equally invisible, even as a pictorial artist. What she illustrates in her text adds significance, but so does what she doesn't illustrate, what remains unspoken.

Moominland Midwinter is the only Moomin book to talk directly of death, through the beautiful Lady of the Cold, a real snow queen in the tradition of Hans Christian Andersen. When she bends her 'beautiful face' over the foolish squirrel who has forgotten the time, he is inevitably lost, bewitched by her cold blue eyes. The Lady of the Cold is not shown in any illustration; on the other hand the dead (deep frozen) squirrel is. The thinking behind this can be found in one of the drafts for the book's illustrations, a sketch of the squirrel beside which Tove has written: 'Let the children imagine for themselves what the Lady of the Cold looks like.' This was the point where the artist stopped and let the reader take over and form his or her own pictures. The author can open the door to the unknown but she does not tell us what can be found there. The figure of death elucidates the text as one aspect of the whole, of existence and of the cycle of time. Too-ticky kindly explains that when you're dead, you're dead: 'The squirrel will become earth all in his time. And still later on there'll grow trees from him, with new squirrels skipping about in them. Do you think that's so very sad?'

Moominland Midwinter is a novel that shakes the Moomin world to its foundations, a winter tale that calls new beings onto the stage and gives those who are already there broader roles. Little My becomes a tough counterweight to the sensitive Moomintroll, a realist who lives in the present and interrupts his sentimental summer dreams. 'Remember last summer when ...,' he starts, but she immediately interrupts: 'But now it's winter.' Like Too-ticky, she is one of the innovators in the enchanted winter, one of those who show how traditions must be changed and transformed, and how sometimes they vanish altogether: a silver tray may become a toboggan and a tea cosy may be used as a piece of warm winter clothing, while an old garden sofa may breathe its last breath as a winter bonfire. When Moomintroll finally opens the door of the house and the heavy snow rushes in in front of him and the spring winds swirl around the drawing room, everything is open and ready for the great transformation. The paraffin lamp he carried through the winter, the porcelain stove that gave him a feeling of security, the Ancestor who was his relative – all this is still there inside him, but does not fill the whole space. The present has become more important than history, he thinks: 'But things that happen now really are more interesting than those that happened a thousand years ago.'

'One has to discover everything for oneself,' Too-ticky tells Moomintroll, 'and get over it all alone.' Tove liked explaining that the name Tuulikki (from Finnish 'tuuli') means 'little wind', a wind that changes things and cleans the house. In *Moominland Midwinter* she blew through Moominvalley and renewed it.

The Great Journeys

The year after *Moominland Midwinter*, Faffan died. 'It happened terribly quickly,' wrote Tove to Tooti on Midsummer Day 1958, but at the end he saw 'pictures on the wall, beautiful sculptures of young men and women'. 'It's terribly hard for Ham,' she continued; 'they must have loved each other much more than I was able to understand.'

That applied to herself, too. When war and politics were no longer part of the order of the day, her relationship with Faffan had changed. Their relative positions were different. Now it was Tove who was the family celebrity and her father's hopes that she would become an artist, 'a great one', had come true. 'He's as proud as a turkeycock,' wrote Ham when Tove was honoured as the Moomin Queen in Stockholm in 1957. No one had been more indignant than he when a Swedish professor of art speculated that Tove had pinched the idea of Moomin from the artist Verner Molin's figure 'the dark sow' (which resembles the black Moomintroll). 'Almost as if I'd been accused of murder,' wrote Tove to Tooti. That was Faffan and art in a nutshell.

Many people wanted a share of Moomin's celebrity and income. The accusation of plagiarism was nonsense, but it was blown up by the newspapers. A Professor Aron Borelius wrote a long article in *Sydsvenska Dagbladet* under the aggressive title 'The Dark Sow – Moomin Speculation Explained' and later returned to the subject in *Expressen*, where he even suggested Tove ought to pay damages. She unwillingly defended herself in *Expressen*. She would rather have kept quiet, but those round her considered a response necessary. 'I Could Not Have Been Influenced' was the title of her reply: 'In the early 1940s, when Verner Molin first exhibited his dark sows, I was in Finland. At that time it was unfortunately impossible for me to see the exhibitions of my colleagues in Sweden, so I could not possibly have been influenced by his work.' When Molin exhibited in Stockholm in 1942 Tove had been imprisoned in Helsinki by the war. Many hurried to Tove's defence, and an energetic *Hufvudstadsbladet* reporter traced Moomintroll's debut back to *Garm* in 1943.

A year earlier than this furore (1956), the Moomin strip series had in fact looked at genealogical origins. The Moomins had once been classified as hippopotamuses and shut up in zoos. They had only been let out after they had been reclassified as 'real Moomintrolls'. The board of directors offer their apologies, said the strip. But Tove never received any apology from the dark-sow camp in Sweden.

In the spring of 1957 Tove had gone with her parents to Stockholm. The NK department store was holding a Moomin event and she had undertaken to appear at City Hall during a scout evening, with Astrid Lindgren present, among others. 'This trip is a bouquet for my parents,' Tove wrote. It was also a mark of love. Afterwards Faffan burst into a song of praise about the 'dream journey'. There had been hiatuses between her and her father, jarrings, breaking points: 'his outer life was as clear and simple as his inner life was complicated,' as she wrote to Tooti the midsummer when he died. But she had always been his daughter. After some happy days on Bredskär a few years earlier, they had written to each other more personally and warmly than ever before. Both kept the letter they received then in their wallets. 'Dearly loved Tove,' Faffan had written, 'I feel a little sad when I think of those wonderful days I was able to have on Bredskär. Say hello to wonderful Tooti.' Tove had replied at once: 'I think I understand you better than you could ever imagine,' she had written, warmly signing herself 'Noppe', one of her childhood nicknames. In the background was their trip to Paris long ago.

'I must have loved Faffan an awful lot despite him being so difficult,' Tove told Tooti at midsummer in 1958. When he died she had just won an award in Sweden for her illustrations to *Moominland Midwinter*: the Elsa Beskow plaque. But she refused to leave the island and Faffan's world. Gebers had to collect the plaque on her behalf.

In the autumn of 1959 Tove and Tooti spent a couple of months in Greece and Paris. It was their first long journey together, carefully planned and long anticipated. Tooti had won a travel grant and been given leave of absence from the Academy of Art, where she was a teacher. Tove wanted to escape from trolls and humans. She needed to get her breath back and think about painting again. They studied Greek, filling a notebook with words, phrases and translations, all neatly written out by Tove. They both had the same plan for the journey: to make preparations in advance but leave room for improvisation. The strips had finished and Tove had given the publishers her second picture book, *Who Will Comfort Toffle?* She had dedicated it 'To Tuulikki'. It was a happy trip.

But it had been difficult to leave Ham and even more difficult for Ham to see Tove going away. In their time they had travelled together to London, France and Stockholm on Moomin business, and after Faffan's death Ham had become ever more dependent on Tove and the family. She had moved in with Lasse on Jungfrustigen in Helsinki but spent weekends with her daughter

Fishing on Bredskär. Tooti, Tove and Ham.

in the studio. Now Tove wanted to go abroad with her lover and not with Ham. It was a difficult moment and Tove's notes bear witness to a drama of jealousy, sadness and melancholy. But she had made up her mind. She needed to get away: 'I'm sure this will be a good productive journey,' she wrote to her mother at the end of October just as they were leaving. Letters came pouring in from the Greek archipelago and the little hotel in Paris at Place de la Contrescarpe where Tove and Tooti spent Christmas and New Year.

Tove described her experiences in her letters, in much they same way as she had done when writing from Paris in 1938. 'I never stop thinking about you,' she wrote. 'We are so close it isn't easy for us to be separated for any length of time.' 'But it'll be wonderful when we meet again,' she added reassuringly. Tove felt a need to talk about the journey and stress how necessary it had been: 'I know you're happy I got the chance to make a real journey after the strip misery so as to be able to bury that properly and make a fresh start. And I feel the great change in my surroundings is calming down old things and building up new ones.' She also worried constantly about Ham's health. Long after, in her short story 'The Great Journey' Tove would deal with more or less the same problem: two women plan a journey and it is not easy for one of them to leave her mother. But the woman in the story makes the agonising decision to travel with her mother and leave her lover behind.

Tove and Tooti crossed Europe, taking the train through Germany and Switzerland and stopping in Lugano before moving on through Yugoslavia and Italy. Greece exceeded all expectations. Here Tove began working in oil pastels, and they settled for several weeks on Mykonos, island of cats and shellfish. The shells on the shore had been 'imported' from fisheries outside Delos, she told Ham, but that made it 'more alive' and less decorative. Some years later she would work a similar importing of shells (from Moomin to his mother) into her sea novel, *Moominpappa at Sea*.

At the end of November they boarded a train to Paris, where each had earlier lived, worked and studied. Now they experienced the city together. To her friend Maya Vanni, Tove wrote: 'I would never have thought life could be so happy and peaceful, so friendly day after day and week after week.' They celebrated Christmas in their hotel room at 6 rue Blainville, buying mistletoe in place of a Christmas tree, and at the beginning of January began to prepare for their return. A week before they left Tove wrote to Ham: 'The journey's over and I'm quite ready to come home.'

CHAPTER 12

A Need for Expression

It's a beautiful thought, to meet a writer only in her books.

'Correspondence' from Travelling Light

After *Moominland Midwinter*, Tove was hailed as a genius. Prizes streamed in: the Elsa Beskow Plaque, the Rudolf Koivu Prize, the Swedish Literature Association's Prize; and the book became a huge success. By the late 1950s the Moomin world had no boundaries. It lived in books, pictures and strip series, it was literature, art and pictures. Moomin was both a concept and a trademark. To be 'Moomin-minded', as one of the strips had it, became synonymous with a lifestyle to dream of, modelled on a world one could simultaneously long for and recognise oneself and one's environment in.

The Moomin world expresses our longing for something beyond ourselves, but it never simplifies. 'We begin a new life' is the title of one of the strips Tove made in the 1950s, an inimitable reconciliation with the impulse to accept certain doctrines uncritically. In this strip, living freely without inhibitions is set against the pressure of Judgement Day, a Dionysiac prophet set against one fixated with sin, guilt and punishment. Moominmamma, with a curtsey to both, settles the dilemma. The teachings of both prophets, she summarises, are certainly comfortable, but not practical for ordinary folk.

The Moomin philosophy of life was debated by literary people and students at universities all over the Nordic countries. Among the most active was the young poet Lars Bäckström in Uppsala, writing about Moomin teachings. Tove Jansson became a celebrity writer in demand for readings and lectures, expressing views she would later bring together in her essay 'The Deceitful Writer of Children's Books'. In Stockholm 'Moomin fever' had broken out among the students, according to the programme secretary of the student union in an invitation to Tove. This was in February 1957, and that the event would be a success was considered self-evident. The crowd that packed the hall set a public record when Tove came to read from her forthcoming *Moominland Midwinter*. Writers of the calibre of Astrid Lindgren, Lennart Hellsing, Harry Kullman and Åke Holmberg were there too, but Tove and Moomintroll were the star attractions. 'Queuing for Moomin Tove', reported *Stockholms-Tidningen* the next day. In Uppsala the venue had to be changed, but it was still overcrowded and ended with standing room only. The student union at Heimdal recorded one of the biggest public events in its history.

More invitations flooded in, from Helsinki University and Helsinki School of Economics, from the student unions of Trondheim and Oslo, from the universities of Lund and Gothenburg and, in the early 1960s, from Åbo Akademi in south-western Finland. Tove was proud and happy her 'doodlings' were able to provide such entertainment in academic circles, but she rationed her appearances. Speaking in public taxed her strength, sapped her energy and wrought havoc with her concentration. All in all, it had become a question of protecting her identity as a painter: 'my true profession, so badly neglected in recent years,' as she put it, politely turning down a hopeful student leader in the spring of 1960.

Contemporary students read the Moomin strips and books and invited their creator to their universities and colleges, attracted by the vitality, power and easy unrestricted freedom of the Moomin world. They were interested in the new children's literature that was developing, and *Stockholms-Tidningen* reported that half the students gave up a dance rather than miss a discussion on children's literature led by the critic Eva von Zweigbergk. Tove herself kept out of this. She was willing to talk about her own writing, but that was all. Moomin had reached the universities, but it would be a long time before her books and strips, like other literature for children, were accepted in seminar rooms. A literary-historical dissertation on the Moomin books written by Harry Hackzell was submitted in Stockholm in 1964, but it was not until the 1980s that academic research into Tove Jansson was taken at all seriously.

'Moomin fever' is a fair description of the intensity of the hectic last years of the 1950s, particularly in Sweden. The second Moomin play, 'Troll in the Wings', first performed at Helsinki's Lilla Teatern in 1958, was a smash hit in Stockholm. 'Parnassus went on pilgrimage to the theatre,' wrote Birgitta Ulfsson, who played the theatre rat Emma. 'An unqualified triumph,' remembered Lasse Pöysti who played Moomintroll: 'Quite simply, Moomin humour worked in Sweden.' Tove was there in Stockholm, of course, together with the company and their director, Vivica Bandler. 'Great reviews everywhere,' she reported to Tooti, except for 'the bitter Ebbe Linde', who grumbled 'terribly'. Tove described the rehearsals, premiere and 'general hullabaloo'. Among other things, Lennart Hyland gave the Moomin gang twenty minutes on TV. Later the play was produced in Gothenburg (1960), but once again the combination of Moomin and Gothenburg didn't really work. Yet when it continued on tour to Oslo the same year, it met with greater success than ever. Here it became real theatre. Tove went on herself at the first performance, as the hind legs of the lion. 'The best performance I played in all my fifty years in the theatre,' recalled Lasse Pöysti in his memoirs.

Once Tove had put the Moomin strips behind her, it was for good. Something 'absolutely cut and dried', she confided to Maya Vanni: 'I might just as well try to remember past toothache.' The brutal comparisons strewed around her letters and notes were necessary if she was to get back to painting and regain her self-respect. She had 'forced her brain to work with trivial ideas which made real ideas disappear' and comic strip artists were never respected as serious visual artists. Lasse, about to take over the strips, was also thinking of taking up sculpture again. But, as Tove confided to Maya, you couldn't be a sculptor, have friends in the Artists' Union, and put your name to a comic strip, all at the same time. Comic strips and art simply didn't mix; 'I know. And I'm not exaggerating.'

At this time she was able to claim happily in letters to both close friends and professional acquaintances that the commercial Moomin star was 'setting'. 'It won't be long before no one will ever again want trolls made of marzipan or soap, or wear them pinned to their bosoms. My life has been quietening down and at last I've been able to begin painting again, with all the boldness and fear you'd expect after such a long break.' Like living in a 'dreadfully threadbare marriage' was one of her many descriptions of what it had been like working on the strips. 'By the end I was drawing with hatred,' she wrote, 'and if I'd continued it would have killed the artist in me altogether.' Worst of all had been the loss of love: 'There was no longer anything in my work to make me happy.'

She often set down similar thoughts in writing: 'I have no regrets and I'm grateful for the experience the strips have granted me, even if it has been like nothing so much as a two-edged sword.' When she talked about being set free after seven years of 'toothache', it was pleasure – as always – that was central to her thoughts. It was as if a weight had been lifted from her, so that she could see everything in a new light. Her perspectives had opened up and she calmly settled down just to 'be' until 'the joy of activity begins to flow – not as a duty but as a necessity'. After she had drawn the last line of the last strip in July 1959 she celebrated her divorce with Tooti and Ham and two bottles of Dopff Dry – a wine from Alsace. Now at last she could again concentrate on things she wanted to have time for.

The First Letter from Åke

'I think in the last four months I've done more painting than in the previous ten years,' noted Tove in April 1960, as the craving to paint and make pictures affected everything she did. In her business correspondence she held up her painting like a protective shield to ward off offers and requests.

There were exceptions. One of these was Åke Runnquist of the publishing firm of Bonniers in Sweden. He suggested she might like to illustrate a Swedish translation of Lewis Carroll's *The Hunting of the Snark*. In her answer Tove took care to make clear she was a painter; the letter had been addressed to her as 'The Author Tove Jansson', not 'The Artist'. The letter dropped through her box during the hectic final phase of the strips, in May 1958, but she couldn't resist Lewis Carroll, the Snark and

'A New Beginning', oils, signed 'Jansson – 59'.

Åke. *The Hunting of the Snark* proved to be the beginning of a collaboration that lasted thirty years, involving a dozen books and a deep friendship. Åke himself had translated Carroll's text together with Lars Forsell – who met Tove at a reception in Helsinki – and he was convinced the book's 'bizarre and amusing collection of characters' would appeal to Tove's imaginative approach as an artist.

That settled the matter, even though Tove had planned to keep the summer for painting. But she insisted that she must be allowed to work without pressure of deadlines. If not, the whole thing would end up in 'that category of meaningless frenzied activity which (together with Moomintroll) has been tormenting me in recent years. And it would be badly done.' She made no offer of negotiation, but asked for immediate information on the book's format and the number of colours for the cover, and demanded the full text together with the Swedish translation. She made suggestions for vignettes and begged for a 'fullgrown' cover, 'preferably fantastic in design but very refined in colour', and asked eagerly: 'May I do you a couple of full-page illustrations?' She had never seen Henry Holiday's original illustrations or the work of any other Snark illustrators, but this would prove a definite advantage. It was the poem's lack of pictures that made her want to draw ones that had nothing to do with Moomin. 'Hell, what a chance to have a go at the classics,' she exclaimed to Maya.

Previously, Tove had illustrated about a dozen books by other authors, mostly when she needed such work to earn a living. A couple of picture books in the 1940s, Solveig von Schoultz's *Nalleresan* ('Teddy's Journey', 1944), a course book for learning English, the Finland-Swedish children's writer Lilli Forss-Nordström's fairy tale play for children, *Våren vaknar* ('Spring Awakens', 1951), Erik Gardberg's *Zebra Sebulon och andra djursagor* ('Sebulon the Zebra and Other Animal Tales', 1952), which carries Tove's signature as illustrator, and several collections of light informal pieces, some of them now lost. But after the Moomin fever, only Lewis Carroll and Tolkien found a place on her work table.

The Hunting of the Snark was something new for her. Difficult but interesting, was her verdict; 'pure modern nonsense verse', as she told Maya in August 1958. This was an exclusive

Croquet match. Illustration for Alice in Wonderland, *1966.*

commission, a classic, a collaboration with the prestigious publishers Bonniers – who had once turned Tove down – and an original text in the same spirit as her own. The trio of Runnquist, Forsell and Jansson suited each other. The book reviews were respectable (as Åke Runnquist put it), but nothing more. Lewis Carroll has never been a major figure in Sweden, still less this particular absurd and extremely Anglocentric narrative poem. It was not reprinted. But the publishers were happy; the pictures were of the 'highest class' and Tove had tried a new form of expression. From the first, Åke talked of placing it abroad, and Tove's illustrations for both *The Hunting of the Snark* and *Alice in Wonderland*, which she did some years later, have both been published in Lewis Carroll's homeland.

Åke also made a new translation of the super-classic *Alice*. For him there could be only one illustrator: Tove Jansson. When the offer came at the beginning of 1965 she was illustrating her next Moomin book, *Moominpappa at Sea*. Although busier than ever, she couldn't resist the temptation. She could feel the attraction of Carroll's text in her bones. It contained sheer 'horror', and had been a favourite since childhood. Once, when asked by a publisher to name a book or author she would like to illustrate, she had answered unhesitatingly: Edgar Allan Poe.

Alice opened before her once more the prospect of doing 'horror' illustrations. 'The story is terrifying and can in no way be seen as an idyll, but it causes shivers of pleasure,' she told Åke in February 1965. The *Alice* story provides a form of surrealism, a reality 'above' what one first sees and experiences. And this was what she wanted to show in her pictures: a pathological nightmare worthy of Hieronymus Bosch – this was the direction in which her thoughts were moving. But Åke rejected these wild plans to turn *Alice* into a 'horror story'. What he wanted was to 'emphasise reality more than the macabre'. 'In any case my pictures are as nice and easy to understand as they always are,' she explained bitterly after they had discussed the matter. In her letters to Maya she wrote sadly of the publishers' – Åke's – determination to turn *Alice* into a pleasant idyll that would be a suitable partner for the welfare state. But there is nothing idyllic about Tove's illustrations. Alice and the cat, together in a field with tall waving grass and large flowers, have been given a sense of heightened reality through Tove's use of colour, the circling bats, the pure brushstrokes and the absence of detail.

The Lewis Carroll texts challenged her quality as an illustrator. As she told Åke, to attempt *Alice* after John Tenniel's emblematic pictures was daunting: the Carroll text had already been illustrated definitively. Åke, for his part, was convinced Tove's version would be 'something absolutely extraordinary' and his hopes were fulfilled. When he had the *Alice* illustrations in his hand in autumn 1965, he immediately telegraphed: 'Congratulations on *Alice*, you have created a masterpiece.' There was talk of following up with the second *Alice* book (*Through the Looking Glass*), but nothing came of it.

Give Me a Picture

'Pleasure' and 'necessity' were always positive words for Tove in relation to her writing and painting. 'When there's no picture and no project, no desire to express myself comes and I feel panic.' Tove wrote with an intensity that bordered on obsession about herself as a visual artist and about the process of making pictures and painting canvases. Writing became a way of talking about art and of coming to terms with it, and her notes about making pictures often had the character of settling a discussion with herself. Both as artist and writer Tove was hard on herself, sometimes little short of implacable. Once she had achieved a

A marked change in style. 'Still-life', oils, 1964.

new point of view, a new way of seeing, earlier pictures and art lost their significance. She was capable of describing still-lifes and figurative representation as almost 'ridiculous'. In April 1960:

> A few oranges set against a blue background seemed to me totally meaningless as a picture and a woman at her toilet quite simply absurd.

> Interiors, landscapes, still-lifes – nothing but colour spread over a tablecloth, with enormous effort and no inspiration whatever.

> There have been so many attempts and so many failures, endless pauses and trying again.

> And my feeling of guilt has increased, year by year, to a constant, compact feeling of indisposition which has made it steadily harder and harder for me to paint.

I knew without self-pity that this was my last chance, now that the contract to do the strips has come to an end. If I didn't manage now, I'd never again be up to it or feel like it. Now I'm seeing colours.

And 'pictures' sometimes. ...

Give me a picture, a longing to express myself. It doesn't have to be much, but it must be *something*, a little pleasure, a small necessity.

Her beloved colours. She was talking about 'painting' rather than 'colouring', about getting away from the figurative by turning the canvas upside down – at least, that was her reasoning. In the spark of a painting, as she nicely put it, there may perhaps be the 'need to express myself and something of what I want'.

It was not easy for her to liberate herself by painting. 'I'm simply desolate,' she wrote, in one of her innumerable quarrels with the Moomins – one of the most drastic of them. It was January 1961. 'I shall never again be able to write about those happy idiots who forgive one another and never realise they're being fooled.' Moomin, she wrote, was naturally never 'an expression' of herself, but an expression of 'wishful dreaming'. The strips she had created had done more than anything else to kill her pleasure:

Strips are the deadly enemies of all forms of storytelling. Now I've nothing more left to say. I wrote my last book out of compassion [*Who Will Comfort Toffle?*] and the one before that was about loneliness [*Moominland Midwinter*]. My first books were about happy childhood and the joy of being an amateur, with a little escapism. Now there's no more material, and it's the same with painting. ... I used to show the beautiful, abundant profusion of the world. But how do you set about showing an empty room!?

That question remained constant, even (as we have seen) when it came to the art of illustrating a story, but now it was given another, more dramatic significance. It was not a question of portraying the empty room but of creating it. Words and narrative couldn't do it, subject matter withered away, ideas became constricted. Even so, new stories and new books did come into existence. Her desire to write lived in symbiosis with her farewell to the Moomins. She wrote stories 'to get herself going', and spoke of

Tales from Moominvalley (in Swedish 'The Invisible Child and Other Stories') as her last book. But it was going to need more writing than that before she could get away from the valley of the Moomin stories. *Moominpappa at Sea* and *Moominvalley in November* were still to be written.

Spring-Cleaning the Painter

All talk of difficulties, openings and possibilities in painting are a search for a repertoire, a way of thinking, an innovative form of painterly perception. Colour can mean something in itself, still-lifes can be given less distinct contours and pictorial forms can be scaled down or freed up. Tove conquered studio, palette, canvas, colour and form all over again. The desire to paint was a synonym for pleasure, a longing to express herself.

> My work is no longer my enemy, and I've travelled a long way to get that far. But it isn't yet my ally yet, either. Absolutely not a friend I can trust and be sure I can keep even when I can't give him all my time and attention. It's as if nothing but a doorstep or a membrane divides me from calm confidence in my profession, from the joy that can be found in serious work.

What mattered was to be found in painting. That her way of making art was changing is clear from the canvases she exhibited at the beginning of the 1960s. These are more open to interpretation by the eye; they build on power and feeling, shake up colours, peel off forms and have one-word titles like 'Balcony', 'Veranda', 'Shells', 'Seaweed', 'Mountain' and 'Boats'; all of these appeared in her exhibition of spring 1962. A great deal of colour and a great deal of painting. She was developing a more 'abstract colourist figurativism', in the words of Erik Kruskopf, but at the same time the change was also wider and greater. The shifting boundaries between figurative and abstract painting had been part of her art for a long time. Painting abstracts was not about becoming modern or moving in a particular artistic direction and stepping over some boundary. For Tove it was a question of seeing, of changing perspective, of painting unspoken things so that they remained unspoken on the canvas yet open to interpretation by the viewer.

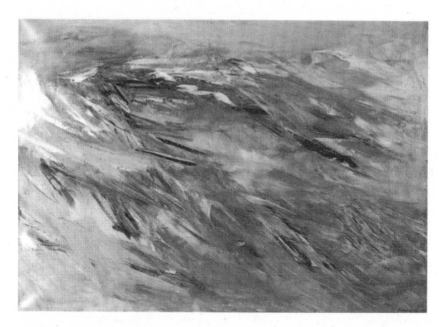

'Eight on the Beaufort Scale', oils, 1966.

Such painters as the Franco-Russians Nicolas de Staël and Serge Poliakoff were now important to her; they featured (with many others) in *Modern Painting – Contemporary Trends* (1960), one of the most important art books in her collection. Her shelves were full of books on French painting, on the Impressionists who were her favourites, on Renoir, Manet and Monet, books about Cézanne and her beloved Matisse, about Braque and Gauguin. The repeated trips she made to Paris with Tooti were above all devoted to painting, as had been her early visit in 1938. Paris was and would continue to be the city of pictures for both of them. On their working trips they spent months in the studios for artists in the great complex of the Cité des Arts, by the Seine. Tooti had a studio of this kind in the spring of 1968 and Tove spent two months there. The climax came in spring 1975, when they shared the same studio for six months. Then Tove painted self-portraits and also used Tooti as a model (see colour plate 29). These were portraits of an entirely new kind. The close-up painting of the artist's own face is unflattering (sometimes known as the 'ugly' or 'angry' self-portrait), while 'The Graphic Artist' shows Tooti at work. Herself and her work in a double portrait, seen through both herself and Tooti.

The 1960s saw a rapid succession of one-man shows. The first opened in 1960 at Galerie Pinx in Helsinki and was followed by four more in 1962, 1963, 1966 and 1969. The last of these was a shared exhibition with Tooti at the Museum of Central Finland in Jyväskylä. The exhibition programme was printed in graphic black and white: simple, clear and undisguised. Tove presented herself with a new face, as indeed she had ever since her first exhibition of the decade at Pinx, a gallery with a modern tendency. The new painter depicted herself in new clothes and her self-portraits were in a state of transition. No more of the woman who had drawn the Moomin strips, who had drawn herself together with her characters in various combinations. Now she was showing portraits of herself on her own, in the setting of her studio (1959). Abstract canvases formed a background and and she herself was dressed in a simple top and trousers. She was a humble 'New Beginner', as she called this portrait. This was a very different image from her egocentric and powerful self-portraits of the 1940s, set against figurative Renaissance-style landscapes.

She was creating herself anew, breaking with tradition, stepping forward as an unassuming novice. She was expecting no new breakthrough, at best some 'semi-sour' criticism, and she had no plans to become 'entirely sour' herself if this was what happened. The main thing, she told Maya before the vernissage on 31st October 1960, 'is for me to show what I'm busy working at, and to leave the exhibition behind me'. After the vernissage, she summed up some of the criticism for Tooti: it was 'just so'. Some of the critics were 'really friendly'. She drew particular attention to the fact that Vehmas (the sometimes nitpicking but influential Einari Vehmas in *Uusi Suomi*) was really 'amiable, considering it was a question of Vehmas on the one hand – and me on the other'. But she didn't read them all immediately. She wanted to wait till she could get a total picture. 'Then perhaps they'll cancel each other out,' she told Tooti, 'and that will mean, when all's said and done, that nothing ultimately catastrophic will have happened.' The most important thing, despite everything, was to show herself as a full-scale painter.

Part of this process was a change of signature. She now signed herself 'Jansson' rather than the familiar 'Tove'. 'Tove' was associated with the Moomins, with illustrations and figurative painting, but 'Jansson' could be anyone. By using her surname as if it was a first name, Tove rejected her image as Moomin writer and illustrator, keeping her distance on her own terms. To the art public she now became a 'Jansson' (while as an illustrator she would always remain 'Tove').

Now in the middle of her personal spring-cleaning, she needed to strip away old layers and clear clutter out of corners. In the early 1960s she did up her studio, modernising it and developing its surfaces to create a new environment for her art and her literature. The architects Reima and Raili Pietilä (Tooti's brother and sister-in-law) redesigned the tower, adding a long bench right under the high windows and a balustrade under the studio ceiling. This last became a place for files and folders, correspondence and wardrobes, with a screened-off sleeping space. A spiral staircase led down into the little room with the mirror, chest of drawers and divan and the small bookcase and the sewing-cupboard that Tove had painted in the 1940s. Down in the studio itself there was room for various benches, tables and bookshelves, together with paintings, easels and Steinlein posters from Paris. And, as always, there was the sculptor's turntable Faffan had used to carry his work in progress, and the sculptures of women and the model ships Tove had built. Choosing whether to have a kitchen or a bathroom – there wasn't room for both – was easy: bathroom. A refrigerator and a couple of cooking rings in the fireplace would have to serve as a kitchen. She blew things away, tidied up and built afresh, a progressive change reflected in her pictures and stories. Change in the Moomin books had long been expressed by the upheaval of catastrophe.

What was old was broken up and ground down – that is how she put it in her notes – and in the resulting dust her work found new expressive power. In February 1962 she wrote:

> ... the exposed studio ceiling with its cork boards trickled black dust over the cat and me. Now they're digging deep holes in the walls to hold the soupente bench and that dust is white. The dust I myself have caused is grey. I'm living in a mist, and footsteps mark narrow paths across the floor between dramatic Ionesco piles of personal belongings, sculptures, books, objects (you can scarcely call them furniture), and my own half-dry paintings that scramble round the walls. An utterly surrealistic world in

the crooked little room [the anteroom to the studio]. But the mighty studio itself is empty and has an impersonal smell, full of rubble and common sense.

When the new studio was finished she wrote of beauty and balance, a setting with 'serene' bow windows, strong white surfaces, a calm high staircase. 'It's all as terribly pure and simple as in a church, or the inside of a freshly-rinsed shell.' This down-to-earth quality was paralleled in the new order, with its workbenches, cupboards and drawers where everything had its place. 'Ready, waiting, filed, classified'; there were drawers for paper of different thicknesses, for paints, manuscripts, theatre, verses, letters, notes, exhibitions, fans, photographs and 'two metres of business correspondence'. This white matter-of-factness creates an almost frightening effect in her description, but opens like a new world ready to receive life – an empty surface ready to be filled with pictures and writing. At the same time her archive began to grow on the shelves. Tooti had moved into a flat around the corner in the same block, on Kaserngatan. They could find each other through long attic passageways, also explored by the cat, Psipsina.

Life on the islands was facing new horizons too. They had left the house on Bredskär and built a low cottage on Klovharun, the forked island out on the Gulf of Finland, the angry rock as Tove often called it. Now she began writing about family, lighthouse and sea, about herself as the daughter of a sculptor father and about a Moominvalley with no trolls. She wrote about stones, large boulders and the hill in *Moominpappa at Sea* and *Sculptor's Daughter*. It was a longing for new lines, new expression, new places to look out from. It transformed the world of the Moomin stories, and it transformed her pictures and her writing.

The year Tove was working on the stories that would become *Tales from Moominvalley*, her shrewd essay 'The Deceitful Writer of Children's Books' was also published, in the periodical *Horisont* (1961). The editor, Kaj Hagman, had asked her to write about the qualifications and prerequisites necessary for a children's writer. Her essay further developed views she had already expressed in her academic lectures, particularly in a talk she had given for students in Oslo the previous year: 'The Secret Motives of a Writer of Children's Books'. A serious business, Tove claimed, that reveals the writer as a 'very self-centred and infantile

The studio transformed – 'like a freshly washed white shell', 1962.

creature' even if she can't be taken seriously for a moment. Yet she is serious. Here we find Tove's theory of the child's feeling for a balance between 'the excitement of the everyday and the security of the imagination' in its fullest form. This had become a mantra for characterisation in her Moomin world. But the typical Moomin feeling for catastrophe, so stubbornly loved by readers, journalists and academics, was only a part of a wider argument. Tove's essay also discusses something else: what it is that drives a writer to choose to write a book for children.

To 'abreact' was an expression Tove often returned to in

connection with the conditions for creativity – writing or painting as part of a cleansing process, a cathartic development in the Freudian psychoanalytical sense – to speak, write or paint oneself free. The cleansing effect of art, the cleansing effect of anger, the cleansing effect of action. When she was on the island she could abreact – she often wrote about it in her letters – by doing heavy physical work, like chopping firewood or carrying large stones. A writer of children's books could have a need 'to give free expression to some surplus or excess, or to reproduce – and thus experience – something lost or unattainable'. One can write for pleasure ('I can't leave it alone'), and if the writer is not writing specifically to amuse or educate children, one must assume that 'he' is indulging his own childishness.

> Either what has been half-lost or finds no place in adult society. A very easily overlooked form of escapism.

> Perhaps this is why the most convincing children's books are full of symbols, of identification and self-obsession – and have so little to do with the immature reader.

> But I believe the immature reader is often spellbound by what is unspoken and disguised.

> This risky but meaningful undercurrent is not incompatible with the child's own inaccessible sense of mystery, tenderness and cruelty. And fear.

The writer's own urges and needs are essential if writing is to occur, whereas the existence of the reading child is not. This was a bold concept, modern for its time, cleverly formulated by a truly 'deceitful' writer of books for children. The idea of the children's book as 'camouflage' rests on these prerequisites: the writer as manipulator writing a story either to satisfy a childish need of his own or to give free expression to a 'fatal' naivety. 'So he ends up writing a book for children in which people are nice to each other. Something he certainly would not have done if he'd been writing an [adult] novel or a collection of stories.'

Tove worked from this theoretical basis in her short stories and novels for adults. In these, people are not 'nice to each other', and this troubled the critics. In the same way, in her more persuasive children's books there is play with this dangerously meaningful undercurrent. For the benefit of the reader, she expounded her theory of the importance of not narrating or illustrating everything. There must be a point where the writer stops but the child goes on. 'Some threat or a magnificence that is never explained. A face that is never entirely revealed.' This was something Tove had long practised in her Moomin books.

Writing this essay on the deceitful nature of the writer of books for children was not merely a discussion of her own methods, but above all a way to 'abreact' – to give free expression to her own role as Moominmamma and writer of children's books. The painter in her was determined to become visible again.

The Loving Toffle

The picture book *Who Will Comfort Toffle?* (1960) has a significant place in the process of transformation. Tove threw herself into her painting, but words and storytelling refused to let go. Besides her work on *The Hunting of the Snark*, Åke tempted her to write a short essay on Elsa Beskow for Bonniers Literary Magazine (*Bonniers Litterära Magasin*) in 1959. The incentive was Stina Hammar's new biography of Beskow. Under the title 'The Fairy Tale Within Reality', Tove wrote of Beskow's ability to leave room for the reader's imagination.

For herself, in her notes, she wrote about her desire to paint, but the urge to tell stories would not go away. No sooner had she buried her comic strip troll and celebrated her freedom, than she created a new picture book. In the summer of 1959 she wrote the text for *Who Will Comfort Toffle?* in narrative verse, in which strophes of six iambic pentameters are followed by strophes of six iambic heptameters with end-rhymes on the pattern ababcc/aabbcc.

Who lives inside this little house? It's Toffle all alone.

Poor Toffle doesn't notice quite how lonely he has grown.

Outside he hears the Groke's shrill howl, Hemulen's heavy tread.

As nervously he lights his lamps to guide his way to bed.

Around him forest creatures close their doors against the night

And keep each other safe from harm
    with smiles and warmth and light,
But Toffle's feeling cold and sad, with no companion near
He burrows under bedclothes, body shivering with fear,
So Who Will Comfort Toffle, tell him, 'Hush now, it's okay.
Life's bound to seem much brighter
    when tomorrow comes your way.'

'An epic in verse', is how Tove described the finished manuscript to Maya at the end of the summer; it consisted of '14 verses with 12 lines in each'. She was in the middle of drawing the pictures, partly in Indian ink and partly as double spreads in colour. Her working title was 'The Romantic Tale of the Lonely Toffle'. The format was to be the same as for *The Book About Moomin, Mymble and Little My*, but 'without holes or other novelties'. What distinguishes the book is something entirely different: 'No Moomintrolls', as she told Maya. It is an important distinction that one needs to see in writing. There are no trolls in the book, not even in the margin of any of the pictures. Other figures have taken over the scene, just as in *Moominvalley in November*, though that still lay ten years in the future. Now it was 1959 and she was writing about the creatures that move in the world round Moomin: Toffle and Miffle, Fillyjonks and Hemulens, Mymble, Snufkin, Too-ticky, Booble and Little My. *Who Will Comfort Toffle?* is the story of The Others.

The picture book was part of Tove's transition from strips to painting, a forum where text and pictures could tell a story and be painter friendly at the same time. It was a story she wanted to work on in peace so as to achieve the right perception, but as always she was having a difficult struggle with pleasure. At the end of the summer she told Vivica: 'I'm aiming at feeling joy in my work, freedom and a childish craziness, though it isn't going very well. But in any case I shan't let the book out of my hands until it's good. It might take several years until I '*see*'. But she had finished the book before she and Tooti went to Greece that autumn.

In *Who Will Comfort Toffle?* the painter in Tove Jansson is working with broad surfaces, pure forms, and open and extended lines. The black contours she used in *The Book About Moomin,*

Och knyttet gömde brevet i sin ficka,
det första brev han nånsin hade fått,
dessutom var det skrivet av en flicka
och detta gjorde knyttet mycket gott.
Han blev med ens så modig, stark och glad,
han tog ett kallt, men lyckligt månskensbad,
sin kappsäck tömde han på allt och satte sig i den
och rodde ut på havet i den långa dyningen,
två skor låg kvar på stranden och en hatt med stenar i

New stories, new pictures. From Who Will Comfort Toffle?

Mymble and Little My were now replaced by white edges around
the actors. There are cut-out elements (découpage) in *Who
Will Comfort Toffle?* too, a flatness of form that exposes the
symbolism, giving it an archetypal atmosphere. She purifies the
themes, removes what is inessential in the setting and brings out
the figures. The pictures are figurative, but the pure, simplified
forms have an abstract effect. The big picture of Toffle on the
beach is done like a canvas in which the colours and lineaments
of shore, sea and horizon flow into one another. The line of
boulders stretching out to the sea rests like a series of blue half-
moons on the pink water; the shell on the beach is large and
white just as it says in the text. There, between shore and sea, the

story turns a corner, stuck in a borderland where all the longing in Toffle finds expression: 'So Who Will Comfort Toffle and remind him that a shell/Is nicer when there's somebody to show it to as well?' In both her painting and her writing Tove returns to borderlands of this kind again and again: the shore, the sea, the bay, the island. *Who Will Comfort Toffle?* is about having the courage to cross the border, to go over the line between the well-known and the unknown. A picture book where the painter and the writer in Tove Jansson meet.

The story is a lesson in love about learning to express oneself. The lines about having the courage to speak have become therapeutic classics: 'They'd know that he was there if he would only say hello.' All who are fearful, unsure of themselves and miserable can identify with the lonely Toffle, who nevertheless gradually comes to meet his counterpart and learns to speak the silent language of love:

> Now Toffle looks at Miffle. They exchange a timid smile
> That says as much as words, perhaps, but only for a while

It may seem that Toffle and Miffle have fixed roles, he as the rescuer and she as the rescued. But the lesson in love has a different purpose. It portrays the process of finding courage, irrespective of woman or man, girl or boy, Toffle or Miffle. At first Tove worked with a female Toffle, as can be seen from her manuscript. But as the text began to develop in verse, 'she' was crossed out and replaced by 'he'. By this time the text had as its title 'The Romantic Tale of the Lonely Toffle' and the same structure as the finished book. It is not clear from the draft if the struggle with the Groke and the great salvation would have been achieved by the female Toffle as principal character, or whether she would have saved a Toffle or a Miffle.

The Letter

Who Will Comfort Toffle? allows space for the reader in a new way – through a letter. Tove loved the more adventurous forms of communicating by letter, and she wrote of letters in bottles, the method used by Miffle, both in her diaries and in the Moomin books. Such a letter plays a decisive part in *The Moomins and the Great Flood*. This deals with a sender in need, whose message is often smudged and difficult to read. As it is in *Who Will Comfort Toffle?*

> In shallow water near the shore, mysteries are afloat.
> Toffle can see a bottle and inside it there's a note.
> He paddles out to rescue it, to see what it might say.
> If it was signed, the sea has washed its signature away,
> But Toffle has the moon which is the perfect reading lamp.
> He'll work it out, although the words are blurred and damp.
> He reads aloud, 'I'm terrified! Won't someone come and help?
> Won't somebody protect me when the Groke begins to yelp?
> If you are strong and wise and brave, please will you call or write?
> I'm just a little Miffle and it's very nearly night ...'

This sorrowful text has a decisive influence on the recipient's fate, as in classic letter-literature. But Toffle himself has no ability with the pen, which means the reader has an important task, if the lesson in love is to achieve its desired result. Each reader can himself or herself write the text that will guide the love story to a happy conclusion. This is what the narrator proposes:

> So Who Will Comfort Toffle now? Will someone lend a hand
> And help him write to Miffle so that she can understand?
> (Find some writing paper. You won't need a stamp.
> Just stick the letter on a rosebush
> where you're sure Miffle will see it.)

The narrator gives immediate proof of the letter's effectiveness. The roses change colour from white to red, the colour of love.

'If I'm addressing any particular sort of reader, I'm addressing a Miffle,' said Tove in an interview with Bo Carpelan a few years later (1964). She demonstrated it in this picture book. With it, she opened her own letterbox wide. Hundreds of children wrote comforting letters to Toffle and Miffle, but they usually didn't end up in any rosebush but in Tove's letterbox, whether with a stamp on or not. 'To Miffle, Moominvalley, perhaps near Helsinki, Finland' is just one of the addresses that reached her. One letter writer took the story literally and sent the letter in a bottle with the instruction to ask 'Mummy' to iron it if it got wet. (Tove later used this one in her short story 'Messages'.)

Behind the Toffle book lay a reader's letter from Sweden that became part of the Jansson storyteller's myth and has often been repeated. Tove herself gave various versions of it over the years, but in essence it remained the same. On the manuscript for a lecture (dated 1963), written in one of her workbooks, she set down its background: 'Actually the story was the result of a letter from a child. It was signed "Toffle". "You don't know me," he wrote, "But I'm one of those miserable little ones who are always on the outside, that no one ever notices or invites anywhere or looks at when they speak. I'm afraid of nearly everything."' Tove went on: 'I suppose the simplest way to give a Toffle self-confidence is to find him a Miffle, someone even more frightened than he is. So I sent my Toffle out to find Miffle and save her.'

One of these 'Toffles' was a certain Karl Sundén in Sweden, no child but sixteen years old. His letter tells of his longing for Moominvalley and how difficult it is for him to be brave. 'You gave me the idea of Toffle,' Tove later wrote to him, but there were many 'Toffles' among those who wrote to her. She described one of them, a boy who addressed his letter to Snufkin, as the 'original Toffle' in her letters and notes. But there were Toffles everywhere and she wrote to them all. Letters had to be answered, particularly those written by children. She had believed this ever since childhood and insisted on it all her life, even when it became a huge job. She loved telling the story of how Per Olov as a small boy wrote to the President of France and asked him to get rid of the Foreign Legion. But no answer came from the President, so Ham answered instead. 'The President would think the matter over,' she wrote.

A Best-loved Book

Who Will Comfort Toffle? became one of Tove's best-loved books in Scandinavia, both by children and adults. Its success was immediate, and once again it was considered that Tove had surpassed herself. She was particularly delighted by a review by

Bo Carpelan in *Hufvudstadsbladet* that was lyrical in both form and content, and introduced by the following tribute:

Wonderful is in truth the story-world of Jansson, Tove
Exotic but nonetheless substantial just like Almqvist, Love.

(Almqvist was a great nineteenth-century Swedish romantic poet and social reformer.)

'A fairy tale for our times,' declared Eva von Zweigbergk in *Dagens Nyheter*, detecting the great 'world terror' lurking in the 'fierce and awful Groke'. In other words, she detected the threat of a third world war in the book.

Who Will Comfort Toffle? has been filmed, dramatised and staged with and without music. 'No actual "play" exists,' wrote Tove to a Danish theatrical agency that had put two questions about the book to her: 'I have been very free about giving permission for performances, with no contracts and no fees either, so far as I am aware.' A very typical answer. Her list of dramatisations of the book lists some thirty productions of Toffle, many more than for any other of her books, and still more could always be added. Theatre schools, amateur groups and small theatres with no financial basis to speak of performed their own dramatisations of Toffle. It was difficult to say no or, more accurately, easier to say yes. So she answered one particular theatrical agency: 'Wouldn't it be easiest if you just write that so far as I'm concerned, it's plain sailing?'

She was not so keen on having it adapted from verse to prose as was done for a German-language edition for Austria in the late 1970s, though she allowed it nonetheless. 'Benziger Verlag were unwilling to publish the book in verse, explaining that children don't like verse. Haha!!!' she wrote to Thomas Warburton at Schildts. But they were not altogether able to escape verse. The deceitful author divided the text into rhythmic sections, added a rhymed song (for Toffle) as an ending and forbade the prose version to 'go any further'.

In *Who Will Comfort Toffle?* Tove wrote of the deep need for closeness that exists in us all, mediated via a Toffle and a Miffle. 'It is difficult to imagine anyone this book could not relate to,' declared Bo Strömstedt. For Tove, it was her declaration of love for Tooti. She dedicated the book 'To Tuulikki'. 'Oh, Tooti, how much I miss you!' she wrote as she was finishing the book in

September 1959. She was alone on the island. 'Do you realise your book is as good as finished, even the title page and the final vignette. Now all that's left are the front and back covers and a bit of work on the Indian ink. I'm in the middle of writing out the text in pencil, half done.' She had altered the position of some of the pictures, cut down on the Indian ink (as they had discussed) and longed desperately to show the whole thing:

> I've made a double-page spread of the section about the letter in the bottle, in colour – and the same thing with their meeting at the end. Which is better. Now the Indian ink drawings are only right at the beginning and end. That makes a better whole. It'll be such fun to show you.

Who Will Comfort Astrid?

'God bless you for Toffle!! But who will comfort Astrid if you don't agree to the proposal I'm now going to make to you?' An appeal tumbled into her letterbox one day in November 1960. The Swedish publishers Rabén & Sjögren were planning a new translation of J.R.R. Tolkien's *The Hobbit* and there was only one person in the world who could draw in the way the book 'needed' – Tove Jansson.

'Think it over,' wrote Astrid Lindgren, the Swedish creator of the famous Pippi Longstocking books. 'Don't say no at once.' She knew very well that Tove loved to 'sit and paint beautiful pictures', but this was Tolkien. 'When people read the book they will have the illustrations in front of them, drawn by Tove Jansson, and will tell themselves that this will be the children's book of the century, and will live long after we are dead and buried.'

Big words, but this was not what attracted Tove. She was deeply involved in painting at this point, but she saw in Tolkien a chance to enjoy terror and 'horror', just as she had with *The Hunting of the Snark* a couple of years earlier. Tolkien was even 'more gruesome than Poe' – the highest praise she could bestow. To her his books were sort of 'horror stories'. 'Write to me soon, I'm waiting impatiently,' wrote Astrid at the end of her first letter, and within a week Tove had decided. But she needed

Astrid Lindgren and Tove Jansson in Stockholm, 1958.

plenty of time, just as she had for Lewis Carroll. An exhibition
of oil paintings had just become a possibility, and during the
spring she needed a long 'painting period'. So there it was. In
the summer of 1961 she sent her illustrations to Astrid.

Tove Jansson did not know Astrid Lindgren well. Their
friendship had never extended beyond official events, as she
reminded Astrid much later, but it did exist at a distance. They
had appeared together at literary events in Stockholm and
had met in Helsinki too, and when Rabén & Sjögren published
a serialisation of *Finn Family Moomintroll* in the children's

347

magazine *Klumpe Dumpe* in 1957, they had exchanged a couple of letters. That had been the full extent of their literary co-operation. The Tolkien project was unique in various ways. Two of the internationally best-known writers in the Nordic countries were working together on the same book, but neither of them as author; instead their roles were publisher and illustrator. The translator was a third leading writer, Britt G. Hallqvist. It was a no less exclusive trio than had come together for *The Hunting of the Snark*.

In her usual way Tove soon provided Astrid with a work plan: the number, size, execution and placing of the illustrations, the relationship between text and pictures, an instruction that 'slender' introductory vignettes should extend horizontally at a certain distance along the title of each chapter. Her instructions were to the point, precise and practical. The Tolkien pictures had to speak for themselves as an expression of the *artist* Tove Jansson, not of the illustrator of the Moomins. This must be part of the purification of her artistic repertoire, in which for the time being she was pushing the Moomin characters out of the limelight.

Tolkien perfectly fitted Tove's weakness for 'horror', but she had no interest in entering into the world of his characters. His landscape was what fascinated her. 'The characters are commonplace: dwarfs, goblins, elves, black demigods – but the scenery is seductive in its macabre ferocity,' she told Tooti just after accepting the commission. She had been tempted in the same way as she had been by Lewis Carroll. The text resonated with her own inner world, with her love of the drama involved in expressing catastrophe: 'Forests of living horror, coal-black rivers, moonlit moors with fiery wolves – a whole world of catastrophe that I know I can respond to in pictures so long as people don't put pressure on me.' As for the figures, she was thinking of making them 'really small' or simply inventing new goblins and elves. The scenery was what mattered. Some of the characters did become 'really small', and others, to the disgust of many Tolkien fans, were cheekily reinvented. Indignant critics also wrote that she hadn't 'bothered to take into account the many meaningful details with which the author has taken the trouble to enrich his characters'.

For Tove it was important to keep her Tolkien illustrations

entirely separate from the Moomin world. She devised a way of subverting her own technique and creating a new style of drawing. 'I have tried to free myself from my "Moomin style" with its careful line-drawing and painstakingly filled surfaces,' she confided to Astrid. She drew more freely, with no black lead under the Indian ink. This particularly applied to the vignettes, one of her specialities:

> The only way to escape my own technique was to draw on poor quality paper (i.e. paper I did not respect) and to draw each figure freely again and again, 20, 40, 60 times till it looked fairly free. You understand. Then I glued the result together. That's why so many of the vignettes look like patchwork, but of course people won't notice this once they're printed.

The vignettes consist of small figures set beside one another that share in a spontaneous movement, almost a sketch-like Impressionistic reproduction in black lines. This was a painstaking method, which could capture gesture and impression in the moment, and she took it further in the illustrations for her short-story collection *Tales from Moominvalley*, which was done at the same time. Sketching directly in Indian ink was very different from the more 'regular' Moomin illustrations, as she put it to Astrid. She preferred not to carry it to extremes, but emphasised that the new technique affected the whole. For full-page illustrations she was compelled to use her 'usual pearl-knitting', but went over each one several times and expressed the hope that 'they don't really look like Moomins, do they?' It had been a long time since the days when as an artist she sneaked her Moomin-signature into other writers' books.

'Dear marvellous Tove, send me the hem of your cloak so I can kiss it! I'm so happy with your wonderful little Hobbit that I can't find words to say what I feel. He is exactly the sort of ingeniously moving and charming little creature he should be, and he has never been done like *this* in any edition,' wrote Astrid to Tove in July 1961. Both publishing house and publisher were delighted, but the cover ran into trouble. Some felt it looked more like a book for adults than one for children, with too small a Bilbo against too large a landscape. The main character needed to be in the foreground; in Astrid's words, he had to 'catch the

The bridge over Rivendell. Illustration for The Hobbit, 1962.

eye' without too much background, so as to 'stand out clearly on bookshop counters'. This was the exact opposite of what Tove had intended. To her the most important thing was the dramatic potential of the scenery, but she fell into line and redesigned the cover – though she did it much against her will. The new picture showed Bilbo ready for battle with a mountain chain in the distance behind him, plus a band of warriors on horseback and a dragon floating overhead.

Thus, to please people who published children's books, she 'made the picture more childish' (an expression she would often use during the 1960s). This sort of adaptabiliuty took a heavy toll on her in the long run, and the relationship between Moomintroll and troll freedom, between books for children and books for adults, became increasingly critical with the publication of her subsequent Moomin books: *Tales from Moominvalley, Moominpappa at Sea* and *Moominvalley in November*. It was also the main reason why she later left her Swedish Moomin publisher Gebers (Almqvist & Wiksell) and went over to Bonniers for her new books for adults.

This new edition of *Bilbo, The Adventures of a Hobbit* came nowhere near to becoming the 'children's book of the century'; rather the opposite. It made no impression on critics or readers, and still less on Tolkien experts. It only achieved one edition with Tove's illustrations, in 1962. Readers saw Jansson where they would have preferred Tolkien, and some of the pictures gave particular offence. The severest criticism was later directed at the representation of Gollum, who appeared as an ordinary man with a crown of seaweed on his head – what could have been more 'wrong' for a text that cried out for 'correct' illustrations, complained the magazine *Arda* in 1987.

Other, more tolerant, voices referred to 'strongly atmospheric' and unusual Tolkien illustrations. The problem was the unfamiliar quality of the pictures. *Interpreting* Tolkien was as bad as swearing in church. Yet even the severely critical *Arda* admired one illustration: the dwarves with their horses on the bridge over Rivendell. Rabén & Sjögren used it as their 1962 Christmas card.

351

The Invisible

The relationship between Tove and Moomin, like all true love stories, was seasoned with anger and hostile outbursts. 'No one would accept me as a painter,' she told Eva Konikoff when they exchanged letters in 1961 after several years' silence, writing in English. 'It's been rather rough – as every comeback is, I guess ... They only see me as the famous Moominmamma. I ended up in an empty space.' She felt out of touch with her earlier work habits, she added, 'and going nowhere'. Her first exhibition 'was turned down', but in March (1961), she would have another. At the same time she was illustrating her new book, a collection of stories for children called 'The Invisible Child'.

What she had to say had the same common denominator both on canvas and in writing: the idea of the invisible. In the Moomin books she took more and more figures off the stage, reducing the family and writing about those who moved on the fringes, like Toffle. She wrote about a Moomintroll who wants to experience his invisible surroundings (*Moominland Midwinter*), of a Moominpappa who wants to be a lighthouse keeper and a Moominmamma who paints herself as one of several Mammas on the whitewashed wall of the lighthouse (*Moominpappa at Sea*). By late November the family has left its valley, and the result – *Moominvalley in November* – is a Moomin book with no Moomins in it at all. This process took a long time. Moomin had become part of Tove Jansson whether she liked it or not. In her painting she was working with dissolved forms, blurring any direct representation, letting anyone who liked imagine themes for themselves. But it was a complex process. The most terrible thing was that the artist in her had made herself invisible as a painter. When she resumed exhibiting people couldn't see Jansson, only the famous Moominmamma.

Her story collection *Tales from Moominvalley* (in Swedish 'The Invisible Child') is part of her longing to express herself. 'I've begun writing short stories for young people, and I notice I'm beginning to grow up. Maybe there's no harm in that,' she told Maya in summer 1961. She talked of *beginning* to write in a short format and linked this to change in herself as a writer – she was still writing for children, but was herself beginning to be an adult. This enabled her to distance herself from writing for children in a sort of double movement that would now mark her future writing. The new short stories were also about her longing to write herself away from children – or, to put it another way, to render the child invisible.

Tove herself often used the English term 'short stories', even if her collections were described in Swedish simply as tales or 'noveller'. 'I love the short story,' she wrote in a note in the 1990s: 'concentrated and united around a single idea. There must be nothing unnecessary in it, one must be able to hold the tale enclosed in one's hand.' She wrote five more story collections after *Tales from Moominvalley*. She was now walking in the footsteps of Chekhov spiced to some extent with Poe. On the one hand was concentrated expression and a richly satisfying atmosphere; on the other dramatic effect; denouement at one single point. The short story as a form pursued Tove throughout her writing career. She had started in 1934 when she was twenty with 'The Boulevard' (illustrated by herself) in *Helsingfors-Journalen*, and set a final full stop with 'Messages' (1998). Then as always she combined painting with story-writing.

It is significant that she linked writing in a short form to 'being grown up', even when she was writing 'short stories' for the young. The young writer of the 1930s wrote no tales for the young. The short story belonged in the adult world. Making a collection for children could be transformed into an aesthetic experiment. One of her provisional titles for *Tales from Moominvalley* was 'Childish Stories'; other alternatives were of a more general character, like 'Mixed Tales' and 'Mixed Stories'. The collection consists of nine stories, four of them featuring the Moomin family, among them the 'invisible child' that gave the book its original Swedish title.

The characters are motivated by various trials involving longing, desire and dreams. On his way home one April evening, a nameless Snufkin meets a nameless 'creep' – one of the invisible – and is unable to find the tune for his spring song before he can see the creep in its own right. Moominpappa is drawn to the Hattifatteners and is shorn of his defining lineaments as a troll and a father, while Moomintroll's overwhelming love for a splendid gold dragon ruins his self-confidence. The process of finding oneself and achieving visibility is the recurring theme, as in *Who Will Comfort Toffle?* The theme looks different depending on

'The Invisible Child', 1962. In Tales from Moominvalley.

the individual: a Whomper with too much imagination, a Fillyjonk who believes in disasters, a Hemulen who loves silence, a child who becomes invisible. 'The Spruce Tree', which closes the collection, was written many years earlier, as we have seen, for a Christmas number of *Svenska Dagbladet*. Here, too, the process of individualisation that marks Tove's other stories is missing.

Invisibility is the main theme of the book, most clearly expressed in the title story. Ninny (as Too-ticky explains) is a little girl who has been frightened into invisibility by the sarcastic woman who looked after her. With the Moomin family, she becomes visible again step by step, mainly through Moominmamma's care and attention (and Granny's Household Remedies). First her paws reappear, then her body up to her neck and the ribbon in her hair. But her face is still invisible, till she listens to a bit of advice from Little My. This fits in with the instinct to abreact – so important for Tove herself – and in the story it is a question of literally biting back. 'Believe me,' says Little My to Ninny, 'you'll never have a face of your own until you've learned to fight.' When Ninny sinks her (invisible) teeth into Moominpappa's tail (he had been pretending he wanted to push Moominmamma into the sea), she becomes a living proof of psychological truth. Her face appears and Little My is full of praise: 'I couldn't have done it any better myself!'

In its portrayal of Ninny's reduction of herself the text is concrete and it is complemented by the illustrations, but is at the same time made abstract from the point of view of understanding.

When she finally shows her face, Ninny has called forth her true nature, and nearly becomes worse than Little My (at least in Moominpappa's view). The expression to 'show one's face' comes more than once in Tove's writing, and she spoke of Moomintroll's transformation in *Moominland Midwinter*.

Among other things, the reviewers wrote of Tove Jansson as a therapist, moralist and educationalist, and the story has been used in various therapeutic connections. She read a good deal of psychological literature and went into analysis for a couple of years in the 1960s, with a 'head doctor'. It was all about the demands made of her, celebrity and dreams of being left in peace. It was of course disturbing, she wrote, but it did inspire a belief in change. But most important of all was the American psychologist Karen Horney, and in particular her famous book *Neurosis and Human Growth: The Struggle toward Self-Realisation* (1950, published in Swedish in 1953). Its basic theory is that the divergence between the ideal self and the real self sets up a conflict which hinders self-realisation.

Horney's theory of the tyranny of the inner imperative was especially significant. In Tove's copy of the book this chapter is full of underlinings. According to Horney, there are three kinds of neurotics: the expansive, the self-effacing and the resigned. These are outlined in the story collection: the self-effacing Ninny, the expansive Moominpappa and the resigned Fillyjonk. 'Karen Horney formulated what is important, simple and clear, actually before I read her books,' wrote Tove rather cryptically, but admitting willingly that Horney was a revelation of her own writing; Tove actually used the English word 'revelation'.

Several of Horney's books can be found in Tove's library (*Our Inner Conflicts* and *Feminine Psychology*). Tove's notes often deal with the inner demands of the self – everything that is converted into compulsion and duty, pleasure, work, love, family, celebrity. 'My friendliness and consideration for others are no more than a neurotic attitude,' she wrote in 1966: 'Not even my conscience is honourable, often just a hysterical reaction because I was not able to fulfil the excessive demands that Horney calls the "inner commands". Unfortunately she is right.' As always Tove's view of herself is implacably critical. She describes herself in terms of the honest deceiver she will later write a novel about.

Her enormous correspondence was and continued to be one of her greatest touchstones, and she nearly always referred to it in interviews and articles. The compulsion to answer letters dominated her completely. As a writer Tove Jansson was able to express the necessary revolt against the tyranny of the inner commands (as in the short stories), and Tove as a person needed to do the same. 'I have tried to explain my aversion to the correspondence, but probably consideration for others has made my repugnance much too vague,' she noted in 1966. She sought strength through her writing. The invisible child was, quite simply, one aspect of herself:

> Like the Invisible Child I must learn to be angry; and show it. Probably I show it too much at the beginning, and for this reason too I need a margin of isolation. Hopefully my face will gradually develop.

The faces of her characters developed, too. At the beginning of the 1960s 'Moomindom' became a more general human wisdom and the various characters began to lose their particular identities as Whompers, Hemulens, Moominpappas and Fillyjonks and became generalised individuals. 'My characters are usually a camouflage for 'models of human behaviour,' as she put it in an early working note, but they also widen my functional margins: 'I mean, a particular Mrs Smith cannot be placed in completely unimaginable circumstances and situations, but one can work so much more freely with a Mrs Fillyjonk who in any case doesn't resemble anything one is accustomed to.' The stories in *Tales from Moominvalley* work in the opposite sense. They present a Mrs Fillyjonk and a Mr Hemulen (whom we have learned to recognise), but strip off their camouflage. They have become more human, while the readers down the years have become more Moomin-like.

The story 'The Fillyjonk Who Believed in Disasters' is a text of this kind. When the tornado comes the Fillyjonk abreacts with all her characteristic Fillyjonk exaggeration: fear, inner panic, a duty to protect family heirlooms like pieces of sculpture, cut-glass chandeliers and mahogany furniture. The storm strikes, turning everything upside down and having a cleansing effect. It is followed by a tornado (at sunrise) that whisks up all her possessions, furniture and memorabilia and hurls them out into

Laughter; sketches for 'The Invisible Child'.

space: 'All is washed clean and swept away!' When the tornado has done its job it dissolves and is no longer 'needed'. The story could just as well have been told about a Mrs Smith as about a Fillyjonk, about any middle-aged woman living in the neighbourhood. Only the name would have needed changing.

This is one of the kinds of purifying force that recurs in literature when abreaction requires it – the multiplicity of catastrophes is one of the most obvious. For Tove herself the power of the elements, the expressive reformation of nature through storms and tempests was always important as a rebirth. One of the biggest storms to hit Bredskär – the most magnificent she had ever seen, she told Maya in a letter in the summer of 1959 – contained a tornado. But to her great disappointment she missed experiencing it:

> The whole cottage shook and it took two of us to open the door. A tornado (pillar of water) ten metres high seems to have passed the island, according to the pilots. What a shame that we didn't see it go past. The boat, which had been pulled up on the shore, was carried many metres over the sand by the wind

and the whole island was filled with a thrilling atmosphere of catastrophe. [...] Now there's a compact rampart of seaweed round the shore and everything has been rinsed out and washed clean after the long drought.

A Writer of Children's Books for Adults

With *Tales from Moominvalley* the debate about Tove Jansson as a writer of books for children moved to a higher plane. One reviewer was surprised while reading it by an indignant grandchild insisting on his right to the book, and the critics racked their brains over the age of its readers: 'Is this Tove book more for adults than for children?' wondered Gudrun Mörne yet again, but left the question to the children to decide. Both Bo Carpelan and Lars Bäckström followed the same train of thought. 'A collection of fairy tales' of such moral and psychological sophistication has more to tell adults than children,' stated Bäckström. Tove was amply living up to the image of the deceitful writer.

Distinguishing between fairy tales (for children) and short stories (for adults) seems always to pose a dilemma for critics and literary scholars. Tove won the *Stockholms-Tidningen* 1963 prize for Finland-Swedish culture for this story collection. In his article on the prizewinner, Per Olof Sundman faced the burning question squarely: 'Is Tove Jansson a writer of children's books?' The initial answer was an unhesitating yes. At the same time the stories were more than 'mere fairy tales for children', but 'in all their deceptiveness, their poetic gentleness, their bizarre and sometimes slightly macabre fancies' were also reading for adults. This was a clear illustration of Tove's camouflage thinking, especially as Sundman also included *Moominland Midwinter* (as much a book for adults as for children) and *Who Will Comfort Toffle?* – more for 'us oldies' than for 'our children'. But *Tales from Moominvalley*, brought together as 'a collection of stimulating tales for adults', was despite everything the praiseworthy breaking point.

All the many twists and turns in this major article were of course intended as the highest praise. The aim was to justify the children's writer Tove Jansson as prizewinner and explain the nature of this short-story collection. Not just for children, but perhaps most of all for adults. This feature was to recur down the years, with many variations, in reviews, articles, interviews, essays and dissertations of various academic kinds.

The movement towards a writing involvement with adulthood was emphasised by Tove's choice of the short story as form. In its physical form *Tales from Moominvalley* carried no obvious signs of being a book for children. It formed no part of any series (in Sweden the earlier Moomin books had appeared as part of a series called 'Robinson Books'), was not described as a children's book and had nothing but a picture, the author's name and the title on the front cover. The back cover carried only a minimal description of the stories and talked of a wonderful new book by Tove Jansson 'for all ages' (first edition). Everything hinted at a distancing from the form of a children's book, except the illustrations. Short-story collections for adults are not usually illustrated. Perhaps *Tales from Moominvalley* will be my last children's book, Tove told Eva while working on the pictures in spring 1962. 'You realise,' she went on, 'that writing for children was a really good "rubbish dump" for my "naïveté". Now it seems my books are getting increasingly adult and I have a strong feeling that the door to childish fantasy is about to close. I shall never be able to write "adult" books.' But that was exactly what she was capable of and wanted to do.

After Tove had finished the illustrations for the short-story collection, she prepared an exhibition. She was on the verge of new travels with Tooti and at the end of 1963 they went to Portugal, Spain and Ibiza, where Lasse had settled with his daughter Sophia. It was a journey she had longed for. To Ham she wrote happily: 'I'm busy with a new book.'

CHAPTER 13

The Woman Who Fell in Love with an Island

The island is high but bare with a sort of vigorous shrubbery in the middle thrown together by the storms, and also clad with glorious flora around the shore.

Letter to Eva Konikoff, 14th August 1946

'An astonishing number of people go about dreaming of an island,' Tove wrote in her essay 'The Island' in 1961. She herself had been in love with islands all her life. Islands relate to loneliness and closeness, openness and separateness. They are a metaphor for freedom. 'We live here on this island, and people who come to bother us should stay away,' says Grandmother menacingly in *The Summer Book*. There is room for shyness and exclusivity in such a view, laced with a strong feeling for home. 'It feels safe to be on a little island, a bit like being at home,' wrote Tove to Ham in the autumn of 1959, when she had just landed on Mykonos. Islands were a way of life, both at home and away, and that idea had been rooted in her since childhood. 'Have you read "The Man Who Loved Islands"?' (a D.H. Lawrence short story), she wrote to Tooti when they were planning to build on Klovharun in the spring of 1963: 'How about the woman who fell in love with an island?'

Lawrence's story could have been specially written for Tove. Her first love was Kummelskär, the largest and most beautiful of

The house on Bredskär, 1957.

the chain of uninhabited skerries west of Glosholm in Pellinge archipelago. Then came Bredskär and finally Klovharun. To own an island was her dream, and she was already discussing it in the earliest interviews she gave in the 1940s. There was a beacon in her dream from the first. One of the islands to which she went on expeditions as a child was Glosholm, whose lighthouse was built high with little windows and a ramshackle staircase that led up to the light. Tove had been allowed to climb it for herself. This experience stayed in her mind and was brought into *Moominpappa at Sea*, 'maybe a trifle dramatised', said Tove later, in her short text 'Dream of a Lighthouse' – written for the Finnish coastguard authorities. When her Moomin family step into the dark lighthouse, the drama is like a Hitchcock film. The staircase winds up into the tower, long and rickety and creaking under Moominpappa's footsteps: 'A little daylight filtered through holes in the thick walls, and in each hole the silhouette of a large motionless bird could be seen. The birds stared down at them.'

The Jansson family's criss-crossing of islands and skerries in Pellinge (Glosholm, Laxvarpet, Nyttisholmen, Tunnholmen) became stories in her early diaries, on Tove's part given added zest by her reading of exciting adventure tales. Just thirteen, she described an expedition to Tunnholmen in August 1927:

> We landed at the same place as before and everyone except me went off to fish. I sat down to read 'The Amazon of the Desert' [by P.N. Krasnov]. They came back almost at once and we went to the interior of Tunnis to pick raspberries. It was boiling hot and Per Olov and I went ahead to the shore and bathed there. After a while Pappa came and said we were going to move on to another shore. When we got there we put up the tent. Meanwhile a great bank of cloud rose up behind the forest and soon from the sea too. Thunder rolled menacingly. Soon a few drops of rain fell. We'd already been in a hurry, but now we moved with terrifying speed. Pappa set the sail against the open side of the tent, Per-Olov insulated it all around and dug a channel for the water. Mamma busied herself with the potatoes and I carried all the gear to the tent. Finally we moved everything into it and everything was saved and the potatoes ready. By now it was really pouring down outside and thunder was rolling. Though not too near us. We ate our food and had no end of fun. For a while after the 'storm' was over they went fishing again and I buried myself in 'The Amazon of the Desert'. It's terribly exciting!

Story and reality blend into one another and the scene with the tent, rain, thunder and insulation with moss is like a mirror image of the wonderful expedition in *Finn Family Moomintroll* in which the sail is made into a tent, Moominmamma stops up its sides with moss and the Snork digs a ditch around them for the rain water. As Tove herself put it, it has just been dramatised a bit and, above all, transformed into a living part of the world of the Moomin family.

In Tove's writing the island becomes a place where one can look for arguments and develop them, a 'topos', in the language of classical rhetoric. The island is a place for adventure, renewal of life and transformation, a place where one can build up one's life and create a world of one's own. Tove did not actually leave home until she moved to a studio in 1944, but long before that she had built places to live in Pellinge in the form of huts, cabins and small structures. After her first hut, strengthened with planks and roofed with fabric, she had a little shed on Sandskär, then an exotic cabin with a reed roof, canvas tent and wooden floor at Laxvarpet (the bathing place in greater Pellinge), and a structure near her beloved grotto, with walls and roof, windows and steps. In the summer of 1947 the Windrose House developed on Bredskär, and in autumn 1964 a temporary structure was knocked up on Klovharun. Building a house was building yourself, both as troll and human. When Moomintroll plans his house on the lighthouse island in *Moominpappa at Sea*, it is a low cottage, a structure utterly different from Moominpappa's phallic upwardly aspiring lighthouse ideal. This low building was Tove's model for her cottages on Bredskär and Klovharun. Her dream of a beacon where she could look after the light never became reality. But it stayed long with her in various forms. As part of her last great attempt to be allowed to build on Kummelskär in 1961, she suggested she would be able to look after the lights.

The island assumes various bodies, expressions and forms in Tove Jansson's books; it can be found narrated, painted, drawn and documented in novels, short stories, literary documentaries, painted canvases and films. In *Moominpappa at Sea* she combined her own island dreams with Moominpappa's longing for something beyond the confines of Moominvalley. He sets his inner compass for the lighthouse on the island among the outermost skerries, an island so small that, in Little My's words, it's like a bit of fly-dirt on the map. This is where the Moomins will try out a new life.

To the Island

Tove never got Kummelskär. There was always some kind of fish that might be disturbed by construction work – herring, cod, white fish, salmon. 'They won't allow any building because of the herring,' she told Eva in 1947, 'but I've started negotiations for another island. I want my island, and I mean to have it!' Opposition merely made her more determined. At least at Bredskär

Sjöblom och Brunström

The pirates from Kråkö. Nisse Sjöblom and Sven Brunström.

she got nearer to the horizon and the outermost chain of sker-ries. When family and friends began to swarm in to limit her freedom and solitude began trickling away, she would start look-ing for a new island. The pilot Alex Karlsson had indeed sug-gested this as early as 1947 when Kummelskär first came into the picture. But the road to Klovharun, which formed part of the Pellinge conservation area, became a long-drawn-out process: an agonising vote on whether she should be allowed to build there or not, a long wait for building permission and an attempt to stop the whole process at the last moment. The story is told in *Notes from an Island* (1998), in which it is interwoven with notes on the building process, partly by Tove herself and partly by Sven Brunström, the 'pirate' from Kråkö who got everything under way. 'We can't wait,' he had said. 'The only thing to do is to make sure that the roof beam is in place. Then there can be no way back.' They both kept notes during the process of building, about both island and cottage; in the book Brunström's notes are intertwined with Tove's to make a double text, allowing two different perspectives.

Brunström's laconic notes have been preserved in three small diaries, written in parallel with Tove's own diary entries.

'The hut is ready, not much left to do,' he noted when the cottage was nearly finished in the summer of 1965, while Tove for her part wrote, 'Now it's beginning to look fine and ready. Excitement in the air, the cottage nearly finished. Endless little jobs all day.' On 14th July completion was celebrated by a dinner, according to Tove 'with whitefish and vodka, candles and red cloths, accordion, record player and dancing – a real party till 2.30 at night.' Brunström noted next day: 'Extinguishing the still burning embers. Done. Home 4pm. PS 11.30am to Bredskär to fetch Mrs J. When we got into the boat at Bredskär we could hear "On a Blue Field Shall I Tarry" from somewhere and saw someone splashing, it was Tove.'

The whole thing was a work of 'opposition' and with all its drama the process of building it became an extremely happy adventure for Tove. She lived with the builders, carried stones, aligned boards, laid bricks, made food, shot ducks and helped with nearly everything, all she had dreamed of and longed for. In a text written before *Notes from an Island* she gave a straight account of the whole process, from the negotiations to the day when the building permit finally arrived. She veered between experience and reflection, disclosing her tendency to 'dramatise' and convert experience into fiction, but above all she wrote powerfully about a woman who fell in love with an island. It was a story of conflict, construction and happiness.

Long before Bredskär I tried to get permission to live on Kummelskär, the beautiful, wild scene of childhood expeditions [see *Moominpappa at Sea*] with its beacon – I so wanted to look after the light – but it wasn't possible. I tried many times. When Tooti and I wanted to move from Bredskär we tried yet again. There was a meeting in Borgå about the matter, but a summer resident with great influence in Pellinge, Dr V, convinced them that we were undesirables so it came to nothing. On our last day on Bredskär I realised it was now or never, and drove the boat to Dr V's island (he had many) and said we would try for Klovharun, I knew he was the townees' prophet – and a remarkable agreement was reached; a notice was put up on the wall of the local general store: Dr V Recommends that X and Y be allowed to live on Klovharun on condition they neither own it nor lease it out to others until Jansson's death, when the whole will return to the village community. And we promise to make a donation (an approximate sum!) to the Pellinge Fishing Association. No 'legal papers!' Yes or no. The answer was yes, so we started the process of getting a building permit in Borgå. Later it transpired that Dr V had talked to my friend the lawyer (he didn't know we knew each other) and had said this would never go through, they would never let us have a permit on such vague grounds, ha ha.

But we did get the permit. And when we started building, a Pellinge pilot, a bigwig in the Fishing Association, wrote to Borgå council and demanded that the construction work had to stop because it was disturbing the cod. We found this out by a roundabout route. And we also found out that construction cannot legally be stopped once it has reached the roof ridge and the roof beam is in place.

We had to hurry, but we trusted that the council's mills would grind slowly.

We got help with the building from Kråkö, near Borgå – the Pellinge village community themselves could scarcely be considered – and it was Brunström (there is an authentic description of him in 'Midsummer' in *The Summer Book*, and his friends Sjöblom, a carpenter, blaster and busdriver – Charlie, a former seaman, and sometimes Helmer, a crane operator. The people of Pellinge *didn't like* the people of Kråkö. They called them pirates. (Brunström really *was* a pirate.)

So we got going; it was already well into autumn.

While all this was going on Tooti was travelling in the south. I think I've never been so happy as during those weeks when the roof beam had to be raised; we hammered away as if our lives depended on it! We slept in the Bredskär cottage (myself discreetly in the soupente) and early every morning took the boat out to Harun [as described in 'Blasting' in her short-story collection *The Listener*]; it was a stormy autumn, 6–7 on the Beaufort scale all the time. Eventually it started snowing. I made food for us on Harun under tarpaulin, mostly fish, sometimes I went at dawn with Brunström further out to sea where he shot birds. We all became friends, naturally. When it reached 8 Beaufort it was 'bedtime', one had to wait then.

It was like a competition, a downhill race on skis – and they really enjoyed fooling the Pellinge people!

Perhaps I could write about it sometime? Brunström kept a diary throughout, and I wrote it up later. And in fact, when we got up to the roof beam the permit from Borgå commune arrived! But none of it had been in vain; I could have sent roses to that wicked pilot at the Fishing Association and thanked him for a wonderful adventure! Then came next spring and Tooti was there and building continued and the cottage progressed and everything was fine. But best of all had been that uncomfortable autumn when we worked at fever pitch in 'opposition'!

The chapter in *The Summer Book* ('Midsummer') named by Tove in the text depicts the mysterious Eriksson, a pseudonym for Brunström, the man who travels between the islands in a nameless boat. When one talks to him it feels natural to lift one's gaze above the horizon. Sometimes he throws ashore small presents, a small salmon or a rosebush, on his rare visits. He is the friend who never comes 'too near', above all the man with a special gift: 'Eriksson was the man who fulfilled dreams.'

This was the part Sven Brunström played for Tove during that wonderfully difficult autumn of 1964.

The Melancholy of Guilt

Things had been cramped on Bredskär, and the summer of 1963 had been marked by the family crowding in, too many guests and too little time for work. Even so Tove completed six canvases of 'uncertain appearance', cobbled together with 'unbelievable effort', comic songs for Lasse's musical *Crash* (including the acclaimed 'Psychofnatt' song) and did a little 'welfare work' in the form of pictures for Save the Children. But her work was giving her no pleasure. 'It's as though I no longer have any desire to do anything and it just gets worse – I don't know what to do,' she told Maya in August. There were so many people on the island: Tove and Tooti, Ham, Lasse and his wife, Nita Lesch, and their year-old daughter Sophia. The summer was full of 'friction' and she couldn't strike any sort of balance with the island. She kept busy decorating, doing housework and arranging things, but 'it seems as if there's no point in anything. It's just the same with work, with everything I do, it's as if I'm desperately trying to play a part I'm not suited for and haven't learned properly.' She longed for Klovharun, which she and Tooti had been planning for during the spring, and to be free to be a pioneer again.

Leaving Bredskär was difficult because of Ham. They had lived together in the archipelago ever since Tove had been little, and after Faffan's death they had come even closer than before. The plans for the new island affected their relationship and everything was transformed into what Tove called a 'melancholy of guilt', like before the trip to Greece. Her determination to have a life of her own became for her mother various forms of threat, whether from a new island or travel. Ham was afraid of being alone or abandoned, of being in the way, and Tove's decision clearly conflicted with her maternal will and created jealousy. 'You have to understand,' Tove confided to Maya, 'that Ham sees Klovharun as an enemy, and her hope that she may die before I move there has a very negative effect on the feelings of spontaneous pleasure one associates with the realisation of a long-held dream.' This was a painful love, full of powerful conscience, responsibility and demands that cancelled out her own longing. Her dream of a wild island created competitive love between the women she loved, Tooti and Ham. 'It's awful that everything I touch simply turns to bad conscience,' she went on, 'and it's quite clear that I can expect no pleasure. You understand, if everything I have tried to do, and sacrificed, and fought against, and given from my heart's desire, has merely resulted in Ham feeling she's in the way [...] and wants to die and is unhappy – then it's all been utterly pointless. Just a single huge fiasco, not improved by the fact that Tooti is uncomfortable too, and nervous as a cat and thinks I've decided to put Ham before herself.'

This emotional trap was painful for all three, but 'the archipelago situation' (as Tove called it) was a drama that could sort itself out with time. The last summer on Bredskär (1964) was more harmonious, something she for her part felt she should thank the 'Pappa book' for, because, she told Maya, it 'has done so much to relieve the pressure of the island complex and to smooth the way for a positive summer of togetherness.' Writing through her problems, she let Moomintroll plan a cottage, just like herself. And she never relaxed her grip on her new island. On the 'angry little skerry', as she often called Klovharun, she and Tooti had put up their tent for five happy days during the

Tove on the island of Klovharun.

strenuous summer of 1963. They had cut reeds, built fireplaces, laid nets, done carpentry and planned the woodpile. A wild, beautiful, exhilarating storm marked their last day. Tove's diary sums up her feeling for the island in a few brief sentences: 'Grade six storm, rain. Only just saved the boat. Sea a witch's cauldron, breakers like a cannonade. Tent torn. Supremely beautiful.'

Before building started in autumn 1964 Tove went alone to Klovharun, lived there in her tent and went through her book on Moominpappa and the sea. The island was cold, withered and wet. Desolate and peaceful. And she was 'very happy'.

To the Island Again

In autumn 1965 it was time for the Moomin family to come to terms with themselves and move from their home in Moominvalley to a solitary island with a lighthouse. Tove worked on *Moominpappa at Sea* during her trip to Spain and Portugal during 1963-64, far from all the islands in the Gulf of Finland; writing it took her barely two years. When the first reviews reached her, she didn't even know the book had been published. The news was brought to the island by Brunström. She wrote to Tooti: 'Brunström read in *Borgåbladet* (the local Borgå newspaper) about *Moominpappa at Sea* which had clearly come out. All he knew was that the reviewer had ("presumably") liked the book and believed that adults could read it too.'

Moominpappa at Sea is the real breaking point between Tove's writing for children and writing for adults, a coming to terms with her narrative of the Moomin world, much more dramatic and subversive than what was to be her last Moomin book, *Moominvalley in November* (first published in 1970). It had not been easy to start a new book after *Tales from Moominvalley*, and it was getting harder and harder to write for children. She did not yet believe she could write for 'grown-ups'. She was moving in a zone beyond the boundary between children's writing and adult writing, a paradox she was to work with in her two last Moomin books. One provisional title she experimented with – at a very late stage – was 'Pappa and the Sea. A Story for Big Children'. When the deceitful writer for children had explored the concept of abreaction she had given her own position as balanced between children's literature and adult literature. In *Moominpappa at Sea* she gave deceitfulness a literary face. Leaving Moominvalley and the family she was writing about, she had steered her way towards another narrative. The back cover of the new book announced:

Far out at sea lay the Island.

It was virtually deserted. There was a lighthouse, but the light had gone out. There was a fisherman living there on a headland, but he kept silent. To this island Moominpappa brought his family, wanting to guard and defend them.

It was a different sort of island. Quite different from Moominvalley, where everything was as it should be. To tell the truth, things were going to be really terrible on the island. It came near to changing them all – except for Little My. And the reason was the sea, which they really couldn't understand. What they needed was a storm, that someone should be rescued and that the light should be lit again. The sea might have had a bad character, but it was a good enemy. Did you think that this novel was *only* about the Moomin family? Read it one more time – you can certainly do that – and you'll find out.

Sketch for a chart for Moominpappa at Sea.

The island, the lighthouse, the fisherman, Moominpappa, the family and the sea are the basis of the story. But the description has been completely de-Moominised – apart from concepts like Moominvalley and Moomin family – and it is altogether a story about fathers, families and islands in general. The characters have become less specific and the names are consistently given in general terms, without Moomin prefixes – they have become mother, father and troll, a form of naming already used in *Tales from Moominvalley*.

Of interest in this context is a largely unknown short story titled (in Swedish) 'An Unfortunate Affair'. It was written for the 1966 calendar of the Writers' Association of Sweden, *The Winter Street* (the theme of which was 'the galoshes of happiness'); in it, terms like 'Hemulen', 'Whomper', 'Gaffsie' and 'Mrs Fillyjonk' act as a familiar guide to the reader, but are set in a new context. The famous Hemulen (artist) and the self-effacing Whomper (secretary of a cultural society), brought together by a forgotten pair of galoshes during the aftermath of a party, could equally well have been called Andersson and Svensson. But names like Hemulen and Whomper give an immediate clue to their personalities. This is yet another illustration of the diminishing tension between Moomins and humans that can be found in *Tales from Moominvalley*.

Moominpappa at Sea (its Swedish title is simply 'The Father and the Sea') is classified as a novel on the back cover in the Swedish-language editions and for Tove this was an important statement. Its dedication reads 'To a Father'. The novel may be about a Moominpappa, but it can equally well refer to any other father; it is about the Moomin family, but is also about any other family. The picture of Moominpappa on the cover indicates that it is a Moomin book, but its outward appearance gives no other indication of its being so. It was the same for *Tales from Moominvalley*. The Swedish-language text on the back cover of *Moominpappa at Sea* was retained in later editions, even if phrased in a more 'child-friendly' manner.

But Tove failed in her attempt to stop it being published as a children's book. Her publishers in Sweden wanted no changes compared to her earlier books, apart from the cover and its text. Of course it was clear that Tove particularly intended the book for adults but at the same time it was definitely meant for children went the somewhat contradictory reasoning. Her earlier readers, went the argument, must once again be able to identify with her. However, 'this slipping over into adult literature seems not to have presented any difficulties', wrote the editor to Tove. This was clearly a relief to the publishers. Tove Jansson and the Moomin books were a sure-fire publishing success, and there was the risk of losing a wide readership if she were to go over totally to writing books for adults. For Tove the publishers' attitude was a great disappointment and when a couple of years later she presented them with *Sculptor's Daughter* (1968) – which is not a children's book – the gulf between them grew wider. Her publishers in Sweden refused to accept a photographic cover design showing a little girl in a sculptor's studio, like that used for publication in Finland. They wanted a drawing to emphasise that this was another Tove Jansson book. So after her *Moominvalley in November*, when the argument about the cover was repeated in similar fashion, Tove moved to Bonniers for publication in Sweden.

Many reviews also went into the question of children's book versus adult book, exactly as in Brunström's reference to its first critic, but they seldom went deeply into the matter. Benevolently positive and naïve, as Tove summed up the 'Pappa criticism' for Tooti. 'They haven't noticed any difference,' she went on sarcastically, but 'see the Moomins as just as cosy as ever! Oh well, in a way it's quite reassuring.' But most of the reviewers were not especially interested in whether the book was meant for children or adults. Ideology and class were more important on the agenda of the age, and the Moomins' superficially gender-determined way of life was an easy target in the socially aware 1960s. The Moomin books represented easily the most seductive brand of conservatism of the time, wrote Karl-Erik Lagerlöf in a series of articles on books that 'defined the age' in *Göteborgs Handels- och Sjöfartstidning* (1972). 'Mothers must stay at home with their children, always in the house. Fathers must dedicate themselves to loving their adventures. If you show consideration for your neighbour you will save the world. God loves the simple-minded and everything is in the best possible hands.' Tove was a major figure; her books had a wide reach and were able to influence 'the ideal upbringing of a wide range of readers'.

But in fact Tove was moving backwards and forwards in time. As a family drama, *Moominpappa at Sea* is in line with the constructive concept of family developed in earlier Moomin texts. The extended family of the 1940s, which in a spirit of free collectivism increased the size of the dining table and moved in more beds, was now reduced to a nuclear group consisting of mother, father and child, with Little My as a corrective. *Moominpappa at Sea* is the story of a family under stress, of a father and a mother each separately in search of an idea. The child no longer plays the leading part, and the story can be read as an accommodation with the welfare state on a symbolic level. What motivates them as they cross the sea to the isolated lighthouse island is that the family, as Moominmamma states, have been having things too easy.

Moominpappa at Sea introduced a new tone to the literary criticism of the Moomin books. Until the 1960s and 1970s set them in the ideological firing line, they had seldom been read in a contemporary light. In *Dagens Nyheter* Christer Dahl condemned the terrible Moominmamma as a representative of 'illusory security', and 'at least as dangerous as the Groke'. Just like other literature, the text was scanned against contemporary signals, and it was felt necessary to condemn the Moomin world for its clear lack of involvement with society. 'The Moomin philosophy comes dangerously near a flight from reality,' wrote an anxious reviewer in *Nya Argus*, but took comfort from the opportunity to 'forgive' Tove thanks to her 'captivating language' and 'deep humanity and understanding'. At least one could calmly (and without a guilty conscience) continue to love the Moomin family.

It was with *Moominpappa at Sea* that the debate about the Moomins' escapist middle-class lifestyle really took off. This would also pursue Tove when she began to write other books. 'Sculptor's Daughter – Committed Escapist' was the heading of an interview in *Hufvudstadsbladet* when her childhood memoir was published in 1968. She was of course aware of the description, but at the same time and with 'increasing astonishment' noticed that her latest books 'despite everything do have something to do with society'. She placed *Moominpappa at Sea* in this category. It became her own coming to terms with her narrative of the Moomin world. Calling the book a 'novel' was an important declaration of intent. Her need to express herself constantly drove her across artistic borders, just as it created the transformations in the Moomin books.

Transformation was once again the key word in *Moominpappa at Sea*, as it had often been before. The journey to the lighthouse is necessary for the father, who moves from unemployed Moominpappa – to a considerable extent condemned as superfluous by his family – to lighthouse keeper, author, scientist and living troll. For the family, Moominmamma, Moomintroll and Little My, the journey to the lighthouse becomes the beginning of a great rearrangement of the order of things, even if My (according to her creator) doesn't change. But the novel is also the story of a writer undergoing change.

Father's Book

The movement towards a new form of Moomin writing was connected with leaving Bredskär and the Jansson family crowd. I have 'abreacted hugely through this book,' wrote Tove on a couple of occasions, and for the most part it's about Faffan. 'If it weren't a touch pathetic and exclusive I'd dedicate the book to him,' she told Vivica in the summer of 1964. The dedication, always important, gives the story direction. The first page of one of the sheaves of manuscripts for the book was dedicated 'To my Father', but this was changed to 'To a Father', thus bringing together her special father and all other fathers as 'a' father in a less clearly defined form. In fact, what she was writing came to deal with a father in the 1960s, and a few years after *Moominpappa at Sea* came *Sculptor's Daughter*, the manuscript of which for a long time went under the title 'I, the Sculptor's Daughter', which served both as a definition and as a summary of its origins. The warrior and monumental artist Viktor Jansson, often described by Tove as a 'melancholy man', was now in the shadow of his famous daughter. When she wrote about her father in the years after his death, she gave herself the role of the listener, the giver, the stronger of the two. It was as if writing could tempt him out of the darkness of his studio and give him a face, so that she could talk with him.

Moominpappa at Sea is the father's book and yet another father story within the Moomin literature. In Moominpappa's memoirs she had given him a place on the stage as a playwright; he is adventurer, romantic, escaper, protector and veranda-father all in one. He is the father who cannot assert his masculinity without his family. He is the writer who creates himself by writing up his notes and research work and other fragments while working on his dissertation about the sea. The novel *Moominpappa at Sea* begins with a sentence that brings together the father's problems, his feeling of being unnecessary and invisible among the people who more than anyone else should notice him and pay him attention: 'One afternoon at the end of August, Moominpappa was walking about in his garden feeling at a loss. He had no idea what to do with himself, because it seemed everything there was to be done had already been done or was being done by somebody else.'

He has become virtually invisible and, even before her collection of short stories, she had planned to write about an invisible Moominpappa. But she transferred this idea to her story about Ninny and sent Moominpappa off with the Hattifatteners instead. 'The Lonely Family' was one of the many possible titles she had in mind for her new book, but she put Pappa first and let the individual take precedence over the collective. The first illustration of Pappa on the island also relates to his loneliness. He is on watch outside the tent (in which Mamma is sleeping), and the man–tent–sand composition is clearly related to Robert Högfeldt's well-known watercolour 'The Hermit' (of which Tove's family owned a reproduction). The same picture is also described in her next important island book, *The Summer Book*.

In summarising her new book for Vivica she discussed family memories:

> It has naturally ended up melancholy, despite all my efforts and despite a positive ending in which pappa, mamma and troll find their way out of their lonelinesses and become a family again and the light is finally lit on the beautiful hostile island to which pappa has dragged them in order to assert his manhood and restore his self-respect. My is with them as a necessary contrast in les brûmes nordique [sic] and the Groke moves into the foreground. Apart from that only a fisherman whose territory has been disturbed and who jumps about in the background and wants to be left in peace.

Many people read the manuscript of *Moominpappa at Sea*: Lasse, Tooti – who 'with the patience of an angel and two fingers' typed it out – Maya and a good many more. But the most important was Lasse, at least so far as the language was concerned. He went through the book a couple of times and suggested several 'word changes', which Tove found entirely justified. For herself, she tried to lighten the 'entirely grown-up sad bits', as she told Tooti.

To the Lighthouse

'I was very little when I decided to be the lighthouse keeper on Kummelskär,' says the narrator in *Notes from an Island*, and goes on: 'It's true that there was nothing but a single flashing light but I planned to build something much bigger, a mighty light that would be able to oversee and take care of the whole Gulf of Finland – that is, when I was big and rich.'

There are lots of books about lighthouses and storms on Tove's bookshelves in the studio, placed in the most accessible position above her workbench. These include such classics as *Om fyrar, fyr och känningsbåkar* ('On Lighthouses, Lights and Identification Beacons'; 1835–36), which contains among other things a chapter on 'Lights in the Gulf of Finland'; also William Blasius's English-language study, *Storms: Their Nature, Classification and Laws* (1875). During her work on *Moominpappa at Sea* she carried out exhaustive nature studies and her manuscript material contains observations on winds, flora, birds and the movements of the moon. She noted, for example, that cranes migrate from August to October and long-tailed ducks at the end of September in the outer archipelago. In the summer of 1964 she made a close study of the lights in the archipelago with her childhood friend Albert (Abbe) Gustafsson. He was responsible for those along the coast.

With *Moominpappa at Sea* Tove took her place in the tradition of lighthouse narratives with Edgar Allan Poe, Jules Verne, Arvid Mörne, Jacob Paludan Møller and, not least, Virginia Woolf, author of the famous novel *To the Lighthouse*. The lighthouse has magnetic attraction no less for Moominpappa than for the father in Woolf's Ramsay family, but there is no immediate connection between the two texts, even though both share the same passion for the symbolism of the lighthouse.

To the lighthouse. From Moominpappa at Sea.

The lighthouse marks the boundary between land and sea, warns of the danger of running aground and indicates a safe channel while threatening calamity and presenting a shining objective. It shows the way home but can equally be a sign of parting, and is connected with loneliness, exposure, longing, guiding, surveying, power and safety. Seen from a psychoanalytic point of view, the lighthouse in the 'pappa book' stands for the father's lost manhood. His inability to light it makes the image extremely clear. He is literally unable to recharge the batteries. But in actual fact the lighthouse represents above all a movement (navigation) towards something new. It will give him an objective as father.

'Why should we move to a lighthouse when we're already living in a tower?' Moominmamma asks in one of the 1950s strips, 'The Moomin Family and the Sea' (1957). It is a synopsis for *Moominpappa at Sea*, containing as it does the attraction of the lighthouse, his failure as custodian of the flame and his battle against the sea. The tower has been the troll's architectural ideal ever since his days behind the tiled stove, and seen in this light Moominmamma's question is undeniably justified. An obsession with towers (described by one researcher as 'turriphilia') applies no less to the trolls and their creator. The tower is a place for solitude, individuality and isolation, everything that Pappa pours into his longing for the lighthouse. He wants to be a solitary, just like Tove herself. In a letter to Ham at the time of *Moominpappa at Sea* she writes of her 'wild solitary enthusiasm'.

The first lighthouse keeper in the Moomin books appears as early as the first book, a boy in a tower who uses his shining red hair to guide sailors. From the very beginning the lighthouse plays a part in the unification of the family, and in *Moominpappa at Sea* it assumes monumental importance in their transformation. It is 'endlessly high', 'gigantic', quite simply 'something unbelievable'. The lighthouse guides, but gives no instant light. If anything is certain it is that lighthouses give light, insists Pappa, but the crux of the matter is precisely that there is no such security. The light will remain out until the original lighthouse keeper lights it again. The Pappa in the strip series is searching for the light as an idea, an isolated, highly secluded and romantically fenced-in place, with the right atmosphere for writing 'a book about the sea's majesty written in a lighthouse', possibly under the title 'The Horizon and I'. The tower as a place is connected with writing (as, for example, for Stephen Dedalus in James Joyce's *Ulysses*). Many analogies between lighthouse keeper and writer exist. But in *Moominpappa at Sea* the effect is different, with no trace of the strip series' exhilarated playfulness with the subject of Pappa's writing ambitions. His compulsion towards words grows through a search for writing that can make clear connections (the secrets of the sea) that he does not understand.

The tower has been seen as an antimodernist image; the lighthouse has been described as a last outpost against the modern, as a landmark from a bygone age. This is where the unnecessarily explained Moominpappa is at home. He wants to recreate a time when he was 'pappa' and to follow his genealogical history, if in a modified form. In one of the first strip stories Moomintroll's ancestors were professional ship-wreckers of the time-honoured kind, who attract ships onto the rocks by means of lights along the coast. The lines come together, even if his inheritance from his ancestors has been blunted by time. 'My forefathers never had to worry about finding the right way,' it says when before the journey to the island Pappa sniffs at the wind and switches on his 'sense of direction'.

In her writing, Tove combined her philosophy of islands and lighthouses with the transformation of the Moomin family. Her work on the book was a new start for her as a writer. As always, pleasure and necessity were the key words. 'I'm thankful', she told Vivica in 1964, 'that I've been able to write for a long, connected period with real pleasure, an absolute necessity – nowadays a rare phenomenon.' She ascribed to her trip to Spain (a present from her friends, led by Vivica) the effect of enabling her to give birth. She was writing the book all the time, Tooti remembers. *Moominpappa at Sea* is a story of pleasure lost and regained, presented through Pappa's researches into sea and lighthouses; he struggles laboriously, searches, measures, writes and ponders. When the family rescues a load of drifting planks, he immediately starts building shelves, even though the wood is wet. ' "I know wood shrinks when it dries," he said. "But I can't wait. You don't mind if there are a few cracks in the kitchen shelves, do you?" "Not at all," said Moominmamma. "Go ahead. Hammer away while you're in the mood." '

To hurry while you feel like it, not to wait but to act, is the thematic mantra of the story. It challenges the tyranny of demand and is an exhortation to listen when necessary. The movement towards the lighthouse is transformed for Pappa first to a series of acts he thinks he should fulfil: to work (as a lighthouse keeper), to get food (by fishing) and at the same time to give protection and thus be transformed into a real 'pappa'. When he turns to his own needs the perspective changes. The process is much the same for Mamma and troll, but their expectations are different. To use Karen Horney's formulation (now a psychological cliché), one can say that they 'realise' themselves. This even applies to the cold Groke, whose temperature is raised by Moomintroll to the point at which she dances. The symbolism is almost too clear, but at the same time frighteningly distinct: a puzzle with a lost piece (first applied in the wrong place), a lighthouse whose light cannot be lit, a living island, a bottomless stare (a deep pool of water) and a search for coherence. *Moominpappa at Sea* can easily be described in Jungian terms as a journey through the unconscious in a search of the 'Self', towards an initiation. But the story moves in various directions.

It goes more deeply into the basic Moomintroll story. Pappa runs off again, but this time takes the family with him. It is his

Moominpappa on guard alone. From Moominpappa at Sea.

masculine principle, father's law (after Freud), that drives him to the island. The subject is man's duel with the sea and the forces of nature, as in Hemingway's *The Old Man and the Sea*, the literary twin of the title, but Pappa has both Mamma and troll at his side. The story sets Pappa and Mamma at opposite poles in an entirely different way from before. The point of departure is their gender-coded roles as 'Mamma' and 'Pappa'. When Pappa wants to fulfil his identity as a father he subordinates himself to Mamma.

This brutally alters her role as carer and her identity as Moominmamma is stripped away from her. 'You sit still and take it easy,' says Pappa to Mamma when they have landed in their boat on the island's sandy beach, and she obeys while Pappa 'scrambled about in the boat organising things'. She gets it into her head that everything is presumably just as it ought to be. 'In time she would probably get used to being looked after, perhaps she would come to like it. Even now she slept for a moment or two.' Gradually she creeps into the nest that Pappa has built, a tent made from sails and oars, turns round once or twice on the mattress, sighs and goes to sleep. Rituals are broken, she neither hands round sweets nor makes up beds, but the greatest change is her rejection of her handbag, which she uncompromisingly sets away from herself on the sand. Her bag is the symbol of her identity as *Moominmamma*, the closed space in which everything needed can be immediately stored. For Moomintroll (her child) this is a sure sign that the whole thing is a 'real change, and not just an adventure'. The lighthouse and its lamp play a part in this transformation for everyone: for Mamma, who controls the oil lamp in the valley; for the Groke, who follows the light towards the island; and for Moomintroll, who lets the light shine as a guiding beacon to show her the way.

The transformation is built on a play of contrasts: valley versus island, earth versus rock, Mamma versus Pappa, text versus picture. In her lighthouse novel Tove etched in her artistic identities as painter and writer in a new way. Her thinking about writing had changed. *Moominpappa at Sea* set reflection at the centre.

Mamma *al Secco*

While Pappa looks for change through writing and words, Mamma works with pictures. In *Moominpappa at Sea* she becomes an *al secco* painter (like Tove when working on the altarpiece at Östermark), adding murals to the whitewashed walls of the lighthouse. Mamma has no tempera or watercolour, but uses material she finds in the lighthouse: dyes for fishing nets in brown, blue and green, red lead for boats, a little lampblack and a few old paintbrushes. Then she begins to paint; previously she has drawn in indelible pencil, and the colour is absorbed 'right into the plaster and looked intense and transparent'.

This developing painting of Moominvalley becomes the expression for a longing so powerful that it brings the artwork to life and swallows up the artist, as in the famous myth of the Chinese artist Wu Tao-tzu. Mamma paints herself repeatedly, in the form of small Mammas here and there dotted about the valley, like trompe l'œil. The family are not supposed to be able to guess which the 'real' one is. She thus makes herself invisible and, like Pappa, explores her identity. There are many fathers in Pappa and many mothers in Mamma. The many images of Mamma are evidence of her power in the valley; she is everywhere there and everything is stamped with her. 'Couldn't you paint some of us,' Little My asks, 'and not just yourself?' And Mamma answers: 'But you're outside on the island.' Where the family is, as she knows, but she needs to find out where she herself is. When Moomintroll slinks off and doesn't answer questions and behaves like an evasive teenager, she paints a sleeping Mamma by the lilac bushes –

a mother freed from the small child's need for closeness and affinity.

The painting of the valley becomes a hiding place, just as it did for the painter and writer Tove Jansson. She painted the valley, hid herself in it and nearly disappeared into it. There are many images of herself in the books and pictures, but none that can be called the 'real' one.

Moominmamma *al secco* is one of the most beautiful passages in the Moomin books. It calls up a magic from outside the predicament of reality, with a flying bird and mixed colour and light, and pleasure and need are its great driving force. It is a description that shows how art and life can become one:

> One evening the western sky was on fire with the most beautiful sunset she had ever seen. It was a tumult of red, orange, pink and yellow flames, filling the clouds above the dark and stormy sea with smouldering colours. The wind was blowing from the south-west towards the island from the sharp, coal-black line of the horizon.
>
> Moominmamma was standing on the table painting apples on the top of a tree with red-lead paint. 'If only I had these colours to paint with outside,' she thought. 'What lovely apples and roses I should have!'
>
> As she gazed at the sky, the evening light crept up the wall, lighting up the flowers in her garden. They seemed to be alive and shining. The garden opened out, and the gravel path with its curious perspective suddenly seemed quite right and to lead straight to the veranda. Moominmamma put her paws round the trunk of the tree; it was warm with sunshine and she felt that the lilac was in bloom. [...]
>
> She flung her arms round her apple tree and shut her eyes. The bark felt rough and warm, and the sound of the sea disappeared. Moominmamma was right inside her garden.
>
> The room was empty. The paints were still on the table and outside the window the black bird went on circling round the lighthouse. When the colours in the western sky disappeared, it flew away across the sea. [...]
>
> Moominmamma stood behind the apple tree and watched them making tea. They looked a little misty, as though she had been

watching them moving about underneath the water. She wasn't at all surprised by what had happened. Here she was at last in her own garden where everything was in its proper place and everything was growing just as it should grow. [...] She sat down in the long grass and listened to the cuckoo calling from somewhere on the other side of the river.

When the kettle boiled for tea Moominmamma was fast asleep with her head leaning against the apple tree.

Moominpappa at Sea was a major project. It contains a friction between Mamma and Pappa not previously seen in the Moomin books. The story deals with a family under stress, in which the environment is crackling for every member. Moominpappa uses sea and water to explore himself; he does calculations, drags the sea bottom and draws up formulas, but freedom cannot be found in any system. When he lets go and allows life to flow freely, he comes to life again, exactly like the lighthouse when the light is lit. 'All Moominpappa's thoughts and speculations vanished. He felt completely alive from the tips of his ears to the tip of his tail. When he turned to look at the island – *his* island – he saw a beam of light shining on the sea, moving out towards the horizon and then coming back towards the shore in long, even waves. The lighthouse was working.'

The final vignette in the book shows a crossed saw and axe. This symbolises the story. Pappa has tried to establish himself on Mamma's woodpile, the place where she saws out her beautiful wood treasures, but this causes strife. But this is something they can divide, each working on their own things. A note in the manuscript emphasises this co-operation: 'Let Pappa and Mamma share the woodpile. This is important. More important than whether or not the light is burning. Emphasise this in the final vignette.' This is a new meeting between Pappa and Mamma, on equal terms this time, a long way from the romantic rescue described in Pappa's memoirs.

The sizzling vision of ruin that Pappa describes to himself at the beginning of the book – the dramatic destruction and disappearance of the valley in fire – is a picture that speaks clearly of his relationship with the valley and Mamma. She is connected with the earth, growth and life. To Pappa things look different. For him the valley is cramped, stifling, shut in, flammable. 'He had described the burning valley, the white-hot tree trunks, and the fire creeping along the ground underneath the moss. Blinding columns of flame flung upwards against the night sky! Waves of fire, rushing down the sides of the valley and on towards the sea ... "Sizzling, they throw themselves into the sea," finished Moominpappa with gloomy satisfaction. Everything is black, everything has been burned up [...]'

A violent image that shows the power of the lighthouse light and the power of the transformation. Set against it is Moominmamma's *al secco*, the picture of Moominvalley that she paints on the white walls of the lighthouse. Once her longing fades, she is no longer absorbed in her artwork. The same applied to Tove herself, a process she would come to shape in the very last Moomin book. But the picture of the valley still remains, even in a time of transformation.

CHAPTER 14

The Stone and the Story

When they stopped their blasting a great silence descended on the island.

Notes from an Island

The first summers on Klovharun were full of work to get everything in order. 'Now what concerns me is little wild Klovharun,' wrote Tove at the beginning of June 1965. Boats went from one island to another; builders, friends and relatives came and went, the atmosphere was full of building, carrying, cleaning, rinsing, painting, carpentry and chopping. Paintbrushes, pencils and colours had to wait, and the box for her watercolours took on a new function as a cashbox. When payment for the construction work had to be made Tove forgot her hideaway, but a thunderstorm at night refreshed her memory: 'In the middle of the night, thunder, got up and found my half million [Finnish marks] in the old watercolour box. Thank God. Last I knew they were in the toolbox.' On the closely written pages of her diary, starting in the summer of 1965, she described the birth of her new world, fitting up the cellar, clearing a space for the woodpile, building a stone terrace. Ham commuted between Klovharun and Bredskär, which had been completely taken over by Lasse. At last life with the island, the rocks and the sea was beginning.

Klovharun – the island of stones – with the summer house.

But her dream of solitude conflicted with reality. The island soon became a sight and its building famous, and people travelled from far and near to have a look at island, house and writer. There was also a great stream of guests. That first summer Tove soon felt herself 'kaputt' as far as social life was concerned. She longed for the blessing of days free of people, and when three groups totalling some twelve people arrived on the same day she was gripped by a 'certain desperation' (July 1965). Her diaries give roughly the same picture year after year: a mass of visits, welcome and unwelcome, all the time against a background of wanting above all to be alone to work. The island was a place for freedom – where she busied oneself with stone and wood, earth and seaweed – but in a flash it could become a place of no freedom at all. Anyone can land on an island. It was necessary to strike a balance between solitude and social life, between pleasure and discomfort. When 'the Carpelans' (the writer Bo Carpelan and his family) came on a visit together with Lasse and Sophia in the summer of 1969, Tove wrote: 'Nice *for once* to have guests.' But next day it was back to '*Seventeen* strangers came from E. to have coffee, drinks and soft drinks and talk and "look at me". Kiss my arse. Ham and Tooti struggled. Threw stones. Angry.'

She threw a lot of stones on Klovharun. The blasting of the Great Rock on the island so that the cottage could be built provided enough stones for many years' fury – and happiness. She needed it. She lived out her emotions through the stone, abreacting physically ('abreaction' was the key word here too) over and above writing and pictures. The stone summoned up her strength. Tove, herself small and slender, tossed stone, rolled stone, carried stone, worked stone and built in stone. There was no need, she noted in her diary, to write about quiet happy days spent on her own, but stone demanded words, as when she was building in the summer of 1966: 'In the mornings I cemented the sunny north wing – we were always up by 6 – we finished the stone bench and terrace so I moved down to the ravine and began building the woodshed from stone.'

The island *was* stone, from the start a material to work with, to build with and to assemble into new figures and formations. Building on Klovharun started with the blasting of the Great Rock, the stone that lay on the only possible place to build a cottage on the island. Literally the shot of the starting pistol that made the building of her home possible, an explosion that Tove used in a literary sense in one of the stories in *The Listener* (1971), simply entitled 'Blasting'. Life on the island began from the rock, as did her later book, *Notes from an Island*, which started with a declaration of love:

> I love stone; the cliff that goes straight down into the sea and the unclimbable mountain and the pebble in my pocket, and prising up stones from the earth and throwing them aside and letting the very biggest boulders tumble right down the hillside into the sea! As they thunder away I can still enjoy the rank smell of sulphur they leave behind.

Rocks and stones are the new foundation of the family in *Moominpappa at Sea*. In the Moomin books there are stones

'Disintegration', oils, 1965.

in the landscape beyond the valley in islands, mountains and ravines. A pile of stones can turn into an avalanche (*Comet in Moominland*), the magician's hat is found at the top of a mountain (*Finn Family Moomintroll*) and all round Moominvalley Lonely Mountains raise their jagged summits.

It was stone that linked Tove to her father: 'I'm a sculptor's daughter,' she wrote at the age of eighty-two in *Notes from an Island.*

Medals and Revisions

In 1966 Tove was awarded the Hans Christian Andersen medal, long the most important international prize for children's literature. It was an honour she really appreciated, and she celebrated with an improvised crayfish party on the island. She particularly looked forward to this medal: 'I just hope it'll be the sort of medal I can actually wear!' she wrote to Tooti. She was tired of all the 'cheap faience plaquettes', to accept which she had to interrupt her work and leave the island. But now she had a good excuse to go travelling with Tooti again. After Ljubljana, where the prize-giving and a congress were to be held, they would go to Venice and the Art Biennale. The compulsory speech was as always a worry, but her 'presentation' was very positively received. People were even moved, she told Ham, but she 'could not understand why'. 'Happy and scared' was how she summed up her reaction. But once again the medal was a disappointment. 'It is indeed very beautiful,' she said, 'but unfortunately also very large.'

The prize came a year after *Moominpappa at Sea*. Again she was finding it hard to write, and even harder to go on writing books for children. She had reached a sort of no-man's land with the Moomins from a motivational point of view. 'It isn't easy to get started when you've stuck your "family" on a desert island in an all-too adult setting,' as she told her publishers in Sweden in the spring of 1967. Where should they go, 'and what can you do with a troll who has reached puberty?'

In the early summer of 1967 she started revising her Moomin books, starting with the ones she was least satisfied with – *Comet in Moominland* and *The Exploits of Moominpappa* – books she had already reworked earlier. In her diary she kept a record of her work during the summer: 'Comet done, apart from corrections' (6th June), 'Began rewriting Pappa's memoirs' (12th July), 'Comet's cover done' (24th August). She 'corrected the *Mag.'s Hat*' (*Finn Family Moomintroll*) (22nd August) and then began 'also to tidy up the language in *Dangerous Midsummer*' (*Moominsummer Madness*) (17th September).

Tove made mostly minor linguistic changes in her new versions of the two last books, but they can also be distinguished in content from their earlier editions. In the new *Finn Family Moomintroll* the Magician appears in the sky to Snufkin during the storm on the Hattifatteners' island; in the first edition he makes his first appearance in the final chapter. The books' illustrations also had a makeover; she renewed, altered and above all made new versions of pictures that were missing or had been lost. The originals of many of the illustrations had been lost by exhibitors and publishers after she had loaned them out for various reasons. Early in 1968 she complained of the terrible work caused by 'vanished covers and illustrations'. The *Comet* book alone needed more than thirty new pictures. It was an enormous job and, after this, copies were made of the Moomin illustrations so the originals could be kept safely in Helsinki.

The reason for all this activity was the Swedish publisher Gebers's new edition of the Moomin books as so-called 'pocket books' in hard covers. Tove took advantage of this chance to check the books and revise them. She was not the same writer in 1967 as she had been in the 1940s: 'I have rewritten the comet book and M.pappa's memoirs, in part completely, and done a superficial tidying up of the language in the Hobgoblin's Hat,' she told Maya during the summer. 'You know, the sort of thing you do when it's not possible to string together anything new.' She went on:

> But that's fine – I've long been ashamed of those first two books (I mean The Little Troll [*The Moomins and the Great Flood*] and the Comet Hunt [*Comet in Moominland*]) and now when Gebers want to reprint the whole series in pocket format it gives me a chance to revise them; they must at least be reset. Also, I've done new covers for the whole edition – except for the coloured picturebooks, of course.

The Moomin books were given a uniform appearance for their new edition of 1968–69. *Moominpappa at Sea* was altogether new, and, like *Tales from Moominvalley* and the future *Moominvalley in November*, could easily be fitted into the series. In reality she was still doubtful about *Comet in Moominland*, as she admitted to both Maya Vanni and Ham. It's 'a terribly bad book', she told her mother, but even so it has 'some amusing genuine bits. Unfortunately not many.' In her 'tidying up' – the phrase she used for her editing – some of the more exotic features of the Moomin world were lost; for example, an underwater expedition for pearls was changed to an underwater expedition to find round white stones. The silk monkey (loved by many) was changed to a kitten, but the hyenas and the enormous eagle were allowed to stay, as were the poison bush 'of the dangerous Angostura family', the giant octopus and the giant lizard in the cleft full of garnets.

Not everything was altered. The most obvious biblical allusions disappeared, like the ill-omened swarm of grasshoppers from Egypt and a discussion about Moses among the reeds. The characters were tightened and fixed in more permanent forms. In the 1947 version ('The Comet Hunt') Moomintroll hovers between child and adult; in the 1968 edition ('The Comet Comes') he is more clearly presented as a child. Palm wine is replaced by milk, and the expedition to find the comet is renamed an excursion (by Mamma). The suspense is preserved and the greatest horror, the comet, is just as menacing as before, but digressions from the main story have been removed. The text has become more obviously a children's book, above all through its new structure. This is also the case with *The Exploits of Moominpappa*, which now begins with an explanatory prologue, in which Mamma suggests to the depressed Pappa that he should write his memoirs. Pappa's antediluvian (a word Tove was particularly fond of) boastfulness takes on a shyer profile.

All Tove's reflections on the difficulty of writing children's books might seem to have been blown away in conjunction with the revisions. One benefit of the new edition was that she could now bring the books together as a united whole by a single publisher in Finland (this had already happened in Sweden). She felt this gave her a new freedom. 'Söderströms has let Schildt take over *The Comet Hunt* so now I have all the books together in the forthcoming "pocket" series. I gave Söderströms a large abstract picture of cockfighting in relief.' Now the Moomin books would benefit from a collective reprint, and there would no longer be any 'terribly bad book' in the series to worry about or be ashamed of.

But above all, this new edition gave Tove a chance to sweep the Moomins out of the way and set her sights on new writing. The clean-up made room for a new writer and a new form of expression. The stories for *Sculptor's Daughter* began to develop after her summer of revision. The new book would not be illustrated, she told Tooti; it was important to make it clear that this was not going to be a book for children.

Stories of Childhood

After *Moominpappa at Sea* Tove wrote a couple of texts about love. Some 'verses on love' for the composer Erna Tauro, with whom Tove had frequently worked; Tauro needed material for a radio song-competition. One of these texts was 'Autumn Song', which over the years became one of Tove's best-loved songs. She had originally written the lyrics on the island in 1965, for a 'fill-in' book for lovers called *Us*, which appeared with vignettes by Ham in the same year.

Tove the illustrator was working on *Alice in Wonderland*, published in 1966, while the painter Jansson was preparing abstract canvases for an exhibition (1968). New things, because she didn't want to exhibit old ones, she told Tooti in December 1967. She was constantly writing, in notebooks, in her diary and in masses of letters, mostly business correspondence. In folder after folder she filed away enquiries and proposals of various kinds, often requests for new stories or for the republication of old ones. There were letters from newspapers, periodicals, publishers, clubs and schools, but also from private individuals. During the 1960s the weight of the correspondence in her in-tray became even heavier. Requests for the publication of written texts and other material not restricted by various rights got a positive response; otherwise the answer would be no. She rarely wrote new texts to order: 'I shall only start writing another book for children after many years,' she told the hopeful editor of a children's paper in 1968; with the 'best will in the world' she could not produce anything but painting. This was a point of view she had held consistently for many years.

She made an exception with the story 'Our Magic Christmas', published in the 1965 Christmas issue of the magazine *Vi*. The editor had asked for a piece on Christmas recipes remembered from childhood, but Tove offered instead a 'recipe-free' story about Jansson family Christmas customs from both Finland and Sweden as a single mixture, she wrote, giving as an example the family's habit of celebrating Lucia day on the morning of Christmas Eve. This became the beginning of the stories that would constitute *Sculptor's Daughter*, which came out in the autumn of 1968. This was yet another literary turning point for Tove, more emphatic than *Moominpappa at Sea*. It was her first book explicitly for adults, without any pictures or Moomintrolls. She started work on it alone on the island in an atmosphere of autumn, telling Tooti in September 1967:

> Autumn came on my first day alone. I've started to write but of course I've no idea yet what will come of it. The main thing is I've made a start. Not about trolls, it's a sort of continuation of our magic Christmas, childhood troubles. Writing in fully adult

mode yet about what is still a small world. It's not easy but I'm so happy that all things considered I can hold a pen again – and not just sorting out old stuff in desperation.

'I want to work, not play,' she wrote, and her literary writing really got under way that autumn. She worked hard at *Sculptor's Daughter* and was now writing for the sheer pleasure of it, as she stressed in a letter to Vivica: 'I've reached a point in "I, the Sculptor's Daughter" at which I'm rewriting and mistrusting every single sentence. Sometimes I'm happy about my book, sometimes I think it's terrible. You know. But the main thing is I've been writing with *pleasure*.' She worked at her 'short stories' right through the autumn – 'short story' being, of course, an adult concept – and reported to Tooti: 'This evening I've rewritten the "The Iceberg" and made it less literary and knowing. I'm constantly altering the book, a little here and a little there.'

She was writing new things and painting abstracts, and by the time the book was nearing completion towards New Year she was planning to take part in a new exhibition. During her abstract period in the 1960s she painted large canvases with lots of colour and titles like 'April', 'Hurricane' and 'White Dominant'. She was a painter who took up lots of space and showed herself off. A couple of later paintings were called 'Transformations' (1968) and 'Decision' (1969). Her need for self-expression ran parallel in words and pictures. A narrative of childhood in the first person singular and an abstract painting; these were forms of expression steeped in tradition, but for her books and for her pictures the context had been renewed.

Her childhood was familiar long before the publication of *Sculptor's Daughter* and had been made into a personal narrative, alongside the Moomin books and strip series. A sculptor, an illustrator, a home dominated by visual art, summers full of storms and expeditions. In her acceptance speech for the Hans Christian Andersen medal she spoke of her islands, of her parents' work, of Ängsman, of her brothers, of Lotsgatan and 'above all of the hurricanes of the Gulf of Finland'. It was quite remarkable, she commented to Ham. But through interviews, talks, lectures and presentations she had from the first guided her story of childhood and life. Her 'Workbook – Facts' contained the main points, noted down as answers to 'repeated questions'. Now someone else was taking over her story. A remarkable and frightening experience.

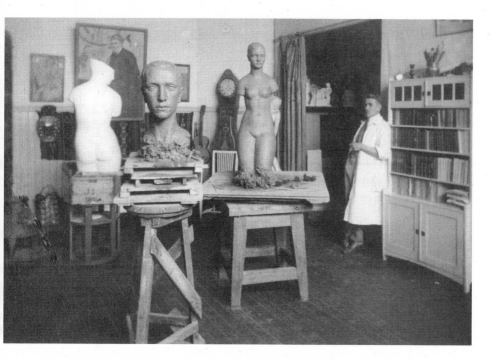

Viktor Jansson in his studio, Lotsgatan 4B.

In *Sculptor's Daughter* she set down *her own* story of childhood. There was the artistic topography, with an artistic couple and the thinking in pictures that permeated their speech and life. A number of the episodes had been described in Tove's early diaries, some belonged to her later years (and many can be recognised from her Moomin books), but the narrative encloses them all. When she writes in the first person as the sculptor's daughter, it is as a nameless 'I'. Identification of this 'I' with the child Tove Jansson has been taken for granted, but the narrator is never called Tove, either by those round her or by herself. Nor do names like Viktor, Signe, Faffan and Ham occur in the text, with the exception of her sculptor father who is addressed as Jansson a couple of times. Places, locations, friends, visitors and persons in the environment do have names, for example, the geologist 'Jeremiah' and the home help 'Anna'. But the family does not need to be named or defined. It is as sacred and self-evident as the art it lives with. The narrator's brother has the name Per Olov but his place is on the fringes of the family which basically consists of Mummy, Daddy and child.

Sacred Sculpture

When writing my first essay on her work, I wrote to Tove Jansson and asked her about her view of gender roles in connection with her books (1974). She referred me to the family background described in *Sculptor's Daughter* in these words:

> He was a sculptor and she was an illustrator. Sculptors could only relate to payment in connection with competitions. These events were triumphantly lavish and wasteful, and between one and the next there was nothing but work for work's sake.

> She worked half the day at a job to earn a living, and for the rest of her time till late at night she drew illustrations in the studio for newspapers and publishers.

> I was never aware of any problems, for example they never talked about money, never about social groups, it was just a question of good art and bad art. We lived together very calmly and freely. Pappa worked, Mamma worked. Work was sacred. They would criticise each other's work.

> After breakfast she would always be at home, that gave a permanent sense of security. He disappeared in the evening but I understood that was what Fathers and sculptors did. When there was a party at our place women were never invited. I learned that friendship between men was nearly as sacred as sculpture.

Art came first, whether good or bad. The roles as sculpting father and drawing mother were as if automatic, but most important was work in itself and for its own sake. *Sculptor's Daughter* is built on an artistically conservative view of gender by those involved, there was a male society of war memories, maritime law and partying, but art in itself was above gender boundaries. When the sculptor Viktor Jansson's daughter was born, it was his ambition that she would become a great artist.

She had outlined stories about mother, father and child many years before. Her new writing was no sudden impulse, but the fruit of a long maturing of thought within herself. Her point of departure was writing for adults, but seen through a miniature world. These stories dealt with a child who saves her mother from death, and with an artist wife who doesn't feel at home in a man's country. The year after Faffan's death (1959) Tove wrote several short texts anchored in childhood and featuring a narrating mother, a sculpting father and a listening child called 'Totto', one of Tove's pet names as a child.

'Once there was a little girl who was awfully beautiful and her mother was awfully fond of her ...'

The child nodded, solemn and appreciative. That was better, she said. You mustn't change the beginning. After that it can go as it likes.

The mother went on and the child listened politely. A mild stream of words, a little slower and higher in pitch when something exciting happened, that was how the soft voice went on, persuasive as a declaration of love.

It spun an isolated world of intimacy for them, it built up walls against everything that was outside. Inside all was warm and soft, blunted and free from danger.

Go back to the beginning, said the child suddenly.

Don't you want to know what happened, the mother asked. No, said the child, start a new story.

So the mild, whispering voice continued: Once there was a little girl who was awfully beautiful and her mother was awfully fond of her ...

The studio was very large and very cold. It was only at the far end near the tiled stove that it was warm. The fire, and the shadows on the floor and the arms that were holding her and the secretive voice that was interested only in her and had time, any amount of time.

Here are mother and child, always together, in a private room of love. Words like 'inside', 'outside', 'intimacy', 'isolated' and 'walls' are set against one another and intertwined with various meanings for mother and child, a symbiosis, at one and the same time both stifling and detached. This is close to the text of *Sculptor's Daughter*, but in the book the child 'I' is one with the narration, neither polite, appreciative nor solemn. The important thing is for each story to begin in the same way; what happened next was not so important. *Sculptor's Daughter* is a narration about mother, father, child, art and love.

Work and love are one theme, sculpture and illustrating another. It was the nearest Tove came to an explicit autobiography, shot through with art and pictures in both language and action. The child sees and names her world through pieces of sculpture, sculptor's turntables, modelling tools, illustrations, plaster-casts, pencils with very soft leads, overall coats of colour and streaks of gold. Art defines the world and gives it life through the language of both mother and father. The forest looks as if drawn by John Bauer (a household god in Tove's childhood), with rocks as if 'Cawan' (Alvar Cawén) had painted them. Most alive of all is mother's shining sackcloth painting, in which forest treetrunks rise from the moss against a fire-red evening sky, a painting that goes 'deep into the wall' and absorbs the viewer – like Moominmamma's mural in *Moominpappa at Sea*. It is possible for the life of the studio itself to be transformed into a painting, like when the child watches her father and his partying friends from her bunk: 'The table is the most beautiful thing. Sometimes I sit up and look over the railing and screw up my eyes and then the glasses and the candles and all the things on the table shimmer and make a whole as they do in a painting. Making a whole is very important. Some people just paint things and forget the whole.' The whole can be found in Bauer.

The daughter's narrative tells of a creative father, but speaks with equal power of a creative mother. From a practical point of view, art has its hierarchy; father sculpts and mother draws for a living, but words are her field. 'Mother's stories' have a natural place in the child's world. Storytelling is seen as no less sacred than art and is made into a ceremony as important as plaster-casting, surrounded with respect and solemnity. 'We turn out the lights in the studio and sit in front of the fire and she says: once upon a time there was.' The words bind together mother and child 'for ever.' And if the storytelling is mother, father is the stone, the hard material that can be shaped and hewn by a sculptor. 'The Stone' is the title of one of the stories, which describes how the daughter finds a stone with silver in it, purposefully rolls it home and up steps and stairs, then loses it and finds it, only to lose it again. Rolling a stone, but not in the same way as in the Moomin book. In this case the stone contains what may be a treasure, something that – as the narrator sees it – could make the family rich. A stone that could earn the family more than the sculptor can.

'Haze', watercolour by Tuulikki Pietilä. Illustration for Notes from an Island, 1996.

Stone is something to define, to take an attitude to and to experience. But this has to happen through individual experience. The geologist in the story 'Jeremiah' is obsessed with stone, and the same is true for the narrator. 'If one wants to collect stones one should be allowed to do so on one's own.' The father works in stone, carves his white women in stone and makes them beautiful, unattainable, controlled. That can't be called into question. The same applies to the code system that defines the family's life, how one draws forest or behaves during a plaster-casting session, how one parties or reacts to a discovery of smuggled vodka. There is no rebellion, no questioning, but there is a different will. The mother can look at her husband and say: 'that may be so, and when she is alone she does it in her own way'. Father sticks to tradition, as it says at one point, and so does the sculptor's daughter. She keeps close to both mother and father, each in relation to his or her own way. Their pictures and art give her a language for describing reality. When in the first chapter the narrator makes a golden calf and she and cousin Karin compete for a sign from God, she works at a piece of 'sculpture', but once it has been criticised she realises what she has done has nothing to do with 'sculpture'.

When Tove writes a book and calls it *Sculptor's Daughter*, she gives the father a leading part. He shapes his home, environment and family through sculpture. At the same time the stories in the book (nineteen of them) shine with concise characterisations of the daughter-narrator and her relationship with her mother. Mummy leads her into storytelling and imagination, while Daddy is responsible for the setting, the dark studio full of white women. Narrative, picture and imagination also become inseparable, as in the chapter 'The Bays'. The narrator gives us five bays and five stories, all about her mother, her father and herself. She makes stories in which life and imagination come together, through pictures from art and storytelling. John Bauer is among those who evoke words, as in his picture of the grieving Princess Sedgetussock, who is transformed into a reed: 'I walk for such a long time that I become tall and thin like a reed and my hair becomes the reed's soft feathery panicle till in the end I take root and begin to swish and rustle and sigh like all my reed sisters and time becomes endless.'

Mother and child, close together as if inhabiting a single body – there are many such scenes in *Sculptor's Daughter*. Several of the Moomin books also climax in the togetherness of mother and troll, but in *Moominland Midwinter* the umbilical cord is cut. In *Sculptor's Daughter* safety can be synonymous with resting in Mummy's tummy, or with resting in the story before the fire or hearing Father whistle at his turntable in the studio.

But it can also be used to describe herself in her own narrative, with no foundation in either mother or father. The fifth bay, 'tiny and beautiful and all my own', contains the daughter's own room with its stones, climbing tree and strong southwesterly wind. A place far from plaster-casting and drawing where the spotlight

shines on herself, not on her mother or father. 'If a thousand
little girls walked past under this tree not one of them would
have the faintest idea that I am sitting up here. The pine cones
are green and very hard. My feet are brown. And the wind is
blowing straight through my hair.'

Moomin's Daughter

In Finland, *Sculptor's Daughter* was one of the autumn's best-
selling Swedish-language books in 1968. Many asked for a sequel, but none was ever planned. 'No, I'm not going to let the
sculptor's daughter grow any older', said Tove in an interview.
'I'm not the least bit interested in trying to describe what happened to her later; it's only the child's way of experiencing things
that interests me.'

Sculptor's Daughter came out with two different covers, one
for Finland and one for Sweden, and at two different times. Tove
handed the manuscript in to Ola von Zweygbergk at Schildts
in January. The book was then 'irrevocably' finished and he
liked it. 'Nice, don't you think?' Tove wrote to Tooti. It came out
in Finland in early autumn, with Per Olov's photograph of the
sculptor's studio on the cover. But there was a problem about the
book's appearance with Gebers, the publishers for Sweden. They
wanted a drawn picture for the cover, and wanted publication to
be delayed until Christmas, to coincide with the release on TV of
a new film by Margareta Strömstedt called 'Moomin and the Sea'.

Tove became increasingly irritated. In an unusually sharp
letter she criticised Gebers's management of 'the daughter':
It had sunk without trace in Sweden, she complained to the
publishers. It had been a matter of advertising, distribution
to reviewers and accessibility in the bookshops. At the same
time she was having strong doubts about Gebers's general
effectiveness (added to which, she pointed out, they were being
careless over the Moomin strips, which they were still being
credited in her own name, without Lasse's.) From Gebers's point
of view Tove was first and foremost Moomin's daughter rather
than the sculptor's. The Moomin books were selling well – a
couple of them were due out in new editions the same year – but
this new book was more uncertain. The size of these editions

was a good indication of the publishers' attitude. Four thousand copies of *Sculptor's Daughter* were printed, as against 25,000 for the original edition of *Moominland Midwinter* and 19,000 for *Tales from Moominvalley*.

The publicity was ambiguous, too. 'Sculptor's Daughter is something new in Tove Jansson's writing. With this sensitive portrait of childhood she takes her place among the important Swedish storytellers.' So went the blurb on the cover of the Swedish edition, a formulation which immediately prompted the reader to wonder whether the Moomin books were important or not. Sven Willner took up the gauntlet in his review: 'Books like *Tales from Moominvalley, Moominpappa at Sea, Moominland Midwinter* and *Moominsummer Madness* are unquestionable masterpieces of modern Swedish prose. But so is *Sculptor's Daughter.*' Greta Bolin included a similar reference to the art of storytelling in her review, and made a point of only mentioning Moomintroll in passing. 'Tove Jansson has been a wonderful storyteller for children,' she wrote, 'and now she is a wonderful storyteller for adults too.'

The 'Moomin's daughter' view inevitably marked the criticism. A book by Tove Jansson without trolls or similar figures was a challenge to some readers. Moominvalley seemed an obvious parallel to the sculptor's studio and the book was read throughout with the Moomin world as a corrective. The new book 'gives us tools we can use to help us research the Moomin world's anatomy', as one critic put it, while for many, quite simply, it was difficult to read the stories without comparing them to the Moomin books. People spoke of 'the Moominvalley of reality' as an alternative to the 'secrets of Moominvalley'.

This biographical reading, with her stories of a child's world seen as a background to the Moomin world, was naturally no surprise to Tove herself, any more than the reviewers' excitement at having discovered a key to the 'secrets' of Moominvalley. But there was extra tension before publication, just as there had been with *Moominpappa at Sea*, and the book's reception was to some extent a disappointment. Tove's first person narrator and self-centred daughter were hopelessly out of step with the times. It was 1968 and, as with the Moomin-father novel, questions about escapism, materialism and middle-class assumptions dominated the criticism. The fiercest of these ideological critics was Yrsa

On the hill. Klovharun, 1969.

Stenius in *Studentbladet*. Her review took the form of an attack on a privileged family and their impersonation of an attitude to life far distant from the 'life-sapping demands of the factory whistle'. Tove Jansson's book was in many ways descriptively charming, wrote Stenius, but self-obsessed and pretentious in its claims to a wider relevance. This perspective did not last long, but for a while it had a significant effect on attitudes to Tove Jansson's writing.

Over the years *Sculptor's Daughter*, together with the Moomin books, has become one of Tove Jansson's most widely translated and read books. Despite her original intention it has also been published in illustrated editions with photographs from the sculptor's daughter's childhood.

While the book was being typeset, Tove was preparing to go to Paris where Tooti had established herself in a studio. Tove continued to write when she felt like it and, as she told Tooti in February, 'this happened quite often'. As always she had plenty to do, with permanent 'duties' that needed to be fixed and 'dealt with'. She read the proofs of *Sculptor's Daughter*, drew thirteen new illustrations for a television production of *Who Will Comfort Toffle?* and made room for various readings in her programme.

She went to Stockholm for the funeral of her much-loved uncle Einar, who died in February. 'He was one of the most important people in my life,' she told Tooti. Their conversation in letter form about Einar gave her great comfort. She had not even been able to talk to Ham about her maternal uncle: 'No one has said so much about Einar as you. We Finnish clams and Janssons, you know. Ten years together do leave some trace.'

They were to spend a month in Tooti's studio at Cité des Arts and then go on to Brittany and London. Lasse and Sophia had moved back to Helsinki, and Ham was living with them. Tove felt free and longed for Tooti and their self-evident togetherness: 'I also believe – in fact I know – that we have an unusually happy and peaceful life together. Despite all the rubbish that could threaten its balance. We've got through that, you see – so there are no dangers any more, things can only get better. At least that's what I think.'

The same year she began to write her last Moomin book.

CHAPTER 15

Dreaming of a Valley

Autumn by the sea had not turned out to be the autumn she'd expected. There had been no storms.

'The Squirrel', from The Listener

With *Moominvalley in November* the writer Tove Jansson moved out of Moominvalley. This is the Moomin book without trolls, a story about a family that, like Godot, is constantly mentioned but never appears on the stage. It tells of a valley with a garden full of flowers, with white lace curtains that flap slowly in the summer wind, with memories of apple blossom, windswept green grass and sunbeams, and of a family. In the present the story describes a valley full of rain, mist, wet leaves and the dark colours of autumn, and tells of departure, farewell and melancholy. The family has sailed to the lighthouse and the house is empty. The valley should be closed, as it says at one point. There is an atmosphere of Chekhov's cherry orchard about the story, of waiting, meeting and forlorn abandonment, and the blows of an axe can be heard even in Moominvalley. But no cherry trees fall. It's just the Hemulen cutting firewood for the winter.

When *Moominvalley in November* came out in the autumn of 1970, exactly twenty-five years had passed since Tove's first book. 'They can't have moved away just like that without saying a word!', exclaimed the Fillyjonk, but that is precisely what the family had done. But they had left a message behind, a message related to tradition and history: 'Please do not light a fire in the stove because that's where the Ancestor lives.' It was signed 'Moominmamma'.

Moominvalley in November is the book about the transformation of the world Tove had started to write about in the 1940s. All the notes about 'no Moomintrolls' for her 1960s books tell of her readiness for a new kind of writing, and are at the same time evidence of how close she was to her Moomin world as writer and artist. It demanded more words, pictures and narration. Pages of manuscript and notes for her November story are crowded with ideas for the title of the book (as had already happened for several other of her books); verbal variations on the concept of abandonment, disappearance and emptiness linked to words of dreaming, longing and memory. 'The Abandoned Valley', 'A Dream in November', 'The Vanished Family' and 'The Happy Valley' are a few examples. In the end she settled on letting the month of November give meaning to her title.

Autumn is the obvious metaphor for change, through colour, decay and putrefaction. Nature withering away and dying down, dissolving in moisture, going to rest; all these are images of disappearance and death, the breaking down that is essential for new growth. Moominvalley is a dream of harmony, of the happy family, as Tove wrote in her notes for the book, and through this November story the dream is peeled back and gives way to something new. *Moominvalley in November* describes a secret garden, as it is beautifully expressed. Relevant to this is some interesting manuscript material that gives a background to this imagery. As with *Moominpappa at Sea* Tove worked on location, in the heart of the landscape, with close studies of earth, stones and plants. She regarded these as natural entities, writing in the forest and making notes. A couple of pages headed 'Notes made in the forest, Storpellinge – 69' bring together short pieces of text and descriptions, a sort of photographic snapshot of the earth's surface or a section of shore or a sandy bottom with interwoven metaphors. These may function as if in a painting with selection and mixture of colours and use of light and shade. 'The last sprigs of blueberry were a powerful yellow-green in the wet forest with a few sodden berries still hanging here and there. The red cranberries were dark as blood. Some hues had grown stronger with autumn, vivid as rowan berries, while others had sunk into the colours of the earth. The mouldering leaves were like wet leather.'

It is from the rain, damp and mist, from the purifying moisture, that something new can be born. When the words have been arranged and edited into a literary text for the book *Moominvalley in November*, new life can spring from the ground in Moominvalley. Unknown forces burst from the decaying soil. In the forest the 'late autumn's secret garden' forces its way with violent force up through the decay: 'a strange vegetation of shiny puffed-up plants that had nothing at all to do with summer'. Everywhere there were 'strong new colours'.

Powerful imagery marks the story, from the title's statement of autumn to the final suggestive sentence in which the Whomper Toft goes down to the jetty to catch the mooring line and tie up the family boat. This is yet another new birth, with the line as a restored umbilical cord connecting family, valley and narrator. 'Moominvalley Revisited' is what Tove called her story in several places in her manuscript, and the return visit affects both the writer and the family, like the miscellaneous creatures who through memories, longing and dreams have made their way to the valley only to find the house empty and the garden deserted.

The most avid seeker is the little Whomper, Toft; who has told the story of the family to himself so often that 'the excitement of repetition' has just become deeper. When the mist one evening lies grey over the story and the valley disappears in darkness and everything 'goes backwards', he decides to find the valley in his dreams, to make his way there and talk about who he was. Toft is the writer Tove's voice in the text, a Tove who has found it more and more difficult to write about the family in the valley. *Moominvalley in November* becomes the story of how 'the valley and the happy family faded and slipped away'.

Towards Paris

So in the spring of 1968 Tove went to Paris. The years after *Sculptor's Daughter* became a time for painting and her feeling for the city of artists remained as strong as ever. Tooti had established herself with graphics, watercolours, gramophone records and books in a studio in the ultra-modern right-angled Cité des Arts, and it was as if she had been living there for ten years, Tove wrote to Ham. The city roared around her, just as it had during her painting spring exactly thirty years before and on her first visit a few years before that (in 1934). 'I think I'm experiencing the city just as intensely as the first time I saw it," she wrote happily to Ham. She noticed little of the later student agitation and political unease – they went on to Brittany at the beginning of April – but Martin Luther King's death hit Tove hard. A disgrace to humanity and the whites, Ham wrote, and Tove replied in a letter that crossed hers in the post. The radio talked of nothing else, people were beside themselves and the consequences would be terrible: 'It's a stain of shame that can never be washed away.'

Tove visited her French publishers and she and Tooti met a few colleagues, including Tooti's old graphics teacher, the painter Juhani Blomstedt and his family, but for the most part they wandered around freely as the spirit moved them. A happy Tove told Lasse and Ham about museums, exhibitions, clubs, mussels (Tove), oysters (Tooti), bookshops and buying new literature: 'We've bought masses of books about daydreams, monsters and the horrible symbols of the subconscious – very stimulating!', she told Lasse at the end of March. At the beginning of April they set of for the coast on a return visit to the old painters' countryside, and in the little village of Ploumanach they found their 'real Brittany'. Here were the light, the scents and the space. They wandered along the shore, picked spring flowers and drew. Tove was very happy. She drew stone, her beloved material, and wrote in exhilaration to Ham about 'incredible boulders' which could be exhibited in the Konsthallen if only a boat big enough to carry them could be found. They finished their journey in London.

'It's comic that I have to go to France to meet colleagues,' commented Tove, but it was important from the point of view of experience and the work situation. Moomintroll had overshadowed her painting during the hectic days of the 1950s, and kept her away from artistic circles and painterly connections. She had been living with a celebrity that stretched beyond her boundaries and out into the world, in circumstances shared by none of her writer and artist colleagues. But she was also a solitary who liked to walk alone, and fame merely made her shyer with the passing years. The island was supposed to be a place where she could get away to work and be alone, but it never did become the refuge she had hoped for. Sometimes her

In the Marché aux Puces (flea market), Paris 1968.

summer days became hectic, and after an unusually hard day of television negotiations, business and visits – it was July 1969 – she exploded in her diary: 'I think I'll move back to town so I can work in peace.'

When in 1972 Tove was placed top of the list of candidates to move into the 'Poet's Home' in Borgå, she declined. She would have succeeded the poet Rabbe Enckell and, one might add, would have been its first female occupant. She realised that the chance to live there was the highest honour available to a writer in Finland, she replied, but she could only say no, thank you. 'I live alone,' she went on, 'in a light and spacious studio and see this generous offer as more suitable for a writer in more serious need of this ideal place for work and family life.' The studio on Ulrikasborgsgatan was her home, her place for solitary painting and writing, and somewhere where the general public and her own public appearances were under her own control. No official 'Poet's Home' could ever be such a place for Tove Jansson.

She also avoided societies, associations and committees (an exception was four years on the committee of the Society of Finland-Swedish Authors). She also declined to accept 'the great honour' in 1971 of joining the Academy of Nine in Sweden (the Academy is an exclusive literary society restricted to nine members elected for life). Long-planned and impatiently awaited travel, and a great deal of work, took up all her time, she told the chairman, Olle Holmberg, and she later gave the same reply to Astrid Lindgren, chair two years later, who particularly wanted to have Tove in the group.

A Summer of Writing

Moominvalley in November would be the last book in the prose fiction series, but not the last Moomin story. Moomintroll would be back. A television series with a script by Tove and Lasse was recorded in summer 1969, and called simply 'Moomintroll'. There was also the text of a picture book illustrated with pictures from the TV series. The old Moomin gang returned to their leading roles, Birgitta Ulfsson (Moominmamma), Lasse Pöysti (Moomintroll) and Nils Brandt (Moominpappa). Vivica Bandler directed; Gösta Ekman played the king who takes in hand Moomintroll's education. But there was more of Lasse's extrovert Moomintroll in this TV production than of Tove's more philosophical characters. By now he had been drawing the Moomin strip series for several years.

The co-operation of her brother was an enormous relief to Tove. 'Thank goodness that he's helping me and we've become partners,' wrote Tove in a note in autumn 1969. The market for Moomintroll seemed insatiable, and there was never enough time.

Summer became one single long need for for 'real' solitude, peace and quiet for work, both for life on the island and for writing, and days without visitors were specially marked in her diary. One such was 18th July: 'A long day *for myself* without visitors. Laid out nets.' There was hardly any time at all for concentration, tranquillity and her own personal experiences. After sharing memories of the archipelago one evening with her childhood friend Abbe before a village audience, she noted with ironic exhilaration: 'Home 11.30 at night with Holmberg in a storm. He couldn't land so I jumped into the sea up to my waist in the breakers and got ashore that way, the first bit of fun I've had for ages.'

But the text of *Moominvalley in November* grew during the summer, on the island and in the forest at Pellinge. By September the streams of visitors had died down and she was alone. She took advantage of the chance to begin work on something new. In the daytime on 8th September she set out nets and that evening noted: 'Late I wrote a short story, "Bang Bang". Maybe it's good. Started another, a mere trifle.' This was the beginning of her short-story collection *The Listener*, her first book after the Moomins. Next day she took up the nets (thirty-eight fish and she cooked nine of them) and commented on her story: '"Bang Bang" *is* good. Finished the other one – nothing more: "Letter to an Idol".' She also did more work on 'Moominvalley Revisited' and made a fair copy of it. The next day she read it through and checked it and in due course began revising. A couple of days later she began a Christmas card for UNICEF, which she finished quickly. Just after the middle of September Tooti arrived, a 'happy day'. A few days later they went home to the city and her summer of writing was over.

'Intensive, close living,' Tove wrote in her succinct notes. They show how hard she was working, how she planned her projects and how she was able to start something new when still finishing her last job. 'Bang Bang' is an expression that says everything about the relationship between pleasure and work. As it says in *Moominpappa at Sea*, you must hurry to get on with things while you feel up to it. When the moment froze and her solitude was lost, she walked over the hill and started throwing stones. For Tove, nothing was more important than feeling free to work. She described the pleasure that freedom could bring in *Moominvalley in November*.

'Moominvalley Revisited'

The story begins with a rebellion. Snufkin packs his tent and leaves Moominvalley, but he is forced to turn back from his lonely wandering. He can't complete the song about rain that was growing under his hat; it lacks five bars, and he can only find them in the valley. In Snufkin, composer and writer, Tove projects how the valley reminds her of itself and opens the way for a return. In *Moominpappa at Sea* she let the family establish themselves on the island with the lighthouse. In *Moominvalley in November* she shows that there are still several bars of a song to be found about the family in the valley.

Those who take over the valley during the family's absence have a variety of desires and expectations of life, but for them it's all about dreams, longing and memory. The Hemulen evokes the picture of a valley where 'everything was simple and ran by itself', where there was 'quite simply' a family. He orientates himself towards Moominpappa. The Fillyjonk remembers uncomplicated companionship which left no room for 'dismal thoughts': she particularly thinks of Moomintroll's mother. Return for her is a way of conjuring up death, fear of decay, worms and everything that can't be tidied away, and Moominmamma corresponds to life. Grandpa-Grumble (the old man) remembers a valley he visited long ago where parties went on all night; whether he only heard people talk about it or whether he read it somewhere is immaterial. He is new in the November story, with no documentation in earlier books. He is searching for his own story, represents an earlier time and finds emotional security in the Ancestor. He is seeking for a pleasure of his own, it says in the notes, and this includes the whole new 'family' that has established itself in Moominvalley. The Whomper Toft is looking for a valley he has described to himself, a shining pleasure garden with Moominmamma as its obvious central point. Mymble is looking for her little sister My and to make a connection. Together they form a new family in the valley but the basic figure, Moomintroll, is missing. It is only when Snufkin comes back that the text remembers him.

This gives many perspectives on the Moomin family: different personalities, genders and ages are confronted with one another and with memories, dreams and ideas. *Moominvalley in November* is the book in which Tove deconstructs the personalities of her characters (as in *Moominpappa at Sea*), yet at the same time sharpens their contours. She added short notes to her manuscript about the motive force of the new family:

I shall tell that dreams matter more than reality.

Snufkin is the one who tells them the truth and he is the only one who stays behind to meet the family when they come home.

The Whomper Toft is the daydreamer who looks for safety and continuity in the idea of the family.

Mymble is the spoilt brat who exploits the family's friendliness and generosity.

The Fillyjonk is looking for them in unconscious terror within her narrow isolation.

To Grandpa-Grumble they are a dream of freedom and simplification, an adventurous excursion back to childhood origins.

In *Moominvalley in November* the writer Tove Jansson introduces herself under a new name, as if derived from her own: Tove has become the Whomper Toft. She speaks as the narrator seeking to call forth the family in the valley, illustrating the impossibility of taking the earlier narrative any further and voicing the possibility of finding a new narrative – this happens towards the end of the book. Toft allies himself with the reader, identifying with those who, like him, long for the family, for Moominmamma and the flowering valley.

He is in fact searching for the idea of the family. The story he tells himself recalls a wild green garden lit by sunshine, with fluttering leaves, grass, patches of sunlight and buzzing bees, a garden with scents of 'summer and safety'. Toft experiences everything through his own internal narrative: 'He had done this hundreds of times before and each time the excitement of going over it again became more and more intense. Suddenly a grey mist descended over the landscape, it was blotted out ...' Toft tries to narrate his way back but fails. The narrow door back to the story-world of childhood is closed for ever. As it turns out, the story Toft tells doesn't come to deal with the wonderful valley,

Dreaming of Moominvalley. From Moominvalley in November.

but with transformations, longing and other things. The grey mist still fills the valley when the Hemulen comes. It confuses him. He had 'in some way' always imagined eternal summer in Moominvalley.

So had many readers, as Ulla Stina Nilsson's review of *Moominvalley in November* so pregnantly expresses. People felt free to express their feelings in the face of this loss. As they came together to read aloud in groups of friends, they would hover uneasily over the prospect of the family's return or – terrible thought – permanent absence. 'The atmosphere of the Moomin house spread through the room. We felt angry, disappointed, cheated ... A fairy tale of uncertainty and frustration! A Moomin book about problems of identity and alienation! Must the Moomin family and Moominvalley also be taken from us! Our last refuge!' People longed for the Autocrat's party (in *The*

Exploits of Moominpappa) and for Thingumy and Bob, and were faced with the realisation that the Moomin family had been 'reduced to a storm-lantern'; they reread the old Moomin books till late at night. 'But even so it's a very fine book,' was Ulla Stina Nilsson's considered judgement.

In her notes for the book, Tove wrote that it must get the reader to think more profoundly. This is an idea fundamental to her writing and was certainly one reason for the somewhat hostile reception reported in this review. People didn't want to have to imagine what the Moomin family might be doing and experiencing, but they wanted to be given a complete story containing nothing too radically different from what they were used to. A sentence like 'There is no family any longer' (from *Moominvalley in November*) could be interpreted as provocation by the Moomin reader who, like the Whomper Toft, longed for the scent of summer and safety.

Nummulites

Closely tied up with the description of the valley in November is the Whomper's new story, the one that replaces the now over-shadowed story of the family in the valley. This is found in the thick book that Toft finds in the attic, thrust aside just like the family album and in its own way also part of the family's history. But it tells of quite different things, 'curious beasts and murky landscapes and nothing with any name that he recognised'. They are transformed to a new story of something secret and earlier hidden in the depths, all written out in a language relating to natural history specimens (as in pictures of nature) that can be read in two ways. These may be pictures of forgotten and extinct animals, or at the same time expressions of a new developing story. Electricity, the power at the heart of, among other things, stormy weather and thunder and lightning, serves in both cases as an expression of life and creative energy.

> Toft had never known before that deep down at the bottom of the sea lived Radiolaria and the very last Nummulites. One of the Nummulites wasn't like his relatives, there was something of Noctiluca about him, and little by little he was like nothing

except himself. He was evidently very tiny and became even tinier when he was frightened.

'It is impossible for us to express sufficient amazement,' read Toft, 'at this rare variant of the Protozoa group. The reason for its peculiar development naturally evades all possibility of well-founded judgement, but we have grounds for conjecturing that an electrical charge was a crucial necessity of life for it. The occurrence of electrical storms at that period was exceptionally abundant, the post-glacial mountain chains described above being subjected to the unceasing turbulence of these violent electrical storms, and the adjacent ocean became charged with electricity.'

Nummulites are primitive creatures that live in the sea and appeared in the early tertiary period; Noctiluca is another form of primitive life, known for its capacity to give light. Its body is spherical and its mouth contains a toothlike outgrowth. Tove took part of her description of Nummulites, Radiolaria and creatures of the species Protozoa (from Greek *protos*, 'first' and *zoa*, 'animals') from Volume IV of Brehm's famous multi-volume *Life of Animals*, which she had in her library. This was the origin of the zoological account that she turned into fiction and made her own to fit the origin of the Moomins. Toft reads that the very last of the Nummulites live deep in the sea. In nature, the Nummulites are an extinct genus.

The Swedish word *Nummulit* can be made into an anagram for the Swedish spelling of 'Mumin', if 'u', 'l' and 't' are removed; thus, a primitive ancestor of the Moomins. Storms and violent bad weather (delight in catastrophes) are one of the life necessities for the species (as they are for Moomintrolls), as is its relationship with the sea. The characterisation is on one level naturalistic, but at the same time typical of a variety of primitive creatures synthesised into one. The creature is the story that grows so big that it bursts its boundaries and becomes impossible to tell. It cannot be harnessed or controlled in any way except

Creatures from Moominvalley in November.

by a return to its original condition – that is how it is in the Whomper's narrative. The Nummulites' life necessities and the history of their development are woven together with the utopia of Moominvalley and made into the history of the Moomintrolls, of their origin and life. The new story thus becomes a basic text on the writer's relationship with her fictive world and at the same time an epitaph for the character Moomintroll.

Moominvalley in November ends with a return – at any rate, at a distance. The Fillyjonk's shadow play, 'The Returning Family', is an omen, an anticipatory invocation of the unseen family that has been discussed throughout the story. But we see no more than their shadows; their actual return does not happen in the story or for the reader. The Moomin family has become an abstraction, connected with something lost or evasive. The whole valley is run down to become a mere show; it pales, dies away, disappears into mists, is darkened by rain. At the end of the story house and garden become a dream, experienced by the Whomper Toft: 'The whole of Moominvalley had somehow become unreal, the house, the garden and the river were nothing but the play of shadows on a screen and Toft no longer knew what was real and what was only his imagination.' The valley had to be purified of dreams, illusions and fantasies (Toft revises his idealised picture of Moominmamma), and it is only after it has been emptied that it can be opened for something new. Once Toft has been cleansed by anger – as in a typical abreaction – and met the family's dark shadows, the dreams disappear and the family can return. He walks towards the sea to meet them and looks around, but the valley is just resting like an 'insignificant shadow' behind him. Dusk falls, 'the land sank away in the darkness', and like the fall of a curtain the sun goes down. The game is over.

> Just before the sun went down it threw a shaft of light through the clouds, cold and wintry-yellow, making the whole world look very desolate.

> And then Toft saw the storm lantern Moominpappa had hung up at the top of the mast. It threw a gentle warm light and burnt steadily. The boat was a very long way away. Toft had plenty of time to go down through the forest and along the beech to the jetty, and be just in time to catch the line and tie up the boat.

Such is the suggestive ending of *Moominvalley in November*. The reader is kept away from the family's return. 'No one other than Toft should meet the family when they came home.' Tove and Toft, the family and the valley, belonged together for always, even if the story was over. The Nummulite had returned to its original primitive form.

Sorrow

Tove wrote happiness and peace into Moominvalley, everything she had dreamed of during the war. The idea of a family in a wonderful valley, where danger lay beyond the horizon, with its roots in the exciting summer world of her childhood, grew into a great story about a family. But families change, just as memories of them do. *Moominvalley in November* was written at a time when Tove had published her portrait of childhood in *Sculptor's Daughter* and was busy with abstract painting. She had a one-man exhibition in 1969 and in the same year also shared an exhibition with Tooti in Jyväskylä. This was a 1960s retrospective, with thirty canvases painted between 1963 and 1969. The programme was printed in black and white, with a photo of Tove showing a serious woman with the arm of her glasses in her mouth. She was launching a new image of herself yet again.

As for writing, she put the books for children behind her and became a writer without portfolio. This had nothing to do with the children's book as a form, just with what she wanted to write and say. The link Toft–Tove–family is obvious to the reader of *Moominvalley in November*, but her preparatory work on the book contains an interesting alternative. For a long time it was Snufkin, the world traveller and apostle of freedom, that she had chosen to stay in the valley to meet the family. Like Toft, he has a link with poetry. Both are storytellers. With Snufkin to receive the family the perspective is opened outwards, but at the same time the course of events puts particular emphasis on him. The family is less important to him than it is to Toft.

In her notes Tove wrote: 'The one who stays behind is Snufkin. He goes down to the sea and sees something approaching, a boat – or is it something drifting, just a stone? Perhaps the mist makes it hard to see, so that he never finds out if it is the family coming back and it is left to the reader's imagination. It isn't so important for Snufkin: if it was just a stone I shall set off for the south, I'll be able to cross the mountains before the frost comes if I get started now.' This would have brought a different conclusion for the family of the valley, more open-ended and more open to thoughts about the family's return. There is no bright storm lantern in it; what Snufkin glimpses could just as well be a stone as anything drifting. The family is reduced to primitive matter, stone or water, in much the same way as the Nummulite is led back to its primitive condition in the Whomper's story. The reader must use his own imagination, noted Tove, and accordingly continued on the aesthetic line she had already established in relation to her Kotka murals in the early 1950s. But what she attempted here was more radical than before. It fitted together with her new writing and with her picture of herself. Snufkin the songwriter is looking for five bars missing from his song about rain in the valley, and once he has found them it is as if the whole story has now been completely set to music – everything is in place. Snufkin and Toft have different perspectives on the family; one keeps apart from them and the other identifies with them. Through them Tove establishes her double view of the family – at the same time dismissing them as a stone and accepting them as a light.

It was within itself that *Moominvalley in November* carried the greatest sorrow. In the summer of 1970 Ham died and after that nothing was the same as before. 'I go about in a great unreality, calm but alien,' wrote Tove to her old friend Atos the day after Ham's death. It was a loss of such magnitude that for a long time Tove could not even speak her mother's name. 'I've a feeling I've been worrying about Ham all my life, and sometimes it's such a burden.' The journeys she so loved had caused difficult separations from her mother, and it had been a relief when their closeness was able to move onto new paths on the island and in town. In the summer of 1970 Tove and Tooti had established themselves on Klovharun as early as May. She wrote up the early summer days in detail as she waited for Ham to join her and expressed joy when she arrived, then her diary remained empty. Ham had been taken ill and died two weeks later in hospital in Borgå.

New painter, new self-portrait. Tove Jansson presents herself at the exhibition in Jyväskylä in 1969 (photo from 1964).

It was an extremely difficult summer. The island had lost its meaning without Ham, Tove wrote to Maya. To Atos and his wife, Irja Hagfors, who had sent a warm personal letter, she answered: 'The summer continues as beautiful as ever and work goes on. Today there's a thick fog; all four windows are white and the cottage seems to be sailing through empty space.' There was nothing for her but work. The text of *Moominvalley in November* was finished, but the illustrations still needed to be done. That meant intensive and uninterrupted work – there were eighty-three of them – and Tove hardly stepped outside the door. Drawing helped bring her close to Ham, but it was very difficult, as Tove admitted. Toft's longing for Moominmamma became her own, and his loss became hers too. There are no pictures of Moomintroll in *Moominvalley in November*, apart from the shadow play 'The Returning Family'.

Later Tove wrote a short, intensely intimate text about an old lady's death in a hospital near the sea. This was the short story 'The Rain' that would be included in *The Listener*. In *The Summer Book* she brought her mother back to life again, as a grandmother on an island together with her son Lasse's little daughter.

Moominvalley in November is in many ways a family book. It was dedicated to Lasse, who became in time Tove's most important critic. His view of the *November* book, one typewritten page, relates in an interesting way to her new writing. Though he considered the impression of autumn overwhelming and the descriptions of nature outstanding, he felt the atmosphere was too grey, sorrowful and colourless. It needed 'something happier and more tangible to take away the atmosphere of unreality and expectation with no one knowing why'. It could be altered without changing the basic idea, he wrote.

His views coincided to some extent with those of the disappointed reviewer, and for readers Moominvalley was a world of expectation. She made a number of changes, but the atmosphere remained one of waiting and uncertainty even in her final version. The idea of Snufkin meeting the returning family shows how far she had been ready to travel from the start. She always wanted to be free, just like her solitary figure with his tent, ready to walk into a forest with hundreds of miles of silence ahead of him.

A New Family

Like *Sculptor's Daughter*, *Moominvalley in November* came out in two editions with different covers for Finland and Sweden. Schildts remained and would remain her publishers in Finland, but in Sweden *Moominvalley in November* was to be her last book for Gebers (a subsidiary of Almqvist & Wiksell). There had been many disappointments, involving their edition of *Moominpappa at Sea* and even more their treatment of *Sculptor's Daughter*, and their determination to force Tove to continue in her role as Moomin-writer Jansson. She was also worried that her books were not being distributed properly. A couple of letters from Åke Runnquist about the difficulty of getting hold of a copy of *Moominvalley in November* added to her dissatisfaction. He suggested trying some of her more recent books in paperback on an adult readership.

This exactly suited Tove. *Sculptor's Daughter* and *Moominvalley in November* were scarcely books for children, she told Åke Runnquist in reply – they would do very well for a paperback edition – but the trouble was Gebers held all the rights. Meanwhile she had another book up her sleeve, short stories of an 'extremely non-Mooministic' type. Ola von Zweygbergk at Schildts was kept informed, but her present Swedish publishers would get nothing more. Referring to earlier discussions, Tove spoke her mind very clearly. 'I think it's a good idea,' she wrote in spring 1971:

> It would widen my readership and establish the step from children's books to books in general that I tried in vain to hint at, first by drawing no illustration of the daughter and using a photograph for the cover and then by having Schildts print two different covers for the November book, I mean for Finland. Gebers chose the more childish alternative.

Black and white, so far as her intentions and irritations were concerned. As earlier, she was worried about the launch, but hesitated about interrupting the series of Moomin books. But several of these had been reissued since Bonniers first asked her if she would like to change publishers, so she decided to offer them her new book: a collection of short stories 'totally without trolls'.

One who goes alone and is entirely free. Snufkin in Moominvalley in
November, *1970.*

The Listener was published by Bonniers in autumn 1971,
followed by *The Summer Book* the next year. She gave no
further books to Gebers, but after a number of years they issued
paperback editions of both *Sculptor's Daughter* and *Tales from
Moominvalley* (1973). Later Tove tried to shift all her books
to Bonniers, 'Moomintrolls and all', but failed after several
attempts. Gebers, publishers of the Moomin books in Sweden
since 1949, would not let go. When Tove later brought out a new
picture book, it was under the Bonniers Junior imprint.

Moominvalley in November examines the idea of the family
as a form for existence and survival and reviews the power
and magic practised by the family in earlier books. As with
Moominpappa at Sea, a stream of self-realisation runs through
the book, nearly all of it portrayed as a coming to terms with
ideas and concepts about the various members of the family.
'You can't become a Moominmamma just by moving the dinner
table out of the house,' Mymble tells the Fillyjonk. In the end
Nummulites look like nothing but themselves, as it says in the
Whomper Toft's book, and this also applies to each member of
the temporary family in the Moomin house.

Like *Moominpappa at Sea, Moominvalley in November* is a
book about pleasure, and most of all about storytelling. When
Toft wishes that 'the whole valley was empty, with space for
bigger dreams', and that it needed 'detachment and silence to
be able to form them carefully enough', the writer Tove was
expressing her own desires and longings through him. It was

a case of telling it so it could be seen. For Tove, Moominvalley was something she had to leave behind if she was herself to be seen.

The Ancestor, symbol of the ur-troll of the stories, is described in *Moominvalley in November* as 'somebody with shaggy grey hair, angry close-set eyes and a tail. The nose was unusually large.' Angry close-set eyes and a tail, that is half the description of the narrow-snouted figure from the *Garm* pictures of the 1940s, who stepped into a story and became a Moomintroll. But the Ancestor's snout is not narrow, but on the contrary is described as unusually large. It has grown too much for the writer who once drew it. But even if Tove felt she had finished with books for children, she would never be finished with the family in the valley.

CHAPTER 16

Journeys with Tove

I live here and there, answered Snufkin, taking out three cups.

Comet in Moominland

In the letters that passed between Tove and Atos after Ham's death, surviving sparks of their former intimacy can be detected. 'You write to me so beautifully I want to hug you,' wrote Tove: 'I think it's rather wonderful that we both feel? happily grateful towards each other – not guilty-grateful! – it's extremely important to me too.' He wanted her to illustrate a volume of his aphorisms, but making pictures for other people's books was something she had given up long ago. Her gentle refusal was prompted by the possible relationship between text and pictures, too. 'It'll be a fine book,' she wrote after reading it, 'but it doesn't need pictures, not even abstract ones. They would irritate rather than stimulate.' That had always been her basic belief.

But she had something else to tell Atos now they were writing to each other again, 'remarkable things' about an old dream near fulfilment. It was July 1971: 'Tooti and I are going to go Round the World!'

The direction – Japan – has been determined by a job I shall do in Tokyo; that leg will be paid for by the Japanese. Then Hawaii, and San Pedro, you know, the place where Taube [Evert Taube, a famous Sweidsh singer] took gasoline on board and where

Tooti's maternal aunt lives, and Mexico and by multifarious ways (including a paddlesteamer!) up through the States to New York. I haven't yet quite realised it's true. Tooti's studying English 4–5 hours a day and the Map of the World is constantly open.

She wrote in the same mood of excitement to Åke Runnquist, who was busy publishing *The Listener*. Now she and Tooti would make the 'Great Journey' they had longed for for so long. It would start with work – the 'job' in Tokyo – and would then develop into an entirely personal trip.

They had been preparing for a long time. During the spring they devoured quantities of books about Japan and the other places and, as she had told Atos, the map of the world was always open. A large notebook was made into a 'round-the-world book' and between its cloth covers grew a personal guide with notes, commentaries and lists of sights, landscapes, culture, museums, beautiful places, nightlife and shopping for Japan, Hawaii, Mexico and the USA. The journey was written out and planned, but allowing for entirely different ideas to develop along the way. This was their basic formula for travel, as Tooti put it concisely in her story of travelling with Tove:

We had the same feelings about how we should travel: to read up and prepare ourselves thoroughly but leave room for improvisation – we needed to be free to go how we wanted and where we wanted. Generally we never booked hotels in advance for our private trips. When we came to a new place we left our luggage at the station and went out and had a look round, and when we saw something we liked the look of we went in – and we always got rooms. If we were happy where we were staying we stayed as long as we felt like it; if we weren't happy we went on. It was a great freedom and we never once formulated it in words; it functioned automatically.

A long period of this undefined freedom lay ahead of them. The journey lasted eight months. It was a relief to Tove to venture out on something new and of her own and to keep a distance from all the places and islands and the studio and apartment on Jungfrustigen that breathed Ham. Many years had passed since she had last been able to live without facing a flood of letters. But of course letters still had to be answered. Those that seemed most urgent were dealt with by Lasse, and the rest piled up to

Tove with Ernest Benn (right) at her London publisher's party to celebrate the launch of Moominvalley in November, *autumn 1971.*

wait for her return. Everyone who wrote was sent a card which read: 'My sister, Tove Jansson, is abroad and will not be returning to Finland before next summer. Since it is uncertain where she will be and when, she has asked me to keep all her letters till she can answer them herself. With best wishes.' The card might be signed by either Lasse or Per Olov. From her travels she sent close-written picture postcards to her family and friends.

They set off in October 1971, at about the same time as her new short-story collection *The Listener* came out. She managed to escape the reception of her first book since the Moomins (she kept the reviews to read after she got home). This was a relief. The journey started in London with work, business meetings and PR. Her English publisher, Ernest Benn, wanted to celebrate twenty years of co-operation and also bring out *Moominvalley in November* in English. The publishers' party was a highlight, with Tove giving a celebratory speech and gentlemen wearing

Moomin ties (white trolls against a blue background) – just like one of her most memorable receptions of the 1950s. Her programme was packed with interviews and public appearances, but whenever they had the chance, Tove and Tooti would venture out into the London crowds on their own.

Her horror of official events and ceremonies plagued her as always. It was something she never got used to. She told Maya: 'Big party in my honour with masses of people, just imagine being so scared of official events that it isn't until afterwards that I realise the whole thing was fun.''We've met enough people to last me for the next five years,' she went on, 'and I've talked enough for ten.' The social round conflicted with her need to be alone, but she was like a fish in water when she had to be. The shy Tove was in fact a born performer with exhibitionistic features. She was terrified of the public, but enjoyed attention. She liked learning speeches in new languages, and was happy to practise Japanese for Tokyo, learning 300 words that in Swedish would take two minutes but in Japanese, even for a native Japanese speaker, would take a good many minutes longer, as she reported in an interview. Her teacher had been a Japanese architect (from Reima Pietilä's office) who drilled her in pronunciation, intonation and speech rhythm; he would speak first and she would repeat after him. By speaking in Japanese – for an audience of 800 – she showed great respect for the host country, and it was inevitably a success. She stood out in photographs like a shimmering figure of light, giving her speech in an elegant close-fitting dress and page-boy haircut, holding bits of paper with notes to help her memory.

London was a rehearsal for the really big performance. Japan – the country, the people, her reception – was an 'incredible experience, captivating and frightening'. She and Tooti were received like queens, but the superlaunching of the Moomin world was hard work, involving TV, radio, press, interviews, talks, book signings and drawing. 'It's going so quickly I can't be scared any longer,' she wrote, comparing her time in Japan to a downhill ski race of people, meetings, appearances and exhibitions. The Moomin books were in the process of being published there, and she had to meet publishers and translators and, not least, confer with Fuji Telecasting, which was producing drawn Moomin films for TV. The Moomin books came out in one go between 1968 and

Tove Jansson and Tuulikki Pietilä as guests in Japan, 1971.

1972. They had many different translators (only one of whom knew any Swedish), who worked from both the English and Finnish editions. Naturally this led to mixed results, especially as the Moomin books are full of names and creatures without parallels in the dictionaries. On the other hand the later books were translated directly from Swedish. Today all Tove Jansson's books are available in Japanese.

The translations and the television series were launched together, but the filming was a horror. In Tove's words, a dreadful production. The characters had been distorted till they were unrecognisable, Moominpappa gave Moomintroll a thrashing and war broke out in Moominvalley, a world fundamentally

429

different from the one in the books in which to all intents and purposes violence is banned. Also, the trolls had been given different colours. Tove dealt with the matter at once. There was nothing she could do to stop the films being shown in Japan, but it was quite otherwise for other countries. When later a new series of films was made (starting on television in 1991), both content and production were strictly controlled – by both Tove and, most especially, Lasse. This version was sold to many countries.

The great breakthrough in Japan – the new 'Moomin boom' led to later filming and another visit (1990) – has been given many explanations. The Japanese publishers saw the books as a response to an increasing need for togetherness at a time when family life was changing. Families were breaking up and their members moving off in different directions. The Moomin books presented a family which gave every member freedom yet at the same time held them together, a positive combination of an older era and a new one. It has been said that the books were a counterblast to the stream of pedagogical literature, and people emphasised Moomintroll's happy-go-lucky nature and easy-going good humour (particularly developed in the film series) – though an appeal of this kind scarcely has national boundaries.

Tove herself came nearest to the nub of the matter in her essay 'Islands', which she wrote especially for Japan; it is dated October 1971 and marked 'In Tokyo'. In it she brought Finland and Japan together by changing the specific to something held in common under a single concept: freedom. She started from her earlier essay, 'The Island', and told of her powerful early longing for an island, of her life's two islands in the Gulf of Finland and of what an island could give in the form of freedom and solitude. She then shifted her gaze from the islands of Finland to the mountains of Japan, two different kinds of place on opposite sides of the world, but with similar symbolic value:

> Japan and Finland are both countries with long shorelines and innumerable islands. We have many tens of thousands of islands. Only a very small number of them are inhabited. In Japanese literature I have often come across mountains, cool mountains where one can hide to rest or gather strength for a particular

task. With us it is the islands which are a symbol of constructive solitude, for summer living and for the chance to live freely and naturally.

She demonstrated her own and the trolls' landscape and loaded it with meaning through a landscape both she and her new readers could recognise. She had been asked many questions about loneliness as a concept, a condition and a need, and her Japanese essay gives an unusually open account of the importance of solitude for her writing: 'I have noticed that being alone, for good and ill, and freedom, and responsibility, and compassion play a large part in what I write. I think one writes more about one's unsolved problems than about the solutions one has reached; one describes more than one explains.' Freedom, she is saying, is not freedom if it can't cope with solitude.

This is the thought that runs through many of the texts in *The Listener*. One of the earliest was 'The Squirrel', which brings together solitude, the topography of the island and in the long run Tove's writing as well. In order to be able to write, the woman in the story must come to terms with her own solitude. The squirrel (which one day appears on the island) both helps and hinders this process. An island can be a place to hide, Tove wrote in her essay, and it has this function for the woman in the story. The arrival of the squirrel turns everything upside down. 'Sometimes one has to escape so as to be able to return out of pleasure and not out of compulsion,' Tove wrote in her essay. Escaping sets up both the woman on the island (through the squirrel) and Tove herself (through her great journey). Pleasure as always was the keyword. Asked to name a fee for her Japanese essay, she chose a Hokusai, the artist whose picture of the great wave glimmers with freedom.

Japan was the beginning of a new era for Tove, the time of the moving pictures. 'I want to make pictures that are alive,' says Jonna as she films in the short story 'Travels with a Konica' in *Fair Play*: 'I want motion, change.' She continues: 'My film is my sketchbook.' It was in Japan that the little 'Konica' cinecamera was bought and, always loaded with reels of 8mm film, it became a constant companion on her travels, on the island and in her work. No other camera was ever even mentioned. The Konica became an extra eye and a third narrator of life and travel. All this material from twenty years of filming has since been made into a trilogy of films:

one about the Great Journey of 1971–72, 'Travel with Tove' (1993), 'Haru, the Island of the Solitary' (1998) and one about travelling in Europe, 'Tove and Tooti in Europe' (2004).

Freedom

Their journey to freedom started when they took their places on the jumbo jet to Honolulu. They had survived the downhill run to Japan and months of travel still lay ahead. They were on their way. 'Just imagine, Maya,' wrote Tove ecstatically from London, 'just imagine *just travelling*, free!' It would be a journey with adventure, peace and discoveries far away from Moomin business and correspondence and every sort of responsibility. While travelling Tove wrote when she felt like it, freely and simply, in note-books. Many of her later texts began life while she was crossing the North American continent. After Hawaii, where they landed in 'calm and warmth and mild slowness', they crossed to Los Angeles and San Pedro on the coast (where Tooti's aunt was living) and then on to San Francisco. They travelled in Arizona, gambled in Las Vegas and researched small towns in Mexico. Then came the big dream: New Orleans, where they settled in the old French Quarter for a month. 'I think this is the best thing of the whole journey, this happy, beautiful, peaceful town so full of music! We're not tourists any more; we're living here, pre-paring food at home, in an ordinary room with our own back yard where vegetables grow,' Tove told Maya in March 1972. She began writing here. She completed *The Summer Book* – which she had been working on for a year – and started some new sto-ries. She sat in their little kitchen scribbling away at breakneck speed, 'wonderfully happy', Tooti remembers.

Travelling was vital for Tove and Tooti. They had both travelled a lot early in life, before they met, and each had found a like-minded travelling companion in the other. Tove loved the very word 'traveller' ('that beautiful old-fashioned word,' as she called it in her short story 'Locomotive'), and travel had enormous consequences for her writing. The journeys to France and Italy in her early years when she was an embryo artist and trainee painter had been important for her painting and for the Moomin books. After she became a celebrity, travel became meaningful

Tove and Tooti on their Japanese travels, 1971.

in other ways. It made possible longer continuous stretches of work, widened her perspectives, gave her new impressions and had the ability to bring peace. Travel became a free zone of concentration and time that she could call her own. During her trip to Spain at the beginning of the 1960s ideas began to 'flutter under her hat'; that led to *Moominpappa at Sea*. Distance could sharpen one's sight and bring a deeper understanding of what was otherwise too close. When she was writing *The Summer Book* in the little kitchen in New Orleans, at the time calling the book 'The Sophia Suite', she was approaching the landscape in a new way, and seeing the island in the story with new eyes. But she was also writing herself into her new landscape. For her novel *Sun City*, her stay in St Petersburg, Florida was essential.

Once Tove had begun to write about the Moomin world she had worked at great speed and when she made a serious start on her post-Moomin writing it was the same. The eighteen stories that made up *The Listener* were published in 1971, *The Summer Book* the next year, and two years after that the novel *Sun City* (1974). She revisited Moominvalley in the picture book *The Dangerous Journey* (1977), and this was followed by her story collection *The Doll's House* (1978). Two novels, two collections of stories and a picture book inside eight years. She also wrote the libretto for a Moomin opera (1974) and scripts for television, also finding time to paint and slip in some Moomin drama. But even later than this she was still living with the Moomins. She created Christmas calendars and Moomin puppet plays for Swedish and Polish TV. She wrote several Moomin songs, a repertoire she had laid the foundations for in the 1950s with the staging of her Moomin plays. In the 1970s the Moomin world was exhibited in three-dimensional form and ended up in a museum. The first of these exhibitions was 'The Moomintroll' (1974), in which illustrations, sketches, drawings and early watercolours were shown at Hvitträsk outside Helsinki together with an exhibition of Faffan's smaller sculptures.

In 1987 the Moomin world became a permanent exhibition under the name 'Moominvalley' at the Tampere Museum of Art, using a large number of original illustrations, sketches, early watercolours and other pictures, cartoons and illustrations. At the heart of this exhibition is a two-metre-high Moomin house roofed with 6,800 wooden shingles made by Tove, the whole thing put together with the help of Tooti and Tove's friend Pentti Eistola, who had first knocked on Tove's door with an early version of a Moomin house in 1958 and was to become one of her closest friends.

The house – this great Mooministic dolls' house – had great success on tour in Sweden. It had been exhibited for the first time at the 1979 International Biennale of Illustrative Art in Bratislava. The house included a large series of tableaux – eventually there would be forty-one of them – representing scenes and situations from the Moomin books. This concept grew from Tooti's hands (she had wanted to be a sculptor from the start); small figures to begin with, then interiors, scenes and the whole landscape. In the spring of 1980 the house was exhibited at the Finnish Museum of Architecture, and in autumn the same year at the National Museum in Stockholm. This was where Tove had wandered as a picture-obsessed three-year-old with Ham in the spring of 1918, while Viktor was at the front in Finland, longing for his wife and pictures, burning with ambition for his daughter to become an artist. Now she had become world-famous and was exhibiting her own art.

The Listener

The Listener was the first book to come from Tove's new publishers in Sweden. She wrote to Åke in April 1971: 'So Ola von Zweygbergk will offer Bonniers on my behalf the short-story collection, *The Listener*; it is already being set and the cover has been finished.' She added: 'I hope you like it.'

She was nervous before publication. 'You can feel a cold wind on your legs when you step outside a Moominvalley,' she wrote. It needed courage to venture out onto a new literary field, but she had been feeling as if shut up in a vacuum. When she was finding it most difficult to write, she had a piece of advice from Ola von Zweygbergk at Schildts. 'Do some reading while you are waiting for the pleasure to return,' he said; 'why not Chekhov?' She would often tell this story as proof of the value of publishers.

In 1971 she presented herself as a new writer. This was a Tove Jansson with loneliness and obsession on her literary agenda, a

Tove Jansson who let her characters excel at self-analysis – all in eighteen short stories without valleys or Moomintrolls. Some reviewers reacted predictably. 'Tove Jansson cannot disown the Moomintroll in herself,' one writer insisted, while another considered she had moved out to the fringes of Moominvalley: 'That's the whole thing in a nutshell.'

As for Tove, she wrote to Åke that she was very much 'afraid of disappointing those who had expected a new Moominvalley,' but he had assured her of the publisher's delight at having published the book. He himself had chosen 'The Squirrel' and 'Letter to an Idol' as his favourites, but did not want to expect too much. It was difficult to sell collections of stories, especially if they were texts that obstinately refused to relate to the literature of their time: 'People can always accept memoirs, but it can be quite another thing with short stories, especially when they don't give a damn for most of the literary fashions of the day.'

Tove expected no miracles – 'I know it's hard to sell short stories,' she told Åke in reply. But by early 1972 *The Listener* was into its third printing and the reviews, all things considered, had surpassed all expectations. 'It's a long time since any book has had a better reception; it has even done better than Harry Martinson [the Swedish Nobel prizewinning writer] after he was rediscovered,' wrote Åke in a letter that reached her after her long journey. 'It's been selling really well,' he went on, especially 'bearing in mind the Swedish public's resistance to short-story collections.' Sending her a bundle of reviews, he assured her they were 'suitable reading even for a very shy person.' It was no exaggeration.

The Listener was the first book by the new Tove Jansson and the reviews poured in. Many were remarkably detailed and emotionally charged, focusing strongly on Tove as writer and human being. Some of the critics viewed Tove from a sort of private perspective, while some 'gave' her to her readers, and others were thankful for her very existence and burst into various kinds of declarations of love. 'What worthiness and dignity, what respect Tove Jansson commands when she writes about people!' exclaimed Jacob Branting in *Aftonbladet*, ending: 'Thank you for existing.' Many articles of this kind were written. Literary comparisons flew in various directions; Hjalmar Gullberg was mentioned, and Harry Martinson (to whom Åke had referred),

Epictetus (whom Harry Martinson had quoted), Kerstin Söderholm and masters of the short story like Chekhov and Kafka. In *Svenksa Dagbladet*, Göran Schildt spoke of artistically refined short stories, while in *Hufvudstadsbladet* J.O. Tallqvist waxed lyrical about the winged pen that hovered over Tove's new writing.

Many drew comparisons between the new writing and the Moomin books. 'The parallel is inescapable,' stated Sven Willner: 'There is no Moominvalley in Tove Jansson's short stories, no peaceful place of refuge. But nothing can be really dangerous.' Margareta Strömstedt identified a Moomistic catastrophe mindset, transformed into dexterously balanced living. For many reviewers Tove Jansson was a writer who would last for ever like the Moomin books, and no one was aggressively negative. But in *Folktidningen Ny Tid*, for which Tove had once drawn a Moomin strip and where she had been hailed as a writer of fairy tales by Gudrun Mörne, she was given an honest lecture. Tove should have taken a break after 'her trolls' and waited before writing a new book, wrote Aili Nordgren severely, adding, 'Writing a good short story is a difficult and demanding art.'

A critical perspective that became particularly clear from *The Listener* onwards was the conflict between the writer's will, the shaping of the work in hand and the reader's expectations – this above all else marked her reception after the Moomin books. Göran Schildt summarised it effectively in his review: 'Among Tove Jansson's innumerable friends and admirers, there must be many who ask themselves why the writer who created Moominvalley and all its deathless characters so stubbornly persists in painting extremely conventional canvases in oils and writing conventional fine literature.' Schildt's explanation is based on the changes in the Moomin world. The dream of a closed and isolated work of art (Moomin) has been dissolved by himself: the characters have stepped out of the books, almost become living beings and ended up in new contexts. The 'over-optimism' of the Moomin world had reached its boundary: 'Helplessness, loneliness and insecurity have more and more demanded her attention. It is to enable herself to deal seriously with them that she has turned her back on Moominvalley and stopped writing for a readership made up of those who either are children or would like to be.'

Tove began writing short stories at the same time as she finished *Moominvalley in November*. It was a part of her longing to express herself, nothing more unusual than a writer or artist turning in a new direction after finishing a particular piece of work. This is quite clear from her diary entries. 'Letter to an Idol', in which a young woman plucks up the courage to write to a famous writer, was one of her first short stories. 'No more,' noted Tove in her diary, but at the same time another short story flowed from her pen – and 'this one is good'. These were stories of the highest non-Moministic kind, as she described her new writing, in contrast to the Moomin books. In *The Listener* she examined herself and her art through humans and not through trolls. It was a matter of showing that she could work with words in new ways and the short stories use a language cleared of unnecessary words, with an economy and astringency that would be characteristic of her future writing and become ever more pronounced. 'Words are dangerous,' she wrote in *Moominvalley in November*, and this view is stressed again and again in the later stories and novels.

The Listener Herself

With its harsh language, the collection steers clear from themes and settings that might be familiar from the world of her earlier writing (if one knew that world). Tove now writes of events and activities nearer herself: 'Rain' describes the illness and death of an old woman (Ham), 'Blasting' describes the blasting of rock on an island (Klovharun) and 'Black-White' looks at an illustrator's struggle with paper, Indian ink and terror in fiction and reality. 'A Love Story' deals with an obsessive attempt to finish a work of art.

The love story concerns the relationship between an artist on a travel grant in Venice and the marble sculpture of a female bottom: a 'perfectly achieved free-standing behind', the 'rounded fruit of an artist's love and insight'. When his wife plans a theft in the name of love the perspective changes to a different love story – between the woman, the man and art. The illustrator in 'Black-White', who is busy with an illustration job for a mediocre anthology of horror, turns the horror inwards towards himself and his own life. The project becomes a reworking of what is inside him, what is unsaid in his well-ordered life.

> It is what is not said that interests me, he thought. I have drawn too clearly, one should not make everything clear, that's how it is. [...] I have spent too long reproducing what I see. Now I shall try something new and entirely my own; what is merely hinted at is much more important than what is clearly shown. I see my pictures as a slice of reality or unreality cut at random out of a long and inevitable course of events; the darkness I draw may continue for any length of time. I pierce it through with slender and dangerous shafts of light [...] I make my own pictures and they follow no text. Someone will come and provide an explanation for them.

It is possible to see Tove Jansson between the lines in this piece, a Tove Jansson who does not want to write and draw with absolute clarity, who wants to surrender herself to what is hinted at and not to the obvious. A writer making 'fine literature' in Göran Schildt's sense, rather than writing about a Moominvalley. That Tove did not want to illustrate *Sculptor's Daughter* was part of her new image. But the Moomin books are in fact full of things hinted at and left unsaid; that was a programme she had adopted early on.

Only Tove Jansson herself could know the price she was paying for her creative power, implied Schildt, seeing the short stories in *The Listener* as illuminating insights into art and life. The ability to understand and respect one's neighbour was the important thing. It made her into 'something like the listener she depicts for better or for worse in the title story'. This is the most interesting comment in the whole harvest of reviews.

The short story as a form was close to her: 'I have had to listen more than I have wanted to and now I like silence,' she wrote in a note. Like Tove herself, the listener can be a 55-year-old writer who draws aside from the world and her friends in order to write about new worlds. The story deals with the 55-year-old aunt Gerda, who has transformed her great family map into a work of art. Gerda, described as a very good letter writer, has changed from a listener into someone who narrates and researches instead of listening. She has devoted herself to others, written letters, sent cards of congratulation, assembled portraits designed to show the brilliance of others, stuck in spangles, listened and been on hand. Then comes the great transformation: she stops listening. Her letters become impersonal, her style becomes magniloquent and long-winded and she only writes on one side of the paper (with time the grand style became a tendency in Tove's letter writing too). This change happens over a long period, a process that begins with a map of people and relations:

> Now she only formed words in short, intensive sentences each of which summarised a particular piece of knowledge. Each was intended for someone who listened very carefully. Did you know that it was your fault that he died? Do you know that you are not your daughter's father? That your friend doesn't like you? And the map would be changed at once and Aunt Gerda had drawn her first gold line. It was a terrifying and irresistible thought-game and *it was called the killing words*. It could only be played in the evening, by the window. She realised words of this kind could only come separated by long intervals, if they were also, sometimes, actually uttered. Eight or nine words could be enough for extensive and lengthy changes in the great plan on the dining-room table. And later, at the right moment, new words for a new listener and again the picture would change. You could predict and calculate the moves in the same way as when you play chess against yourself; Aunt Gerda remembered some lines from a poem she had read when she was young: ... they sat, both of them, at a chessboard beautiful to behold, with alternate squares silver and gold ... She would draw her lines in silver and gold and wait, perhaps for a long time, then draw another line. She had plenty of time and the material was inexhaustible.

'The Listener' is a story about power and wilfulness, about the will to alter expression and creativity. To play chess with oneself is to move one's characters on the squares, to have an overview and be in control. The image of a game of chess (also found in Tove's painting 'The Family') has been taken from the nineteenth-century poet Tegnér and the poem Gerda read in her youth was his *Fritiofs saga*, in which Björn and Fritiof play chess on a board coloured in gold and silver. Words, just like chess, can lead to checkmate. The danger of words is a concept Tove will return to again and again. She reduces, pares away and 'boils down', as she called her method. This can even be seen in the physical size of her books, which get slimmer and slimmer.

Tove and squirrel, late 1940s.

'"The Squirrel"', Tove told Åke, 'is the story I like best and I rewrote it many times.' (Eight manuscript versions exist.) Like 'The Listener' it was close to her, and it centres on one of her key settings: the island. This is the place for solitude, writing and isolation, and the woman struggling to write on her isolated island can easily be taken as the portrait of a writer like Tove herself. 'The Squirrel' is a story about the difficulty of writing – about the power of words – and of attempts to overcome this

441

difficulty: strict rituals for work, eating, drinking, sleeping and being alone. Life on the island is all system and order, from the glass of Madeira in the morning to writing habits. First comes the paper, then the pens and lastly the words: 'On the table lay the paper in orderly white sheaves, always placed in the same way with pens beside them. Any sheets of paper she'd already written on lay hidden against the surface of the table, because if words lie face down there's a chance they might change during the night; you may suddenly come to see them with a new eye, perhaps with a rapid flash of insight. It is conceivable.'

All these rituals are broken by the squirrel that 'one windless day in November' appears just before sunrise. It has a pervading double symbolism, as an interruption of her solitude and as an opportunity for wordless communication. But above all it becomes a living expression of the change the woman is striving for. Her struggle with the squirrel, for example over the woodpile, is paralleled by her struggle with her writing. She hates it and she can love it. She can compare herself to the squirrel when she sees herself in the mirror. Her face is exactly like the squirrel's indeterminate grey-brown: 'like the November earth; squirrels become grey-brown in winter but they don't lose their colour', unlike the writing woman, they acquire a new colour. They transform themselves and acquire a new expression.

'The Squirrel' is a text about words, a struggle with those words that want to become a story, words that want to live a life of their own outside the writer's control and authority. The same applies to the squirrel, which ends up outside the woman's control and leads its own life. Fundamentally this is the conflict between pleasure and need, the will to write against the need to write. The story begins almost exactly as it ends, with a figure seen early one morning at the landing place. But now the squirrel has been transformed into a human being. 'One windless day in November, near sunrise, she saw a squirrel at the landing place.' That is how the story starts. It ends with the woman at her kitchen table; she has built up the fire in her stove and screwed up the wick of her lamp and is writing at great speed: 'One windless day in November, near sunrise, she saw a human being at the landing place ...' It is as near as makes no difference to a literal illustration of those thoughts about the concept of the short story that Tove later summed up as the principle of concentration and textual unity: 'Nothing must be superfluous, one must hold the story enclosed within one's hand.'

The Summer Book

Summers became quieter and brought fewer visitors in the 1970s; 'thank goodness' no great invasions, Tove reported to Maya in the summer of 1971. She wrote as much as she could, and shortly after her return from the Great Journey (May 1972) she was able to tell Åke that a new book was nearly ready. It started as part of *The Listener*, but it was no collection of stories:

> It's nice to be able to say that my next book is neither short stories and not a Moomin book for Gebers. It is called *The Summer Book* and features a very old woman and a very small girl together on an island. I wrote a number of sections of it while I was busy with *The Listener*, they didn't fit together with the rest and I laid them aside for later. I did go on with them afterwards a bit during the journey. Soon you'll get a sample to judge, but I want to go through the book again and try to change what I can to make it better.

The Summer Book – a minor masterpiece in Åke's words – brings together three lives and three generations, a six-year-old girl, a father and a very old grandmother on an island in the Gulf of Finland. It takes the family through twenty-two concentrated chapters of strictly controlled vocabulary. Most of the chapter titles are brief and descriptive: 'The Morning Swim', 'Moonlight', 'Dead Calm', 'The Robe', 'The Cat', 'The Cave' – like the catalogue of a series of pictures at an exhibition (a similar technique is used in *The Listener*). The story centres on the island, drawn on the cover, the variable setting for Grandmother and Sophia. The characters relate to Tove's own world, with Ham as the grandmother, her brother Lasse as the father and Lasse's daughter Sophia as the little girl.

Tove sometimes claimed to have based the three individuals on her relatives and at other times denied it. 'I have tried to describe the friendship between my mother and my brother Lars's little daughter,' she told an American publisher in 1974, adding 'Mother died three years ago, aged 88.' The island can

Two comic strip artists: Tove and Lars, 1978.

be identified as Bredskär with the Windrose house. But beyond these direct lines to a Janssonesque reality, a life goes on within this family triangle that is transformed into a story – with significance far beyond the contours of the little island. Tove depicts the idea of summer.

This is no Moomin book for Gebers, as Tove had told Åke; the Moomin world had been transformed into a literary world of such dignity that it also shines through in other texts. So it was with *Sculptor's Daughter* and *The Listener*, and it broke through in *The Summer Book* too. The characters, the valley and the other settings have been transformed into concepts and names that can interpret her other books. Now it is her readers, not the writer, who are looking for a wider space for interpretation. It is possible to relate these books to a general Moomin text, as some reviews and articles have pointed out. Ruth Halldén saw Tove Jansson as a great violinist who had grown tired of the violin and was now trying out her talent on the piano. She had achieved 'well-earned world fame' for her illustrated Moomintrolls and having now left them behind, found herself in 'a difficult artistic predicament'. This view recurs in the reviews. It was noticed

444

that the enchanter who had created the Moomin world was now writing short stories and novels about the difficulties, sufferings, obsessions and desires of human beings, but that she was also able to write about human happiness was difficult to take.

Several lines in Tove's writing cross in the *The Summer Book*. Here is the island, a milieu she knows as intimately as her own pocket, the secure hillside where a cat licks its lips after a night's hunting, a meadow full of flowers, rocks reaching down to the water, the boat's engine throbbing out at sea at night, the storm and the summer days. But it is also a place with unexpected combinations of culture and nature, pink false teeth against black earth, a mini-Venice of sea-carved wood in a little swamp. There is a family which contains the roles of mother, father and child but in a formation in which grandmother and child can be placed on an equal footing and kept apart. The father has many projects, plants an entirely new garden, parties, fishes, draws, fetches the post – but he is not involved in the game played out between Sophia and her grandmother. But the family has become so well adjusted that their joint life functions of itself:

> When the south-west wind was blowing, the days seemed to follow one another without any kind of change or occurrence; day and night, there was the same even, peaceful rush of wind. Papa worked at his desk. The nets were set out and taken in. They all moved about the island doing their own chores, which were so natural and obvious that no one mentioned them, neither for praise or sympathy. It was just the same long summer, always, and everything lived and grew at its own pace.

The father in *The Summer Book* is in the background, he is repeatedly described as 'just working at his desk', a permanent image. The focus rests on the child and the old woman, each egocentric in her own way. Relating to each other, they research the island and their other surroundings, play, learn and share experiences. Above all they discuss the premises of life and death each from her own separate perspective. Some of these debates end with aphoristic sentences that describe the fragile balance between loneliness and friendship, young and old, life and death, love and hate. An example is the observation Sophia makes about her headstrong cat, which cannot be tempted to give more love than it feels inclined to: 'It's funny about love,'

Sophia said. 'The more you love someone, the less he likes you in return.' 'That's very true,' Grandmother observed. 'And so what do you do?' 'You go on loving,' said Sophia threateningly. 'You love harder and harder.'

Like *Sculptor's Daughter*, *The Summer Book* gives codes about how to behave, live on an island and approach it: everything has its rituals and rules. 'An island can be dreadful for someone from outside. Everything is complete, and everyone has his obstinate, sure and self-sufficient place. Within their shores, everything functions according to rituals that are as hard as rock from repetition, and at the same time they amble through their days as whimsically and casually as if the world ended at the horizon.' In *The Summer Book* the grandmother is able to teach Sophia; in *Sculptor's Daughter* the narrator codifies herself according to how her father and mother perform in different situations. There is a model for how to behave. This can apply to a cat and it can apply to the few visitors. 'Hunt! Do something! Be like a cat!' shrieks Sophia at the great white cat Fluff. He prefers his warm bed to the morning storm, unlike his wild predecessor Moppy, whose greyish-yellow colouring blended with earth and stone. Anyone who doesn't behave according to the code ends up unavoidably excluded. (The purring Fluff is taken back to his previous family and the headstrong Moppy is able to return to the island, where he is in his natural element.)

Change

The Summer Book, together with *Sculptor's Daughter*, is the most Moominlike of Tove's books. This has to do with the topography, the island, the sea, the rocks and such Moomin commonplaces as the expedition, the sleeping place on the shore, and the love of storms and violent weather. As Tove herself wrote, it is no Moomin book, but it is a story that writes itself as a naturalistic shadow of the Moominlike, comprehensible to anyone who sees Tove Jansson's writing in a wider context. There is no sharp boundary between the different parts of her writing.

Grandmother's moments of rest during her time with Sophia are assigned to selected patches of sand and spots of earth where the view gives a picture of the surrounding nature. Compare two

Illustration for the German edition of The Summer Book, *1976.*

configurations of the same idea. One can see Moominmamma from the Moomin summer in *Finn Family Moomintroll* in more or less the same places. In *The Summer Book*:

> Between the arm of her sweater, her hat and the white reeds, she could see a triangle of sky, sea and sand – quite a small triangle. There was a blade of grass in the sand beside her, and between its sawtoothed leaves it held a piece of seabird down. She carefully observed the construction of this piece of down – the taut white rib in the middle surrounded by the down itself, which was pale brown and lighter than the air, and then darker and shiny towards the tip, which ended in a tiny but spirited curve.

In *Finn Family Moomintroll* there is a similar scenario:

> Moominmamma clambered down to a little patch of sand which was hidden by some fearsome rocks. Here clumps of blue sea-pinks grew and the sea-oats rattled and whistled as the wind forced its way up their narrow stalks. She lay down in a sheltered spot from which she could see only the blue sky and the sea-pinks that waved over her head.

The manuscript of *The Summer Book* followed Tove during her Great Journey; at the time she called it the 'Sophia Suite'.

She had begun the book in the summer of 1971 and finished it (as we have seen) in the following year in New Orleans. As with *Moominpappa at Sea*, travel proved a stimulus, giving power to her writing and detachment from her home environment. Her notebooks from the journey contain sketches for the cover, pictures of Sophia and her grandmother, and draft versions of the closing lines about the boat whose thumping motor is likened to the beating of a heart. The idea of writing about a little girl and an old woman had originally been Ham's, and it did not immediately take root in her daughter.

When her mother died, the telling of the 'Sophia Suite' became a way of keeping her close in descriptions of the Ham that Tove and her brothers had lived with on the islands. She put in events and experiences from a Hamlike life: a grandfather who had loved storms, a grandmother with a past as a Girl Scout leader, phenomena we know from Tove's stories of her childhood, a time that could be remembered, visualised and narrated many times. But in *The Summer Book* she also tells of the great change. The final chapter, 'August', describes the slow ending of summer, preparations for the winter and departure from the island. Everything moves nearer to the house and changes place and at the same time the landscape is transformed. August is the month that stands above all others in her stories of summer and the islands; it is the month when she herself was born and the month she gave to Moomintroll: a month of melancholy, change and memories, a time of expectation and sadness, as in *The Finn Family Moomintroll*:

> It was the end of August – the time when owls hoot at night and flurries of bats swoop noiselessly over the garden. Moomin Wood was full of glow-worms, and the sea was disturbed. There was expectation and a certain sadness in the air, and the harvest moon came up huge and yellow. Moomintroll had always liked those last weeks of summer most, but he didn't really know why.
>
> The wind and the sea had changed their tone; there was a new feeling in the air; the trees stood waiting.

August belongs to both summer and autumn, a border crossing when nature glides from one condition to another. It is part of the process of change, something that happens every year in more or less the same way. No matter whether one is a human or a Moomintroll one takes part in change, which is in fact a leave-taking. In *The Summer Book*:

> Grandmother had always liked this great change in August, most of all perhaps because of the way it never varied: a place for everything and everything in its place. Now was the time for the traces of habitation to disappear, and, as far as possible, for the island to return to its original condition. The exhausted flowerbeds were covered with banks of seaweed. The long rains did their levelling and rinsing. All the flowers still in bloom were either red or yellow, strong patches of colour above the seaweed. In the woods were a few enormous white roses that blossomed and lived for one day in breathless splendour.

The last chapter features only Grandmother and her relationship to time and the island. It describes her movements on the island in detail, how she polishes doorhandles, scours the rubbish pail and washes clothes, and how she takes leave of her room by looking closely at everything. She spends a particularly long time in front of 'the pretty picture of the hermit in his open tent against a sea of desert sand with his guardian lion in the background. How can I ever leave this room, she thought.'

We see life through Grandmother's eyes in this last chapter, and all likenesses and pictures can be related to her, from the island's wish to be uninhabited again to her reflection on the hermit, an artistic depiction of solitude. Nature's rinsing out of herself becomes an image of the vanishing of time, a time which is not Grandmother's. In the final lines she looks out over the sea at night, hears boats pass by and becomes aware of the smell of autumn. Life throbs out on the water and the imagery is sharp and clean, without a trace of sentimentality. A passing boat doesn't enter the channel but heads straight out to sea:

> Its slow thumping passed the island and continued out, farther and farther away, but never stopping. 'Isn't that funny,' Grandmother said. 'It's only my heart, it's not a herring boat at all.' For a long time she wondered if she should go back to bed or stay where she was. She thought that she would stay for a while.

'All good art is life, and everything that is an expression of what is living and real must make the world a better place,' said Tove when she accepted the Mårbacka Prize in 1972, the year *The*

Summer Book was published. She talked about reading, about Selma Lagerlöf (the Swedish writer who was the first woman ever to be awarded the Nobel Prize for Literature, in 1909), books and writing for children, and launched an attack on the informative, minatory and revelatory type of children's book.

But the life of good art is also valid for a book like *The Summer Book*. It is exactly this feeling of something living and real, the play between Sophia and her grandmother with the silent father in the background, which has made it into a classic among her books. It has been published in many editions and as early as 1973 Tove recorded it complete for Swedish Radio. It has been filmed and dramatised, and has had exceptional international success, with translations into English, German, Italian, French, Dutch, Japanese, Spanish, Norwegian, Polish and many other languages. It is not far-fetched to link its success with its Moominlike quality, and the identification of the island with freedom. In Argentina it was published with a picture of the Andes on the cover, another symbol of freedom (1977).

In the USA the book was published by Pantheon and was advertised prominently in the *New York Times Book Review* and the powerful *Publishers Weekly*. It later appeared in paperback. Tove herself was astonished at its international success. 'I am amazed how much is happening with my "adult" books, I never for a moment believed they would be published outside Scandinavia.'

As we have seen, she was careful to keep *Sculptor's Daughter* free of illustrations, and the same restriction was initially applied to *The Summer Book*. When a couple of years after it was first published the German publisher Paul List raised the subject of pictures (they wanted five or six), she was doubtful, but gave in. 'I haven't drawn anything for more than five years,' she wrote to Bonniers' foreign department in 1975, 'and have always made a point of illustrating books at the same time as writing the text, while the book was still close inside me.' A year earlier she had said no when her American publisher suggested pictures. Her reasoning was true to her artistic belief that some things should not be made explicit. The faces of the old woman and the child should be left to the reader's imagination. But when she finally got to work on illustrations for the German

Sophia and Grandmother, from the 1976 edition of The Summer Book.

edition she produced no fewer than seventeen, eight of them whole-page. Her arguments in favour of these pictures, made for a book she had not intended to illustrate, give interesting practical insight into the relationship between text and pictures. She was very anxious that the book should not be mistaken for a children's book because it had pictures in it. For this reason it was appropriate that the book should be classified as a novel:

> I've tried to draw the grandmother and the child from behind so that the reader can imagine their faces, and tried hard not to

make typical children's book illustrations. But in any case, *can* the book please be described as a 'novel' to be on the safe side, on the cover? (or something like that). People who leaf through it could be put off by some little drawing or other showing a child, that I was unable to avoid ...

No picture in the illustrated edition shows either the grandmother's or Sophia's face, or even the father's. To reproduce literary figures who carried within themselves memories of living people was impossible; to give the grandmother a face would have been equivalent to drawing Ham. It was different with the setting. Nature is reproduced exactly in 'accurate reproductions' of the 'milieu *The Summer Book* describes', in Tove's words. The illustrations came to have importance for her and became part of the process of seeing the past – bringing it back to life. Several new editions were published abroad and she later wrote to Åke: 'I'm pleased with the illustrations.' Since Tove's death a new (and again very popular) English edition of *The Summer Book* has come out (2003), with an introduction that includes photographs of the island, the house, Ham and Sophia and of the writer herself on the cover and inside. This has made concrete the biographical framework in the same way as for *Sculptor's Daughter*. But the title of the book has remained, just as Tove once wanted it: *The Summer Book, A Novel*.

Sun Cities

The novel *Sun City* saw a total change of scene. From the island in the Gulf of Finland, the family with grandmother, father and child, to oldies in their rocking chairs on the verandas of boarding houses in Florida, USA. Tove had met these people eye to eye during the Great Journey. Together with Tooti she had moved into the Butler Arms (the name taken straight into the novel) in St Petersburg on Tampa Bay in western Florida. This was one of the 'sun cities', places of sunshine, silence and rest for older people. She began writing about the Sun City while she was there. The earliest manuscript sketch can be found in her round-the-world book.

They had made their way to St Petersburg to see the ship used in the film *Mutiny on the Bounty*, but she was more powerfully

Postcard sent to Maya Vanni from St Petersburg, Florida, April 1972.

impressed by the old people. Tove sent a picture-postcard of the *Bounty* to Maya in April 1972, but the close-written lines tell mostly about the city's oldie essence: 'St Petersburg, the pensioners' city in which a third of the population are over 70, embedded in peaceful and subtropical greenery in white wooden guesthouses – and we lived there too, but were known as "the girls". You should have seen Tooti asking the little oldies for a dance when music from the beginning of the century was being played on the veranda piano! (The few men no longer had the strength.) We had a delightful time, utterly unexpected.'They'd planned to be there several days, but stayed longer.

Sun City started as a short story but grew into a novel. When Tove wrote to tell Åke about her new book (June 1973), she had paused in her writing for Moomin work (a Christmas calendar for Swedish television), which knocked a great hole in her work on the book. Now she was trying to get started again: 'It is a novel, but best not to talk about unfinished work – if all goes well

I'll offer it to you for the publishers' opinion in December.'When Åke had received the manuscript he wrote of his good fortune in getting it to read. The publishers had no real new Jansson on their list for 1973. At about the same time a portrait of Tove was commissioned for the collection of portraits of writers at the Bonniers villa Manilla, at Djurgården in Stockholm. It was signed 'Kenneth Green', the English portrait painter who once rented Tove's studio.

The new novel was a story about the commercialisation of death, about human loneliness and the need to communicate, and about the inexorable march towards old age, with its threat of the loss of one's speech, memory and freedom of movement. But the term 'sun city' also symbolises the hope of a last refuge, a place of light, serenity and rest. Before the text of the novel the reader is presented with an extract from an 'American brochure' about 'Sun Cities': 'those wonderful peaceful cities where we guarantee eternal sunshine and paradise on earth, as refreshing as old wine ...'

It was a path in her writing whose outspoken focus on ageing and older people and their unpredictable attitudes to life predictably troubled some critics, who longed for the subtle tenderness of earlier Jansson texts. Behind their words, as they struggled to sound positive, lurked doubts about the text. Caj Lundgren in *Svenska Dagbladet* started by calling Tove a poet with 'magic gifts', but he was uneasy: 'It is with a certain unease that one begins to read her new novel, *Sun City*, whose action is astonishingly enough placed in a pensioners' paradise in Florida.'Tom Sandell in *Hufvudstadsbladet* called *Sun City* a wise book, containing many of the 'basic truths' of life, but insisted that as a novel it was not a success – it was either too long or too short. Too long because the lives of the old people are too lacking in incident to be the stuff of novels, despite an attempt at 'variations of theme'; it can't sustain the reader's interest for 190 pages. Too short because too many 'individual people' are assembled at the heart of the novel: 'By giving her description greater psychological depth, a more long-drawn-out narrative background of for example the most important events in the past of the most important characters, this could have been avoided.'

Tove had attached to the book a (photographed) handwritten text for the back cover which many of the reviews quoted. It was a presentation and an explanation at the same time, a message from the writer who had met the sun cities face to face:

> I travelled through America, through Florida, and came one night to a city that was completely silent. Next morning it was equally silent and empty. The open verandas lay there in their greenery with long rows of rocking chairs, all turned towards the street. The peace was almost sinister. And then I understood that the city was one of the sun cities, those cities for old people where sunshine is guaranteed throughout the year. Everything has been prepared for rest and old age, inexorable and ideal.

She called the city 'St Petersburg' but, she wrote, it could equally well have another name. The serenity was only to be found offstage, as if a curtain had been drawn behind the verandas to hide the forces inside the people. To counterbalance the oldies is Linda – who looks after them – and Bounty Joe, her lover, the man who guards that symbol of the desire for something else, the ship *Bounty*, site of the mutiny of mutinies.

> I have tried to write a book about being old. And described the love between two very young and beautiful people who live in the city of the old. In America, and very strongly in Florida in particular, a new faith is arising that Jesus is about to return, now, at the last moment, and it is the young who are expecting his return. I have let Bounty Joe be one of those waiting. He is a guard on the film ship, the mutiny ship *Bounty*, which is anchored in St Petersburg harbour. The whole city, as I experienced it, is a sort of last resort for departure and arrival, an open possibility to anywhere. The sun city is a loveable, frightening and intensely living city.

Writing about the end of life, about the decay of body and senses, about death as the only future, was in no way what people associated with the poet with the magical gift. She had written about ageing earlier, in the form of Grandpa-Grumble in *Moominvalley in November*, and Grandmother in *The Summer Book*, but old age is more starkly and grimly portrayed in *Sun City*, where it is, above all, inexorable. In the Moomin books growth and change, welcoming new events and the impulse to break loose bring life and transformation, but *Sun City* only describes the time when movement is carried forward to the last place, to the room where the dream of life must end. When Mrs Elizabeth Morris goes below decks on *Bounty* and ends up in a polished and shining world of wood and brass, what she sees is the empty room that is death:

> The high windows cast rectangles of light right up to her feet. And when one dies, thought Mrs Morris, with sudden interest, I mean when one leaves one's room … It could be possible, it might perhaps be thinkable to have a big shining room free of everything and clean like a deck. No wastage or disorder, no sign of everything that hangs round an exhausted life: habit and forgetfulness, the refuse of the days, life's polluting slush. Suddenly she remembered: 'There was a slow creaking in the ship's hull,' presumably a sentence from the adventure books she had loved so much.

Sun City is a story that reminds us of the decay of the body, of the slow disappearance of speech, of the fragility of memory, a story of the desire or affinity that can give old age substance, and how this in turn can vanish too. It may be the worship of an old star, an attempt at a new love or an affinity that has passed its sell-by date years before; or the will to draw back into oneself, completely to avoid talking or communicating with the surrounding world. The novel *Sun City* looks forward to texts like *The Stone Acre* and the short story 'Messages' in her last book. Lines run backwards from it to the Whomper Toft's maxim that words are 'dangerous', and the Listener's game with words that can kill. Words are the theme of the story about the city of sun: the old vaudeville star Tim Tellerton (who lusts after young Joe) is in search of company without words, there are two elderly sisters who never speak to each other and Mrs Morris ponders the possibility of replacing conversation with the written word:

> To be able in silence to exchange messages written on the pages of a notepad […] A voice opening up in a face can be frightening at close quarters, the unconsidered words of the moment that demand an immediate answer. It must, thought Mrs Morris, it must be possible to find an acceptable margin for reflection. The time that writing allows, a mute message, could allow room for thought. Nearly everything we say to one another is marked with haste and thoughtlessness, with habit and fear and the need to make an impression.

This could have been said in Tove's later novel *The Stone Acre* by Jonas, the elderly journalist who is writing a biography of someone he hates.

When Tove wrote *Sun City* she was heading for her sixtieth birthday, which came in the year the novel was published. She was halfway between the two ages she was describing, on the one hand the beautiful young Linda and her lover Bounty Joe, on the other the old exemplified by Mrs Peabody, Mrs Rebecca Rubinstein, Mr Thompson, Miss Frey and many more. Both were areas unknown to her, particularly the world of the young, and she absorbed herself in studies of the phenomenon of the Jesus folk (from *Time* magazine) and motorcycles. She was able to study the oldies on the spot. There is also in *Sun City* Karen Horney's only 'conscious influence', according to Tove herself, an example of detachment theory, but it had escaped everybody, she noted:

> No one has noticed that Peabody is a loathsome creature. Poisoned with syrup, in a word. Perhaps this type of person is very common and just glides by, a little grey snake that hides in the sand and seldom manages to bite. And when she does sink in her poisonous teeth in total submission there is so much else, so much that is more dramatic to find fault with. She squirms in her pangs of conscience. I could have written a whole book about Peabody, but now I've used her and it is therefore impossible to use her again. Pity.

The Great Journey, her mother's death and her reading of Karen Horney, all became parts of this otherwise very different book *Sun City*. 'It's best to get going before you get too old,' said Tove before departure, and the opening ceremony in the sun cities' silent rooms became certain confirmation of this.

Sun City was launched as a Book of the Month, which overwhelmed Tove: 'Something absolutely fantastic!' she wrote to Åke. But it didn't sell anything like as well as *The Listener* or *The Summer Book*, and it never went into paperback. In fact, it never had any real chance of success. The change had been too great. This was not the Tove Jansson everybody knew and loved, but a Jansson who obstinately persisted in writing 'fine literature', to borrow Göran Schildt's expression. *Sun City* has long lain dormant in the backwater of Jansson writing and has not been reprinted. Curiousy, in America, the land of the sun cities, where it came out in 1976, it reached two editions and a paperback.

Sun City occasioned a spat between Bonniers and Schildts over foreign rights. In Tove's archive the relevant letters have been marked with phrases like 'huge consternation', etc. This quarrel between her publishers was painful to her. Åke Runnqvist wanted to take over responsibility for foreign rights, until then controlled by Schildts, so as to be able to place the books with new publishers. One possible redeeming spark came when Tove's old English publishers were slow with an option. As Åke wrote to his colleagues at Schildts, there are always some authors who touch one more than others. For him, Tove was such an author: 'I think there are very many more people who would gain a huge amount of pleasure from reading her books, and one of my most fervent wishes is that this should come about so that more people may share my delight in them. This is the motive force behind everything I have done in this connection.' Tove was one of the greatest writers writing in Swedish today, he went on, but she had been poorly served, not least by her previous publishers in Sweden: 'One could have wept tears of blood last autumn when after her fine advent calendar the whole country was discussing Moomintroll and in the bookshops not even the smallest advertisement could be seen, not to mention anything else to let people know that Almqvist & Wiksell publish eight Moomin books.'

All in all it was a criticism of Schildts, something that deeply distressed Tove. Loyalty, and in particular loyalty to her publishers, was deeply rooted in her and her relationship with Schildts was virtually sacred. 'They have helped me and looked after my muddled literary life virtually from the start,' she told Åke with unaccustomed frankness, 'and they have spared me thousands of worries':

> When I was young and was signing idiotic contracts with obscure publishers, Schildts cleared up my mistakes as far as they reasonably could. If they want to continue looking after books abroad I'm perfectly happy. If Schildts can come to any agreement with Bonniers it would be best if that could be arranged between the two publishers.

This cut right between Åke Runnquist on the one side and Ola von Zweygbergk and Thomas Warburton on the other. This is quite clear from the correspondence. But after a heated exchange of letters they reached an agreement to put before Tove. This settled the matter and the subject was dropped from their correspondence.

Drama in Paris

Autumn 1974 saw the premiere of the Moomin opera. The spring had been getting on top of Tove, and she had been taking too much on herself: 'too many *different* kinds of jobs, and it's hard to get them done,' as she told Vivica, who was her opera consultant. 'Of course I should be happy and thankful, and I certainly would be if I weren't so tired and worried about not getting things finished. Anyway, my book *Sun City* is ready, proofs and covers and all.' The autumn was a busy time too. 'It's all happening at once,' Tove told her friends: an exhibition of drawings was on tour (the Moomin illustrations from Hvitträsk), a story from *The Listener* was coming on TV ('The Children's Party' under a new title, 'The Snake in the Sitting-Room') and there was work leading up to the premiere of the Moomin opera. In the midst of all this she was getting ready to go to Paris.

One of these 'jobs' was the libretto for the 'Moomin Opera' in two acts (with roughly an hour's running time) that was being produced for the Finnish National Opera in Helsinki by Ilkka Kuusisto. It was based on Tove's characters, particularly from *Moominsummer Madness*, and was to be sung in Finnish. The printed programme came in the form of Moominmamma's handbag, folded to make a compartment in which cards with the names of singers, producers and other participants had been inserted. But how could a human being sing opera dressed as a Moomintroll? In plays the trolls' snouts could be thrown aside, but for the opera they were combined with loudspeakers.

There was more drama in Paris. In the studio in the Cité des Arts Tove felt 'blank' and exhausted after a year of 'trouble' and overwork. The idea of spending the spring in Paris writing and working at first frightened and worried her. The building felt like an enlarged Lallukka, with long corridors, black plastic furniture and everything else grey-gold – there was nothing positive in Tove's description to link it to the artists' home in Helsinki. It was very difficult for her to get started. She began to write, got stuck, pretended she was writing and tried everything to get her pen going, she told Vivica in February 1975:

> When I couldn't write [...] I started painting out of sheer desperation. And continued with my jaw clenched. Tooti's relief is touching. I shall be interested to see what it turns out to be. Something is beginning to move, perhaps. I *can* do it, I know that after such a long life, I even *see* sometimes, but what I can't do without, what is hardly within reach any more, is *pleasure*. That is what I'm waiting for.

As always, pleasure was crucial, but she needed to work, there wasn't anything else for her. Her need to express herself constantly drove her on and when she started painting – something she hadn't done for five years – she 'stuck her teeth into it', regardless of the result. First she did a still-life with 'a nice leek and apple and a view and self-portrait and interior', but she was not interested in doing a large canvas. It started as a portrait of Tooti, continued without a model and later began to resemble Tooti's mother: 'an angry Mamu. God forbid she should ever get to see my "Mother-in-law".' She also produced her portrait of 'The Graphic Artist' (Tooti), a painting into which she worked the vital concepts of work and love (see colour plate 29).

They worked away for all they were worth at the Cité. The city no longer tempted them with the 'expectation of discovery' of their younger days. Instead they settled down with potted plants, kitchen utensils and treasures from the flea market and built themselves a home in the studio. 'We're really happy,' Tove told Maya. 'Tooti has immersed herself in graphics and I haven't seen her so radiant for several years.'

The studio should have been a private zone, but even so many found their way there on business of one kind or another: a Frenchwoman who had translated Moomin without permission, a Japanese woman who wanted to learn how to write children's books (Tove devoted three days to her), a gentleman from Tove's London publishers with a request for more Moomin books. This irritated her. There was also a 'terrible fuss about "children's books" and "adult books". Bonniers were nagging. I ought to be madly flattered but I'm just upset.' She concluded: 'Every time they start fussing I just feel *less* desire to write.' Her writing block was first loosened by a dramatic piece, a future vision for television that was abandoned. This was 'The Window', which reached TV the next year. After that came a new commission, for a piece 'on death'. This would become 'The PE Teacher's Death'.

During the 1970s Tove wrote several plays. The thriller-like 'The Woman Who Borrowed Memories', seen on TV in 1977, was something of a breakthrough. 'Tove Jansson's plays are getting more and more like Samuel Beckett's,' wrote Bengt Jahnsson in *Dagens Nyheter*: creepy isolation, hopelessness in relation to a solitary person. In Beckett's 'Happy Days' a woman buries herself in her memories; in Tove Jansson's play she has them stolen from her. 'Tove Jansson has developed into a master of icy insecurity,' wrote Margareta Sjögren in *Svenska Dagbladet*. It was precisely this kind of atmosphere that Tove did want to write about, the frightening abyss that can be found in every person, what are called 'horror stories' in direct realism. To have one's memories stolen is like having one's identity stolen. 'No one has any idea how much [Ray] Bradbury I've been reading,' she wrote in exhilaration to a correspondent after working on 'The Window'.

Tove Jansson was now a major figure and prizes rained down on her during these years. In 1970 she shared the Heffaklumpen Prize for Swedish Children's Books with Astrid Lindgren and the same year won the Swedish Literature Association Prize. The year 1972 brought her the Mårbacka Prize and the Swedish Academy's Finland Prize. A couple of medals (which fascinated her) were the Albert Gebhard Medal and the 1976 Pro Finlandia Medal. A year later she won the top prize of the Foundation for the Promotion of Literature, and in 1978 the Topelius Prize and Rudolf Koivu Prize. She also won awards in Austria, France and Poland, and an Honorary Doctorate at Åbo Akademi (to which she presented manuscripts and letters) in 1978, and, at long last, the City of Helsinki Culture Prize for 1980.

This was roughly a prize a year in Finland and Sweden, but great honours were still ahead of her. When the Swedish Academy awarded Tove its Major Prize in 1994 on the occasion of her eightieth birthday, genius and taste finally caught up with the times.

The Most Dangerous Journey

One journey still needed to be made and that was to Moomintroll's best-known landscape. In *The Most Dangerous Journey* Tove returned to her valley, a 'Moominvalley Revisited' in picture-book form. More than fifteen years had passed since *Who Will Comfort Toffle?* and a good many since *Moominvalley in November*. Now Tove called out her characters again, and travelled with a little girl called Susanna through menacing landscapes to a remote Moominvalley full of sun, friendliness, flowers and colour. The road there was filled with figures from the books and strip series, and trials along the way recapitulated typically Moomin catastrophic events: a devastated seabed, a volcanic eruption, an eclipse of the sun, a snowstorm.

It was fun making the pictures, Tove said, and the new picture book was related to both her psychological horror dramas and her blazing painting in Paris. Negotiations began again for the transfer of all the Moomin books to Bonniers in the mid-1970s, but once more they failed. She had many other Moomin projects on the go at the time, above all the major exhibition with the Moomin house, tableaux and illustrations from the books and strip series. In addition, a photographic picture book called *The Scoundrel in the Moomin House* came out in 1980, based on the constructed house and with photographs by Per Olov. Its short text was mainly a guide for expeditions of discovery by the reader.

In *The Dangerous Journey* Tove painted a new story about the road to Moominvalley. It was as though she was clearing the path that the Whomper Toft had lost in *Moominvalley in November*, and filling it with dangers and violent landscapes that gave expression to her multiple relationship with the Moomins who were never far from her, whether she wanted them there or not. She kept them out of the way for most of the story. Unlike *Who Will Comfort Toffle?*, *The Dangerous Journey* is not a story without Moomintrolls, but Tove keeps them firmly in the valley, that land of warmth, friendliness and colour – everything she dreamed of during the war years. The garden is starred with flowers, fruit hangs heavy, chestnuts bloom – everything is happening at once in a stylised flowering model piece. It is a picture that responds to the eternal Moomin longing expressed by so many critics

Susanna reflected in the water. From The Dangerous Journey.

faced with her other books. In this valley 'the grass is if possible even greener than before', as all the passionately longing Moomin readers are informed, thus assuring the writer's status as a creator of fiction. The Moomin family of trolls and friends has been painted for ever into a Moominvalley.

It is a world to visit and a world to leave, exactly as Susanna shows us in a parallel to the Moominvalley pictures that Moominmamma paints on the walls of the lighthouse in *Moominpappa at Sea*. Like Moominmamma and the painter in the Wu Tao-tzu myth, Tove steps into her own pictures. She stands for the working imagination that makes the trolls visible again, for her readers of course, but above all for the writer-cum-artist who had said nothing about Moomintroll for many years, at least not in book form. The invisible family accompanies her on *The Dangerous Journey* and becomes visible again at the end of the book.

When Tove turned back to the Moomins it was in the first instance as a painter, not as a writer. For *The Dangerous Journey* it is the pictures, not the text, that come first, reversing her usual order of work. She tells the story in pictures rather than words, like the Whomper Toft in *Moominvalley in November*. The pictures feature dramatic scene-setting, but stand still in relation to the movement of the narrative. In some of them, the characters seem to have been transferred from one square to the next as if frozen. They resemble tableaux and indeed the pictures for *The Dangerous Journey* were finished at about the same time as Tove and Tooti started their major work on the Moomin exhibition tableaux. They were also busy with a film. In a letter to Maya Vanni, Tove described work on the island in summer 1976: 'On the first of July Tooti turned her back on graphics and since then we have mainly worked on the "tableaux"; our shelves are full of small figures, monsters, buildings, properties and furniture, and so long as the weather allows it and the light is right Tooti is filming. It's going to be "The Comet is Coming" and I've been busy with a synopsis according to all the rules of art.' She certainly was busy.

The Dangerous Journey is markedly metafictive in character, a story about the artist's road to the world in Moominvalley, about the power of imagination and about adventure as art. Susanna's literary sister is *Alice in Wonderland*, and like her adventurous predecessor in Lewis Carroll's books, she ends up in a country where everything goes backwards or contrariwise. She welcomes the danger, sees her own reflection in the adventure and, like Alice, is accompanied on the journey by her cat. She is presented as an experiencing child and as a storyteller with the power to stage-manage the development of events. It is she who has called forth the dangers – as in the picture of a deserted seashore with silent birds flying around, a red sky and an empty sea, an image charged with a restrained Hitchcock-like atmosphere:

> Beside the cliff, beneath the rocks, the sea had drained away.
> No wet, no blue, no waves, no splash – it was as plain as day
> The sea was gone, and, in its place, only a gaping void –

A dreadful sight (but one Susanna secretly enjoyed).
'I've got special powers,' she smiled.
'All this is down to me.
I'm just a little girl, a child,
But my mind has moved the sea.'

A journey in the footsteps of a Tove-esque childhood, full of pictures and stories. *The Dangerous Journey* pays homage to Swedish children's book illustrator Elsa Beskow and the painter John Bauer, upgrading deep childhood impressions in a new context. It starts like the Beskow picture book *The Flowers' Festival* with a midsummer night's dream, in which little Lisa meets the midsummer fairy in the meadow; her eyelids are smeared with poppy juice and she steps into the flowers' secret and expressive world. On Tove's journey Susanna's glasses are changed, and meadow, flowers and world take on new forms and perspectives. Her dangerous journey passes through a couple of Bauer's pictures, Princess Tuvstarr staring at her reflection in the water of the fishpond and a painting of Lapps in a snowstorm. There are no soft lines or rounded contours in the desert landscape of this dangerous journey; it is sharp, thorny and rugged. Moominvalley lies embedded among high mountains, woods and waterfalls.

The Dangerous Journey is very much the work of the painter Tove Jansson, full of dark, intense colours that have been mixed to make new watercolour nuances. They tell the story of what was the most dangerous journey of all for the writer: turning back to a world transformed into a place without Moomintrolls.

The 1970s were a time when Tove's versatile artistic talent once more saw the light of day in prose, painting, drama and song lyrics. After Paris and the portraits of herself and Tooti her painting levelled out to a great extent and the pen became her main tool. But Moominvalley tempted the painter in her one more time. She made sparkling murals for a day nursery in Pori designed by Reima Pietilä, Tooti's architect brother.

The murals (see colour plate 31) were called 'The Hobgoblin's Hat' and she did them in 1984 at the age of seventy. These large scenes, full of Moomintrolls and other figures, are perhaps among the most beautiful of Tove's Moomin paintings. They are expansive in form, full of colour and movement, like memories of a story from the past, a dream mixing time and trolls together. It was the same with the watercolour that became the cover for my own doctoral thesis in 1988. Tove had originally painted the flowering dream landscape in the 1930s, but added wandering trolls to the picture more than fifty years later.

CHAPTER 17

A Time for Words

*But the hours they all vanish and the sunset time grows long
and somehow I can't find in me a single little song, to tell of
expectation and how sadness comes with spring and of one
who walks alone and free and never owes a thing.*

'Snufkin's Spring Song'

*Sometimes he was able to play with the idea of attaching
himself to a traveller. A Traveller! That beautiful, old-
fashioned word.*

'Locomotive', from The Doll's House

Summer 1976 found Tove on Klovharun writing new short stories.
'We're at work' was how she summed up island life in a letter. As
always her various fields of activity crossed one another and the
short stories kept company with dramatic writing of one kind
or another. She wasn't satisfied with everything she was doing,
and wrote frankly to her friend Maya about some pieces she had
sent in to a competition announced on the radio:

> Can you believe it, they bought '3.50 am', that is to say the inferior
> radio play. Among other things, [Walentin] Chorell won 5 prizes
> and sold a dozen items. Chorell and I the only Swedish names.
> It was amusing, there were 745(!) entries. Since then I have
> written a synopsis of 'The Fillyjonk Who Believed in Disasters'
> for Finnish TV.

Drama was an important work area for Tove during the 1970s and 1980s and she listed many television and radio productions, sometimes adding self-critical commentaries. 'Not good, naïve', she wrote of her radio play 'The PE Teacher's Death'. This later found its way as a short story into *Travelling Light*; in fact several of the stories in that collection started life as plays (for example, 'The Window' for TV). When she couldn't write anything new she rewrote, arranged, started again and altered. This was an important part of her way of working as an artist. For *Travelling Light*, reworking drama was a convenient solution for the problem of having too much to do. Self-criticism was sometimes hard to handle.

'I'm looking for something absolutely not for children,' Tove told Åke Runnquist at midsummer 1976. Åke had become one of her most important critics and she showed him the stories for her next collection. She wanted to develop a hard-boiled style and this caught on. It had a superficially impassive tone, as he wrote, 'in which the course of events is told and nothing else', but he was most impressed by the 'double depth' he glimpsed in a pair of other stories. In their letters they discussed the placing of the stories, a constant general theme in her story agenda, and the discussion about 'the order of the train' in *The Doll's House*, which I quote below, was typical of Tove's correspondence with Åke. She weighed things up, talked them over and gave explanations for them, both to her publisher and to herself. Variation was essential, the title was vital, and stories with similar themes could absolutely never be placed next to each other.

> For example, not the flower child and the white ladies hand in hand; all drinking ladies! Then there are three stories that in a way take up the phenomenon of *exploiting* people: 'The Principal Role', 'The Parasite', 'Locomotive'. "The Great Journey' and 'The Doll's House' both indicate homosexual relationships. Then as far as possible I have tried to keep stories with first-person narration apart and also stories that deal with very old people. [...] So shall we call the book 'The Flower Child', then? Naturally with a cover picture that has nothing to do with the title.

But this wasn't at all how it turned out. Two more stories were added, one of them 'The Doll's House' (the other was 'Art in

Nature'). This became the book's obvious title, also as a tribute to one of Tove's great favourites among story writers, Katherine Mansfield, who had published a collection with the title 'The Doll's House'.

The Doll's House became yet another 'new' Tove Jansson book in its mixture of typical Jansson motifs to do with the conditions of art and penetrating studies of human obsession, alienation and attempts to live. 'Together with *The Summer Book*, this is your most striking book,' wrote Åke in August 1978, adding in brackets '(which is scarcely comparable)'. He waited with bated breath for reactions and to find out 'how long some of your fans will be able to take cold steel'. Tove answered, elated: 'I sincerely hope some people will be shocked by my hard-boiled approach. Do you know, I sometimes wonder whether the nursery and the chamber of horrors are really as far apart as one might think.' Their friendship deepened with the years, and when Tove came to Stockholm they often went to the Opera Cellar to talk under the wanton fin-de-siècle arabesques, as Tove put it. Sometimes Åke would express some literary points in their correspondence with a limerick (he was particularly good at them) and she would answer in the same way. But the most important thing was the confidence she had in him: 'It was always so peaceful meeting Åke; there never seemed to be any hurry and you knew most things would work out fine.'

The title 'The Doll's House' clearly refers to the artist's desire to build a permanent, sheltered and well-defined world, a structural pattern typical of Tove's writing. It also applies to the storyteller's lust for power. For the upholsterer Alexander in the title story, constructing things is synonymous with freedom – the freedom for him to make all the decisions: 'I build everything exactly as I want it. I decide. The ground floor and first floor face the sea. Then comes the drawing room.' It might belong somewhere in Germany – the attic is from Paris. 'I shall have to see,' says Alexander.

This is reminiscent of Moominpappa building a model lighthouse in *Moominpappa at Sea*, but it represents a different artistic freedom. In this case there is no firm basic concept of outlook and placing as there is for the lighthouse, but the opportunity that construction gives for imagination is the same.

Similarly, making a collection of short stories itself permits the building up of a house in which the writer can place her 'dolls' in flats, which may be distributed here and there in towns like Helsinki with direct access to Janssonesque rooms, streets and avenues, or travel destinations like Hawaii, America or London. Collections of short stories are always dolls' houses in the sense that they can be populated and furnished just how the builder wants. They become an expression of the writer's will and in effect know no limitations. Alexander's answer to his flatmate Eric, who talks about his 'doll's house', can be taken as the writer Tove Jansson's reply to those who compare her books for adults with the Moomin books: 'It's not a doll's house. It's going to be a real house.'

Not everyone could take the cold steel and the volume was given a mixed reception. One reviewer spoke of cruel stories, another of clichés, a third of an 'intermediate book', while others wished Tove Jansson didn't know so much about 'such gloomy matters'. The 'homosexual' relationships in 'The Great Journey' and the title story, 'The Doll's House', were hardly mentioned at all by the critics. The reviews of *The Doll's House* drew much the same picture as had the reviews of *Sun City*: one wanted to read Tove Jansson, but expected material different from that which was actually to be found between the covers of the book. Most dissatisfied of all was the reviewer in *Folktidningen Ny Tid*, Tatiana Sundberg, who was even more severe than her predecessor who had reviewed *The Listener*, and had no time at all for Tove's hard-boiled approach: 'The most gruesome aspect of the stories is that, in practice without exception, communication is destructive because it is consistently a question of extortion and exploitation'; the reviewer felt the need of a wind to blow 'holes in the haze and reveal the sky' and was clearly longing for the world of the Moomin books: 'We are an awfully long way from Moominvalley and all we can know is that some queens reign for a very long time.' In contrast, Merete Mazzarella summarised the pattern of reactions to the new Jansson books:

There has long been a tendency to be unwilling to take Tove Jansson seriously as a writer for adults but to want to try to drive her back into the Moomin world, but in *The Doll's House* as I see it she has written her best book for adults so far – even deeper and richer than her 1971 story collection *The Listener* with which it otherwise has a lot in common. The style is simple, clear and disciplined.

The Doll's House sold badly and the publishers partly blamed its unusual cover as a miscalculation. Unlike the covers of *The Listener* and *Sun City*, it had not been drawn by Tove herself but was completely different, an aquatint signed by Tooti and printed in black, showing house walls full of windows that seemed to be climbing upwards. This was a long way from any pictures Tove might have been expected to relate to, a long way from any doll's house in the traditional sense. Very many people were 'astonished and a bit frightened', Åke reported, lamenting the pitiful impression it made: 'It's a damn shame the book's literary interest was treated so loosely.'

The Doll's House, too, was never reprinted (though it has recently emerged in English, entitled *Art in Nature*). It contains several of Tove Jansson's sharpest stories, expert depictions of human dreams and desires, such as 'The Doll's House', 'The Cartoonist' and 'The Great Journey'.

With *Sun City* and *The Doll's House*, two successive books had gone less well than expected, and Tove was more affected by the critics than she showed in her letters. Tove's next book, *The True Deceiver*, would not appear till 1982. Writing was increasingly becoming a battle with pleasure and words.

Writing Oneself

One of the stories Tove had been working at on the island had been 'Locomotive'. It features a man obsessed with the idea of the train. He has never actually set foot on a train, but the word 'traveller' has a special sort of ring for him. It becomes a synonym for being free: 'To go off, out, away ... And while you're being carried away everything you've left behind is irreparable and final, while what you are approaching has not yet stated its claims. You are a traveller, and for a short time you are free.'

The hunger of the two world travellers, Jansson and Pietilä, was not satisfied by their round-the-world trip. Travel opened new areas of freedom from their ritualised working lives and provided a variety of settings for the short story's statement about the freedom of travel. They took their Konica to islands and cities in Europe, to Iceland, Corsica and Ireland, to Venice, London, Vienna, Madrid, the Faroes and the Lofoten Islands. The endlessly whirring Super 8 gradually produced the film 'Tove and Tooti in Europe', subtitled 'A Documentary on 8mm Film'. Tove never got to see it, but it features extracts from her short stories read by the film's narrator and interspersed with Tooti's travel memories. Travel was an art for them both, the traveller an observer and the journey an experience, in this film about 'old Europe', as it is called in the presentation. They travelled light. This was how the young Tove had lived as a traveller in 1930s Europe, and when much later she put the idea of travel into words in one of the stories in *Travelling Light*, the principle was the same: 'My bag was as light as my happy-go-lucky heart,' says the travelling first person narrator. The traveller has no ties, with no responsibility for what lies behind him and with no possibility of foreseeing what lies ahead. What he has is 'Just a huge serenity.'

Her travels were no less important than before, but the landscapes and places demanded less space in her books. Tove wrote about what was most relevant to her. Words and pictures had always been there for her, from the beginning with miniature books and diaries, through illustrations and cartoons to reflections on art, professional identity and freedom in memoranda and literary texts. She wrote about painters, illustrators, authors, letter writers and travellers and at the same time she wrote about herself in a state of change. She had constructed her ego from various sources. Drawing comic strips, building a doll's house, illustrating books for children, growing up in an artists' home, studying at art schools, being drawn herself and becoming a celebrity – all this belonged to her life and work as an artist and writer.

'Every canvas is a self-portrait,' Tove told her friend Eva Konikoff the autumn after the war, and this relates to all her work as an artist. But she did not document the person Tove Jansson and never invited others to interpret her works against the background of her life. For her what mattered most was to find ways of expressing herself that she could constantly change. As a visual artist she had started with a drawn self-portrait in

Travels with a Konica. Italy, 1979.

1933 and finished with a painting of herself more than forty years later in 1975. There was not just one, but many different Tove Janssons: her signature Tove, her signature Jansson and the writer Tove Jansson. As Tuulikki put it, she had a thousand faces.

Her time for visual portraits in oils, Indian ink and drawing was over by the mid-1970s. 'Just at the moment I am compelled to write, every day, I must define things exactly. Pictures aren't enough,' says the narrator of 'Locomotive'. She was faced with writing under compulsion, framed by her own and others' 'refusals', a verbal wrestling whose pursuit of words became a theme for the stories themselves. In her letters she wrote repeatedly about the loss of pleasure, but also about the delight of working when this relaxed. The growing importance of words became decisive for her portraits of herself. 'It just gets harder and harder to write,' she confided to Maya as she struggled with her novel *The True Deceiver*. But through all the agony she kept going. In roughly ten years she produced three novels: *The True Deceiver* (1982), *The Stone Acre* (1984) and *Fair Play* (1989); three collections of stories: *The Doll's House* (1978), *Travelling Light* (1987) and *Letters from Klara* (1991). Then followed her Klovharun story, *Notes from an Island* (1996), and one more collection of stories, *Messages* (1998).

473

Letters from Klara was Tove's last book with Åke Runnquist, who died in the spring of 1991. He was never to see the book in print. Their letters had inaugurated a conversational – and highly critical – process that became very important for Tove's path into writing, not least after they abolished the concept 'deadline' at Tove's suggestion. When she was working on the texts which later became the story collection *Travelling Light,* in May 1985 she wrote to him:

> Busy with several more stories – it's such a relief to have no deadline, one can try to write and rewrite again and again and give things a chance to mature on their own terms and perhaps gradually understand which stories should be abandoned forthwith and which ones will do. The order of stories in the book is going to be important; the same themes seem to be repeated, for example oldies, islands, journeys, I have to keep them separate. It's fun working at the moment. And I'm happy to know you're being Very Critical.

She was 'Very Critical' herself too; she rewrote, crossed out, altered, scaled down and in the slender novel *Fair Play* that followed *Travelling Light,* she ruthlessly wrote up the editing process for the short-story writer Mari, as experienced by her partner Jonna in the chapter 'Killing George'. It is a cruel self-portrait, frank and detached at the same time, a painful but vital process: 'these short stories that never get finished but just go on and on and are rewritten and rejected and taken up again, all these words that change place and are switched round and I can't remember how it was yesterday and what has happened with them today, I'm tired!' *Fair Play* is a remarkable book, as it writes so frankly about what was a definite reality for Tove and Tooti themselves: their life in work and love in their studios, on the island and while travelling wth the Konica.

The appeal of the Moomins continued as great as ever, with exhibitions, translations and general business. 'This business correspondence is terrible,' sighed Tove in the mid-1970s (and the situation didn't change with the passing of time). The letters poured in and out of the studio, swelling the piles of papers and brown cardboard archive folders that grew until they creaked. Naturally it was possible to deal with some of the business by telephone, but Tove preferred to deal with most of the proposals, negotiations, contracts and enquiries by letter. Walt Disney got in touch in 1975 about the film rights of the Moomin books and *Who Will Comfort Toffle?* They returned to the matter after Tove's death; according to Sophia Jansson they wanted to buy 'everything'. The Moomin books' home in Sweden was also in question. Åke Runnquist had wanted to bring all Tove's books together under the same roof. When the books were sold off at the end of the 1980s he saw his chance to try again. Tove agreed: 'Oh yes, I've heard that Norstedts have sold off all their Moomin books and I think it would be wise, as you say, to attack again and try to take them over. Last time you nearly pulled it off – even though they changed their mind at the last minute.' But it didn't work this time either, and Gebers (Almkvist & Wiksell) brought out new Moomin editions a couple of years later.

The 1980s saw the first considerable books and academic studies about Tove's writing; there were new exhibitions, and a new initiative from Japan involving Moomin films was on the way. 'A Moomin boom,' as Tove summed up this new commercial interest. 'There is so much happening!' she wrote to Åke in the summer of 1985. At the time she was working on new stories (for *Travelling Light*) while Tooti was preparing a retrospective exhibition in Tampere. The novel *The True Deceiver* was on the way to becoming a film, and a dramatisation of the story 'The Doll's House' was being planned for TV. She was thankful for the quiet of the island; hardly any guests and no raids to speak of. 'We've been able to work in peace,' she wrote. But in the midst of everything came a longing to travel. Travel was a necessity, and at the beginning of August they went to the Faroe Islands to see, at long last, 'the World's Biggest Waves'.

Streaks of exhaustion can be detected in some of her notes, a longing for calm and seclusion. She often talked of tasks and events that needed to be 'cleared up'. Even travelling, which otherwise brought peace and quiet, could seem hard work, but once she had got started and was sitting on the plane she felt free. A trip to Vienna in 1982 gave much more than she had expected, especially once her dutiful participation in a 'Discussion on Children's Books' was over. 'It's only now I realise how tired I have been,' she wrote, 'and that this trip wasn't just one more thing to get through, but that I should be happy and calm and very thankful.' In this letter (sent to Maya) she drew pictures of herself and her fellow travellers, as she had during her earlier major trips. She was really happy.

One major job was a revival of 'Moomintroll in the Wings' at Dramaten, the Swedish National Theatre in Stockholm, in spring 1982. Tove wrote a new script for this old 'chamber play' from the 1950s. It had been staged then in a theatre where the auditorium, in Tove's words, was no larger than a couple of buses, but now her characters would stand on a big stage of national importance. She did a lot of rewriting and the whole project worried her, especially work on the scenery and costumes. She needed to get to know the spaces, the stage and the auditorium to be able to work properly and that took time. 'A fabulous family show,' wrote Susanne Marko, reviewing the play in a long article in *Dagens Nyheter*, though she had reservations about the length of the second act and the many theatrical parodies – altogether too much oriented towards adults. But all in all it was a success for the old Moomin gang, who came together in the theatre one more time: Tove Jansson, writer; Vivica Bandler, director; and Lasse Pöysti, the former Moomintroll who was now head of Dramaten.

The painter Jansson had laid down her brushes, knives and palette, but even so Tove worked on pictures and visual thinking in film scripts (*The Summer Book, The True Deceiver*), drama and exhibitions. But she was not always allowed to join in. She would have very much liked to help with the filming of *The True Deceiver* but had to be content with reading about it in a newspaper: 'Of course they didn't want me around,' she told Åke in summer 1985. The next year saw the opening of the great Tove Jansson Exhibition at the Museum of Art in Tampere, to which she had contributed illustrations, pictures and tableaux. Drawings from *Garm* that she had rediscovered in the attic at the beginning of the 1980s (exhibited for the first time in Helsinki in 1983) went there too, together with the tableaux and the Moomin house. 'It seemed a good idea to have all the material in one place,' she wrote, like a professional archivist, while enjoying the freedom and emptiness in the studio.

Tampere was a joint project for the artists Jansson and Pietilä. An exhibition of Tooti's graphics opened at the same time as the Moomin exhibition, and these shows initiated a longer collaboration with the museum. 'She was busy with a passepartout for us both and packed in utter glory,' wrote Tove happily, adding that some 'impressive men' from a removal company had promised that Tooti could have a job as a packer any time. Later, in the spring of 1986, they hung their exhibitions and she passed the time until these opened by working on the stories destined for *Travelling Light*. It's a good thing when texts have time to lie idle and wait 'until one suddenly *sees*, understands what one has the possibility of improving, and what one wants to compress, expand or leave out altogether'. That was her method and she stuck to it.

Tove devoted the whole spring to work. 'We have been really unsociable,' she wrote, 'but that's really important if you want to get anything done – and it's so peaceful. We meet in the evening. Tooti offers her fine food, then we work some more or just read or watch TV.' Sometimes they visited their extra archive, the little flat known as no. 45 (in the same block) to 'make copies of this or that. It's a good room, so quiet – and no telephone.'

'Silence', 'serenity', 'peace' and 'quiet' – these were the words Tove was now using to describe her life.

New Pictures

As I have said, Tove wrote no real autobiography, but a handwritten manuscript six pages long elegantly summarises what she liked to tell about her life, growing up in a world of art, school, art schools, scholarship travel and the beginnings of writing:

> I don't remember very well what I really occupied myself with in those first years, just that I was deeply interested. When I was fifteen, to the relief of everyone I was removed from school to try to become an artist; that woke me up and I became very interested again.

> The art colleges, wherever they were, seem with hindsight to have been very much alike, but in fact it was us, the students, who all behaved in much the same way; following our teacher regardless of whether he painted with a brush or a palette knife, then suddenly totally against him, leaving college in mid-term to found a dissident group, turning a rented room into a bohemian studio (very easily done), changing styles and lovers with the

same happy nonchalance, to leaving home with maximum fuss – yes, it was a glorious time!

But your first trip abroad on a travel grant changed everything. You began signing your canvases and dating them and submitting them to general exhibitions, which either refused them or sent you a mention that you stuck into a book. No matter whether the criticism was good or bad, it could block your work for some time to come; you stopped abruptly, terrified of what you had done or no longer believing in it.

It was the same when I started writing.

Later it became possible to imagine choosing between 'making an impression on' and 'giving expression to', but that was much later.

Pictures and art had been with Tove from birth and when she was no longer working at the easel she summoned up visual art, both her own and that of others, through words. There are endless references to artwork and artists in what she wrote after the Moomins. In *The Listener* she paid tribute to the American artist Edward Gorey in the short story 'Black-White', and another to 'Venus Kallipygos' (literally 'Venus with the pretty bottom') in 'A Love Story'. *Sculptor's Daughter* is full of sculptures and drawings by John Bauer; in *The Summer Book* the picture 'The Hermit' by Robert Högfeldt has an important place, and there are references to J.M.W. Turner and the 'package' artists Christo and his wife Jeanne-Claude in *The Doll's House*.

In *Letters from Klara* the first person narrator in the story 'Karin, My Friend', paints a large picture of the wise and foolish virgins for her Uncle Hugo, who is married to her mother's sister Elsa. In this story Tove describes her first trip abroad on her own in 1934, when she stayed with Ham's sister and her family in Germany. The foolish virgins were the subject of her only sacred painting, in the church at Östermark. In the story they are depicted together with Christ at Uncle Hugo's request, but the artist's portrayal of Christ is not a success:

I had thought to make Christ less mild than he is usually shown, to bring out something of his critical force, the controlled violence I expected from him – but it wouldn't come right. I moved him further and further away till he was scarcely more than a phantom of light; I had worked at his face with such desperation that its surface became blurred and coarse.

Uncle Hugo shook his head and said, 'I see you are getting further and further from Him, you are no child of God. Those who are not friends of Christ cannot portray him. But we'll hang it up anyway.'

The pictures are inserted in various contexts to give them significance. What is least relevant is the art for art's sake that Tove had talked of as a young painter in the 1940s. Now she was using art to describe reality in the fictive worlds of short stories and novels. It was a question of getting people *to see*, as it says in *The True Deceiver*.

There is a fine example in 'Locomotive', which in many ways is a key story for understanding Tove's view of creative art. It contains traces of the thoughts about pictures and interpretation that she had long been writing about in her notes, all expressed through Turner's famous painting of a speeding train ('Rain, Speed, Steam'). This is used to illustrate 'the idea of the train' for the locomotive-obsessed narrator, but for the writer behind the story its significance is quite different:

> The painter Turner has conveyed in a very convincing manner the train's breakneck speed and power but he conceals the locomotive's face, so to speak, in steam and mist; One knows but one cannot see. His painting of the forward-rushing train depresses me deeply. He's not really painting the locomotive at all but only himself.

The velocity in the picture has no more significance than an Impressionist flicker of colour (as, for instance, in Monet's painting of Gare Saint-Lazare). Rather it is a question of what the painting contains behind its painted layers of steam, speed and mist. Turner paints himself by hiding his face. One knows, but one cannot see. These were the sort of 'double depths' Åke had been referring to, and for Tove herself the staging of variant interpretations became more important than ever when she stopped painting pictures.

It was as a painter that she was working in those stories, like 'Art in Nature', that deal with classic questions on the nature of art, such as the concept of knowing without seeing. The story begins with number 34 in the great exhibition, a package tied with string that some of the visitors wonder about opening. A security guard gives information about the originator of this school of art (a 'foreigner') and its technique: for example, sculptures and whole mountains can be packaged – a reference to the artists Christo and Jeanne-Claude (who are never named in the text of the story). But the question is 'Where can the boundary between art and nature be drawn?' A couple have bought a canvas and have had it packaged. It is abstract, representing two chairs turned a little away from one another, but in private the couple disagree on how the chairs must have looked and what it is that the painting shows. They know they have a picture, but they don't know what they can see. Each person sees what they can, says the guard, suggesting they should leave the canvas inside its package: 'Since a work of art can be almost anything and one only sees what one wants to see, you might just as well not bother unpacking it and simply hang the whole package on the wall. Then you won't need to quarrel.'

'Chairs', oils, 1960.

Like many of the stories in *The Doll's House*, 'Locomotive' refers, like the author behind the story, to pictures and descriptions that Tove presents in various connections. The packaged picture (as its buyers remember it) resembles a canvas by the painter Jansson, with chairs standing turned a little away from one another (1960). The man obsessed with the idea of the train loves beautiful 'antediluvian words' (like Tove herself); he is skilled at drawing and as a child would tell himself stories on his long road to school, a child who staged quantities of dramas in his imagination and made himself master of life and death through words and stories:

> Sometimes I was a captain, and let the ocean-going steamer hit a reef, or an iceberg, and everyone and everything on board would be shaken up for a single anxious instant, then with a terrible scraping as if of tearing metal the ship would continue on its voyage, but for how long? Only I knew that. I was an emperor and made life and death decisions. I closed schools, I forbade the entire populace to produce children. It was a glorious game, both in the morning and on my way home.

Thus Tove wrote about the power and opportunities open to the storyteller, but the unhampered games played on the way to school were later transformed into a search for words and meanings that could conjure up pictures. Like Turner, she portrayed herself. But let her face stay hidden inside the package.

Work and Love

Work and love continued to be Tove's life during her time of words. Summers on the island were calmer with fewer guests and more periods of extended peace. 'We have been able to work without interruption,' she wrote early in the autumn of 1980, and this was how she described many summers during the next few years. But when focusing her attention for a new book, an exhibition or some new Moomin presentation, she would want to get away from the beaten track. She longed for more effective isolation than was possible on Harun, and planned somewhere else to live for part of the early spring of 1981: 'for March and April Tooti and I have had the idea of renting an empty cottage

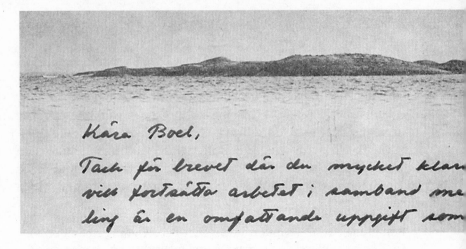

'My island'. A letter to Boel Westin, 1980.

on an island *away from* any channel through the ice, I mean, a place where one will be able to work in peace – but also if necessary ski to the bus on the mainland. We'll fix telephone and electricity.' This stay would give them a breathing space after the great Moomin exhibition at the National Museum. 'We're fine,' she told Åke, 'but in a hell of a rush. This Moomintroll is getting too big for his boots.'

Life on the island was no longer running on the same lines as before and, even if it was calmer, with fewer guests and more time for work, the atmosphere was not the same. When her old friend Albert Gustafsson suddenly died in 1981 a large part of the happiness that came with the island and 'things of the archipelago' was lost. Tove had become part of the population of Pellinge archipelago and had been friends with 'Abbe' since childhood. He had always been there at 'the Bay' (Eidisviken) where the Janssons had been his parents' tenants and as children Tove and Albert – he frequently appears in her early diaries – had played at 'Red Indians' together in the environs, and had built wooden horses, bathed and sailed during the summers of the 1920s. And it was Abbe who in 1962 had built *Victoria*, a boat that danced on the swell, strong and supple, made of 'mahogany, four metres long and clinker-built', the most beautiful boat on that whole section of the coast, according to *Notes from an Island*.

But getting older also meant not being able to do as much as before. All the time they were on Harun, Tove and Tooti slept in

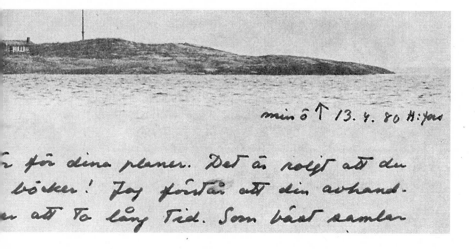

their tent, keeping the cottage for guests, preparing food and working. 'We're living in the tent as usual,' Tove told Maya in 1980, but the storms aren't as enchanting as they used to be:

> One night there was a horrid storm from the north-west and the tent turned into a pool of water. We guarded the boat in turns, all night long. We can't pull it up on land, you see, so it leaps about like a mustang held by its four ropes and if anything breaks that'll be it. We took refuge in the cottage of course but it shook, really shuddered, and there was a downpour. I always used to think storms were so exciting, but now I get a bit anxious.

It was of course very different from earlier times and, even if life on the island was still possible, it was getting a little rough at the edges. Worst of all were the break-ins that afflicted them for a couple of years, together with wild sharp-shooting exercises by the defence forces. These things were not just a disagreeable intrusion into their vital privacy, but also an encroachment on the whole concept of solitary island life.

The first break-in happened the year Abbe died, and it upset them and drained their strength: 'horrible with a break-in that happened at the cottage while the defence forces were busy shooting again; the soldiers had broken windows – the idiots, there was a key hanging on the wall – and taken away most of what we cared about – to the value of about 8,000 marks'. A year or two later burglars broke in again and this time it felt as if the whole island had been polluted. Broken windows and bottles were spread over the little sandy beach and meadow. Now shutters over the windows and locks had to be fitted to the cottage. It felt 'decayed', but in the midst of it all Tove worried about 'all the shipwrecked lovers who are used to coming in to warm themselves, fix something up, work on their engines. The villains never realised that the key was hanging beside the door. Ha. And on top of that, they dropped the guestbook in the sea. I found it full of seaweed.'

At the same time she was grateful they had been able to keep their paradise undisturbed for so long. The threat to their freedom, growing older, not being able to manage or do things, friends and relatives getting worried about them – all contributed to plant a thought that grew into a possibility: leaving the island. Tove wrote: 'We have lots of friends who worry about us, a great nuisance. Take care – and what do you do out there day after day? Blow soap bubbles,' Tooti tells them. They cleaned and tidied up the island and the cottage, and moved things to town so as to let the house gradually turn into a fisherman's cottage with bare walls and quiet surfaces. They devised ways of making things easier for the heavier jobs – like sledges, for example, but as early as the year before her seventieth bithday Tove noticed that she was getting stiffer. There was less she could do and she was getting more careful.

It was a very difficult decision to leave Klovharun. Tove had lived among the islands since childhood, and had first dreamed up her ideal of a solitary island when still very young. In a beautiful letter written to Eva Konikoff the year after the war she evoked a longing so powerful one can still feel it. She was on her beloved Kummelskär, the island she desired so passionately but was never able to have. Per Olov had sailed her out with Atos, to celebrate her birthday with crayfish and rockets and sleep in the heather rolled up in a sail. Lasse was with them too. 'I don't think you've ever been to Kummelskär,' she told Eva: 'It's almost twice as far from Pellinge as Tunnholmen – a magnificent wild rocky island with two sailing marks and two small beacons.' During the whole period of the war it was mined and inaccessible, but now she was indescribably thrilled to see 'her' island again, 'the one I like best'. It was here she wanted to live and make her home. 'When I lay there looking up at the crowd of stars I was overcome by a strong desire really to live on that island – or own it.' It was the furthest out to sea, unprotected, with no fresh-water spring, and no land where you could grow things, or woods. It was the solitary Tove's dream. I could have masses of mineral water with me, she planned, and cook in seawater, and buy lots of tinned food and jars and the boat would be pulled up on rollers because there isn't any harbour.

> You'd love the wild precipices, ravines and lagoons on the exposed side where even in calm weather the sea strikes breakers. That night we climbed up on the highest rock and watched the sea thundering white in the moonshine. The island was scarcely real – it looked more like a moon landscape or a dream.

She lived with that dream all her life. The island had lived in her body since childhood but now she was no longer in balance with the landscape. It was affecting her work. On the island her work was built on 'the calm, the monotony of the days'. But the sameness of living alone can come to resemble petrification: 'You must beware of desert islands if your work isn't going as it should. Because then the horizon can turn into a hoop of iron and the monotony of the days become merely a relentless confirmation of the fact that you can't get started. It is as if existence on an isolated skerry involves a sort of intensification of what you are, what you feel and what you do.' Intensification was the key. She felt this on Kummelskär and lived with it on Harun. The archipelago off the southeast coast of Finland was 'the landscape I love more than all others', she wrote, 'and no other place has contributed more to my work'.

They began preparing to leave the island as early as the beginning of the 1980s, and their very last day there came ten years later. On 30th September 1991, Tove signed a gift deed for the cottage, which she sent complete with an inventory to the Pellinge district Residents' Association. The cottage could be kept open for hunters and fisherfolk from the district as it always has been, she wrote, and continued: 'To cover costs the Residents' Association could levy a fair rent on such people as sea-scouts and divers and visitors who happen to pass by.'

When Tove left her island she left a lifelong passion behind her. The world grew smaller and the space she had available to live and work in shrank. In *Notes from an Island* she made a declaration of love to the savage island in words, showing how she had captured it, tried to tame it, lived with it and finally been forced to leave it. It is a text that together with Tooti's etchings of the landscape and views of the archipelago evoked the island for her and helped create it for her readers. 'Tooti and I are fine,' she wrote in July 1992. 'Being in town in summer doesn't feel as strange as we expected, more peaceful at all events. And we don't have to throw our rubbish into the sea – and we have running water and TV and so on.'

The Black Novel

The question of the stories' profitability recurred in her writing time and again. Painting was now a thing of the past and there were only words left to refuse to do what she wanted them to. The desire to write and the duty to work refused to coincide, and she tried various ways to get started on writing. 'I write on the sly,' she said, for example, during work on *The Stone Acre* in October 1983. When a few years earlier she had complained to Åke about how difficult she was finding her work, she got a long answer:

> I understand that with your strong sense of duty you are upset to be finding writing so hard going, but I think there are no particular reasons for you to feel such pressure. I think your publishers and even your readers understand quite clearly that you are less able than most writers and artists to write to order. Few books make such a strong impression as yours of having matured to the point where they have become self-evident. Try telling your inner voice to go to hell sometimes, let yourself enjoy a bit of fun and relax about both the doll's house book and the novel! They will be more than welcome when they come, but the most important thing is for them to be just as you want them. I believe everyone will be happy if you wait until then. In the meantime, if there's anything I can do, all you have to do is ask!

The doll's house book was the picture book *The Scoundrel in the Moomin House* (1980), and the novel she was working on was *The True Deceiver*. 'I have been struggling on stubbornly and laboriously for a couple of years with a novel that has been getting me down,' she confided to Maya in 1980. Versions of the text went backwards and forwards between her and the publishers, and a beautifully handwritten version of the first chapter rests in Bonniers' archive.

In *The True Deceiver* she wrote a black novel, much fiercer than the stories in *The Doll's House*. She wanted to write about power and relationships, about the struggle between two women, Anna Amelin and Katri Kling, apparently different but alike deep down. Which one best fits the description 'the true deceiver' varies according to the context. In the writer of children's books, Anna Amelin, who draws books with flowery rabbits in them, Tove portrayed the years of Moomin business when she was looking after nearly everything herself. Anna carries on an extensive business correspondence, but her large house contains not so much as the shadow of an archive. To the house comes Katri, firmly determined to take charge of Anna, her financial affairs and the house, and to provide a future for herself and her brother. With her she brings her wolf-like dog. The battle between wild beast (Katri has yellow eyes) and rabbit reaches no real conclusion and no real answer is given to the question of what is right and what is wrong. Everyone is a fraud, from the children who scoff at Katri and her beloved little brother, to the businessman who is cheating Anna over her accounts. 'This is a precise composition, a work of perfectly achieved symbolism, but it is a book that lacks any joy in life,' wrote one reviewer. *The True Deceiver* may seem like an unusual novel by Tove Jansson, but its merciless view of life is in fact one of the characteristic features of her books for adults.

'When you write a book you do it for yourself and you describe various sides of yourself in it,' said Tove in an unusually frank interview before publication. 'Every seriously written book is a sort of self-portrait. I was interested in the concepts of honour, self-deception and responsibility.' The critics latched on to this, seeing Anna and Katri as two sides of one and the same person. One can believe that Anna is the true deceiver, but perhaps Anna is rather a portrait of the author as we have created it, wrote Berit Wilson in *Dagens Nyheter*. In the person of the writer of rabbit books, Anna Amelin, Tove writes among other things about having a bad conscience over unanswered letters, and through Katri Kling she writes of the duty of being efficient and organising life properly (perhaps at the same time giving a portrait of the secretary she never had). There is also a battle of words played out between the rabbit and the wolf. Katri even goes so far as to try to answer letters in Anna's name and practises forging her signature.

The True Deceiver was a disturbing analysis of the dissimulation and self-deception that afflicted her readers in real life. It is played out in an archipelago landscape in a small village that one could imagine existing somewhere near Tove's own island home. This was risky and the story was not to be taken as an impression of real life. 'None of the characters in this book have prototypes in reality, just as the village cannot be found on any map,' as the flap of the dustjacket warned.

Tove's second novel of the 1980s, *The Stone Acre*, came only two years later and was quicker to write. Here the paring down of words was given one of its strongest expressions, both in theory and practice. It contains 108 extremely sparse pages that tell of the retired journalist Jonas, a man who has spent his life working with words. Now he has to write the biography of an elderly newspaperman called Y. Jonas despises Y and his words won't do what he wants, refusing to attach themselves to the paper. His daughters invite him to the archipelago so they can look after him, but his writing merely gets harder and harder. 'Have you thought what "In the beginning was the Word" means?' he asks one of his daughters. He has tried to write her a letter, but can't get beyond 'Dear Maria'. The words close themselves up; they become dangerous and have no wish to be written or spoken. Jonas finds his biography is beginning to get more and more like an autobiography, and when he finally buries his laboriously composed pages in the field full of stones it is a ritual act: turning the written words to stone is necessary if he is to be able to start again.

The Stone Acre is the most savage story about writing and speech among Tove's later books. A 'stone acre' is a place where water has washed away everything except stones and rocks – a clear and powerful image. 'One must wash the words and start again from the beginning,' thinks Jonas. There is no substance in the field, and that is how Jonas sees writing.

The new novel got a big response that was less Moomin-fixated than before. It clearly appealed to men and a remarkable number of those who reviewed it were also men. But the range

Tove Jansson in her studio, 1982.

of reactions to it was great, from those who saw the book as just as dead and boring as the biography Jonas is trying to write to those who saw it as a reflection of Tove's own development. 'Skilful instances of stripping oneself bare and a finely honed narrative technique, together with psychological realism united with rich symbolism,' wrote Magnus Ringbom. A study in human wisdom, stated Caj Lundgren in *Svenska Dagbladet*, defending the brevity of Tove's writing; his view was that *The Stone Acre* may seem like a short story stretched out to look like a novel, but that it contains more human wisdom than many books of double the length. The problems with words and their dangerous qualities that Tove was writing about in these two novels were also problems she herself had wrestled with. She was working at various ways of coming to terms with this difficulty. Anna Amelin is the wordless writer whose publishers write her texts for her, the journalist Jonas buries words and the writer Mari in the forthcoming *Fair Play* searches for new words to tell stories with, and to change and exchange.

Tove reached seventy in 1984, at about the same time that *The Stone Acre* came out. Her next book came out in the year she reached seventy-five. This was her great novel about work and love, written over a bare 115 pages in the form of 17 short narratives or stories.

Fair Play is the story of the life Tove and Tooti shared in studios, on the island, at work and travelling with the Konica, a life the story makes little attempt to disguise. Here is a description of the family wall in Tove's studio; here are themed evenings watching feature films on TV; here are stories from the island and descriptions of working together. It is an impression of Jansson-Pietilä life in cross-section; the rooms, the landscape, the views; even the view towards the harbour in Helsinki is included, the view they could see when they crossed the attic between Tooti's flat and Tove's studio.

In *Fair Play* two women, an artist and a writer, have long been living together. Jonna is a graphic artist and Mari writes short stories. Mari's mother (like Ham) helped start the Girl Scout movement in Sweden. The links between Mari and Tove and between Jonna and Tooti are obvious, like the whole setting. The writer makes no secret of the fact that she's writing about her own life, but directs the text like a game with two players. Here are all the readers' letters that have been sent to Mari. How should she answer an admirer who wants to know about the eternal truths? Jonna doesn't worry herself about the matter, but has a practical solution: 'Try once and for all to write down the meaning of life and take a photocopy so you can use it again next time.'

The real leading parts are played by work and love. 'The Letter' is the title of the last story. Jonna has had the offer of a studio in Paris for a year but hesitates to leave Mari. But the letter to Jonna also gives Mari an opportunity and is transformed into a proof of her love, closely intertwined with work. To give her beloved the freedom to travel, as Mari does, is to become aware at the same time of a possibility: 'She began to anticipate a solitude of her own, peaceful and full of possibility. She felt something akin to exhilaration, of a kind that people can permit themselves when they are blessed with love.' This is work and love at their very best.

Fair Play was given a big review in *Helsingin Sanomat*, whose critic Suvi Ahola saw it as a frankly autobiographical story. Others thought Jonna and Mari were two different sides of the

The attic passageway between Tove and Tooti's flats.

same woman. But few wrote about love between woman and woman or about homosexuality as a narrative.

Summer 1989 brought them four happy months on the island. In a letter to me, Tove wrote: 'Imagine two people alone together for four months on a desert island without getting angry with each other more than twice! Three times, says Tooti, but it didn't last long.' They went out as early as the middle of May so as not to miss the beginning of summer – the most beautiful time of all: 'If you're able to work Harun is the best place imaginable, but a paradise of tranquillity can be horrible if you can't get started, let's see, up to now I'm comforting myself that *Fair Play* hasn't yet been able to come out and I'm planting and pottering about and practising just existing.' Memories of the break-in had faded; they were kept busy by aggressive seabirds and Tove thought sadly of her gull Pellura, which used to land outside the window and tap for food.

They travelled again, the year after *Fair Play*, to Japan, this time with Lasse. There were new Moomin films to be launched and Moomintroll was about to conquer the world again, as the newspaper headlines announced. Books about Tove were being published in Japan and the comic strips were coming out in Japanese with photographic material on the writer and illustrator. The next year (1991) the new television series 'In Moominvalley' started in Finland (in both Swedish and Finnish) and in Sweden. Eventually more than a hundred episodes were made and sold to over a hundred countries.

'I'm very tired,' wrote Tove in 1992, defending herself against the 'Moomin boom' – it was beginning to be frightful. New projects and the launching of books and strip series were going on all the time, and there seemed to be no end to them. The following year she and Tooti visited their favourite city, Paris. It was to be her very last journey.

Messages

It seemed perverse to write any more after *Fair Play*, but the short-story collection *Letters from Klara* came out in 1991, as did a facsimile edition of *The Moomins and the Great Flood*. Helen Svensson at Schildts had persuaded her to allow this, but Tove insisted on adding a foreword so 'readers won't think this new edition is pure dementia'. She also had a retrospective exhibition of paintings, illustrations and Moomins in Turku, Tampere and Helsinki.

But the world really seemed to have shrunk after they left Harun, and when later in the 1990s new flats were built in an attic conversion in the Helsinki building they shared, the passage that led from Tove's studio to Tooti's flat was shut off. Now Tove lived mostly with Tooti. Her legs weren't up to going down in the lift, crossing the yard and taking the (other) lift up to the studio. She was feeling much older, but still working at new stories for the collection that became known as *Messages*. Now she was looking back at her childhood and youth and the war, and rereading her letters to Eva Konikoff. 'This should make a short story: In praise of friendship and about how difficult it is to paint. But not a whole book because I'm not up to talking about the war,' she wrote in July 1993. A couple of years later: 'Since *Notes from an Island* I've only managed to get together seven short stories and it seems there may be nothing more, really a relief I think – I just have to get used to it.'

This was in 1997, the year before *Messages* was published, a book that became her swansong (an expression she often used).

She had her doubts before publication, however, and blamed her publishers for planning yet another new book:

> Now Schildts and Bonniers want to bring out a 'selected stories', you know, and I decided to be difficult because it seemed to me cheating to mix old and new together. Now I've given in, so there'll be a book coming out this spring.

Many of the new stories had direct links back to her early life. She wrote about her mother's brothers, her letters to Eva and about the student painters' graduation day at the Ateneum, and constructed a story out of her conversations with Samuel (Sam Vanni). This text was taken almost word for word from her diaries of the late 1930s. She had made literature out of herself and made no effort to disguise people, places or events. In 'My Beloved Uncles', Torsten, Einar, Olov and Harald all run riot in Stockholm, where 'Mother's father preached in the Jacob Church' – as was, in fact, the case – though the writer at the same time cheerfully set out to destroy mythical pictures she had herself created. Ängsmarn might be taken as the model for Moominvalley, but there were reservations: 'I'm sorry, but they didn't even have shells around the flowerbeds.'

The war was the most difficult time in Tove's life, and the impossibility for her of writing about it recurs in her notes for the story 'Letters to Konikova'. The hardest thing was to find the right feeling and tone: 'I have to preserve my reverence for our friendship and also a naiveté I have since lost, it's going to be difficult,' she mused. 'I can't write as though I were still young, these letters which still move me are embarrassing; they can't be reproduced in their original form but I must not tidy them up and make them more literary.' Authentic material caused her problems, and the Konikova letters became a long-term project. There are notes on the subject from as far back as 1991 onwards, with sketches, drafts and rejected versions. She planned a novel set against the Winter War and Eva's brave new life in America (to be illustrated with Eva's photos of Harlem), but in her usual way boiled the material down to a short story.

The words turned out to be too difficult to control, and she was unable to inspire them with life. 'It's dangerous with old letters, and difficult to understand that they come from a world that no longer exists if you can't breathe life into it – and I can't,' she noted in 1993. She spent a long time pondering over how to loosen the trap of reality. It involved wakening a Tove who had thought painting the most important thing in the world and restoring life to what she had written long ago – either what she wrote now would be be in tune with the authentic letters or it wouldn't. It did work in the story she finally called 'Letters to Konikova', a text constructed from the letters she had actually written and now threw out in various directions.

Letters

There is something about Tove Jansson and her art that wakens passionate feelings, an urge to communicate, to love and to own – more than everything and everyone else interested in doing business with the world of the Moomins.

The short story 'Messages' – the very last that Tove published – is evidence of this urge, a collection of extracts from letters, greetings and textual fragments of various sorts. These are all directed to the same recipient, a person called Jansson who is a well-known artist. They include everything from affectionate everyday greetings – 'Hi coming later heat the soup' – to business transactions, demands, questions, threats, bizarre accusations ('It was you who murdered Karin Boye'), comments and claims on varying degrees of closeness and communication: 'My cat's died! Write at once' and 'Don't say you're old and tired, I shan't stop writing – I'll never let you go!' The whole mixture is a documentation of human nature, of the claims, desires and parasitical activities that celebrity exposes. Here are three typical examples in different genres: 'We look forward to your esteemed reply soonest re Moomin motifs on toilet paper in pastel shades', 'Hi dear unknown fairy tale auntie, we're a group of young folks with ideas! What d'you think? Are you up for it?' and 'Hi! We're three girls in a mad rush with our essays about you so could you help us by saying in just a few words how you started writing and why and what life means to you and then a message to young people you know the kind of thing. Thanks in advance.' (The last an expression Tove particularly loathed.)

'Messages' is an SOS from an author overwhelmed by fame, admiration and letters, and it shows at the same time how

Tove Jansson in her studio, 1990s.

deceitfully the author works. All letters, all greetings, appeals and desires can be turned round and become literature in her hands – most of the ones used are authentic. She uses them to write a short story about the importance of consideration for others and integrity, and at the same time seizes control over her readers, hijacking their messages and transforming them into a literary text. The author sends out her own message by returning these words sent to her over the years. And she calls her revenge on these words a message.

Tove answered readers' letters all her life. It made enormous demands on her time, but it was a principle she would never renounce. 'Not answering would disturb my work even more than answering,' she insisted, sorting her correspondence into piles, sometimes classified with phrases like 'wants something', 'begs an answer' or 'can wait'. 'I need to tidy up my conscience,' she noted one June day in 1982 when she had gone through piles of letters that had been lying there since the previous December.

Now she had got through her housework and felt relief. But there were limits. A hopeful child who wanted the near eighty-year-old Tove as a penfriend was sent a tip about a club for penfriends of a suitable age. She eventually mastered the art of bringing an exchange of letters to a suitable conclusion. A letter signed 'with worried greetings' from the famous author, Tove Jansson, would not encourage further correspondence.

The short story 'Correspondence', with its poetic imagery, gives a frank and finely tuned summary of the relationship between reader and author. Here the admirer's omnivorous love comes up against the author's need for seclusion. The whole story consists of eight letters from 'Tamiko Atsumi' or 'Tamiko' to 'Dear Jansson san', giving many people an idea of the reality of Jansson correspondence. A gentleman on his way to Japan even asked Tove for Tamiko's address, and some reviewers were convinced she had published authentic letters from a Japanese reader unaltered. But Tamiko is no flesh-and-blood human being. She is a merely a representative letter writer, in whom Tove has summarised her experience, giving it a Japanese stamp and transforming it into a story of love for an author. The letters also afford a glimpse of the background to Tove's popularity in Japan. She was the writer of solitude and freedom, and reading her work gave rise to many thoughts:

> Then I think about snow and how to be alone.
> Tokyo's a very big city.
> I'm learning English and studying very seriously.
> I love you.
> I dream one day I'll be as old as you and as clever as you.
> I have many dreams.

The more demanding young Tamiko's letters become in their longing for the author, and the more concretely she expresses her longing, the more Jansson san draws back. Her reaction to Tamiko's suggestion of a meeting is unmistakable:

> *Dear Jansson san*
>
> Thank you for your very wise letter.
> I understand the forest's big in Finland and the sea too
> but your house is very small.

It's a beautiful thought, to meet a writer
only in her books.
I'm learning all the time.
I wish you good health and a long life.

Your Tamiko Atsumi

The author's message couldn't be clearer. The charming wish for good health and a long life was often to be found in the letters from Japanese readers that flooded through her letterbox. They were words Tove liked very much, and now (in the story 'Messages') Tove returned the greeting her Japanese readers had been sending to her for so many years. She used them as the last words in her last book:

Dear Jansson san,

Take good care of yourself in this dangerous world.
Please have a long life.

With love

The Last Story

When *Messages* came out Tove was eighty-four years old (1998). 'I've only got together seven stories,' she wrote the year before and 'it looks as if there may be nothing more, really a relief I think – I just have to get used to it.' But of course it was painful not to be able to write any more in the way she was used to. Work was the most important thing in the world for Tove Jansson; work and love, in that order.

'This is a sort of report,' she wrote to me in August 1998. The house was being done up and was wrapped in fabric, but she and Tooti had got used to living a twilight life and listening to the men working outside their windows. The world was shrinking, but the sound of a cement-mixer reminded them of the building of Klovharun and the workmen's songs were like a message from the outside world. The singer she liked best specialised in sad ballads. Tove was trying to keep as active as she could and was working with her papers and her archive. She wanted to keep the house clean and tidy:

I went to the little Topelius park at the corner but they had taken away the benches to frustrate the local drunks. So now

I've worked out a new way to get exercise; I walk backwards and forwards in my big studio and move papers from one pile to another, labelling the piles carefully – and tearing up everything I can!

Isn't it a good idea to try to create *some* sort of order in time and not leave one's chaos as a *burden* for someone else to have to deal with?

Actually it has been quite interesting, I mean not only incredibly boring – I've been able to find cardboard boxes relating to my work (I mean my written work, there isn't the slightest note about my painting and illustrations).

Naturally, new material comes tumbling in every day (except Sat Sun). But I try to put each paper in its place, at once, to avoid these *piles* that build up so easily everywhere.

Don't you agree that I'm right to try to keep the house tidy in this way?

I've torn up all my private correspondence, totally.

Not yours – and what you have – or my letters from Tooti.

Tove was weak during her last years and became seriously ill with both lung and breast cancer during the 1990s. She withdrew more and more from the public eye and gave very few interviews. For her eightieth birthday on 9th August 1994 she was celebrated as a world-famous queen of words and pictures with exhibitions and a three-day international researchers' symposium in Tampere. It required a considerable effort, but she was present throughout, listening to the papers, shaking hands with delegates and admirers and letting herself be spoken to, photographed and stared at.

This was her last official appearance. In the summer of 2000 she suffered a severe stroke, after which she was cared for in a nursing home for the best part of a year. She died on 27th June 2001 in Helsinki, the city where she had been born one Sunday in August, a few weeks before Finland entered the First World War, in the city where she had worked, loved and lived for eighty-six years. She is buried in Sandudd cemetery in Helsinki, in a family grave with Faffan, Ham and Lasse, who had died the year before.

The announcement of her death included lines from 'Snufkin's Spring Song', about solitude and freedom, aspects of life that had always been vitally important to her. Faffan, she once said, had warned her never to stay with the same art dealer and had often expressed his contempt for people who ensured themselves a pension and saved up for their old age – you had to stay free in all respects and at all times.

'Solitude has a hundred faces,' she wrote, and her books, pictures and stories are a living witness to this fact. The Groke, Toffle, Jonas, Anna, Jonna, Mari and all the others – all solitary searchers, each in his or her own way. But here the key figure is Snufkin, the creative narrator who seeks to express himself through images of words and music, through poetry; he is freedom and solitude in one. The spring song in praise of freedom that bears his name describes the demands made by the artistic life:

I wander through the forest very early in the spring
the spring I have been waiting for and missing.
With heaven full of wings and with the earth full of the paths
of all the creeping things that have now woken.
I wander where life takes me in my ancient greeny hat,
I play my tunes in daytime and I play them in the night
And I keep nothing around me because I always must be free
to find new songs and sing them to my own sweet melody.

I'd like to sing a ballad to the clear cool springtime stream
and silent tunes to the moon's pale curving crescent
and small songs with harmonica for the flight that each bird flies
and a song in solitude's most gracious honour.
But now the hours are passing though the sunset lingers long,
and somehow I can't find in me a single little song
to tell of expectation and how sadness comes with spring
and of one who walks alone and free and never owes a thing.

Tove speaks in Snufkin's words: 'I must be free/to find new songs and sing them to my own sweet melody.' Snufkin's spring song is just as much about the writer who brought him to us and showed us how he lives and what he looks like. He sings of searching, of pleasure and will, about the artist himself, and of the eternal longing to find new ways of expression and of the final farewell to art that must one day come to all.

Tove Jansson grew up in a studio world where life was centred on art and work. But in the studio there was also a big set of bookshelves which she never forgot, shelves that reached to the ceiling and where she was free to search all the way from the big art books at the bottom near the floor up to the novels and poetry. It was where she learned the most important lesson of all; as she put it herself: 'to find the Pictures and the Words: the things that will never end'.

The winged pen.

ACKNOWLEDGMENTS

Godparents

Some of Tove's fifteen godparents. On the left, Signe Hammarsten-Jansson, Elin Hammarsten with Tove, and Viktor Jansson; on the right, Fredrik Hammarsten.

There wasn't enough room at Tove's christening party for all her godparents, a happy crowd of relatives and friends. In the photograph they assemble with baby Tove in the middle, safely held in her maternal grandmother's powerful arms.

This book about Tove and her words, pictures and life has godparents, too. Sophia Jansson and the Jansson family allowed me to work freely in the studio and archive in the years after Tove's death in 2001. They and Tuulikki Pietilä allowed me house room at no. 45 among the files and Moomins. Per Olov Jansson has also made photographs available to me.

Then there are all those who have helped me in archives and libraries in Finland and Sweden: Mirja Kivi of the Moominvalley Museum in Tampere, Petra Hakala at the archive of the Swedish Literature Association in Helsinki, Martin Ellfolk in the Manuscript Room of Åbo Akademi, Gun Grönros at the Brage Press Archive in Helsinki, Barbro Ek at Bonniers's archive in Stockholm and the staff of Helsinki University Library, the Royal Library in Stockholm, the Swedish Institute for Children's Literature in Stockholm and the Finnish Institute for Children's Literature in Tampere. Also the San Michele Foundation for a stay on Capri and the Centre Culturel Suédois for a stay in Paris, places where parts of the book were written. Lilga Kovanko, who generously allowed me to read Tove's letters to and from Vivica Bandler before they were deposited with the Swedish Literature Association in Helsinki, Pentti Eistola, who read the manuscript, and my two most faithful readers, Gunnar T. Westin and Göran Rossholm. To all these trolls and humans – the warmest thanks.

The book's most loving godparents have been Helen Svensson and Tuulikki Pietilä: Helen, Tove's publisher at Schilds Publishers, who became such a good friend during my work on the book, and Tuulikki, always known as Tooti, Tove's deeply loved life companion. Tooti (who died in 2009) helped me in every imaginable way, giving me an enormous amount of information and entrusting me with material of the most personal nature. It is to her that I dedicate this book about Tove.

Tove Jansson was at the same time open and secretive, intimate and distant, in a manner all her own, and had she not had confidence in me I would not have been able to write this biography. Her atmosphere has come to meet me every time I walk into the beautiful tower studio at Ulrikasborgsgatan 1 in Helsinki. Tove's unswerving respect for the integrity of work stamped the whole of her colourful life and I hope it has coloured my book too.

Boel Westin

Chronology

1914 > Born Helsinki, 9th August.

1917 > First surviving drawing, 2½ years old.

1920s > Makes many small illustrated books.

1922 > First summer in Eidisviken, Pellinge archipelago (1921 in Rödholm).

1928 > First publications: verses and illustrations in *Allas Krönika*; illustrations in *Julen*. Works on stories *Osynliga makter* (Invisible Forces) and *Matilda och konsten* (Matilda and Art) and makes her own newspapers for sale.

1929 > Comic strip *Prickinas och Fabians äventyr* (The Adventures of Prickina and Fabian) serialised in *Lunkentus*. First drawings in *Garm*.

1930 > Comic strip 'Fotbollen som flög till himlen'(The Football that Flew to the Sky) in *Vårbrodd*. Leaves school. Starts at Stockholm Technical School.

1931 > Offers a picture book to Bonniers, which is rejected.

1933 > Makes picture-book *Hemkomsten* (Homecoming) for her family. First drawn self-portrait, for *Humoristerna* (The Humorists), Salon Strindberg, Helsingfors. Picture book *Sara och Pelle och Neckens bläckfiskar* (Sara and Pelle and the Octopuses of the Water-Sprite) published in Swedish and Finnish. Comic strip *Palle och Göran gå till sjöss* (Palle and Göran Go to Sea) for Allas Krönika.

The Jansson family move to the Lallukka artists' home. Tove finishes her studies at Stockholm Technical School and starts at the Ateneum. First illustrations in *Lucifer*. First cover picture for *Julen*. Editor of *Ateneum* newspaper (to 1936).

1934 > Travels in Germany: Stettin, Hamburg, Berlin, Dresden, Munich, Velbert, ends her journey in Paris. Starts in the painting class at Ateneum, interrupts her studies twice during the following year. First short story, *Bulevarden* (The Boulevard), published in *Helsingfors-Journalen*.

1935 > Member of the Finland Artists' Association. First cover for *Garm*. Publishes short stories *Kliché* (Cliché) and *Stadsbarn* (A City Child).

1936 > Publishes short story *Brevet* (The Letter). Escapes from Ateneum.

1937 > Together with Ham, illustrates Ella Pipping's *Jag, en fyll-i-bok för nyblivna föräldrar* (Me, a Fill-in Book for New Parents). Elected to the Guild of Artists. Exhibits her first oil painting. Takes part in several exhibitions. Studio in Fänrik Stålsgata. Leaves Ateneum permanently.

1938 > Publishes short story *Bryggliv* (Life on the Landing-Stage). Studies in Paris during the spring, then travels and paints in Brittany. Publishes short stories *Skägget* (The Beard) and *Quatz' Arts*.

1939 > Takes part in several exhibitions, including the Nordic Exhibition in Gothenburg. Rents several workrooms. Travels to Italy: Verona, Florence, Rome, Naples, Capri. Publishes short stories *Aldrig mera Capri!* (Capri Never Again!) and *Hyra rum* (Renting a Room).

1940 > Publishes short stories *San Zeno Maggiore, 1 stjärna* (1 Star) and *Fiolen* (The Violin). Takes part in the Young Artists' Exhibition. Exhibits together with four colleagues at Stenman's Daughter gallery in Helsingfors; exhibitors call themselves 'The Five Young Things'. Takes part in exhibitions in Gothenburg, Stockholm and Oslo. Two cartoons published in *Folket i Bild*. Draws a large number of postcards and greetings cards.

1941 > Paints in Åland, superintending an exhibition by young artists from Helsingfors. Paints glass in Tullbommen restaurant in Helsingfors. Paints 'Self-Portrait with Fur Cap'.

1942 > Writes poems. Moves to studio on Fänrik Stålsgatan. Exhibits 'Familjen' (The Family). Paints self-portrait 'Loboan'(The Lynx Boa).

1943 > First solo exhibition at the Bäxis Gallery, Helsingfors. The Snork first appears in *Garm*. Illustrations for Brita Hiort af Ornäs' *Lill-Olle och harpalten* (Little Olle and the baby hare). Meets Atos Wirtanen.

1944 > Moves to studio at Ulrikasborgsgatan 1. Paints windows for girls' school in Apollogatan. First Moomin book submitted to Söderströms Publishers in May. Summer in Åland: paints, writes and meets Atos' family. Illustrations for Solveig von Schoultz's *Nalleresan* (Teddy's Journey), Martin Söderhjelm's *Om flugan Maja* (Maya the Fly) and Ole Reuter's *Learn English*.

1945 > Mural paintings for Strömberg's factory at Sockenbacka. First Moomin book, *The Moomins and the Great Flood*, published in Sweden.

1946 > Second Moomin book: *Comet in Moominland*. Second solo exhibition at Kunstsalongen, Helsingfors. Illustrates *Magazine 1946*. Meets Vivica Bandler.

1947 > Paints two frescoes in the Town Hall cellar, Helsingfors. Writes poems. Builds the Windrose house on Bredskär. Illustrations for Carolus Sjöstedt's *Bröderna Borgs bedrifter* (The Exploits of the Borg Brothers). Draws comic strip series *Mumintrollet och jordens undergång* (Moomintroll and the Destruction of the World) for *Ny Tid* (up to April 1948). *Comet in Moominland* published in Sweden. Söderströms turn down *Finn Family Moomintroll*.

1948 > Third Moomin book, *Trollkarlens hatt* (The Hobgoblin's Hat), published by Holger Schildts. Travels in Italy with Sam and Maya Vanni. Goes on alone to Brittany.

1949 > Mural paintings for a kindergarten in Kotka. *Trollkarlens hatt* (The Hobgoblin's Hat) published in Sweden. First Moomin play *Mumintrollet och kometen* (Moomintroll and the Comet) premiered at Svenska Teatern, Helsingfors. Elected to the Writers' Association in Finland.

1949–50 > Publishes two short Moomin stories, *Mumintrollets julafton* (Moomintroll's Christmas Eve) and *Mumintrollet – rulltrappan* (Moomintroll – the Escalator) in *Nya Pressen* and *Småbarnens julstjärna* respectively.

1950 > Fourth Moomin book: *The Exploits of Moominpappa – Written by Himself*. From now on the books are published simultaneously in Finland and Sweden. The third book, *Trollkarlens hatt*, is published in England as *Finn Family Moomintroll*.

1951 > *Trollkarlens hatt* published in USA as *The Happy Moomins*. Illustrates Lilli Forss-Nordström's book *Våren vaknar* (Spring Awakens). Travels with Vivica Bandler to Italy and North Africa, finishing in Paris.

1952 > Paints murals in the Society Hotel in Fredrikshamn and for Technical School in Kotka. Illustrations for Eric Gardberg's *Zebran Sebulon* (Sebulon the Zebra). Designs costumes and décor for ballet version of Yrjö Kokko's *Pessi ja Illusia*. Awarded Svenska Dagbladet prize for Finland-Swedish literature. First Moomin picture book: *The Book About Moomin, Mymble and Little My*; published in both Swedish and Finnish.

1953 > Last drawing for *Garm*. Paints murals for the student residence Domus Academica. *Moomintroll and the Comet* produced at Gothenburg municipal theatre. Awarded Nils Holgersson Plaque for *The Book About Moomin, Mymble and Little My*. Comic-strip studies in Fleet Street, London. Paints altar-piece for Östermark church.

1954 > Fifth Moomin book: *Moominsummer Madness*. Danish edition of *The Moomins and the Great Flood*. The Moomin strips begin in the London *Evening News*. Paints murals for Karis coeducational school and Nordiska Föreningsbanken bank in Helsingfors. Travels to London and the French Riviera with Ham.

1955 > Moomin play produced in Wasa theatre. Third solo exhibition in Konstsalongen. *Helsingfors: The Moomin Books* translated into Finnish. The Moomin strips begin in the Swedish and Finnish newspapers *Svenska Dagbladet*, *Politiken* and *Ilta-Sanomat*. Meets Tuulikki Pietilä.

1956 > Publishes short story *Granen* (The Spruce Tree) in *Svenska Dagbladet*. Publishes *Moomintrollet på kometjakt*, a reworking of *Comet in*

Moominland. Publishes *The Exploits of Moominpappa* in a partly revised edition. Publishes *Finn Framily Moomintroll* in a new edition with minor alterations. Major Moomin promotion in department stores: Stockmann in Helsingfors, and later NK in Stockholm. Paints murals in Aurora children's hospital, Helsingfors.

1957 > The Moomin comic strips begin publication in book form titled *Mumintrollet* in Swedish. Sixth Moomin book: *Moominland Midwinter.* Journey to Stockholm with Ham and Faffan.

1958 > Faffan dies at midsummer. Awarded Elsa Beskow Plaque in Sweden and Rudolf Koivu Plaque in Finland for *Moominland Midwinter.* Meets Pentti Eistola, builder of the first Moomin house. Premiere of second Moomin play *Troll i kulisserna* (Troll in the Wings) at Lilla Teatern, Helsingfors. Writes Moomin songs for the play.

1959 > *Troll I kulisserna* produced in Stockholm. Illustrations for Lewis Carroll's *Hunting of the Snark.* Writes essay 'Sagan inom verkligheten – Den ärliga Elsa Beskow' (The Fairy-tale within the Reality – the Honesty of Elsa Beskow) for *BLM.* Last Moomin comic strip drawings. Painting 'Nybörjare' (A Fresh Start). Three months' journey to Greece and Paris with Tuulikki Pietilä.

1960 > Solo exhibition at Galerie Pinx, Helsingfors. Second picture-book, *Who Will Comfort Toffle?* published. *Troll I kulisserna* produced in Oslo. Lars Jansson begins to draw the Moomin comic strips.

1961 > Essay 'Den lömska barnboksförfattaren' (The Deceitful Writer of Children's Books) published in Horisont.

1962 > Seventh Moomin book: short story collection *Tales from Moominvalley.* Illustrations for J.R.R. Tolkien's *The Hobbit.* Solo exhibition at Galerie Fenestra, Helsingfors.

1963 > Solo exhibition at Husa art gallery, Tammerfors. Awarded Stockholms-Tidningen Culture Prize.

1963–64 > Long journey to Portugal, Spain and Ibiza with Tuulikki Pietilä. Begins to build cottage on Klovharun. Awarded Anni Swan Prize for *Tales from Moominvalley.*

1965 > First summer on Klovharun. Eighth Moomin book: *Moominpappa at Sea.* Publishes *Vi* (Us), a romantic book for lovers written with Ham. Short story *Vår magiska jul* (Our Magical Christmas) published in *Vi.* Writes 'Höstvisa' (Autumn Song) for Erna Tauro.

1966 > Solo exhibition at Galerie Pinx, Helsingfors. Illustrations for Lewis Carroll's *Alice in Wonderland.* Short story *En ohemul historia* (An Unfortunate Affair) published in *Vintergatan.* Awarded Hans Christian Andersen Medal. Award acceptance speech 'Några ord i Ljubljana' (A Few Words in Ljubljana) published in *Nya Argus.*

1968 > New revised editions of the Moomin books *Comet in Moominland, Finn Family Moomintroll, The Exploits of Moominpappa* and *Moominsummer Madness.* In Paris during the spring with Tuulikki Pietilä, working at Cité des Arts, goes to Brittany. First book for adults: *Sculptor's Daughter*. Shooting of Margareta Strömstedt's TV film *Mumin och havet* (Moomin and the Sea).

1969 > Solo exhibition at Galerie Pinx, Helsingfors. Exhibition together with Tuulikki Pietilä at the Alvar Aalto Museum in Jyväskylä. TV serial *Mumintrollen* written with Lars Jansson. A book with the same title is published with pictures from the TV film. Becomes committee member of the Finland-Swedish Writers' Association (to 1973).

1970 > Ham dies in July. Ninth and last Moomin book: *Moominvalley in November*. Shares Expressen's Heffaklumpen Prize with Astrid Lindgren.

1971 > Changes her publishers in Sweden, leaving Gebers/ Almkvist & Wiksell for Bonniers. Short-story collection *Lyssnerskan* (The Listener) published. Major concentration on Japan with Moomin books and films. Travels round the world in eight months (into 1972) with Tuulikki Pietilä, from London and Amsterdam via Japan, Hawaii, USA and Mexico. Writes essay 'Öar' (Islands) in Tokyo.

1972 > Publishes *The Summer Book*. Prize from the Swedish Academy, awarded the Mårbacka Prize.

1973 > Awarded the Albert Gebhard Medal. 'Mumintrollen' becomes a Christmas calendar on TV in Sweden. *Bilbo – A Hobbit's Adventures* published in Finnish with Tove's illustrations.

1974 > The novel *Solstaden* (Sun City) published. *Muumiooppera* (Moomin Opera) staged (in Finnish) at the Finnish National Opera in Helsingfors. Exhibition of Moomin illustrations at Hvitträsk in Esbo, Finland.

1975 > Spring in Paris with Tuulikki Pietilä, working and living at the Cité des Arts. Paints the 'ugly' self-portrait.

1976 > Awarded the Pro Finlandia Medal. Starts building the Moomin House with Pentti Eistola and Tuulikki Pietilä. *Fönstret* (The Window) drama broadcast on TV.

1976–77 > Writes dramas, including *The PE Teacher's Death*, *The Daughter* and *Ten to Four*.

1977 > Awarded major prize of the Foundation for the Promotion of Literature. Publishes picture book *The Dangerous Journey*. Drama *The Woman Who Borrowed Memories* shown on TV. 1978 Presents manuscripts and other material to Åbo Akademi. Awarded honorary doctorate by Åbo Akademi. Publication of short story collection *The Doll's House and Other Stories*. Journey to Poland, where the Moomin stories become puppet theatre on TV.

1979 > Exhibition of the Moomin House in Bratislava. Travels to Vienna and Italy. *Sommarön* (The Summer Island), a TV film based on *The Summer Book*.

1980 > Exhibition 'The Moomin House' opens in Helsingfors. 'Moomin' exhibition opens at the national museum in Stockholm. Publishes photo-picture book *Skurken i muminhuset* (The Scoundrel in the Moomin House) with Per Olov Jansson. Awarded culture prize by the city of Helsingfors. 'Moomin' exhibition tours Sweden.

1982 > Novel *The True Deceiver* published. Travels to England and Ireland with Tuulikki Pietilä. Play *Mumintroll i kulisserna* (Moomintroll in the Wing) staged at Dramaten, Stockholm.

1983 > Journeys to Paris and Karelia with Tuulikki Pietilä. Exhibition of pictures from *Garm* at Konsthallen, Helsingfors.

1984 > 'The Hobgoblin's Hat' mural for kindergarten in Pori. Publication of novel *Stenåkern* (The Stony Field). Bonniers' Christmas book: *Två berättelser från havet* (Two Stories from the Sea). Travels to Norway, The Faroe Islands and Scotland with Tuulikki Pietilä.

1985 > Three months in Spain with Tuulikki Pietilä.

1986 > Donation to Tammerfors Museum of Art (Moomin House and tableaux with Tuulikki Pietilä and Pentti Eistola). Tove Jansson exhibition opens at Tammerfors Museum of Art. TV drama *White Lady*.

1987 > 'Moominvalley' exhibition opens in Tammerfors. Short-story *Karin, min vän* (My Friend Karin), special edition for the Gothenburg Book Fair. Short-story collection *Resa med lätt bagage* (Travelling Light) published.

1988 > Travels in England and Scotland with Tuulikki Pietilä.

1989 > Novel *Rent Spel* (Fair Play) published.

1990 > Journey to Japan with Tuulikki Pietilä and Lars Jansson.

1991 > New Moomin films made in Japan. Short-story collection *Brev från Klara* (Letters from Klara) published. Pictures from *Garm* exhibition in Tammerfors Museum of Art. Publication of facsimile edition of *The Moomins and the Great Flood*.

1992 > Retrospective Exhibition at Amos Anderson Museum of Art, Helsingfors. Awarded Selma Lagerlöf Prize.

1993 > Awarded the Finland Prize. Travels to Paris with Tuulikki Pietilä, her last major journey. Retrospective Exhibition at Åbo Museum of Art. Publication of *Visor från Mumindalen* (Songs from Moominvalley), a collection of lyrics with music.

1994 > Tove Jansson's 80th birthday. Retrospective Exhibition of paintings, drawings and other illustrations at Tammerfors Museum of Art. International Tove Jansson Conference in Tammerfors. Awarded Major Prize by Svenska Akademien (Swedish Academy).

1995 > Awarded title of Professor.

1996 > Publishes *Anteckningar från en ö* (Notes from an Island) with pictures by Tuulikki Pietilä.

1998 > Publishes story collection *Meddelande* (Messages).

1999 > Film *Haru – De ensammas ö* (Haru – The Island of the Solitary), made with Tuulikki Pietilä.

2001 > Tove Jansson dies in Helsinki, 27th June.

TOVE JANSSON'S

Published Works

Works published in English translation.

Books for children

Sara and Pelle and the Octopuses of the Water-Sprite (by 'Vera Haij'), Helsingfors & Stockholm, 1933.

* *The Moomins and the Great Flood*, Helsingfors & Stockholm, 1945.

* *Comet in Moominland*, Helsingfors, 1946, Stockholm 1947.

* *The Hobgoblin's Hat* (published in English as *Finn Family Moomintroll)*, Helsingfors, 1948, Stockholm 1949.

* *The Exploits of Moominpappa. Written by Himself*, Helsingfors & Stockholm, 1950. Revised as *The Exploits of Moominpappa. Noted down by Tove Jansson*, Helsingfors & Stockholm, 1956. Further revised as *Moominpappa's Memoirs*, Helsingfors & Stockholm, 1968.

* *What Happened Next?* (published in English as *The Book about Mymble, Moomintroll and Little My)*, Helsingfors & Stockholm, 1952.

* *Moominsummer Madness*, Helsingfors & Stockholm,1954.

* *Moomintroll & the Comet*, Norrköping (Sweden), 1956.

* *Finn Family Moomintroll* [revised edition}, Helsingfors & Stockholm, 1956.

* *Moominland Midwinter*, Helsingfors & Stockholm, 1957.

* *Who Will Comfort Toffle?* Helsingfors & Stockholm, 1960

* *The Invisible Child and Other Stories* (published in English as *Tales from Moominvalley)*, Helsingfors & Stockholm, 1962.

* *Moominpappa at Sea*, Helsingfors & Stockholm, 1965.

* *The Comet is Coming* (published in English as *Comet in Moominland)*, Helsingfors & Stockholm, 1968.

* *Moominvalley in November*, Helsingfors & Stockholm, 1970.

* *The Dangerous Journey*, Helsingfors & Stockholm, 1977.

The Scoundrel in the Moomin House [with photos by Per Olov Jansson], Helsingfors & Stockholm, 1980.

Songs from Moominvalley [with Lars Jansson and Erna Tauro], Helsingfors & Stockholm, 1993.

Comic strip series

Prickina's and Fabian's Adventure,
Lunkentus, no.10-16, 1929.

The Football that Flew to the Sky,
Vårbrodd 1930.

Palle and Göran Go to Sea, Allas
Krönika, no.21, 1933.

*Moomintroll and the End of the
World*, Ny Tid 3/10 1947-2/4 1948.

* *Moomintroll 1-8* comic strips
[5, 7,and 8 with Lars Jansson],
Helsingfors & Stockholm,
1957–1964.

Books for adults

We. A Romantic Book for Lovers
[with Signe Hammarsten-
Jansson], Helsingfors 1965.

* *The Sculptor's Daughter*,
Helsingfors & Stockholm, 1968.

* *The Listener*, Helsingfors &
Stockholm, 1971.

* *The Summer Book*, Helsingfors &
Stockholm, 1972.

* *Sun City*, Helsingfors &
Stockholm, 1974.

* *The Doll's House and Other
Stories* (published in English
as *Art in Nature*), Helsingfors &
Stockholm, 1978.

* *The True Deceiver*, Helsingfors &
Stockholm, 1982.

The Stone Acre, Helsingfors &
Stockholm, 1984.

Two Stories from the Sea,
Stockholm, 1984.

Karin My Friend, Stockholm, 1987.

* *Travelling Light*, Helsingfors &
Stockholm, 1987.

* *Fair Play*, Helsingfors &
Stockholm, 1989.

Letters from Klara, Helsingfors &
Stockholm, 1991.

Notes from an Island [with
Tuulikki Pietilä], Helsingfors &
Stockholm, 1996.

Messages, Helsingfors &
Stockholm, 1998.

Articles, essays, other short stories

Hey, Hurrah for Mannerheim
[signed Totto], Allas Krönika
no.21, 1928.

The Cake, Astra no. 4, 1933 [no
author's name given].

Cliché, Helsingfors-Journalen,
no.12, 1935.

The City Child, Julen, 1935.

The Boulevard, Helsingfors-
Journalen, no 25, 1936.

The Letter, Helsingfors-Journalen,
no. 6, 1936.

Life on the Landing-stage, Svenska
Pressen, 28/8 1937.

The Beard, Lucifer, 1938.

Quatz' Arts, Svenska Pressen, 30/7
1938.

Capri Never Again, Christmas
1939.

Renting a Room, Svenska Pressen, 23/9 1939.

San Zeno Maggiore: 1 Star, Lucifer, 1940.

The Violin, Julen, 1940.

Moomintroll's Christmas Eve 1949, Småbarnens julstjärna, 1949.

Moomintroll – The Escalator, Nya Pressen, 19/12 1950.

When the Park Keeper Became Luminous, Dagens Nyheter, 28/11 1953.

The Spruce Tree, Svenska Dagbladet, Christmas edition 1956.

On drawing and story-telling, Svenska Dagbladet, 1/12 1956.

Indifferent to Influence, Expressen, 1/4 1957.

The Fairy-tale Behind the Reality: the Biography of Elsa Beskow. Bonniers Litterära Magasin 1959, pp. 419-420.

The Deceitful Writer of Children's Books, Horisont, no.2, 1961.

The Island, Turistliv i Finland, no.2, 1961.

Our Magical Christmas, Vi. no. 50-51, 1965.

An Unfortunate Affair, Vintergatan, 1966.

A Few Words in Ljubljana, Nya Argus, no. 18, 1966.

Security and Terror in the Child's World, Skolbiblioteket no. 3 1967.

Sailing a boat at night..., Dagens Nyheter, 6/7 1969.

Security and Terror in Children's Books, Författarförlagets Tidskrift, no. 4 1974.

Balancing Terror and Security, Hufvudstadsbladet, 5/3 1978.

Moomin, Exhibition Catalogue 438 at the National Museum, 1980.

The World of Children, Samtiden, no.3, 1984.

Tarzan the Incomparable. Children's Books, in Barnboksförfattarnas litteraturhistoria, ed.Annika Holm & Siv Widerberg, Hedemora, 1984.

Atos my Friend, Astra no. 2, 1996.

Dreaming of a Lighthouse, Meriväylä Merenkylky laitoksen ajankohtaislehti, no. 4, 1998.

Once in a Park, in *Travels with Tove: Memories of Tove Jansson*, ed. Helen Svensson, Helsingfors, 2002.

Letters

* *The Letters of Tove Jansson*, ed. Boel Westin and Helen Svensson, Schildts, 2014 (forthcoming).

Drama

Moomintroll and the Comet, 1949.

Troll in the Wings, 1958.

Crash (song lyrics for Lars Jansson's 'naivistic drama'), *1963*.

The Moomintroll, 1969.

Moominvalley, 1973.

The Moomin Opera, 1974.

The Snake in the Sitting-Room, 1974.

The Window, 1976.

The Listener, 1976.

The PE Teacher's Death, 1976.

The Woman Who Borrowed Memories, 1977.

The Daughter, 1977.

Ten to Four, 1977.

Moomintroll in the Wings, 1982.

The Doll's House, 1986.

White Lady, 1986.

The Leading Role, 1988.

The Great Journey, 1988.

Illustrations for other books

Carroll, Lewis: *Alice in Wonderland,* trans. Åke Runnquist, Stockholm, 1966.

- *Alice in Wonderland,* New York, 1977.

- *The Hunting of the Snark,* trans Lars Forsell and Åke Runnquist, Stockholm, 1959.

Forss-Nordström, Lilli, *Spring Awakens.* Fairy play for children, Helsingfors, 1951.

Gardberg, Eric. *Zebra Sebulon and Other Animal Stories,* Stockholm, 1952.

Hiort af Ornäs, Brita. *Lill-Olle and the Hare-skin,* Helsingfors, 1943.

Mårtenson, Gunnar. *The Colonel's Wife and Her World,* Helsingfors, 1942.

- *The Colonel's Wife Before Her Hearth,* Helsingfors, 1943.

- *On Further Reflection,* Helsingfors, 1946.

Numers, Lorenz von. *A Feeling for Words,* Helsingfors, 1945.

- *Two Bearded Doodles,* Helsingfors, 1943.

Pipping, Ella. *I* [with Signe Hammarsten-Jansson], Helsingfors, 1937.

Reuter, Ole. *Learn English* (two parts), Helsingfors, 1944–1945.

Schoultz, Solveig von. *Teddy's Journey,* Helsingfors, 1944.

Sjöstedt, Carolus [signed Don Carlos]. *The Exploits of the Borg Brothers,* Helsingfors, 1947.

Söderhjelm, Martin. *Maja the Fly,* from *Little Stories About Little Creepy-crawlies for Little Children.* Helsingfors, 1944.

Tolkien, J.R.R. *Bilbo: The Adventures of a Hobbit,* trans. Britt G. Hallqvist, Stockholm 1962.

Photo Credits

The author and publishers have made every effort to trace the copyright owners of all the photographs in this book. If any acknowledgements have unfortunately been omitted, we apologise and ask the copyright owners involved if they could write to the publishers for the error to be corrected. Moomin Characters administer the rights to illustrations by Tove Jansson. Photographs of Tove Jansson's artwork are by Per Olov Jansson unless otherwise stated.

Text photos

Private ownership: 65, 70 , 85, 97, 99, 107, 111 , 116, 137, 138 , 141, 149, 174, 270, 279, 282, 286, 288 , 292, 296, 301, 307, 308-09, 326, 333, 364, 389, 409, 453, 480, 486-87

From Tove Jansson private archives: 12, 14, 14, 15, 16, 18, 20, 22-23 , 24, 30, 34, 39 , 40, 43 , 45, 47 , 48, 50 , 52, 54, 56, 63 , 67, 79, 81 , 82, 86, 92 , 95, 103, 118, 121 , 129, 131, 144, 147, 151, 156, 163, 169, 182, 187 , 196, 199 , 209, 231 , 233, 235, 250, 273, 285, 290, 319, 337, 357, 395, 427, 429, 433, 501, 510

Others: Goran Algård: 361. *Beata Bergström*: 304. *Pentti Eistola*: 387, 473. *Karl Heinz Hernried*: 347. *Lars Jansson*: 228. *Per Olov Jansson*: 2, 369, 403, 444. *Len Waernberg*: 420. *Boel Westin*: 489, 491. *Helsinki Swedish Adult Education Center*: 217. *Ateneum Art Museum, Helsinki*: 27. *Royal Library, Stockholm*: 126. *Pressens Photo/Scanpix*: 222. *Tampere Art Museum*: 122, 165. *Åbo Akademi*: 171, 178-179 , 371.

Colour Section

[1] Book 44 from Tove Press, 1925. Private ownership.

[2] The Adventures of Prickina and Fabian. Tove's first comic strip, in the children's magazine *Lunkentus*, 1929. Private ownership.

[3] Ensittaren (The Lone Sitter), 1935. Private ownership.

[4] The Road to the Technical School, Stockholm. From 'Hemkomsten' (Homecoming), autumn 1930, a picture book for her parents. Tove Jansson's private archive.

[5] Walking home at night in Stockholm. From diary 1931. Tove Jansson's private archive.

[6] One of the maps of Tove's territory in Paris, 1938. Tove Jansson's private archive.

[7] 'Self-portrait with Fur Hat', oils, 1941. Private ownership.

[8] Rembrandt's self-portrait of 1640 © National Gallery, London.

[9] Moominpappa in Rembrandt pose, cover for *Muminpappas bravader* (*The Exploits of Moominpappa*), 1950. Private ownership.

[10] 'Hotel Room', 1938. Private ownership.

[11] A watercolour from 1930 with one of the earliest Moomintrolls. Private ownership.

[12] Closely written pages from the diary for 1944. Tove Jansson's private archive. Photo Nisse Petersson.

[13] Sam Vanni's portrait of Tove Jansson, oils, 1940. With permission from BUS 2007, Finland.

[14] 'Still-life with Shell', oils 1945. Private ownership, photo Matias Uusikylä.

[15] 'The Lynx Boa', self-portrait, 1942. Private ownership.

[16] Frescoes for the restaurant, Helsingfors City Hall, 1947.

[17] 'Red Cape', 1964. Private ownership.

[18] 'Still-life', oils, 1966. Private ownership.

[19] Temple, chalk, Greece, 1959. Private ownership, photo Matias Uusikylä.

[20] Illustration from the picture book *The Book About Moomin, Mymble and Little My*, 1952.

[21] Toffle on the beach. From the picture book *Who Will Comfort Toffle?*, 1960.

[22] 'The Family', oils 1942. Private ownership.

[23] Sketch of 'The Family' in a letter to Eva Konikoff, 1941. Private ownership.

[24] *Garm*, cover for Christmas number, 1941.

[25] Moomintroll's story about the frescoes. From letter to Vivica Bandler, 3rd February 1947. Swedish Literature Association in Finland.

[26] Performing sketch for the play 'Moomintroll and the Comet', staged in Helsingfors, 1949. Tove Jansson's private archive.

[27] Drawings of the Muskrat and Moomintroll for *Moomintroll and the Comet*, 1949. Tove Jansson's private archive.

[28] Snufkin. For the play 'Moomintroll in the Wings', performed Stockholm, 1982. Tove Jansson's private archive.

[29] 'The Graphic Artist', painted by Tove in Paris, 1975. Private ownership.

[30] Too-ticky and Moomintroll in the winter forest. Suggested cover for *Trollvinter* (*Moominland Midwinter*), 1957. Tammerfors Museum of Art, Moominvalley.

[31] 'The Hobgoblin's Hat', fresco for kindergarten, Pori, 1984.

[32] Tove Jansson with her 1975 self-portrait. Photo Per Olov Jansson.

Index of Works

Book titles below are in italics

Index of People

Boel Westin is a writer, literary critic, and emeritus professor of literature specializing in children's and young people's literature. *Tove Jansson: Life, Art, Words* has been published in six languages, and she also edited *Letters from Tove* (Minnesota, 2020). She has also written on August Strindberg; historical children's and juvenile literature; and animal autobiographies.

Silvester Mazzarella is a translator of Swedish and Italian literature. He learned English from his mother, Italian from his father, and Swedish in Finland, where he taught English at the University of Helsinki. He lives in Canterbury, England.